IET COMPUTING SERIES 65

# Enabling Technologies for Smart Fog Computing

# Other volumes in this series:

Volume 1    **Knowledge Discovery and Data Mining** M.A. Bramer (Editor)
Volume 3    **Troubled IT Projects: Prevention and turnaround** J.M. Smith
Volume 4    **UML for Systems Engineering: Watching the wheels, 2nd Edition** J. Holt
Volume 5    **Intelligent Distributed Video Surveillance Systems** S.A. Velastin and
            P. Remagnino (Editors)
Volume 6    **Trusted Computing** C. Mitchell (Editor)
Volume 7    **SysML for Systems Engineering** J. Holt and S. Perry
Volume 8    **Modelling Enterprise Architectures** J. Holt and S. Perry
Volume 9    **Model-Based Requirements Engineering** J. Holt, S. Perry and M. Bownsword
Volume 13   **Trusted Platform Modules: Why, when and how to use them** A. Segall
Volume 14   **Foundations for Model-based Systems Engineering: From patterns to
            models** J. Holt, S. Perry and M. Bownsword
Volume 15   **Big Data and Software Defined Networks** J. Taheri (Editor)
Volume 18   **Modeling and Simulation of Complex Communication** M.A. Niazi (Editor)
Volume 20   **SysML for Systems Engineering: A model-based approach, 3rd Edition**
            J. Holt and S. Perry
Volume 22   **Virtual Reality and Light Field Immersive Video Technologies for Real-
            World Applications** G. Lafruit and M. Tehrani
Volume 23   **Data as Infrastructure for Smart Cities** L. Suzuki and A. Finkelstein
Volume 24   **Ultrascale Computing Systems** J. Carretero, E. Jeannot and A. Zomaya
Volume 25   **Big Data-Enabled Internet of Things** M. Khan, S. Khan and A. Zomaya
            (Editors)
Volume 26   **Handbook of Mathematical Models for Languages and Computation**
            A. Meduna, P. Horáček and M. Tomko
Volume 29   **Blockchains for Network Security: Principles, technologies and
            applications** H. Huang, L. Wang, Y. Wu and K.R. Choo (Editors)
Volume 30   **Trustworthy Autonomic Computing** T. Eza
Volume 32   **Network Classification for Traffic Management: Anomaly detection,
            feature selection, clustering and classification** Z. Tari, A. Fahad, A. Almalawi
            and X. Yi
Volume 33   **Edge Computing: Models, technologies and applications** J. Taheri and
            S. Deng (Editors)
Volume 34   **AI for Emerging Verticals: Human–robot computing, sensing and
            networking** M.Z. Shakir and N. Ramzan (Editors)
Volume 35   **Big Data Recommender Systems Vols 1 and 2** O. Khalid, S.U. Khan and
            A.Y. Zomaya (Editors)
Volume 37   **Handbook of Big Data Analytics Vols 1 and 2** V. Ravi and A.K. Cherukuri
            (Editors)
Volume 39   **ReRAM-based Machine Learning** H. Yu, L. Ni and S.M.P. Dinakarrao
Volume 40   **E-learning Methodologies: Fundamentals, technologies and applications**
            M. Goyal, R. Krishnamurthi and D. Yadav (Editors)
Volume 44   **Streaming Analytics: Concepts, architectures, platforms, use cases and
            applications** P. Raj, C. Surianarayanan, K. Seerangan and G. Ghinea (Editors)
Volume 44   **Streaming Analytics: Concepts, architectures, platforms, use cases and
            applications** P. Raj, A. Kumar, V. García Díaz and N. Muthuraman (Editors)
Volume 46   **Graphical Programming Using LabVIEW™: Fundamentals and advanced
            techniques** J.C. Rodríguez-Quiñonez and O. Real-Moreno
Volume 53   **Nature-inspired Optimization Algorithms and Soft Computing: Methods,
            technology and applications for IoTs, smart cities, healthcare and
            industrial automation** R. Arya, S. Singh, M.P. Singh, B.R. Iyer and V.N. Gudivada
            (Editors)
Volume 54   **Intelligent Network Design Driven by Big Data Analytics, IoT, AI and Cloud
            Computing** S. Kumar, G. Mapp and K. Cergiz (Editors)
Volume 56   **Earth Observation Data Analytics Using Machine and Deep Learning:
            Modern tools, applications and challenges** S. Garg, S. Jain, N. Dube and
            N. Varghese (Editors)

Volume 57    **AIoT Technologies and Applications for Smart Environments** M. Alazab,
             M. Gupta and S. Ahmed (Editors)
Volume 60    **Intelligent Multimedia Technologies for Financial Risk Management:
             Trends, tools and applications** K. Sood, S. Grima, B. Rawal, B. Balusamy,
             E. Özen and G.G.G. Gan (Editors)
Volume 61    **Access Control and Security Monitoring of Multimedia Information
             Processing and Transmission** Z. Lv, J. Lloret and H.H. Song (Editors)
Volume 63    **Personal Knowledge Graphs (PKGs): Methodology, tools and applications**
             S. Tiwari, F. Scharffe, F. Ortiz-Rodríguez and M. Gaur (Editors)
Volume 64    **Intelligent Multimedia Processing and Computer Vision: Techniques and
             applications** Shyam Singh Rajput, Chen Chen and Karm Veer Arya (Editors)
Volume 115   **Ground Penetrating Radar: Improving sensing and imaging through
             numerical modeling** X.L. Travassos, M.F. Pantoja and N. Ida

# Enabling Technologies for Smart Fog Computing

Kuldeep Singh Kaswan, Jagjit Singh Dhatterwal,
Vivek Jaglan, Balamurugan Balusamy and
Kiran Sood

The Institution of Engineering and Technology

Published by The Institution of Engineering and Technology, London, United Kingdom

The Institution of Engineering and Technology is registered as a Charity in England & Wales (no. 211014) and Scotland (no. SC038698).

© The Institution of Engineering and Technology 2024

First published 2023

The Institution of Engineering and Technology
Futures Place
Kings Way, Stevenage
Hertfordshire SG1 2UA, United Kingdom

www.theiet.org

**British Library Cataloguing in Publication Data**
A catalogue record for this product is available from the British Library

**ISBN 978-1-83953-749-3 (hardback)**
**ISBN 978-1-83953-750-9 (PDF)**

Typeset in India by MPS Limited

Cover Image: Olena T./E+ Collection via Getty Images

# Contents

About the authors                                                            xvii

1  **Introduction of fog computing**                                            1
   1.1   Introduction                                                            1
         1.1.1   History of fog computing                                        1
         1.1.2   Concept of fog computing                                        2
         1.1.3   What is fog computing                                           3
         1.1.4   Why is fog computing                                            3
   1.2   How fog computing works                                                 4
   1.3   Taxonomy of fog computing                                               5
   1.4   Fog computing versus cloud computing                                   14
   1.5   Fog computing and IoT                                                  15
         1.5.1   Are fog computing and edge computing the same?                 17
   1.6   Fog deployment model                                                   18
   1.7   Distributed with the fog                                               20
   1.8   Fog service models                                                     21
         1.8.1   Characteristics of the workload                                25
   1.9   Merits of fog computing                                                26
   1.10  Demerits of fog computing                                              26
   1.11  Application of fog computing                                           27
   1.12  Conclusion                                                             27
   References                                                                   27

2  **Fog computing in the IoT environment**                                    31
   2.1   Introduction                                                           32
   2.2   Models of fog computing                                                33
         2.2.1   Basic structure of fog computing                               34
         2.2.2   Analyzing the literature with the help of scientific publications  36
   2.3   Protocol of fog computing                                              38
         2.3.1   Generic fog-computing architecture                             39
         2.3.2   Fog-computing environment model                                47
         2.3.3   Advanced fog-computing architecture                            49
         2.3.4   Fog-computing tree model                                       50
   2.4   Conclusion                                                             52
   References                                                                   52

3   **Enhance quality of fog-computing environment using SDN and NFV technology**                                            55
    3.1   Introduction                                            55
    3.2   The paradigm of fog/edge computing                      56
    3.3   What are fog nodes?                                     60
    3.4   Connectivity technologies                               63
    3.5   Structure and behavior of fog computing                66
    3.6   Analytic and performance parameters for fog/edge nodes 68
    3.7   Performance enhancement techniques                      69
    3.8   Fog computing use cases                                 74
    3.9   Key characteristics of fog computing                   76
    3.10  Challenges of fog environments                          77
    3.11  5G connecting technology and the fog architecture       81
    3.12  Network Function Virtualization (NFV) and Software-Defined
          Networking (SDN)                                        83
    3.13  Fog data analytics and use cases                        86
    3.14  Advanced fog-computing applications                     87
    3.15  Conclusion                                              91
    References                                                    91

4   **Using P2P pervasive grid improves tunneling architecture and routing scalability**                                          93
    4.1   Introduction                                            93
    4.2   Traditional and pervasive environments                 94
          4.2.1   Traditional fog-computing environment          94
          4.2.2   Pervasive environment                          95
          4.2.3   Background                                     96
          4.2.4   Pervasive grid in IIoT fog computing           96
          4.2.5   Improved tunneling architecture                96
          4.2.6   Enhanced routing scalability                   96
          4.2.7   Case study analysis                            96
    4.3   Proximity services with edge computing and pervasive grids   97
          4.3.1   Ubiquitous networks                            97
          4.3.2   Cutting-edge computing technologies            97
          4.3.3   Advantages of connected data processing        98
    4.4   Developing a platform for edge and pervasive computing  98
    4.5   Coordination and clustering                            99
    4.6   Data access                                            101
    4.7   Context and scheduling                                 102
    4.8   Monitoring ozone events for UV alerts                  103
    4.9   Input preprocessing                                    104
    4.10  Time-series analysis, OSE detection and forecast        105
    4.11  The APT protocol                                       106
    4.12  Design principles                                      108
    4.13  How APT works                                          109

4.14   Default mappers                                                110
4.15   Mapping information                                            111
4.16   Data forwarding                                               111
4.17   Failure detection and recovery                                112
4.18   Mapping distribution protocol                                 113
4.19   Cryptographic protection                                      114
4.20   Incremental deployment                                        115
4.21   Routing policy and mapping                                    116
4.22   Conclusion                                                    118
References                                                            118

5   **Vehicular fog computing and virtualization**                  **121**
    5.1   Introduction                                                122
    5.2   Vehicular and virtualization fog computing                 123
          5.2.1   Virtualization in fog computing                    123
          5.2.2   Vehicular nodes                                    124
          5.2.3   Roadside infrastructure                           125
          5.2.4   Fog nodes                                          125
          5.2.5   Virtualization layer                              125
          5.2.6   Data processing and analytics                     125
          5.2.7   Communication infrastructure                     125
          5.2.8   Applications and services                         125
    5.3   Vehicular mobility models                                  126
          5.3.1   Selection of mobility model                        126
          5.3.2   Data collection and preprocessing                 126
          5.3.3   Model initialization                              126
          5.3.4   Simulation execution                              126
          5.3.5   Data analysis and evaluation                     127
          5.3.6   Iterative refinement                             127
    5.4   Content delivery and caching                               127
          5.4.1   Content caching in vehicular fog computing         127
          5.4.2   Cache placement and management                    127
          5.4.3   Content delivery in vehicular fog computing        128
          5.4.4   Virtualization for content caching and delivery    128
          5.4.5   Performance evaluation and analysis               128
    5.5   Network function virtualization                            128
          5.5.1   Network function virtualization (NFV) overview     128
          5.5.2   Vehicular NFV use cases                           129
          5.5.3   NFV infrastructure in vehicular fog computing      129
          5.5.4   NFV orchestration and management                  129
          5.5.5   Performance evaluation and analysis               129
    5.6   Software-defined networking                                130
          5.6.1   Overview of software-defined networking (SDN)      130
          5.6.2   SDN use cases in vehicular fog computing           130
          5.6.3   SDN controller and network operating system        131

|  |  |  |
|---|---|---|
| | 5.6.4 | OpenFlow protocol and southbound interfaces | 132 |
| | 5.6.5 | Northbound interfaces and application ecosystem | 132 |
| | 5.6.6 | Performance evaluation and analysis | 132 |
| 5.7 | Merits of vehicular and virtualization fog computing | 132 |
| | 5.7.1 | Vehicular fog computing—low latency and real-time responsiveness | 132 |
| | 5.7.2 | Vehicular fog computing—improved scalability and resource utilization | 132 |
| | 5.7.3 | Vehicular fog computing—enhanced reliability and resilience | 133 |
| | 5.7.4 | Virtualization in fog computing—efficient resource management | 133 |
| | 5.7.5 | Virtualization in fog computing—service agility and rapid deployment | 133 |
| | 5.7.6 | Virtualization in fog computing—improved fault isolation and security | 133 |
| 5.8 | Application of vehicular and virtualization fog computing | 134 |
| | 5.8.1 | Dedicated short-range communication | 134 |
| | 5.8.2 | Cellular-V2X | 134 |
| | 5.8.3 | Internet of Things (IoT) protocols (e.g., MQTT and CoAP) | 134 |
| | 5.8.4 | Network virtualization protocols (e.g., OpenFlow) | 135 |
| 5.9 | Quality of service | 135 |
| | 5.9.1 | Vehicular fog computing and QoS | 135 |
| | 5.9.2 | Virtualization in fog computing and QoS | 135 |
| 5.10 | Research vehicular and virtualization in fog computing | 136 |
| | 5.10.1 | Resource management and optimization | 136 |
| | 5.10.2 | QoS and service provisioning | 136 |
| | 5.10.3 | Security and privacy | 136 |
| | 5.10.4 | Vehicular mobility modeling and analysis | 137 |
| | 5.10.5 | Edge intelligence and machine learning | 137 |
| | 5.10.6 | Standardization and interoperability | 137 |
| | 5.10.7 | Energy efficiency and sustainability | 137 |
| 5.11 | Conclusion | 137 |
| | References | 138 |

**6   Smart XSS attack surveillance system for fog computing    141**

| | | |
|---|---|---|
| 6.1 | Introduction | 142 |
| 6.2 | Cross-site scripting (XSS) attack | 143 |
| 6.3 | Key contribution XSS | 145 |
| | 6.3.1 Related work | 146 |
| 6.4 | Smart XSS attack monitoring system | 147 |
| | 6.4.1 Extracted web page module | 148 |
| 6.5 | Smart XSS surveillance system | 149 |
| | 6.5.1 Different types of intelligent XSS monitoring systems | 150 |
| | 6.5.2 Cloud data centers' learning mode | 151 |

|       |       | 6.5.3 | Online mode of virtualized network of fog computing | 153 |
| 6.6   | Modes of smart XSS monitoring system |   |   | 154 |
|       |       | 6.6.1 | Analyzer of the input field | 156 |
|       |       | 6.6.2 | Code embedded in JavaScript | 157 |
|       |       | 6.6.3 | Analysis on JavaScript | 159 |
|       |       | 6.6.4 | Protocol generation | 159 |
|       |       | 6.6.5 | Comment Comparison Tool for JavaScript | 160 |
|       |       | 6.6.6 | Context Finder | 162 |
| 6.7   | Components of smart XSS monitoring system |   |   | 163 |
|       |       | 6.7.1 | Conceptualization, development, and testing | 164 |
| 6.8   | Performance analysis |   |   | 165 |
| 6.9   | Conclusion |   |   | 166 |
| References |   |   |   | 167 |

**7 Spectral image analysis with supervised feature extraction**    **169**
| 7.1 | Introduction |   |   | 170 |
|     |     | 7.1.1 | Supervised feature extraction | 170 |
|     |     | 7.1.2 | Evaluation of supervised feature extraction methods | 171 |
| 7.2 | Remote sensing imaging |   |   | 171 |
|     |     | 7.2.1 | Types of remote sensing images | 171 |
|     |     | 7.2.2 | Hyperspectral remote sensing images | 171 |
|     |     | 7.2.3 | Supervised features extraction | 172 |
| 7.3 | Hyperspectral imaging and dimensionality reduction |   |   | 173 |
|     |     | 7.3.1 | Math functions | 174 |
| 7.4 | Supervised feature extraction in hyperspectral images |   |   | 174 |
|     |     | 7.4.1 | Modified Fisher's linear discriminant analysis (MFLDA)-based feature | 175 |
|     |     | 7.4.2 | Prototype space feature extraction (PSFE) method | 176 |
|     |     | 7.4.3 | Maximum margin criterion (MMC)-based feature extraction method | 177 |
|     |     | 7.4.4 | Partitioned maximum margin criterion-based supervised feature extraction method | 178 |
|     |     | 7.4.5 | Hyperspectral feature partitioning | 179 |
| 7.5 | Experimental evaluation |   |   | 183 |
|     |     | 7.5.1 | Description of datasets | 183 |
|     |     | 7.5.2 | Performance measures | 185 |
|     |     | 7.5.3 | Parameter measures modified MMC-based approach | 186 |
| 7.6 | Conclusion |   |   | 187 |
| References |   |   |   | 187 |

**8 Developing of fog computing using sensor data**    **189**
| 8.1 | Introduction |   |   | 189 |
| 8.2 | Analysis of sensor data formats in smart cities |   |   | 190 |
|     |     | 8.2.1 | Sensor data in the SmartME Project | 192 |

      8.2.2  Sensor data in the CityPulse project                211
      8.2.3  Sensor data in the smart city                       213
  8.3  Pre-cleaned datasets for exploration in the Internet of Things,
       fog, and cloud                                            215
  8.4  Conclusion                                                216
  References                                                     216

9  **Information sharing on mobile IoT-based content aware smart
   home with fog computing**                                    **219**
  9.1  Introduction                                             220
  9.2  Computation offloading                                   221
  9.3  Result routing                                           222
  9.4  Load balancing and efficient deployment                  223
  9.5  Mobility-aware edge computing                            224
  9.6  System design                                            225
      9.6.1  Selection of potential employees                   226
      9.6.2  Networking with coworkers                          227
  9.7  Context-aware work stealing scheme                       229
      9.7.1  Extension for context-awareness                    229
      9.7.2  Task management skills that are both reactive and proactive  230
      9.7.3  Performance of Docker image transfer               231
      9.7.4  Transfer of Docker images                          232
      9.7.5  Distribution of tasks to fog nodes                 233
      9.7.6  Distribution of responsibilities                   234
  9.8  IoT-based smart home                                     235
  9.9  Smart home scenario                                      236
  9.10  ICON is an IoT-based, layered architecture              237
      9.10.1  ICON's design principles                          239
  9.11  Conditional logic with predicates                       240
  9.12  Implementation of ICON                                  242
      9.12.1  The fog-computing system architecture for the
              ICON-based smart house                            243
  9.13  Conclusion                                              244
  References                                                    245

10  **Security and privacy challenges in fog computing**        **247**
  10.1  Introduction                                            247
  10.2  Fog application management                              248
      10.2.1  Application performance                           249
      10.2.2  Approach distributed data flow                    250
  10.3  Fog Big Data base analysis                              251
      10.3.1  Processing of streaming data                      252
      10.3.2  Big Data, Stream Data Analysis, and fog computing 253
      10.3.3  Big Data, Stream Data, and the fog ecosystem:
              machine learning                                  253

10.3.4    Learning under guidance                                    254
10.3.5    Decision trees with distributed nodes                      255
10.3.6    Methods for clustering large data                          255
10.3.7    Tools like DBSCAN and DENCLUE are developed for
          use in Big Data environments                               256
10.3.8    Tree-based incremental clustering                          256
10.3.9    Mining association rules in large datasets with a P2P
          distributed computing architecture                        257
10.3.10   Associative mining in real time                           257
10.3.11   Methods for extensive learning                            258
10.3.12   Large-scale datasets and advanced machine learning        261
10.3.13   Scale-up models                                           265
10.3.14   Different approaches to fog analytics                     265
10.3.15   Other goods and services                                  266
10.3.16   ParStream                                                 267
10.3.17   Cloud-based analytics in the periphery                    267
10.4   Cloud Security Ontology                                      268
10.4.1    Create an ontology for safer cloud computing              270
10.4.2    Ontology: what it is and why it matters                   271
10.4.3    CSO architecture as it is defined and operationalized     272
10.4.4    Cloud computing security requirements                     273
10.4.5    Non-repudiation                                           274
10.4.6    Conceptual software architecture                          274
10.4.7    Domain and scope determination for CSO                    275
10.4.8    Identify the ontology's imperative keywords               275
10.5   Fog security and privacy                                     276
10.6   Conclusion                                                   279
References                                                          280

11  Fog robotics                                                    **281**
11.1   Introduction                                                 282
11.2   Fog robotics                                                 284
11.2.1    Facilitating distributed and shared learning              286
11.2.2    Data security, confidentiality, and ownership             287
11.2.3    Adaptability in resource allocation and placement         289
11.3   Comparison of fog and cloud robotics                         290
11.3.1    The fundamentals of FR design                             292
11.3.2    D2D communication in the FR architecture                  293
11.3.3    In an FR architecture with many fog robot servers         294
11.3.4    Delivery of social robots in this scenario                295
11.4   Deep learning-based robotics                                 296
11.4.1    Transferring simulation learning to the real world        297
11.4.2    Execution environment on a networked system               298
11.5   Fog robot architecture                                       299
11.6   Implementation of fog robotics                               301

11.7  Networking system with execution environment               301
11.8  Advanced robotics using fog computing                      302
11.9  Applications of fog robotics                               303
11.10  Conclusion                                                304
References                                                       304

**12  Cybernetic intelligence in fog computing**                 **307**
12.1  Introduction                                               308
12.2  A model of cybernetic intelligence in fog environment      309
12.3  Data utility in cyborg                                     310
    12.3.1  Intelligent distributed computer network     311
    12.3.2  A model for data-intensive applications in fog
        environment                                      312
    12.3.3  Resources                                    314
    12.3.4  Data source                                  316
    12.3.5  Tasks                                        318
    12.3.6  Use of data in cloud computing               319
    12.3.7  Situational aspects                          320
    12.3.8  Data utility                                 323
    12.3.9  Data life cycle                              324
    12.3.10  Using the data utility model                325
12.4  Content-aware intelligent systems fog computing in cybernetics
    intelligence                                          329
    12.4.1  Social media analytics                       331
    12.4.2  Technical intelligence                        333
    12.4.3  Measurement and signature intelligence        333
    12.4.4  Human intelligence                            334
    12.4.5  Finding humming in the dark                   335
12.5  Using fog/edge computing for context-aware intelligence    336
12.6  Types of cybernetics intelligence                          337
12.7  Conclusion                                                 338
References                                                       339

**13  Further application of fog computing**                     **341**
13.1  Introduction                                               342
13.2  Geospatial technology with fog computing and IoT in agriculture  344
    13.2.1  System to monitor irrigation                 345
    13.2.2  Treatment for insect and disease problems     346
    13.2.3  Controlled fertilizer usage                   346
    13.2.4  Monitoring of greenhouse gases                347
    13.2.5  Cattle tracking and monitoring                348
    13.2.6  Assert the need of tracking and farming systems
        monitoring                                       348
    13.2.7  Agriculture and information and communications
        technologies                                     349

13.2.8   IoT's functions                                                    349
13.2.9   Big data's place in the Internet of Things                         350
13.2.10  The Internet of Things and cloud and fog computing                 351
13.2.11  Sensors associated with plants                                     351
13.2.12  The GPS's function                                                 352
13.3  Big Data-based intelligent fog computing                              352
13.3.1   Computerized information management                                353
13.3.2   Big Data analysis and processing                                   354
13.3.3   The role of the cloud in Big Data                                  354
13.3.4   Cloud computing and geospatial data                               355
13.3.5   Big geographical data                                             356
13.3.6   Technical measures for thermostatic regulation                    357
13.3.7   Efficient and eco-friendly structures are called "green
         buildings"                                                        358
13.3.8   Geospatial data influences thermal comfort in buildings           358
13.3.9   Thermostatic consistency of building equipment                    359
13.3.10  Building materials made locally                                    359
13.3.11  Technologies and protocols for the Internet of Things
         overview                                                          360
13.3.12  Technologies of information and communication
         and of physical location                                          360
13.3.13  Detection and monitoring techniques                               361
13.3.14  The Internet of Things in the cloud                                362
13.3.15  IoT with the advent of Big Data and the cloud                      362
13.3.16  Computing on the cloud: from fog to cloud                          363
13.4  Fog computing in health-care systems                                  364
13.4.1   The proposed system's core functionality discerning
         the equipment                                                     365
13.4.2   Disposables identification, location, and tracking                365
13.4.3   Functionality and design of the proposed system                   366
13.4.4   The future of networking devices                                   366
13.4.5   The field of network analysis                                      367
13.4.6   Implied hardware                                                   368
13.5  Protecting individuality within the paradigm of a recommender
      system                                                               368
13.5.1   The cloud-based recommendation service reference model            369
13.5.2   Definition of risk                                                370
13.5.3   Formulation of the issue                                          370
13.5.4   Modifications of the FMCP protocols                               371
13.5.5   PRR protocol for private relevancy scoring                        371
13.5.6   PGD protocol for private group discovery (private group
         discovery protocol)                                               372
13.6  Conclusion                                                           372
References                                                                 373

**14 Future research directions**                                      **375**
    14.1 Introduction                                                  376
    14.2 Cloud of things: cloud–IoT integration                        377
    14.3 Conclusion                                                    382

**Index**                                                              **383**

# About the authors

**Kuldeep Singh Kaswan** is presently working in the School of Computing Science and Engineering, Galgotias University, Uttar Pradesh, India. His contributions focus on BCI, cyborg, and data science. His academic degrees and 13 years of experience working with global Universities, such as, Amity University, Noida, India, Gautam Buddha University, Greater Noida, India and PDM University, Bahadurgarh, India, have made him more receptive and prominent in his domain. He received his doctorate in computer science from Banasthali Vidyapith, Rajasthan. He has also received a D.Eng. from Dana Brain Health Institute, Iran. He has supervised three PhD graduates and presently supervising four PhD students. He is also a member of IEEE, Computer Science Teachers Association, New York, USA, International Association of Engineers, Hong Kong, professional member of Association of Computing Machinery, USA. He has number of publications also in international and national journals and conferences. He is an editor, author, and review editor of journals and books with IEEE, Wiley, Springer, IGI, and River.

**Jagjit Singh Dhatterwal** is presently working as an associate professor with the Department of Artificial Intelligence and Data Science Koneru Lakshmaiah Education Foundation, Vaddeswaram, Andhra Pradesh, India. He has also worked with Maharshi Dayanand University, Rohtak and PDM University, Bahadurgarh, Haryana, India. He has supervised many UG and PG projects for engineering students and is presently supervising one PhD student. He is also a member of the Computer Science Teachers Association (CSTA), New York, USA, International Association of Engineers, Hong Kong, IACSIT, a professional member of the Association of Computing Machinery, USA, IEEE, and a life member of the Computer Society of India. His areas of interest include artificial intelligence, BCI, cyborgs, and multi-agents technology. He has a number of publications in international and national journals and conferences.

**Vivek Jaglan** is working as a professor and director at Amity School of Engineering and Technology, Amity University, Gwalior, India. He has nearly 19 years of teaching and research experience. His current research areas cover artificial intelligence, neural networks, fuzzy logic, and IoTs. He has presented and published 80+ papers in journals and conferences. He holds a doctorate degree from the Computer Science and Engineering Department, SGV University, Jaipur, India. He has supervised 7 PhD students, 11 masters' students completion and is currently supervising four PhD students. He has two design patents (India), one of the patents "Tooth Brush With Digital Display" design patent, which includes unique features that allow the brush to dispense only the required amount of toothpaste recommended by the dentist and verify that the user has properly brushed their teeth. He has been invited as an expert in the field of artificial intelligence and its approach on multiple occasions.

**Balamurugan Balusamy** is a professor at the School of Computing Science and Engineering, Galgotias University, India. His research focuses on blockchain and IoT. He has published 30 technology books and over 150 journal and conference papers and book chapters. He serves on the advisory committee for several start-ups and forums and does consultancy work for the industry on Industrial IoT. He has given over 175 talks at events and symposiums. He is a member of several associations including IEEE and ACM. He holds a PhD degree on *"Investigations of cloud computing access control techniques"* from VIT University, Vellore, India.

**Kiran Sood** is a professor at Chitkara Business School, Chitkara University, Punjab, India; an affiliate professor in the faculty of Economics Management and Accountancy at the University of Malta; and a postdoc researcher in the faculty of Applied Sciences at the University of Usak, Turkey. Her areas of research cover the fields of big data and finance. She serves as an editor for several refereed journals including the *IJBST International Journal of BioSciences and Technology* and the *International Journal of Research Culture Society*. She earned her doctor of philosophy in commerce with a concentration on product portfolio performance of general insurance companies from Panjabi University, Patiala, India.

*Chapter 1*

# Introduction of fog computing

## Abstract

**Purpose:** In this chapter, including its history, introductions, benefits, disadvantages, applications, and conclusion.

**Methodology:** A decentralized computing facility known as pervasive computing, fog networking, or excessive moisture is one in which data, calculations, storage, and implementations are generated during the most suitable and appropriate place on-premises data centers and the internet.

**Findings:** Other names for fog computing include accumulation of dust and fog networking. The notion of pervasive computing is essentially an extension of cloud-based solutions and the advantages it delivers to the network's edges.

**Practical implication:** This brings the benefits and capabilities of the cloud much closer to the location where data are produced and responded upon.

## 1.1 Introduction

Cloud computing that is extended to the perimeter of an organization's network is referred to as "fog computing," which is a phrase that was developed by Cisco. In certain circles, in addition to the term "edge computing," it is also known as "pervasive computing." The performance of computation, storage, and communications services may be facilitated more easily between network elements and the data centers that handle cloud-based applications thanks to cloud environment. The term "fog computing," which is synonymous with "fog networking," refers to a decentralized computing environment in which computing, storage, and enterprise applications are made available in perhaps the most reasonable and realistic place at any moment along with the continuous spectrum from the data provider to the cloud in Figure 1.1. Fog computing is also sometimes referred to as edge computing [1].

### 1.1.1 History of fog computing

The concept of fog computing can be traced back to 2012 when Cisco first introduced the term. They envisioned fog computing as a paradigm that extends cloud computing to the edge of the network, enabling a seamless connection between cloud data centers and end devices. The goal was to address the growing demand

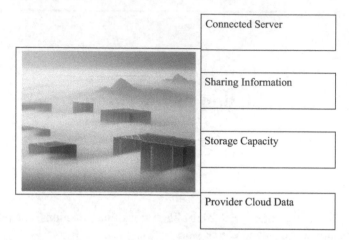

| Connected Server |
| Sharing Information |
| Storage Capacity |
| Provider Cloud Data |

*Figure 1.1   Fog computing*

for low-latency, high-bandwidth applications in the era of the Internet of Things (IoT) and other data-intensive technologies.

In the following years, fog computing gained traction as various tech companies and researchers started exploring its potential. By 2014, the OpenFog Consortium was formed, a collaborative effort among academic institutions, industry leaders, and governmental organizations to standardize and promote fog-computing architectures. This further fueled the development of fog-computing technologies, leading to their integration into diverse fields, such as smart cities, healthcare, autonomous vehicles, and industrial automation.

Fog computing has been a hot topic in the IT industry in recent years, and on November 19, 2015, the OpenFog Consortium was formed. Jeff Faders, Intel's IoT Strategist, is the consortium's first president and Cisco's Sr. Managing Director Helder Antunes is its first chairperson [2].

As of 2021, fog computing continues to evolve and solidify its position as a vital component of the distributed computing landscape, enabling efficient and responsive data processing at the edge fog of the network.

## 1.1.2   Concept of fog computing

- A considerable volume of data is generated by IoT applications. These data have to be analyzed in order to make interoperability choices and to carry out a variety of activities.
- The cloud presents a variety of concerns, such as congestion, extremely high-bandwidth use, delays in real-time answers, and centralized data placement, when these data are sent.
- Cisco invented the phrase "fog computing" in 2012 in order to address these issues encountered by wireless sensor networks in the cloud infrastructure.

- To minimize latency and maximize spectral efficiency, it proposes to move processing closer to the end devices.
- The proliferation of sensor-based gadgets has resulted in an enormous volume of data. Nonvolatile memory and processing are both required for these data. Difficult, expensive, and time-consuming: preserving data in the cloud. It reduces operational time and costs by locating capabilities close to the equipment that will be used [3].

### *1.1.3  What is fog computing*

The phrase "fog computing," invented by Cisco, is often used interchangeably with "edge computing." A dense computing framework at the edge of the network has been referred to as a fog foundation. Such systems are said to include features, such as reduced latency, reduced latency, and wireless connectivity. Real-time analytics and enhanced security are among the advantages. A fog-computing infrastructure, on the other hand, would be able to analyze everything from the network center to the edge of the network. Using fog computing, a system may adjust its signals depending on traffic monitoring in order to avoid accidents or minimize traffic congestion. Cloud-based analytics may also be used to store data for extended periods of time [4].

Cisco's other examples involve rail safety, smart transmission and distribution restoration, and information security. In addition to key enabling technologies like interactive lighting and smart transportation meters, PrismTech Vortex cites vehicle-to-vehicle and vehicle-to-cloud connectivities. Cisco has provided an example of the analytics that may be conducted along a fog network in the picture below.

### *1.1.4  Why is fog computing*

IoT services, such as lower transmission assistance, situational awareness, and geo-distribution, are among the key goals of fog computing [2]. Many operations that need minimal delay between IoT devices and the closest fog web service or cloud service for local data analysis created may benefit from fog computing's ability to extend cloud data center capabilities, such as computation, storage, and networking equipment [5].

The number of fog-based applications is increasing. Unconventional application framework requires considerable platform features that can only be provided if the program is compiled close to the end-users if new use cases for the fog environment are to be realized. All the referenced applications are studied, and their justifications for employing a fog platform are identified.

Augmented reality games, for example, need a latency of less than 10–20 ms for end-to-end latencies (connectivity and processor delay included). Propagation delay from 20 to 40 ms (over communication links) to up to 150 ms (over wireless networks), the distance between an end-user and the closest cloud data center (over 4G mobile networks). As a result, real-world usage of these apps is impossible.

*Run on the internet*: Deploying the server element of these apps in fog platforms would be an easy way to lower the overall latency [6]. Video security cameras and other edge devices generate enormous amounts of raw data on a daily basis, which necessitates optimization of their available bandwidth. Huge network traffic is generated when so much data are sent to the cloud. Fog computing is an intermediary in reducing network traffic for these kinds of applications. In order to preprocess original information at the sources before transferring it to the cloud, fog middlewares are used.

Smartphones, tablets, and other infrastructure components, such as smart IoT devices, have a limited amount of computational capacity. High-complexity applications like image retrieval take a long time to execute on these smartphones. Delegation of authority for certain work to the intermediate virtual machines may affect productivity. When a cloud server is overloaded, the server-side of the running apps may be offloaded to fog servers. Alternatively, offloading might be another option.

For many applications, privacy and security are of utmost importance. There is a large quantity of patient data that may be retrieved via E-health apps in healthcare administration. To ensure long-term accessibility, most recorded data are stored in the public cloud. However, many hospitals are concerned about the theft of personal medical records. By offering storage space to the user or the hospital, private fog minimizes the problem of data privacy and security.

Many IoT sensors and actuators may need sophisticated computers to run and control, such as implementation and condition monitoring, system implementation and switch on/off, and service distribution and incident management. By acting as a middleman, fog computing may supply computational power that not only makes it possible to operate various devices but also lets users tailor the services they get to their own needs [7].

Edge equipment, such as infusion pumps, heartbeat detection systems, and other monitoring devices, have improved in hospitals. As a result, the US suffers from the third-leading cause of mortality each year [8] due to difficulties integrating these devices with patients. Remotely hosted apps that interface directly with the monitoring devices allow for dynamic responses based on real-time data, thanks to fog computing.

In the IoT context, one of the most pressing concerns is the amount of energy used by massive IoT devices. In order to save energy, fog computing allows these appliances to make intelligent choices, such as turning on/off/hibernating.

A pay-as-you-go strategy, which is more common in conventional cloud computing, reduces costs by charging a flat rate per unit of utilization. One-time costs for procuring private fog resources may be better than cloud costs for applications [9]. Reducing network traffic and enhancing response times may be accomplished in part via the use of content parallelization and networking protocols.

## 1.2 How fog computing works

While edge embedded, systems create and obtain information; they lack the computational and storage capacity to execute sophisticated processing and machine learning activities. Despite the fact that cloud servers have the capacity to perform these things, they are frequently too far away to analyze the data and reply in a reasonable timeframe. In addition, when maintaining the confidentiality of data subject to rules in various countries, having all endpoints connect to and transfer raw information to the server through the internet might have anonymity, confidentiality, and legal concerns [10].

Fog reduces the quantity of data transferred to the cloud by doing processing on a data hub in a connected home or on a smart router or entry point. Fog networking enables short-term predictive modeling at the edge, while the cloud handles the source of energy, long-term business intelligence. Fog networking does not replace cloud technology.

## 1.3 Taxonomy of fog computing

Fog computing has suggested classifications, and this is what it looks like. Categorization of edge computing presents a categorization of the current fog-computing efforts. Network architecture is highlighted by the categorization in the following ways.

Configuration of fog nodes: At the edge of the network, the nodes with diverse architectures and settings may support fog-computing infrastructure.

- Node-to-node communication: An edge network's methods for coordinating nodal cooperation among several fog nodes.
- Metric for resource/service provisioning: How to provide resources and services in a cost-effective manner under a wide range of conditions.
- Goals for the quality service.

By introducing edge computing as a middle layer among cloud applications and end applications, the Service Level Objectives (SLOs) were achieved. A network system is appropriate for the situation. Fog computing is an extension of previous computing paradigms that have been implemented in various networking systems. Security is a major issue. Fog computing's security considerations vary depending on the situation. Numerous taxonomic groupings are covered by existing methods and solutions. According to fog-computing features, this taxonomy does not accurately reflect the relative effectiveness of all of the many recommended approaches. Different execution settings, networking topologies, application characteristics, resource architecture, and so on are all taken into consideration and addressed in the work that has been viewed in this study. Due to the complexity of fog computing, it is almost impossible to pinpoint the most optimal solution in terms of structure, service, and security. In the existing studies, fog nodes have been categorized into five different types: servers, networking devices, cloudlets, base stations, and automobiles. In-house web servers may be seen at bus terminals, shopping centers, roads, and even in public parks. In the same way that being light in weight is similar to because of virtualization and cloud computing, these fog servers are cloud servers. The fog server is one of fog computing's most critical functional properties. Fog servers are referred to as microservices, micro data centers, nano servers, and so on in certain studies based on their physical size, while they are classified as cache servers, calculation servers, storage servers, and so on in other papers based on their functions. Fog computing may benefit from a server-based node design that increases computing and storage capability. However, it restricts the extent to which the execution environment may be used [11].

- **Devices for connecting to the internet:** It is feasible that Fog-computing infrastructures might be built using devices like routers, switches, and set-top boxes, in addition to their typical networking duties. Several modern switches and routers include a variety of system resources, such as CPUs, extensible main and secondary memory, and programing platforms. In addition to standard hardware and software components, certain specialized network interface cards, such as intelligent gateways and IoT hubs, have been represented as fog nodes in other publications. Network devices deployed in a dispersed way increase the prevalence of pervasive computing, but the physical diversity of devices has a significant influence on the provisioning of services and resources. The cloudlet is a micro-cloud that resides in the middle of the end device, cloudlet, and cloud hierarchy. Cloudlets may be used to complement MCC by providing mobile device users with cloud-based services. According to a series of studies, cloudlets have been referred to as "Fog nodes." A huge number of end devices may be handled concurrently using cloudlet-based fog computing. Cloudlets, although being deployed at the edge, may nonetheless function as centralized components in certain circumstances owing to structural restrictions. There are still serious issues with fog computing that prevent it from supporting IoT [12].
- **Stations at the ground zero:** An essential part of any wireless network, base stations process and transmit data to and from the mobile nodes. Traditional base stations equipped with particular storage and computation capabilities have recently been deemed viable for fog computing in recent research. Fog nodes may be created using RSUs, small cell access points, and so on, much as regular base stations. Fog-based extensions of cloud radio access network (CRAN), vehicular ad hoc network, and similar networks are better served by base stations. Fog creation using base stations, on the other hand, is complicated by high deployment costs and networking interference.
- **Intelligent vehicles:** Fog nodes may be placed in moving or stationary cars at the edge of a network with computing resources. It is possible to create a highly dispersed and scalable fog environment using vehicles. It will, however, be very difficult to provide privacy and fault tolerance while maintaining optimal quality of service (QoS) in such an environment.
- **Collaboration at the node level:** Cooperative approaches for cluster, peer-to-peer (P2P), and master/slave computation nodes for fog have all been reported in several studies. Cluster nodes in the network may form their own clusters in addition to maintaining a collaborative computing environment. When fog nodes are in close proximity to one another, they might form clusters. The creation of

functional subsystems and congestion control may be prioritized while the nodes are forming a cluster. It is possible to use the capabilities of several fog nodes concurrently by using cluster-based cooperation. It's tough to scale static clusters at runtime because dynamic cluster generation is heavily reliant on the current demand and readily available fog nodes. In both circumstances, the networking overhead is critical to the overall outcome. P2P cooperation is highly popular in fog computing because of the distributed nature of the system. It is possible to do P2P cooperation in a hierarchical or flat manner. There are a variety of ways to classify P2P cooperation between fog nodes besides proximity. For example, virtual computer instances are shared among nodes in a cloud computing environment to optimize resource utilization and deliver scalable and cost-effective solutions to users. It is about P2P cooperation rather than relying on a single node's processed output alone. In P2P cooperation, fog nodes may be easily augmented and made reusable. P2P nodal cooperation, on the other hand, is plagued by problems with dependability and access control [13].

- **Master–slave:** Master–slave nodal cooperation has been extensively discussed in a number of publications. A master fog node typically manages slave nodes' functioning, processing load, environmental protection, information flows, and other aspects. The fog-computing environment may also create a hybrid collaborative network using a master–slave strategy, cluster nodal connections, and P2P interactions. As a result, both the master and the slave fog nodes in order to process data in real time require high-bandwidth communication. There are several aspects that play a role in the supply of resources and services in fog computing, time, energy, application and database context, and more are all taken into account.

- **Time:** Fog computing makes efficient use of time as a key consideration in resource and service supply. The amount of time it takes to complete a job is known as computation time. It's important to keep in mind that the amount of time it takes to operate an application relies heavily on the configuration of the resources it's operating on. In addition, the time it takes to compute a task helps to distinguish between the current and previous periods of different programs and has a substantial impact on fog's resource and power management. The time it takes for data items to be exchanged in a fog-computing environment is referred to as communication time. It has been explored in two ways in the literature: There is a direct connection between the end devices/sensors and fog nodes. To aid in task execution, the network context is reflected in the required communication time. A system's deadline sets the maximum amount of time it may go without receiving a service. Task completion satisfaction has been regarded as a significant QoS indicator in various studies. The delivering services constraint distinguishes between latency sensitivity and latency tolerance applications and games. Service access times in a multitenant cloud architecture, service reaction times, and other time-based metrics such as these may be studied for efficient function and resource deployment and management in sensor networks [14].

- **Data:** Fog-computing literature makes frequent use of input data size and data flow characteristics, two data-centric metrics. The quantity of data that must be processed via fog computing is referred to as data size. There have been several discussions about the computational space needs of requests in relation to data size. In addition, data gathered from a large number of dispersed sensors and devices may have the characteristics of Big Data. Provisioning resources and services based on data load might be a useful strategy in this situation. Data size also has a significant effect on determining whether a computing activity should be performed locally or remotely. The properties of data transmission are defined by the data flow. Event-driven or real-time data flow in the fog-computing environment may have a significant impact on resource and service delivery. In addition, abrupt changes in data flow might lead to dynamic node load balancing. Fog computing's resource and service provisioning may also be analyzed in terms of heterogeneous data architecture, data semantic norms, and data integrity needs [15].

- **Cost:** Fog resource and service delivery may be heavily influenced by considerations relating to cost, both from the standpoint of service providers and customers. It is easy to see how broadband use and associated expenses have a direct impact on connectivity costs in a fog-computing system. Some studies attribute connectivity prices to the upload of data from end devices/sensors and the exchange of data across nodes, while others attribute networking delays caused by broadband problems to network security costs. In a fog-computing environment, deployment costs are mostly tied to the costs of setting up the infrastructure. In several studies, efficient resource and service supply has been linked to cost-effective infrastructure implementation. The cost of deploying infrastructure may be broken down into two parts: the actual deployment of fog nodes in the network, and the creation of virtual computing instances inside those nodes. Fog nodes' computational costs when executing applications or processing activities are referred to as "execution costs." The use of execution costs in resource provisioning and invoicing is rare in fog computing despite its widespread usage in other computing paradigms. Task completion time and resource utilization costs have been used to compute the overall cost of these tasks. Fog-computing resource and service provisioning may take into account migration costs as well as the previously listed costs, as well as charges for security precautions, the most a customer is willing to pay for a product or service [16].

- **Consumption of energy and environmental impact:** In a few studies, fog resources and services have been prioritized based on energy concerns. Fog-cloud interaction has been studied extensively for its energy consumption across all devices, as well as the trade-off between energy and delay at various stages of the process. Previously, the carbon emission rate per unit energy consumption of various nodes was taken into account for resource provisioning objectives in another study. Fog resources may be provisioned according to the energy constraints of end devices/sensors, such as residual battery life and the energy characteristics of communication media. Context refers to the conditions under which a certain thing is found. For resource and service delivery, user and application context has been studied in fog-based research papers. In the future, resources may be allocated to a user based on the user's attributes (e.g., service use history and service relinquish likelihood). Service and resource provisioning may benefit from customer input, such as net promoter score and customer needs. Service provisioning in previous works has taken into account user density, mobility, and network state. The context of an application may be defined as the operational needs of several applications. Prerequisites for task performance (such as processor speed, storage, and storage), as well as network connectivity, and other operational needs might impact the supply of resources and services. The present workload of various apps has also been taken into account as an application context in other research. Fog-computing contexts may also be considered in terms of the execution environment, node character-istics, application design, and so on, and these contexts can play a significant role in providing resources and services. As a result, every piece of background material must be thoroughly examined [17].

- **Goals for the quality of service:** Certain SLOs have been suggested to be achieved using a variety of application platforms, computational models, and optimizations of fog node architecture approach in current research. Almost all of the successfully achieved SLOs are management-oriented and deal with concerns such as latency and power consumption as well as cost, resource allocation, data storage, and other types of applications.

- **Latency control:** Fog computing's latency control essentially prevents the eventual service delivery time from exceeding a predetermined threshold for acceptable latency. A service request's maximum acceptable latency or an application's QoS requirement may fall within this barrier. Some efforts have placed an emphasis on efficient nodal cooperation start to guarantee that com-pute activities carried out by collaborated nodes may be completed within the latency limitation set. It has also been shown that distributing computing tasks across clients and fog nodes may reduce service request computation and com-munication delay. In addition, a low-latency fog network design was presented in another paper to control latency. The primary goal of this project is to find a node in the fog network that delivers services with the least amount of delay.

- **Controlling the costs:** Operating expenses (Operating Expenses) may be evaluated in terms of fog-computing cost management (OPEX). Distribution of fog nodes and their networks is the primary cause of CAPEX in fog com-puting. Fog computing's CAPEX may be kept to a minimum by strategically placing and using an optimal number of fog nodes. According to this concept, the total cost of fog computing is reduced by optimizing the positioning and number of sensor nodes in use. Fog nodes are also referred to as virtual machines launch vehicles and virtual machines in another study. The cost of running data processing processes on these virtual machines varies from pro-vider to provider, and the cost is not always the same. To reduce OPEX in fog computing, it is possible to take advantage of the cost diversity of fog nodes/ providers. According to this, the article proposes a technique to discover the best fog nodes to host Virtual Machine (VMs) in order to reduce OPEX in fog computing [18].

- **Management of the network:** Fog computing's network management comprises, for example, the control of network congestion in the core, the support of software-defined networking/network function virtualization (SDN/NFV), and the guarantee of smooth connection. Network congestion is primarily caused by an increase in network overhead. Because IoT devices/sensors are widely dispersed over the edge, the cost on the core network may be greatly increased by concurrent interactions between end components and cloud data centers. As a result, network congestion will arise, lowering the system's overall performance. In light of this, a layered fog node design has been suggested that allows for the processing of service requests at the node level. As a result, despite getting large numbers of service requests, clouds only receive compressed versions of such requests, which have less impact on the network. There is a lot of interest in virtualizing the traditional networking infrastructure. Virtualized networks are made possible in large part by SDN. SDN is an SDN approach that separates control and data planes from communication gear and puts it into software on different servers. Support for NFV is a crucial feature of SDN. To put it simply, NFV is an architectural idea that enables conventional networking tasks to be virtualized so that they may be done via software. SDN and NFV have a significant impact on cloud-based environments because of their large variety of services. New network topologies for fog computing have been developed to allow SDN and NFV as a result of this; as a result of their physical variety, end devices are able to communicate seamlessly with other entities such as the cloud or fog or desktop computers or mobile devices. As a result, finding resources and keeping the network's communication and computing capacities up to date are made simpler. It is a problem that has already been addressed in fog computing, with new architectures for fog nodes like the IoT hub and fog networking like the vehicular fog computing (VFC). Another development in fog computing is a policy-driven framework for ensuring secure connectivity between devices [19].
- **Management of computations:** Fog computing's SLOs include a high priority on ensuring that computational resources are properly managed. It is possible to estimate computer resources, distribute workloads, coordinate computing resources, and more with fog computing. Resources may be assigned according to certain rules in fog computing so that suitable resources can be allocated, desired QoS can be attained, and an exact service fee can be enforced. According to the current literature, resource estimation strategies are built based on user characteristics experienced QoE, features of service-accessing devices, and so on. Fog computing's workload distribution should aim to optimize resource usage while minimizing computational idle time. More specifically, a balanced load is ensured on several components. A scheduling-based workload allocation strategy has been implemented in a fog-based research project in order to distribute the computational burden across fog nodes and client devices. As a result, both parties' overhead costs are reduced, which raises QoE. In a separate study, a framework for balancing fog-cloud communication delays and power consumption was proposed. Because of their heterogeneity and resource limitations, coordination among various fog

resources is absolutely essential. With fog computing, large-scale applications may be distributed over several fog nodes due to its decentralized nature. Without adequate coordination of fog resources, it would be difficult to achieve the required performance under these situations. In light of this, a paradigm for managing fog resources based on directed graph coordination has been developed.

- **Management of application programs:** Efficient programing platforms are critical for successful fog-computing application administration. In addition to the scalability and compute offloading capabilities, these features aid application administration. Development, compilation, and execution of programs are all made easier with the help of a programing platform, which includes all of the components listed above. Due to fog computing's dynamic nature, ensuring effective resource management and real-time decision-making capabilities are paramount for its successful implementation in applications such as IoT and edge computing. It's quite tough to develop software to handle large-scale applications. Mobile fog, a new development platform, has addressed this issue. Mobile fog's reduced abstractions of programing paradigms make it feasible to build large-scale decentralized applications. As well as the coordination of resources during the implementation, an implementation framework for fog computing was also established in another document. To keep their QoS high even as the number of app users increases and unexpected occurrences occur, apps must be capable of adapting. Application scheduling and service access for users may both benefit from scaling strategies. Fog computing has recently presented an architecture for a QoS-aware self-adaptive scheduler to facilitate the scalable scheduling of data stream applications. Using this scheduler, programs may be scaled up and down based on the number of users and the amount of resources available. It is also simpler to arrange programs in a dispersed form because of the scheduler's self-adaptive capabilities. Fog computing has also offered an adaptive approach for users to choose their service access mode depending on the distance, location, and QoS needs of the service-accessing entities. It is possible to transmit computational activities from resource-constrained end devices to more resource-rich devices via offloading methods. In a mobile cloud environment, computational offloading is a typical occurrence. As part of fog computing's compatibility upgrade support for mobile applications' computation dynamic provisioning in other communication networks has been stressed in various publications lately. Mobile apps' distributed computing and the availability of resources have been examined in these studies [8].
- **Management of data:** Fog computing can't function properly if its information systems SLOs aren't in place. Different research studies have looked at fog computing's data management takes a multifaceted approach. Fog computing's information management approach places a high value on computational intelligence services and preparatory distribution of resources. As an alternative, low-bandwidth aggregation from scattered end devices/sensors may be explored in the interest of improved data administration. End devices/sensors, on the other hand, have limited storage capacity. Storage enhancement for end-entity data storage and data may have a substantial influence on fog

computing in this case. Data processing in fog computing has also been emphasized as a crucial part of storage growth for smart applications.

- **Management of energy resources:** Power management may be provided as a service to various fog computing is being used to connect systems. A cloud infrastructure for fog computing might enable home-based distributed systems to regulate power with customized user control, according to a report. Centralized cloud data centers' power usage may be managed in certain circumstances using cloud services. Data center power consumption is mainly dependent on the sort of applications being executed. By offering infrastructure to support a number of energy-hungry applications, fog computing may complement cloud data centers in this situation. Therefore, cloud data centers will be able to maintain proper power management as a result of reduced energy consumption. Furthermore, carbon footprint emissions can be lowered by carefully controlling the power used in fog computing.

- **Usefulness of networking systems:** The IoT relies heavily on fog computing. Fog computing's usefulness in different mobility, content management, radio access, and vehicle networks are all examples of communication networks that have been emphasized in recent research publications.

- **Internet of Things:** Every device in the IoT can communicate with each other and exchange data. The IoT environment can be viewed from many different angles. Additionally, in various fog-based research studies, this contact has been categorized as either industrial or home-based execution environments. Furthermore, fog-computing systems and service models have also taken into account many kinds of IoT, including networks of wirelessly sensing devices and cyber–physical systems.

- **Access networks for mobile devices/mobile phones:** Fog computing's applicability to mobile networks has also been studied in a number of studies. Fog computing's interoperability with 5G mobile networking has been a major focus of these studies. Compared to current cellular networks, 5G allows for substantially faster connectivity, more signal capacity, and reduced latency in service delivery. Fog computing may be used in various mobile networks other than 5G, such as 3G and 4G. A different study looked at how workloads in fog cloud for mobile communication are allocated depending on trade-offs between power and delay. Individual devices communicate with other network entities via radio connections in the radio access network. CRAN, the cloud-assisted Radio Access Network (RAN), has already piqued the interest of many researchers. Fog computing–based radio access networks have also been investigated as a possible supplement to the capabilities of CRAN [20].

- **Power line communications via passive optical network:** With the introduction of LRPON, backhaul services for homes, businesses, and wireless networks can now take advantage of a new, low-latency, high-bandwidth technology for long-distance communications. LRPONs facilitate network consolidation in addition to providing a wide coverage area. Fog computing has been integrated with LRPONs in order to optimize the network design in this article. Communication over the smart grid's power lines (PLC) is common. Data and alternating current are sent concurrently in PLC utilizing electrical connections. Discussion of fog-computing PLCs in electrical power distribution has been extensive.

- **Internet-based platform for the distribution of content:** Distributed proxy servers supply material and provide good reliability and availability for the end-users via a content distribution network. Many fog-based research projects use fog nodes as they open up opportunities to make content dissemination easier. Users may access fog-based content services with little latency since fog nodes are scattered over the network's edge. The dissemination of high-quality information will run more smoothly as a result.
- **Network of automobiles:** Data interchange and resource augmentation are made possible by vehicular networks, which allow the autonomous establishment of a wireless communication network among cars. Computational and networking resources are made available to cars as part of this network. Fog nodes are vehicles that reside at the edge of a network and are used to promote a fog computing–based vehicular network in several studies [21].
- **Fear for one's safety:** Fog computing relies on an underlying network between end devices and cloud data centers; it has a high level of security risk. However, security considerations in cloud computing are essential to safeguard sensitive data and protect against potential threats or breaches, making robust encryption, access controls, and continuous monitoring critical components of a secure cloud environment. In the literature, fog computing has been researched in terms of information identification, confidentiality, secure data exchange, denial-of-service (DoS) attack, and so on.
- **Authentication:** In fog-based systems, user authentication plays a critical role in preventing infiltration. Unwanted access to fog services is very intolerable since they are utilized on a "pay-as-you-go" basis. In addition to user authentication, the secure fog-computing environment has seen device authentication, data transfer authentication, and instance authentication. End device/sensor data are processed via privacy fog computing. Sometimes, these statistics are discovered to have a strong correlation with users' personal and professional circumstances. As a result, one of the most pressing issues in fog computing is the protection of user security. It has been noted that privacy is an issue with fog-based vehicular computing.
- **Data encryption:** Fog computing is a useful adjunct to cloud computing. Cloud computing is required in certain circumstances for data handled via fog computing. Fog nodes must encrypt this data since they frequently include important information. In light of this, the proposed fog node design includes a data encryption layer.
- **DoS attack:** Because fog nodes have a limited amount of resources, they are unable to accommodate a high number of simultaneous queries. Fog computing's performance may suffer greatly in this situation. DoS attacks might be crucial in causing such significant service outages in fog computing. Fog nodes may be kept busy for a longer length of time by concurrently issuing a large number of irrelevant service requests. Due to the lack of resources, helpful services are no longer accessible. Fog computing has been used to discuss and clarify this kind of DoS attack.

- **Inquiry into the gap and possible future directions:** Rather than relying on remote servers, fog computing makes advantage of cloud resources that are already nearby. Fog computing is critical for supporting widely dispersed end devices and sensors. As a result, fog computing has emerged as a major research area in both academia and industry in recent years. There is an overview of several reviewed publications on fog computing. Many important aspects of fog computing have been discussed already, but there are still some issues that need to be addressed if this field is to advance further. In this section, we will talk about some of the gaps in the existing literature and possible future research directions [22].

Provisioning of resources and services in light of current situation: Fog computing's resource and service provisioning may benefit from context awareness. Fog computing may acquire contextual information in a variety of ways, such as

- Location, time (peak, off-peak), and so on.
- The application's perspective: latency sensitivities, application design, and so on.
- Mobility, social connections, activity, and so on are all examples of user context.

What resources are accessible on the device? How much juice is left in the battery?

The context of a network might include factors, such as bandwidth and traffic.

There are still many undiscovered features of background information, ignoring the fact that several fog-based research studies have taken into account specific information while assessing how resources and service operations might be studied using fog-based research methods [23].

## 1.4   Fog computing versus cloud computing

Many people use the words fog computing and edge computing alternatively because they both entail moving intelligence and processors closer to the location where data are produced. However, the primary distinction between the two is the location of intellect and computing capacity.

- **Cloud technology:** The processing of data and applications in the cloud is time-consuming for huge datasets. Bandwidth issues result from the transmission of all data over cloud channels. Because of distant servers, slow response times and scalability issues arise.
- **Cloud computing:** Instead of displaying and operating from a central cloud, fog operates at the network's periphery. Therefore, it uses less time. Less need for bandwidth, since all data are pooled at a single access point as opposed to being sent through cloud channels. It is conceivable for a fog-computing platform to circumvent reaction time and scalability difficulties by selling tiny machines known as edge servers in direct user view.

## 1.5  Fog computing and IoT

Do not be astonished to learn that about 31 billion IoT devices are now in operation. It is no surprise that we generate 2.5 quintillion bytes of data every day. Clearly, we need advantages over conventional techniques of data management. This is when fog computing comes into play. When an application or device accumulates huge amounts of data, effective data warehousing becomes difficult, not to mention expensive and difficult [24]. Heavy data place a strain on bandwidth usage. It is costly to build Big Data centers to store and arrange this data. Fog computing collects and distributes storage, computation, and network connection services, decreases energy consumption, increasing the productivity and value of the data, and decreases space and temporal complexity. Consider two IoT examples:

- **Sustainable urban:** Data centers are not designed to accommodate the rising demand for smart city applications. As more individuals began to use IoT devices, more information would be transferred and accessible. Fog computing may assist such inadequate facilities and smart grids in delivering the true benefit of IoT application development.
- **Facilities:** The word "utilities" encompasses applications like hospitals, railroads, and enforcement agencies that need the most advanced data delivery infrastructure to enhance their functioning. Knowledge on energy consumption, fractures, and water leaks, for instance, may be utilized to update payment information, save lives, and enhance operations. How cloud technology increases the value of solutions for the IoT and end-users is getting more potent. A significant proportion of data is currently processed in the cloud in Figure 1.2. In addition, here are six advantages that fog computing may provide to the IoT design and development phase.
- **Maximum business flexibility:** With the proper tools, fog apps may be developed and deployed as required. These programs allow the user to customize the device's behavior.
- **Enhanced security:** As a proxy for devices with limited resources, fog computing updates their software and security credentials. It installs fog nodes with

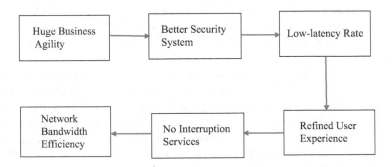

*Figure 1.2   Fog computing enhances solution*

the same policies, processes, and controls as the rest of the IT system. When a large number of nodes process data in a complex distributed system, it is simpler to monitor the security status of adjacent linked devices.

- **Low delay:** Have you noticed how rapidly Alexa responds to requests? This is due to the reduced latency provided by fog computing. Since the "fog" is physically closer to all users (and devices), it is able to deliver instantaneous replies. This technology is suitable for all time-sensitive tasks.
- **Frequency performance of the network:** Fog computing offers rapid and effective data processing dependent on application requirements, available computer resources, and network connectivity. Instead of transmitting information via a single channel, information is integrated in several places. This decreases the amount of data that must be sent to the cloud, thus conserving network capacity and cutting prices significantly.
- **Continuous services:** Fog computing may operate autonomously and provide continuous service, although when cloud network access is impaired. Additionally, because of several linked channels, connection loss is very impossible.
- **Enhanced user experience:** Edge nodes use low-power technologies including Zigbee, Bluetooth, and Z-Wave. Fog computing provides immediate communication between devices and end-users, regardless of network access, hence boosting the user experience. Although fog and cloud computing may seem identical at first glance, they are really distinct levels of industrial IoT solutions. Here are a few distinctions between the two technology solutions:
- **Architectonics:** Fog architecture is dispersed and consists of millions of tiny nodes situated as near as possible to client devices. The design is both hierarchical and flat, with several levels creating a network. Cloud architecture, on the other hand, is centralized. Large data centers are dispersed over the world, which puts them in close proximity to mobile terminals.
- **Communication between devices:** Fog technology acts as an intermediary between software-defined data centers, bringing it closer to end-users. Without the fog barrier, the cloud encounters the electronics, resulting in a lengthy process.
- **Data processing:** In fog computing, data collection and processing occur near the information source, which is essential for real-time management. Fog determines whether to transfer its capabilities to the cloud to process information from many data sources. In a cloud computing approach, the same occurs through distant data centers far from the educational resource.
- **Computational skills:** Compared to fog, cloud technology technologies are more advanced.
- **Quantity of nodes:** In contrast to the cloud, fog comprises millions of little nodes. Due to the instantaneous reactivity between the equipment and end-users, analysis fog provides short-term analysis. Nevertheless, the cloud is designed for long-term study because of its poor reactivity. Because cloud computing employs a variety of security mechanisms and protocols, the danger of cyber-attacks and data loss is significantly reduced. In addition, it has a distributed architecture. Without an internet connection, cloud technology is impossible. Since it is also centralized, cyber risks are more likely.

### 1.5.1   Are fog computing and edge computing the same?

This is a challenging question. To keep things simple, fog and edge computing are virtually the same. Both methods employ computational performance to bring intelligence back to the lowest area network level of the network architecture.

This inhibits the execution of computing activities in the cloud, saving time, resources, and money. In addition, both cloud technology and edge computing may help organizations lessen their dependency on cloud-based platforms for data gathering, which lowers latency difficulties and the time required to make data-driven choices [25].

Perhaps one of the most notable distinctions is the data processing. With a fog node, data are packaged in fog. Computing at the edge interprets information in the system or sensor without transferring it to another infrastructure.

With effective collecting and analyzing data in real time, however, both technologies save time and money when it comes to sustaining procedures. Imagine receiving statistics in near real time that are valuable for improving performance and enhancing uptime. Both fog computing and networking technologies make this feasible.

- **Fog computing and IoT app development in action:** Fog computing stands out as a reliable, dynamic, and cutting-edge technology in a wide range of fields. In this part, we will look at four real-time examples: On the fog platform, data transfer for video streaming applications is well organized. Because of the flexibility and scalability of fog networking and real-time data processing, this is possible. In addition, fog encourages interaction in a virtual full-featured system, allowing real-time video business intelligence for security cameras [26].
- **Monitor and control systems in the healthcare sector:** Future healthcare choices would be incomplete without comprehensive and real-time health data. Data transfer in real time is feasible; however, thanks to the implementation of fog-computing frameworks. "U-Fall" is another key use case, since it automatically identifies a large fall in the event of mild strokes.
- **Playing video games:** Fog computing, like the cloud, puts computational power closer to the players' fingertips. It is no secret that SEGA's fog gaming system relies on the low latency provided by local gaming arcades and centers. So, instead of streaming from the cloud, players would use the local arcade equipment's CPUs to power up their games. The dispersed devices improve the quality of the online gaming experience for many players: a system for intelligent traffic light control; imagine a traffic signal system that is smart uses fog nodes. Multiple sensors on the node interact locally to detect the presence of bicyclists or walkers, as well as the speed and distance traveled by cars. The green light sends out warnings based on the information. Since it already monitors video security cameras, an ambulance may be easily seen by its emergency light and warning alarm. Allowing a vehicle to pass traffic may be done by adjusting the traffic signals in the area [27].
- **In a nutshell:** The IoT solution generates enormous amounts of data every day, and fog computing serves as a partner to the cloud. Data processing near

the source of information overcomes the difficulties of growing data volume, velocity, and diversity as previously stated. It provides companies with more control over their data. Additionally, fog computing enables a more rapid understanding of and reaction to occurrences. A cloud-based analysis is no longer required. This eliminates the need to offload large amounts of data to the core network, which saves money on network traffic. To secure sensitive IoT datasets, fog computing analyzes them inside a company's firewall. In the end, this leads to better company agility, security, and service quality.

## 1.6    Fog deployment model

Fog models may be classified depending on who owns the fog infrastructure and the resources underneath it. In an organization, a third party or a combination of them is responsible for creating, managing, and operating a private fog. It may be installed either on- or off-site. A single entity has exclusive access to the resources of a private fog (e.g., business units). A firm, academic institution, government agency, or a combination of these, creates, owns, manages, and operates a public fog. Fog service providers have it installed on their property. Public fog materials are available to the entire public for free. Several groups in the community, as well as a third party, or a mix of the three, are involved in the creation, management, and operation of the community fog. Typically, the materials are made available only to members of a certain community of organizations that share the same set of issues. It is possible to combine general populace fog computing with cloud applications in a hybrid fog-computing model (i.e., hybrid cloud). Since the fog is devoid of physical resources, it may be advantageous to use this method. The infrastructure has been relocated to a hybrid cloud in an attempt to enhance performance. A cloud infrastructure is expandable, elastic, and capabilities may be accessed on-demand if needed. Because of this, apps depend on the fog models used to deploy them. There are 13 private fog and 17 hybrid fog apps evaluated, with the majority being deployed in a private fog. It is also worth noting that none of these apps are currently being used in public or communal fog. Astonishingly, the applications may be grouped depending on their specific needs and the capabilities of the fog models. It is for these reasons that we conclude that a private fog is the best option. As a result of the high risk to privacy and security posed by apps dealing with personal data, such as wearable devices, many of these applications are better suited to be deployed in a private fog cloud controlled by the user or a third party that the user has confidence in. Similarly, for reasons of security, many companies choose to use a secure cloud to operate autonomous robotic applications.

For applications that are sensitive to latency and resource needs, such as web hosting, the fog platform is the ideal solution.

In the classic cloud approach, you pay only for what you use, which is called a pay-as-you-go (PaaS) model. Some programs, especially those that do not need a lot of flexibility or administration, are more cost-effective to run on-premises. One-time costs for private fog capabilities are less expensive than typical cloud services for similar programs. Fog hybrids are designed to scale fog infrastructures' resources, so they may be used for applications that otherwise would be unaffordable (i.e., computation and storage). As a result, access networks serve as essential building elements for fog platforms since they link IoT devices to the platform. An ultra-low latency and massive data volume network architecture are needed to process and respond to data produced by applications in microseconds. Fog environments allow for the deployment of a wide range of standards and access network types. Because of the dispersion and mobility of fog nodes, wireless communication is critical in this environment. Using wireless networking allows fog communication structures to be flexible, mobile, and reachable. Wi-Fi support at a fog node will rely on a wide range of factors, including the fog node's role and location in a network hierarchy, as well as its coverage and range. For devices and networks with limited resources, LPWAN (low-power wide area network) has been developed as a protocol. It covers a large area and consumes very little power and data. In agriculture, LPWAN technology is well suited to the task. LPWAN-based protocols include LoRa and SigFox.

For long-distance IoT connectivity, cellular networks are the best option. In contrast, all mobile phone network technologies need RF licensing, IP protection, and energy requirements, all of which add up to a substantial price tag. Communication options for the IoT that use the NB-IoT and LTE M protocols are aimed at providing low-power and low-cost IoT communication platforms. IoT connection is predicted to rise because of a new mobile network, 5G. As a further benefit, it promises lower costs, lower power consumption, and lower latency. A wide range of devices are interoperable with IEEE 802.11, the most extensively used local area network protocol. Its power requirement, high data transfer rate, and intermediate range make it ideal for latency-aware fog applications. It was for this reason that IEEE 802.11ah and IEEE 802.11ax (HaLow) were created. The typical structural system of MAC layer protocols was found to be completely at odds with the needs for IoT low-power and multi-hub connectivity. This specification has been the most popular MAC layer technology for the IoT since its debut (IoT). The low data rate and medium range of Zigbee and 6LoWPAN make them excellent for building automation.

Personal area network technologies, such as NFC, Bluetooth Low Energy, and Radio Frequency Identification (RFID), may be useful in wearing fitness equipment, object tracking, and check-in systems (RFID). The size of the fog platforms will be determined by the amount of the region it will cover; many antenna options are available. The live video broadcasting App04 makes use of directional Wi-Fi antennae. The many ways an access network may be used for various applications. There are certain programs that are presented more than once because they use various kinds of access networks and deployment tiers. Real-world test beds are also used for some of the applications being examined. Examples include Power Consumption Management, Vehicle Video Processing, and Vehicle Fog Computing, which explore Dedicated Short Range Communication, LTE, and VFC.

The computers that make up a fog-computing platform are not only physically diverse but also in terms of their processing, storage, and network bandwidth capabilities. Essentially, they are the foundation of fog infrastructures. When compared to standard cloud systems, fog architectures employ modest computational fog nodes or servers scattered throughout a broad geographic region in order to service a greater number of users. A user's latency is highly dependent on where the closest fog nodes are located, as they may be placed anywhere between end-users and a data center. Depending on the application's needs, developers must choose the suitable fog nodes to enhance the application's QoS. In order to better understand how the surveyed apps are being deployed, we investigate several fog nodes. Comparison of prospective fog nodes is using the following characteristics: In general, fog nodes may be divided into stationary and mobile nodes. Static nodes are considered at strategic locations. Small-scale data centers and personal PCs are examples of "static nodes," which are nodes that do not change their locations. Because they are essentially immobile, these devices must be permanently installed. Depending on where they are deployed, static nodes may be further classified into subgroups. Examples include base stations, networking equipment (such as networking equipment), and micro data centers. Setting up and configuring base stations is more challenging, due to their mobility and smaller size. Drones, vehicles, and other node mobility are examples of single-board devices. However, as indicated in this opening paragraph, nodes may be used to consolidate resources longitudinally.

Folio nodes serve as the deployment method for our reference apps, providing a scalable and reliable infrastructure for hosting and delivering applications while ensuring efficient resource allocation and management. Depending on the needs, several of the studied apps might be implemented with one or more possible fog nodes (i.e., computation capacity and proximity). Apps concentrate on near proximity: IoT. When computing resources are needed in close proximity to end customers, single-board PCs are often used. Sensor data from the surrounding environment is collected and processed locally for example. Because of their tiny size, single-board computers may be readily installed and relocated. Traffic congestion management, autonomous driving, and other vehicle-based applications typically make use of the vehicle's built-in computing power to analyze data collected from the roadside. Apps that use drones to move computing resources, such are known as drone-based applications. Using single-board computers, the drone is able to process locally and communicate with other fog nodes in the vicinity. Applications requiring a lot of processing power are often run on laptops or in tiny data centers.

## 1.7    Distributed with the fog

One of the most important aspects of fog computing is its ability to be distributed. If you want minimal latency, you need several nodes spread out over the network, not just one at the network's edge. All users in a designated region may access adjacent resources thanks to the nodes spread. There are two ways that fog-computing systems may distribute their output: In both equipment and software partitioning, the dispersed nodes and the instances and components of programs are shown. For the distribution of hardware, there are two typical options. It is called horizontal node distribution, and it involves having several nodes on the same layer in the design. There is also vertical distribution, which is used when nodes differ for the resources they have (e.g., via a hardware update). To better serve a larger number of users, as a rule of thumb, nodes with even more materials tend to be placed in a greater vertical layer, while those with fewer resources tend to be spread out across a larger area; all of these separate levels are geared toward a single goal: a trip to the endless cloud. To distribute an application across a cluster, replication and multicomponent may be employed. Each element is often a microservice hosted on a different node. As an alternative, a wide range of applications may be duplicated over numerous nodes. A key selling factor for many of the programs that wish to run on top of fog is its dispersion. A regular dispersion of fog nodes is needed when there are a significant number of visitors in a particular application. According to the connected systems that cover the street lights, nodes should indeed be built based on the location of these devices. Replication and horizontal dispersion are both required.

A number of requests rely on the continuous function and replication of the same components across several nodes. Video stream processing, for example, makes extensive use of this technique due to its high computational demands. The purpose of this replication is to reduce latency and increase performance by distributing the copy over many nodes. Fog clusters are tiered such that the edge nodes gather data, which is then delivered to the fog nodes, which analyze it and only give back the results to the cloud for cloud-based applications that need vertical distribution. In the case of data streams, this design is very economical, since only the output results need to be sent. This is an excellent method for reducing internet latency and traffic conditions. Apps that do not need to be distributed at all tend to be edge-only or cloud-based apps, which can operate on either side of a network.

## 1.8 Fog service models

Fog-computing systems, like cloud computing platforms, allow users to access virtualized resources at various levels of abstraction. Depending on whether they provide infrastructure, platform, or software, we may divide them into three groups. To distinguish them from their cloud-only equivalents, we've given them the names Fog-Infrastructure-as-a-Service (FogIaaS), Fog Platform as a Service (FogPaaS), and Fog-Software-as-a-Service (FogSaaS).

- **FogIaaS:** It is possible to employ various types of hardware, including CPUs, networks, and discs, using FogIaaS. A wide range of operating systems and tools are available to the end-users, giving them complete control over how they utilize the resources.
- **FogPaaS:** Customers may utilize it in order to get necessary software products and other capabilities for running multiple and developing software; you may use FogPaaS. A company that develops software testing and deployment processes may be streamlined and cost-effective thanks to FogPaaS.
- **FogSaaS:** It is possible to utilize software programs without having to install them on your own computer using FogSaaS. Using a web browser, users may access the services over a distant network.

According to the service models they use, the reference apps are categorized. As an example, there is just one app for this.

- **Middlewares are essential:** Cloud-based FogPaaS services may be needed as more fog-computing apps are created in order to allow simple application development on fog platforms. We've compiled a list of the most popular middlewares here. The Big Data group first came up with the idea of data stream processing technologies. There was some interest in a fog-computing environment, which might reduce data transfers between IoT devices and cloud servers. There are a variety of systems out there, each with its own unique set of capabilities.

- **Function-as-a-service:** Event-driven, serverless applications may be built with the help of the service. Code or functionality may be developed and managed without the need for servers or server administration. IoT devices may be used in a function-as-a-service architecture, in which a sort of cloud is computing. Fog computing is trying to make use of this. In essence, this is edge computing, where gadgets like IoT and smartphones, web applications, and other endpoints are connected to the cloud technologies exist. Computer networks use message-oriented middleware (MOM) to communicate with one another using MOM. Distributed and heterogeneous components are supported by a software or hardware infrastructure that seeks to provide message reception and transmission. In order to simplify the development of applications for numerous operating systems and network protocols, it has been designed. In fog-computing settings, MOM is utilized to increase the scalability of fog nodes and job scheduling. An ecosystem where apps can operate independently of what they do is what web application servers offer. Typically, they have a variety of service levels, each of which solves a specific issue. A cloud-based database server can provide a variety of functions, including web page serving, container models or services for applications, manufacturing requirements, load balancing over several web hardware, and monitoring and implementation tools. Data centers and end devices may benefit from improved management of and program their computing, networking, and storage resources by enhancing the capabilities of application servers in the cloud. The reference applications make use of a variety of middleware. Middleware is included many times since some applications use more than one kind. Unspecified apps are those that do not specify a middleware type.

- **Data processing methods:** For the fog architecture, it is important to know what kind of data the nodes process in the system. Data volume and processing timeliness are directly linked to this information, which may be found. Cloud computing is generally seen as a dispersed network that may be expanded horizontally to accommodate additional nodes in the event that the current pool of resources is inadequate. The allocation of a single job among several nodes is seldom discussed, despite this fact. It is common for nodes to be able to host a whole job and, as such, to have processing and storage capacity that is tailored to the timeliness of application scenarios. It shows how the apps are organized based on the amount of data they handle. Only a few applications demand a considerable amount of computer power to handle textual data. Delay-sensitive applications may need a lot of time to process sensor data. It is possible that the amount of processing power required will vary based on the kind and quantity of sensors. Even the most demanding programs, it has been found, can handle static graphics or even video in certain cases. Use of specialist hardware, such as graphics processing units, is typically required for this kind of processing.

- **Process automation data:** Sensor data and process automation have led to an ever-increasing amount of data being generated. The number, size, and scale of data created and kept is the most crucial factor in the Big Data community's opinion. Fog is seldom used to store large volumes of data, as we have seen. Fog-computing platforms, on the other hand, are often used to handle data streams that need quick processing or filtering before redelivery to the initial recipients. The quantity of data handled by each software ranges from a few kilobytes up to many terabytes. The great amount of individuals deals with extremely little amounts of data, in the range of kilobytes to megabytes in size, on a regular basis. There is a high demand for real-time operations, which necessitates that data be collected, analyzed, and delivered immediately. Data stream or message-oriented algorithms may need higher storage space when many copies are required to provide high availability and high parallelism. Similar approaches are used when dealing with large volumes of camera-generated data. In many cases, cloud storage is required for apps needing long-term and dispersed retention in fog nodes, such as those that use cameras or personal files (e.g., photographs). A company's customers and IoT devices influence how much data it can store. For applications that use machine learning or deep learning, a large amount of historical data is essential (such as pattern identification from video camera feeds). The significant number of these programs uses private cloud infrastructures that enable managers to set aside a certain amount of storage space for each application.
- **Sensitivity to data speed and delay:** Fog computing's reduced latency between users and resources is a key feature. When parts of the resources are near the end-users, then the widely scattered nodes fulfill a function. Applications seeking ultra-low latencies that may not surpass a few milliseconds regardless of the velocity of the incoming data will be motivated by fog's promised low latency. In the Big Data community, the term "data velocity" is used to describe both the rate at which new data are generated and the time it takes to analyze it. As the number of networked devices and systems grows, so does the amount of data that has to be processed. This is especially true in the field of IoT. According to the application, data output might range from a few kilobytes per second to several megabytes per second. There is a wide range of possible reaction times for different applications, ranging from milliseconds to seconds or even longer. These two metrics are used to classify the reference apps. We can see that most of the programs' input data generation rates are in the MBps or even kBps range. Data production rates of this

magnitude may at first seem manageable, but most applications need a rapid reaction to the data they create. Consequently, any fog-computing platform may struggle to handle an increase in data creation. We've discovered patterns in the apps we've tested. IoT-based apps don't need any latency constraints; however, a large number of other IoT-based applications require low latency for optimal operation. "Low latency" might signify many things depending on the application. Latency requirements for certain apps are quite stringent, but other applications may run with less stringent time limits. Making decisions in the present moment: Ultra-low latency is critical for apps. Decisions must be made quickly in order to prevent collisions, for example, on a fog platform for autonomous cars. User experience of the highest standard gaming and video streaming are two of the most common examples of applications in this area. Rather than endanger lives, long response times might have a negative impact on user experience in these types of apps. In order to fulfill data velocity demands, a humongous fog-cloud computing service must be able to analyze model parameters close to where it was originated and only transport pre-processed data to other fog- or cloud-hosted components.

- **Multiple sources of information:** Data from a variety of different sources must be integrated into a variety of fog applications. A good example of this is App06, which uses drones to deliver items. The recipient's present location and other critical useful data, such as control temperature or the most energy-efficient methods, may be found on the internet; this may be necessary for this application. In order to aid the application's decision-making process, certain metrics must be accessed from outside sources since they are seldom accessible locally. It's possible that there is no established trust relationship between these data owners and the corporations that offer them. Fog applications may have to cope with a variety of security protocols (keys, algorithms, etc.) from diverse data providers since there are a variety of people in charge of independent bodies. There are a variety of data security protocols and methods used by the various providers, which means that the fog application must be able to access and consume data in accordance with these protocols and processes. Data suppliers are included, which organize our reference apps. Specific procedures for the various applications that rely on several independent data suppliers may be required for future fog-computing platforms.

- **Sensitivity to the importance of privacy:** Data are fueling most of the services we use in today's cultures. Data about users are required in order to utilize the service, on the other hand. While many individuals are worried about how their personal information may be used, others choose to keep their personal information private. Apps that monitor physical activity on a user's daily schedule and provide advices on how to live a more healthy lifestyle are an example of this. In spite of their curiosity, the users do not want their daily physical activity to be made public by their neighbors or coworkers. Concerns over European individuals' privacy prompted the European Commission to issue the General Data Protection Regulation. Legal, technological, sociological, and other approaches may all be used to describe what we mean by privacy. The laws and actions that may be done to ensure that only the intended recipient receives personal data are referred to as data privacy in this article. Non-authorized parties should not be able to access an individual's personal information, which is defined as "privacy" under the law. Due to their proximity to the user, fog apps typically gain access to confidential user data. Fog computing, like IoT and cloud computing, has the same privacy concerns. We also deal with data that are ordinarily owned by a user and are located near a fog node in fog computing. Because the position of fog nodes in the vicinity of a user may be determined, the issue of user privacy is made worse.

The three layers of data privacy are as follows:

- The data are open to the public. For instance, a city's street names are open to the public.
- If a number of requirements are met, some of the data may be accessible. Depending on local regulation, a city's list of dangerous streets could be private or public.
- The data can only be accessible by a limited number of people or organizations. Personal health information, for example, is often kept private.
- Security awareness: In any large-scale computer system, data security is a major problem. If you're using fog computing, regardless of whether your IoT data are collected by sensors or is being sent from the cloud, you must assure its privacy and authenticity. Any data transferred should be received at its inevitable conclusion in the same form that it was sent. As a rule of thumb, sensitive information should only be accessible to the data source and its intended receiver. An IoT device's health-related data may be of tremendous value to unauthorized organizations, making it susceptible to attack. This is a good illustration of the need to maintain strict secrecy. The personal health information of about 80 million Anthem customers was compromised because of this breach in 2005. Encryption is utilized in modern technologies to secure data. Therefore, not all IoT devices are capable of handling the computing needs of cryptography. This is a problem. Second, a fog-computing platform may need to handle the importance of secrecy in the fog/IoT domain because of IoT devices' uniqueness. Data leaks may be prevented through context-aware security processes, in which the system switches between various degrees of protection based on its immediate surroundings. Because malware has been detected on nearby computers, a node may switch to a stronger encryption technique. It categorizes the data integrity and confidentiality needs of our reference applications. Obviously, a secure environment is preferred by all applications. We only include those programs on our list that pose a significant risk to their users if their integrity or confidentiality were compromised.

## 1.8.1   *Characteristics of the workload*

Fog-computing systems must be widely dispersed in order to be near their consumers. Thus, they face significant difficulties operating large-scale fog applications, as well as the infrastructure for fog computing. Fog-computing systems must be able to adapt to dynamic workloads, detect, and correct problematic workloads in order to provide the highest possible performance and high QoS.

The workload generated by our reference applications may be divided into two broad groups, each with a handful of subclasses, depending on the peculiarities of their workloads.

• Workload is dynamic and changes based on a variety of factors.
• Fog node position affects the amount of work that must be done.
• Workload fluctuates with the passage of time.
• Depending on how much labor users put in, the workload changes.

Component applications are categorized according to the amount of work they can manage at any one time. As far as we can tell, the majority of fog apps are running at a constant load. During dense fog, sensor data are processed by fog apps. As an example, employ security cameras to take frequent photos and send them to the fog for further processing, as shown in the image. Smart cities, industrial automation, intelligent buildings, and smart grids are just a few examples of where these sorts of applications might be used.

Dynamic workloads were observed in seven applications: three based on geographic location, one on time, and three based on persons. There is no difference between web-based and cloud-based web services when it comes to different applications. On the other hand, fog-based applications can only be utilized under certain circumstances. The number of neighboring sensors may also vary depending on the location. The number of self-adapting stations may be reduced. Depending on how many other fog nodes are nearby, the fog node may establish a connection. Finally, it catches mobile in real-time transport demands, modifying the load.

Fog-computing systems must be designed and operated in a cost-effective way if their workload characteristics are to be understood. For dynamic workloads, fog infrastructure and applications must be created and deployed in a scalable manner. All of these must be included in fog management platforms, including intelligent application distribution and dynamic capital allocation.

## 1.9    Merits of fog computing

• Limit the quantity of information transferred to the cloud
• Reduces the amount of bandwidth used by the network.
• Enhances the responsiveness of the system.
• Storing information near the edge increases the safety.
• Supports freedom of movement.
• Minimizes latency on the network and the internet.

## 1.10    Demerits of fog computing

• The cloud's anytime, anywhere, and data value are diminished by a specific address.
• IP address spoofing and man-in-the-middle attacks are among the security concerns.

- Identification and privacy considerations.
- Information infrastructure for wireless connections.

## 1.11 Application of fog computing

The IoT makes extensive use of the developing technology of fog computing. The network edge receives data and services from the network core via fog computing. Similar to the cloud, the fog provides data, computation, storage, and enterprise applications to end-users.

- Patient monitoring systems in real-time primary healthcare units are being developed.
- Monitoring of pipelines for leaks, fires, theft, and the like.
- Smart grid control has the ability to switch between various sources of energy.
- Smart farms with agricultural applications and irrigation management systems are being used in agriculture.
- Fleet management and vehicle health monitoring equipment for trucks and buses are also included in this category.
- Automated invoicing and reporting of shopping baskets.
- Fire alarms, temperature control, and intrusion detection are all examples of smart home technology.

## 1.12 Conclusion

Fog-computing applications come in many shapes and sizes, and as a result, the pervasive computing platforms built to serve them must be able to handle needs that span a broad spectrum. Researchers hope that these findings will help future fog platform developers make well-informed judgments regarding the capabilities. They may or may not include the kinds of activities that would most benefit from those inclusions. Fogging is a term used to describe a hardware implementation where data, processing, and applications are centered at the edge of the network instead of being on the internet. Service latencies and customer satisfaction are both improved consequently. Fog computing eliminates the need for a return trip to the cloud for analysis, allowing users to react to events faster. This leads to increased organizational capabilities, better service levels, as well as greater safety for enterprises that use fog computing.

## References

[1]   S. Yi, C. Li, and Q. Li, A Survey of Fog Computing: Concepts, Applications and Issues, In *Proceedings of the 2015 Workshop on Mobile Big Data*, New York, USA, 2015, pp. 37–42.

[2]   F. Bonomi, R. Milito, J. Zhu, and S. Addepalli, Fog Computing and Its Role in the Internet of Things, In *Proceedings of the First Edition of the MCC Workshop on Mobile Cloud Computing*, New York, USA, 2012, pp. 13–16.

[3]   S. Yangui, P. Ravindran, O. Bibani *et al.*, A Platform As-a-Service for Hybrid Cloud/Fog Environments, In *IEEE International Symposium on Local and Metropolitan Area Networks (LANMAN)*, 2016, pp. 1–7.

[4]   M. Aazam and E. N. Huh, Dynamic Resource Provisioning through Fog Micro Datacenter, In *IEEE International Conference on Pervasive Computing and Communication Workshops (PerCom Workshops)*, 2015, pp. 105–110.

[5]   O. Salman, I. Elhajj, A. Kayssi, and A. Chehab, Edge Computing Enabling the Internet of Things, In *IEEE 2nd World Forum on Internet of Things (WF-IoT)*, 2015, pp. 603–608.

[6]   H. T. Dinh, C. Lee, D. Niyato, and P. Wang, A Survey of Mobile Cloud Computing: Architecture, Applications, and Approaches, *Wireless Communications and Mobile Computing*, 13, 1587–1611, 2013.

[7]   J. M. Kang, H. Bannazadeh, H. Rahimi, T. Lin, M. Faraji, and A. LeonGarcia, Software-defined infrastructure and the Future Central Office, In *IEEE International Conference on Communications Workshops (ICC)*, 2013, pp. 225–229.

[8]   H. Hejazi, H. Rajab, T. Cinkler, and L. Lengyel, Survey of Platforms for Massive IoT, In *IEEE International Conference on Future IoT Technologies (Future IoT)*, 2018, pp. 1–8.

[9]   W. Shi, J. Cao, Q. Zhang, Y. Li, and L. Xu, Edge Computing: Vision and Challenges, *IEEE Internet of Things Journal*, 3, 637–646, 2016.

[10]  F. Bonomi, R. Milito, P. Natarajan, and J. Zhu, *Fog Computing: A Platform for Internet of Things and Analytics in Big Data and Internet of Things: A Roadmap for Smart Environments*, Springer, Cham, 2014, pp. 169–186.

[11]  S. Yi, Z. Qin, and Q. Li, Security and Privacy Issues of Fog Computing: A Survey, In *Proceedings of the International Conference on Wireless Algorithms, Systems, and Applications*, 2015, pp. 685–695.

[12]  P. Hu, S. Dhelim, H. Ning, and T. Qiu, Survey on Fog Computing: Architecture, Key Technologies, Applications and Open Issues, *Journal of Network and Computer Applications*, 98, 27–42, 2017.

[13]  A. V. Dastjerdi, H. Gupta, R. N. Calheiros, S. K. Ghosh, and R. Buyya, Fog Computing: Principles, Architectures, and Applications ArXiv160102752 Cs, 2016.

[14]  A. V. Dastjerdi and R. Buyya, Fog Computing: Helping the Internet of Things Realize Its Potential, *Computer*, 49, 112–116, 2016.

[15]  C. C. Byers, Architectural Imperatives for Fog Computing: Use Cases, Requirements, and Architectural Techniques for Fog-Enabled IoT Networks, *IEEE Communications Magazine*, 55, pp. 14–20, 2017.

[16]  R. Mahmud, R. Kotagiri, and R. Buyya, *Fog Computing: A Taxonomy, Survey and Future Directions in Internet of Everything*, Springer, Singapore, 2018, pp. 103–130.

[17]  C. Mouradian, D. Naboulsi, S. Yangui, R. H. Glitho, M. J. Morrow, and P. A. Polakos, A Comprehensive Survey on Fog Computing: State-of-the-Art and Research Challenges, *IEEE Communications Surveys Tutorials*, 20, 416–464, 2018.

[18]  R. K. Naha, S. Garg, and A. Chan, Fog Computing Architecture: Survey and Challenges, arXiv:1811.09047 [cs], Nov. 2018.

[19]  A. Yousefpour, C. Fung, T. Nguyen *et al.*, All One Needs to Know about Fog Computing and Related Edge Computing Paradigms: A Complete Survey, *Journal of Systems Architecture*, 98, 289–330, 2019.

[20]  M. Eder, Hypervisor-vs. Container-based Virtualization in Future Internet (FI) and Innovative Internet Technologies and Mobile Communications (IITM), *Seminars FI / IITM WS 15/16, Network Architectures and Services*, 1, pp. 11–17, 2016.

[21]  D. Zeng, L. Gu, S. Guo, Z. Cheng, and S. Yu, Joint Optimization of Task Scheduling and Image Placement in Fog Computing Sup-ported Software Defined Embedded System, *IEEE Transactions on Computers*, 65, pp. 3702–3712, 2016.

[22]  H. Xiang, W. Zhou, M. Daneshmand, and M. Peng, Network Slicing in Fog Radio Access Networks: Issues and Challenges, *IEEE Communications Magazine*, 55, pp. 110–116, 2017.

[23]  J. Santos, T. Walters, B. Volckaeert and F. De Turck, Fog Computing: Enabling the Management and Orchestration of Smart City Applications in 5G Networks, *MDPI Journal Entropy*, 2017, 6, pp. 4–15.

[24]  D. Zhao, D. Liao, G. Sun, and S. Xu, Towards Resource-Efficient Service Function Chain Deployment in Cloud-Fog Computing, *IEEE Access*, 6, pp. 66754–66766, 2018.

[25]  A. Shawish and M. Salama, *Cloud Computing: Paradigms and Technologies in Inter-Cooperative Collective Intelligence: Techniques and Applications*, Springer, Berlin, Heidelberg, 2014, pp. 39–67.

[26]  M. Armbrust, A. Fox, R. Griffith, *et al.*, A View of Cloud Computing Commun ACM, 53, 50-58, 2010. P. Mell and T. Grance, The NIST Definition of Cloud Computing *National Institute of Standards and Technology and Information Technology Laboratory*, 2009.

[27]  R. Jain and S. Paul, Network Virtualization and Software Defined Networking for Cloud Computing: A Survey, *IEEE Communications Magazine*, 51, 24–31, 2013.

*Chapter 2*

# Fog computing in the IoT environment

## Abstract

Fog computing has emerged as a promising paradigm in the field of Internet of Things (IoT), addressing the limitations of cloud-centric architectures. This chapter provides a comprehensive overview of fog computing, focusing on its background, scope, problem definition, aims, and analysis in the IoT environment.

**Background:** The exponential growth of IoT devices has led to an overwhelming influx of data, posing challenges for cloud-centric architectures in terms of latency, bandwidth, and network congestion.

Fog computing, an extension of cloud computing, aims to bring computational resources closer to the network edge, enabling real-time data processing, low latency, and reduced network traffic.

Fog computing leverages the proximity and distributed nature of fog nodes to enhance the performance and efficiency of IoT applications.

**Scope:** This chapter explores the key components and architecture of fog computing, including fog nodes, gateways, and cloud–fog collaboration models, highlighting their roles in the IoT ecosystem.

Various applications and use cases of fog computing in different domains such as smart cities, healthcare, transportation, and industrial automation are examined to demonstrate its versatility.

The integration of fog computing with emerging technologies like machine learning, artificial intelligence (AI), and blockchain is discussed, highlighting the potential for advanced analytics and enhanced security.

**Problem definition:** The limitations of cloud-centric architectures, such as high latency and excessive network traffic, hinder the seamless execution of real-time IoT applications. Centralized cloud processing raises concerns regarding data privacy, as sensitive information may be transmitted and stored in distant data centers. The resource-constrained nature of edge devices in IoT environments necessitates an efficient and scalable computing approach to handle the increasing computational demands.

**Aim:** The primary aim of this chapter is to provide a comprehensive understanding of fog computing's principles, mechanisms, and benefits in the context of the IoT environment. By highlighting the advantages of fog computing, this study aims to encourage the adoption of fog-based architectures for overcoming the limitations of cloud-centric approaches. The chapter aims to identify the potential challenges and research directions in fog computing, facilitating further advancements in the field to fully exploit the benefits of fog computing in the IoT landscape.

**Analysis or observation on fog computing in the IoT environment:** The integration of fog computing in the IoT environment has proven to be effective in reducing latency, improving response times, and enabling real-time decision-making for time-critical applications. Fog computing brings computation closer to the network edge, allowing localized data processing and reducing the need for continuous communication with cloud servers, thus addressing the bandwidth and latency challenges. The scalability and flexibility of fog computing enable the deployment of resource-intensive applications, such as AI-based algorithms and analytics, at the edge, leading to improved efficiency, reduced data transmission costs, and enhanced privacy.

## 2.1  Introduction

The rapid proliferation of Internet of Things (IoT) devices has revolutionized numerous industries, ranging from healthcare and transportation to manufacturing and smart cities. However, the massive influx of IoT-generated data and the need for real-time processing pose significant challenges for traditional cloud-centric architectures. This has paved the way for the emergence of fog computing, a paradigm that brings computational resources closer to the network edge, enabling efficient and responsive IoT applications [1].

Fog computing is an extension of cloud computing that aims to overcome the limitations of centralized cloud architectures in the context of the IoT environment. While cloud computing relies on distant data centers for processing and storage, fog computing leverages the proximity and distributed nature of fog nodes, which are located at the network edge. By decentralizing computational capabilities, fog computing offers several advantages, including reduced latency, improved bandwidth utilization, and enhanced privacy.

In fog computing, fog nodes act as intermediate entities between IoT devices and the cloud. These nodes are typically located at the network edge, such as routers, gateways, or even IoT devices themselves. They are equipped with computational resources and storage capacity, allowing them to perform real-time data processing and analytics closer to the data source [2]. This proximity ensures faster response times and reduces the reliance on long-distance communication with cloud servers.

The scope of fog computing in the IoT environment is vast. It enables a wide range of applications across various domains. For instance, in smart cities, fog computing can support real-time traffic management, intelligent street lighting, and environmental monitoring. In healthcare, fog computing can facilitate remote patient monitoring, timely diagnosis, and personalized treatment. Fog computing also finds applications in transportation systems, industrial automation, agriculture, and many other sectors that benefit from low latency, near-real-time decision-making capabilities.

One of the primary advantages of fog computing is its ability to address the challenges associated with latency and bandwidth in IoT applications. By processing data locally at the edge, fog computing reduces the time required to transmit data to a distant cloud server and receive a response. This is particularly critical for time-sensitive applications, such as autonomous vehicles, industrial control systems, and real-time monitoring of critical infrastructure.

Furthermore, fog computing enhances data privacy and security. Instead of transmitting sensitive data to remote cloud servers, fog nodes can perform localized data processing and filtering, minimizing the risk of data breaches or unauthorized access. This distributed approach to computation also reduces the dependency on a single point of failure, making the system more resilient and robust.

## 2.2   Models of fog computing

The IoT is a transformative technology that connects physical devices, sensors, and objects to the internet, enabling them to collect and exchange data. However, the sheer volume of data generated by IoT devices presents significant challenges for traditional cloud-centric architectures. Fog computing, also known as edge computing, has emerged as a viable solution to address these challenges. It extends the capabilities of cloud computing by bringing computational resources closer to the network edge, where the IoT devices are located.

In the context of IoT, fog computing offers several advantages. By processing data at the edge, fog computing reduces latency and enables real-time decision-making, which is critical for time-sensitive applications such as autonomous vehicles or industrial control systems. Fog computing advantages fog nodes, which are small-scale servers or gateways located at the edge of the network. These nodes have computational power, storage capacity, and networking capabilities to process and analyze data locally. The distribution of computational resources in fog computing enables efficient bandwidth utilization. Instead of sending all the IoT-generated data to a distant cloud server, fog nodes can filter and aggregate the data, transmitting only the relevant information. This reduces the network traffic and conserves bandwidth [3].

Fog computing also enhances privacy and data security. Since sensitive data can be processed and stored locally at the edge, the risk of exposing data to potential threats or breaches during transmission to a remote cloud server is minimized. The scalability of fog computing is another advantage in the IoT environment. As the number of IoT devices grows exponentially, fog computing allows for the deployment of additional fog nodes to accommodate the increasing computational demands at the network edge. Fog computing can support a wide range of IoT applications across various domains. In smart cities, for example, fog computing can enable real-time traffic monitoring, intelligent energy management, and efficient waste management systems. In healthcare, fog computing can facilitate remote patient monitoring, timely diagnosis, and personalized treatment. By processing medical data at the edge, fog computing ensures faster response times and reduces the burden on centralized healthcare systems. Fog computing is particularly valuable in industrial automation, where it enables real-time monitoring and control of manufacturing processes. This improves operational efficiency, reduces downtime, and enhances overall productivity. The integration of fog computing with emerging technologies such as artificial intelligence (AI) and machine learning (ML) unlocks new possibilities. Fog nodes can perform localized AI and ML algorithms, enabling intelligent decision-making and predictive analytics at the edge. Fog computing also offers benefits in the transportation sector. By analyzing data from IoT devices on vehicles and road infrastructure, fog computing can optimize traffic flow, enhance driver safety, and enable efficient fleet management. In agriculture, fog computing can assist in precision farming by analyzing data from sensors and drones. This enables farmers to make data-driven decisions regarding irrigation, fertilization, and crop monitoring, leading to improved yields and reduced resource wastage [4].

The collaboration between fog nodes and cloud servers is another significant aspect of fog computing. Fog nodes can offload certain computational tasks to the cloud when necessary, ensuring a balance between local processing and utilizing the power of the cloud for more complex analysis. Fog computing enables edge intelligence, where data processing and decision-making occur close to the source of data generation. This reduces reliance on the cloud and ensures faster response times for critical applications. The flexibility of fog computing allows for dynamic deployment and resource allocation. Fog nodes can be deployed in a decentralized manner, adapting to changes in the network and accommodating the evolving requirements of IoT applications. Fog computing also addresses the challenge of intermittent connectivity in IoT environments. By processing data locally, fog nodes can continue functioning even during network disruptions, ensuring uninterrupted operations.

However, fog computing is not without its challenges. The heterogeneity of fog nodes and the need for interoperability pose integration complexities. Standardization efforts are crucial to ensure seamless communication and collaboration among different fog-computing platforms. The management and orchestration of fog resources also require efficient algorithms and protocols. Proper load balancing, resource allocation, and fault tolerance mechanisms are essential to optimize the performance and reliability of fog computing in IoT environments.

## 2.2.1    Basic structure of fog computing

The basic structure of fog computing comprises several key components that work together to enable efficient and distributed data processing at the network edge. The following are the fundamental elements of fog computing:

1. IoT devices: These physical devices embedded with sensors, actuators, and communication capabilities generate data in the IoT ecosystem. IoT devices can range from simple sensors to complex machinery or vehicles.
2. Fog nodes: Fog nodes are the core building blocks of fog computing. They are distributed computing devices located at the network edge, such as routers,

gateways, or even IoT devices themselves. Fog nodes possess computational resources, storage capacity, and networking capabilities to perform data processing and analysis tasks.

3. Fog layer: The fog layer represents the collection of fog nodes that form a distributed network at the network edge. Fog nodes are interconnected, work collaboratively to process, and analyze data in close proximity to the IoT devices generating that data.

4. Cloud: While fog computing brings computational resources closer to the edge, it still maintains a connection to the cloud. Cloud servers provide additional storage capacity, advanced analytics capabilities, and access to vast computing resources when needed. Fog nodes can offload certain tasks or transmit data to the cloud for more analysis that is complex or long-term storage [5].

5. Connectivity: Fog computing relies on robust and reliable connectivity among IoT devices, fog nodes, and the cloud. Various communication technologies, such as Wi-Fi, cellular networks, or specialized IoT protocols, facilitate seamless data transmission and control among the different components of the fog-computing infrastructure.

6. Data processing and analytics: Fog nodes perform localized data processing and analytics tasks in the fog layer. They receive data from IoT devices, apply algorithms and rules for real-time analysis, and generate meaningful insights or actionable decisions. This distributed processing capability allows for reduced latency and faster response times in critical applications.

7. Decision-making: Fog computing enables decentralized decision-making, where critical decisions can be made autonomously at the network edge. By processing data closer to the source, fog nodes can respond quickly to events, adapt to changing conditions, and initiate actions based on predefined rules or ML algorithms.

8. Security and privacy: Fog computing addresses security and privacy concerns in the IoT environment. By processing data locally, sensitive information can be kept closer to its source, reducing the risk of data breaches during transmission. Fog nodes can also implement security measures, such as encryption or access control, to ensure data integrity and protect against unauthorized access [6].

9. Application ecosystem: Fog computing supports a wide range of IoT applications across various domains, including smart cities, healthcare, transportation, manufacturing, and agriculture. The flexibility and scalability of the fog-computing infrastructure enable the deployment of diverse applications that benefit from low latency, real-time processing, and distributed intelligence.

10. Management and orchestration: Effective management and orchestration of fog-computing resources are essential for optimal performance. This involves tasks such as load balancing, resource allocation, fault tolerance mechanisms, and monitoring of fog nodes to ensure efficient utilization of computational resources and the overall health of the fog-computing infrastructure.

## 2.2.2   Analyzing the literature with the help of scientific publications

Analyzing the literature through scientific publications is a crucial step in conducting research and gaining insights into a specific field or topic. The following paragraphs provide an explanation of how scientific publications can be utilized for literature analysis, along with a table outlining the key aspects to consider during the analysis process.

1.  Scientific publications, such as journal articles, conference papers, and research papers, provide a wealth of information and knowledge on various subjects. They undergo rigorous peer review processes, ensuring the reliability and credibility of the information presented.
2.  When analyzing the literature, it is important to define the research objectives and identify the specific research questions or gaps in knowledge that need to be addressed. This helps in narrowing down the focus and identifying relevant publications.
3.  One approach to literature analysis is to create a comprehensive database or repository of scientific publications relevant to the research topic. This database can include bibliographic information, abstracts, and full-text articles, enabling easy retrieval and organization of the literature.
4.  A key step in analyzing scientific publications is conducting a thorough literature review. This involves critically evaluating the existing research, identifying key theories, methodologies, and findings, and understanding the current state of knowledge in the field.
5.  During the literature analysis process, it is important to consider the credibility and quality of the publications. Evaluating factors such as the reputation of the journal or conference, the impact factor, and the author's credentials can help in assessing the reliability of the information presented.
6.  It is essential to identify the key themes, trends, and arguments present in the literature. This helps in understanding the different perspectives and schools of thought within the field as shown in Table 2.1.
7.  When analyzing the literature, it is important to identify any conflicting or contradictory findings. This can highlight areas of debate or unresolved questions that can be explored further in the research
8.  Analyzing the citations within the publications can provide additional insights into the relevant literature and influential studies. Identifying highly cited publications can help in identifying seminal works or landmark studies in the field.
9.  It is also beneficial to track the publication timeline to understand the progression of research in the field. This can help in identifying emerging trends, evolving methodologies, and shifts in research focus over time [7].
10. Analyzing the literature through scientific publications also involves synthesizing the information obtained from different sources. This helps in creating a cohesive understanding of the existing knowledge and identifying gaps that can be addressed in the research.

*Table 2.1 Analyzing scientific publications*

| Aspect | Description |
| --- | --- |
| Title | The title should provide a concise overview of the research topic and its relevance |
| Authors | Assess the credentials and expertise of the authors to determine their authority in the field |
| Abstract | The abstract provides a summary of the study, highlighting the objectives, methods, and findings |
| Introduction | Examine the introduction to understand the context, research gap, and rationale of the study |
| Methodology | Assess the research methodology used, including data collection, analysis techniques, and experimental design |
| Results | Evaluate the findings presented in the publication and assess their significance and implications |
| Discussion | Analyze the interpretation of results, the discussion of limitations, and the exploration of future research directions |
| Conclusion | Consider the key takeaways and the overall contribution of the study to the field |
| References | Examine the reference list to identify other relevant publications that can be explored |

11. While conducting the literature analysis, it is important to remain critical and objective. Assess the strengths and weaknesses of the publications, identify any biases or limitations, and consider the applicability of the findings to the research objectives.

12. It can be helpful to use reference management tools or software to organize and annotate the scientific publications during the analysis process. This streamlines the workflow and allows for efficient retrieval and referencing of relevant information.

    Consider exploring both primary and secondary sources in the literature analysis. Primary sources include original research articles, while secondary sources include review articles, meta-analyses, and systematic reviews that provide a comprehensive overview of the existing literature.

13. The literature analysis can guide the formulation of research questions, hypotheses, and the overall research design. It provides a foundation of knowledge and understanding that informs the research process.

14. In addition to analyzing individual publications, it is beneficial to identify patterns, trends, or gaps in the literature across multiple publications. This broader analysis helps in identifying research opportunities and areas for further investigation.

15. Collaborating with experts or researchers in the field can provide valuable insights and guidance during the literature analysis process. Their expertise can help in interpreting complex findings and understanding the nuances of the research area.

16. It is important to keep the literature analysis up to date throughout the research process. Continuously reviewing and incorporating new publications ensure that the research remains current and relevant.

17. The literature analysis should be documented thoroughly, including the methods used, the key findings, and any insights gained. This documentation serves as a foundation for the research and can be referenced in the research report or thesis.
18. Finally, the literature analysis should be presented in a clear and organized manner, highlighting the key findings, trends, and gaps identified. This provides a comprehensive overview of the existing knowledge and sets the stage for the research objectives and contributions.

## 2.3    Protocol of fog computing

A protocol in fog computing refers to a set of rules and procedures that govern the communication and interaction among different components within a fog-computing infrastructure. These protocols facilitate the efficient operation, data transfer, and coordination among fog nodes, IoT devices, and cloud servers. While specific protocols may vary depending on the implementation and requirements of a fog-computing system, there are several common protocols used in fog computing [8].

Message Queue Telemetry Transport (MQTT): MQTT is a lightweight publish-subscribe messaging protocol designed for constrained devices and unreliable networks. It is commonly used in IoT environments, including fog computing, due to its low overhead, small footprint, and efficient data transmission. MQTT enables efficient communication between IoT devices and fog nodes, facilitating real-time data streaming and control.

Extensible Messaging and Presence Protocol (XMPP): XMPP is an open-standard communication protocol initially developed for instant messaging applications. It supports the exchange of structured data and presence information. In the context of fog computing, XMPP can be used for efficient and secure communication between fog nodes, enabling collaboration and coordination within the fog layer.

CoAP (Constrained Application Protocol): CoAP is a lightweight application-layer protocol designed for constrained IoT devices. It is specifically optimized for low power, low-bandwidth networks and enables efficient data transfer between IoT devices and fog nodes. CoAP follows a client-server model and supports request/response interactions, making it suitable for resource-constrained IoT environments [9].

Border Gateway Protocol (BGP): BGP is an internet routing protocol used to exchange routing information among different autonomous systems. In fog computing, BGP can be utilized to establish and manage the routing tables between fog nodes and cloud servers. It enables efficient routing and forwarding of data packets across the fog layer and cloud infrastructure.

Open Fog Consortium Reference Architecture (OFCA): The Open Fog Consortium has developed a reference architecture that defines a set of protocols and interfaces for interoperability within fog-computing systems. This architecture provides a framework for the standardization and integration of various fog-computing components, ensuring seamless communication and collaboration among fog nodes, IoT devices, and cloud resources [10].

*Table 2.2    Key protocols used in fog computing*

| Protocol | Description |
| --- | --- |
| MQTT | Lightweight publish-subscribe messaging protocol for efficient communication between IoT devices and fog nodes |
| XMPP | Extensible Messaging and Presence Protocol used for efficient communication and coordination within the fog layer |
| CoAP | Constrained Application Protocol optimized for low-power IoT devices, facilitating efficient data transfer in fog computing |
| BGP | Border Gateway Protocol for efficient routing and forwarding of data packets across fog nodes and cloud servers |
| OFCA Reference Architecture | Protocols and interfaces defined by the Open Fog Consortium for interoperability and integration within fog-computing systems |
| F2C protocol | Fog-to-Cloud protocol enabling seamless communication and data exchange between fog nodes and cloud servers |
| LWM2M | Lightweight Machine-to-Machine protocol for managing IoT devices, including features like device provisioning and remote management |

Fog-to-Cloud (F2C) protocol: The F2C protocol is designed to enable communication and data exchange between fog nodes and cloud servers. It defines the interfaces and protocols for seamless integration and coordination between the fog layer and the cloud infrastructure. The F2C protocol facilitates resource management, load balancing, and data offloading between fog nodes and the cloud to optimize the overall performance and scalability of fog-computing systems.

Lightweight Machine-to-Machine (LWM2M): LWM2M is a protocol specifically designed for managing IoT devices and their associated resources. It provides a standardized way to communicate and manage IoT devices within a fog-computing environment. LWM2M supports features such as device provisioning, firmware updates, and remote device management, making it suitable for efficient management and control of IoT devices in fog-computing systems.

These protocols as shown in Table 2.2 serve various purposes, including efficient messaging, coordination, routing, management, and integration within fog-computing systems. It is important to select protocols that align with the specific requirements of the fog-computing infrastructure and enable seamless communication and coordination among fog nodes, IoT devices, and cloud resources.

## 2.3.1    Generic fog-computing architecture

Fog computing, also known as edge computing, is a distributed computing paradigm that extends cloud-computing capabilities to the edge of the network. It brings computational resources, such as storage, processing power, and networking closer to the data source, enabling faster processing and reduced latency.

Over the past few years, the architecture for fog computing has indeed been maturing. Several advancements and developments have taken place in this field, making fog computing more robust and practical. Here are some key factors contributing to the maturity of fog-computing architecture:

Standardization: Standards organizations, such as the OpenFog Consortium and the Industrial Internet Consortium, have been working on defining architectures, frameworks, and protocols for fog computing. These efforts help establish a common ground for implementation and interoperability, making fog computing more accessible and easier to adopt.

Hardware advancements: The availability of more powerful and energy-efficient edge devices, such as edge servers, gateways, and IoT devices, has contributed to the maturation of fog-computing architecture. These devices can handle complex processing tasks and run advanced applications at the edge, enhancing the capabilities of fog-computing systems.

Connectivity improvements: The development of faster and more reliable communication technologies, such as 5G networks, has significantly improved the connectivity between edge devices and the cloud. This enables seamless data transfer and real-time interactions between edge devices and cloud services, further enhancing the performance and efficiency of fog-computing architecture.

ML at the edge: The integration of ML and AI capabilities at the edge has been a significant advancement in fog computing. With the ability to process and analyze data locally, edge devices can make intelligent decisions in real time, reducing the dependency on cloud resources tasks and improving overall system responsiveness.

Security and privacy considerations: As fog computing involves processing and storing sensitive data at the edge, there has been an increased focus on security and privacy. The maturing fog-computing architecture incorporates robust security measures, such as data encryption, access control, and secure communication protocols, to protect against potential threats and ensure data privacy.

### 2.3.1.1   Advantages

Table 2.3 outlines the advantages of fog computing, highlighting the key benefits that this technology offers. The advantage of fog computing is its ability to provide low latency. By bringing the computing resources closer to the edge devices, fog computing reduces the time it takes for data to travel back and forth between the devices and the cloud. This low latency enables real-time processing and analysis of data, allowing for faster decision-making and response times. Whether it is in industries like healthcare, manufacturing, or transportation, low latency provided by fog computing is crucial for applications that require immediate actions or real-time monitoring. The fog computing is its ability to enhance data privacy and security. With fog computing, data can be processed and analyzed locally on the edge devices or at the fog nodes, reducing the need to send sensitive data to the cloud. This local processing helps to minimize the risk of data breaches and unauthorized access. Additionally, fog computing allows for data encryption and secure communication between devices and fog nodes, ensuring the confidentiality and integrity of the data. This enhanced privacy and security make fog computing a

*Table 2.3*   *Outlining the advantages of fog computing*

| Advantages | Description |
| --- | --- |
| Reduced latency | Processing data at the network edge reduce the time required for data transmission, enabling faster response times |
| Real-time analytics | Fog computing enables localized data processing, allowing real-time analytics and decision-making at the network edge |
| Bandwidth efficiency | By filtering and aggregating data locally, fog computing reduces the amount of data transmitted to the cloud, conserving bandwidth |
| Improved privacy | Processing sensitive data locally in fog nodes reduces the need for transmitting it to remote cloud servers, enhancing privacy |
| Enhanced security | Fog computing minimizes the exposure of sensitive data during transmission, reducing the risk of data breaches or unauthorized access |
| Scalability | Fog computing allows for the deployment of additional fog nodes to handle the increasing computational demands at the network edge |
| Resilience | The distributed nature of fog computing enhances system resilience by reducing the dependency on a single point of failure |
| Edge intelligence | Fog computing enables localized data processing and decision-making, facilitating intelligent and autonomous edge devices |
| Energy efficiency | By processing data locally, fog computing reduces the need for continuous communication with distant cloud servers, resulting in energy savings |
| Reduced network traffic | Fog nodes perform data processing tasks locally, reducing the amount of data transmitted over the network and alleviating network congestion |
| Seamless connectivity | Fog computing can continue functioning even during network disruptions, ensuring uninterrupted operations in IoT environments |
| Versatility | Fog computing finds applications in various domains, including smart cities, healthcare, transportation, and manufacturing |
| Integration with emerging technologies | Fog computing can be integrated with technologies like AI and machine learning, enabling advanced analytics and intelligent decision-making at the edge |
| Faster insights | Localized data processing in fog nodes enables quicker data analysis and generation of insights, facilitating timely decision-making |
| Resource utilization | Fog computing optimizes the utilization of computational resources by performing data processing closer to the source, reducing the burden on centralized systems |
| Improved quality of service | Fog computing enables low-latency communication, improved responsiveness, and enhanced user experience for time-critical applications |
| Adaptability | Fog computing allows for dynamic deployment and resource allocation, adapting to changing network conditions and computational demands |
| Cost efficiency | By reducing the need for extensive cloud resources and optimizing data transmission, fog computing can lead to cost savings in IoT deployments |

*(Continues)*

*Table 2.3    (Continued)*

| Advantages | Description |
| --- | --- |
| Collaboration with cloud | Fog computing collaborates with cloud servers, offloading certain tasks to the cloud for more analysis that is complex or long-term storage |
| Innovation potential | Fog computing opens up possibilities for innovation and development of novel applications and services that leverage edge-computing capabilities |

suitable solution for industries that deal with sensitive data, such as healthcare, finance, and government sectors.

### 2.3.1.2    Basic rules of IoT with fog

The basic rules of IoT when combined with fog computing:

Edge intelligence: Fog computing enables edge intelligence by bringing computational capabilities closer to the network edge. IoT devices can process data locally in fog nodes, enabling real-time analytics, intelligent decision-making, and autonomous behavior at the edge.

Data localization: With fog computing, IoT devices can process and analyze data locally in fog nodes, reducing the need for transmitting large volumes of data to the cloud. This data localization minimizes latency, conserves bandwidth, and improves response times, particularly for time-sensitive applications [11].

Distributed processing: Fog computing enables distributed data processing across multiple fog nodes. This distributed approach allows for parallel processing, improved scalability, and fault tolerance, ensuring efficient and reliable data processing in IoT environments.

Hybrid architecture: The combination of fog computing and IoT establishes a hybrid architecture that leverages the strengths of both edge and cloud computing. IoT devices interact with fog nodes at the network edge for localized processing, while still benefiting from the cloud's resources for complex analytics or long-term storage.

Real-time analytics: Fog computing facilitates real-time analytics by enabling data processing and analysis closer to the source. With fog nodes performing localized analytics, IoT applications can generate timely insights and respond to events in near real-time, enhancing the efficiency and effectiveness of IoT systems.

Proximity-based communication: Fog computing enables proximity-based communication, where IoT devices can interact directly with nearby fog nodes. This proximity allows for faster communication, reduced latency, and efficient utilization of network resources, leading to enhanced performance in IoT applications.

Context-awareness: Fog computing enables IoT devices to be context-aware by leveraging data processing capabilities at the network edge. Fog nodes can analyze data from multiple sources and provide context-aware services, such as personalized recommendations or adaptive automation, based on local conditions and real-time data [12].

Bandwidth optimization: Fog computing reduces the burden on network bandwidth by performing data processing and filtering locally. Only relevant information is transmitted to the cloud, optimizing bandwidth utilization and reducing network congestion in IoT deployments.

Scalability: Fog computing enhances the scalability of IoT systems. Additional fog nodes can be deployed as the number of IoT devices grows, ensuring efficient processing and management of increasing data volumes at the network edge.

Reliability and resilience: Fog computing enhances the reliability and resilience of IoT systems by reducing the dependency on a centralized cloud infrastructure. With distributed processing in fog nodes, IoT applications can continue functioning even during network disruptions or cloud outages.

Security and privacy: Fog computing addresses security and privacy concerns in IoT environments. By processing sensitive data locally in fog nodes, it minimizes the exposure of data during transmission and reduces the risk of data breaches. Additionally, fog computing allows for fine-grained control over data access and sharing, enhancing privacy in IoT deployments.

Energy efficiency: By performing localized data processing and reducing the need for constant communication with the cloud, fog computing reduces energy consumption in IoT systems. This energy efficiency is particularly valuable for resource-constrained IoT devices with limited battery life.

Dynamic adaptability: Fog computing enables dynamic adaptability in IoT systems. Fog nodes can adjust their processing capabilities based on changing network conditions, resource availability, or workload demands, ensuring optimal performance and resource utilization in diverse environments.

Redundancy and load balancing: Fog computing supports redundancy and load balancing by distributing data processing tasks across multiple fog nodes. This approach enhances system reliability, fault tolerance, and efficient resource utilization, improving the overall performance of IoT applications.

Time-critical applications: Fog computing is well suited for time-critical applications in IoT. By enabling real-time data processing and decision-making at the network edge, fog computing ensures rapid response times, meeting the stringent requirements of applications like industrial automation, autonomous vehicles, or healthcare monitoring.

Edge-to-cloud collaboration: Fog computing establishes a collaborative relationship between edge devices and the cloud. Fog nodes can offload certain tasks or transmit data to the cloud for advanced analytics, long-term storage, or cross-fog collaboration, leveraging the scalability and resources of the cloud infrastructure.

Hybrid data management: With fog computing, data management in IoT systems becomes a hybrid process. Data can be stored locally in fog nodes for immediate processing or transmitted to the cloud for long-term storage, enabling a balance between real-time analytics and comprehensive data archiving.

Adaptation to network dynamics: Fog computing can adapt to network dynamics in IoT environments. The placement and configuration of fog nodes can be dynamically adjusted based on factors such as network traffic, device proximity, or changing environmental conditions, ensuring efficient utilization of network resources.

Seamless device integration: Fog computing provides seamless integration of diverse IoT devices into a cohesive ecosystem. With fog nodes acting as intermediaries, various types of IoT devices can communicate and interact, regardless of their specific protocols or communication standards.

Innovation and future potential: Fog computing opens up new possibilities for innovation and the development of novel applications and services. By combining the strengths of IoT and edge computing, fog computing unlocks the potential for advanced analytics, real-time decision-making, and transformative IoT experiences in a wide range of domains.

### 2.3.1.3    Models of fog computing

There are no predetermined structures or verified models based on empirical study. Various fog-computing ideas will be described here to aid in understanding the fog vision.

*Infrastructure design for generalized fog computing*

Infrastructure design for generalized fog computing involves creating a distributed and heterogeneous system that enables efficient and scalable fog-computing deployments. An explaining the various aspects of infrastructure design for generalized fog computing:

Generalized fog-computing infrastructure design focuses on deploying a network of interconnected fog nodes that can provide computing, storage, and networking resources closer to the edge of the network, where data are generated. The infrastructure should consist of a mix of fog nodes with varying computing capabilities to cater to diverse application requirements. This heterogeneous nature allows for optimized resource allocation and efficient processing of data at the edge [13].

The design should include robust networking mechanisms to enable seamless communication between fog nodes, as well as between fog nodes and the cloud. This involves selecting appropriate protocols, ensuring reliable connectivity, and considering factors such as latency and bandwidth. Scalability is a key consideration in infrastructure design. The system should be capable of accommodating an increasing number of fog nodes and devices without compromising performance. This can be achieved through modular and flexible architectures that allow for easy addition and removal of fog nodes. Redundancy and fault tolerance should be built into the infrastructure to ensure high availability and reliability. This involves deploying redundant fog nodes and implementing mechanisms for automatic failover and load balancing. Security is a critical aspect of infrastructure design. The fog-computing infrastructure should incorporate robust security measures to protect data, applications, and communication channels. This includes encryption, authentication mechanisms, and intrusion detection systems.

Energy efficiency is another important consideration. The design should aim to minimize energy consumption by optimizing resource allocation, implementing power management techniques, and leveraging energy-aware scheduling algorithms.

Centralized management and orchestration are essential for efficient operation of the fog-computing infrastructure. A management framework should be in place to monitor and control fog nodes, allocate resources, and optimize workload distribution. The infrastructure design should incorporate mechanisms for data management and storage. This includes selecting appropriate storage technologies, implementing data caching and replication strategies, and considering data consistency and synchronization across fog nodes. Integration with cloud computing resources is an important aspect of infrastructure design. The fog-computing infrastructure should seamlessly interact with the cloud to leverage additional resources, enable offloading of computation, and support data analytics and decision-making at the cloud level.

Interoperability is a key consideration when designing a generalized fog-computing infrastructure. It should support a wide range of devices, protocols, and communication standards to enable seamless integration with existing systems and accommodate diverse application domains. The infrastructure should incorporate mechanisms for dynamic resource allocation and workload management. This includes load-balancing algorithms, task-offloading techniques, and adaptive resource provisioning based on application demands and network conditions. Quality of service (QoS) guarantees should be provided by the infrastructure to ensure reliable and timely delivery of services. QoS-aware scheduling algorithms, traffic-shaping mechanisms, and service-level agreements can be employed to meet application requirements. The design should consider mobility support to cater to scenarios where fog nodes and devices are mobile or operate in dynamic environments. Seamless handover mechanisms, mobility-aware resource management, and location-based services are essential components in such scenarios. Edge analytics capabilities should be integrated into the infrastructure design to enable real-time data processing and analytics at the edge. This involves deploying lightweight analytics frameworks, ML models, and data preprocessing techniques on fog nodes.

The infrastructure design should take into account the heterogeneity of the fog environment, including variations in computational power, memory, and storage capacities. Adaptive algorithms and resource management techniques can be employed to efficiently utilize the available resources. Service discovery and composition mechanisms are crucial in a generalized fog-computing infrastructure. The design should include frameworks for discovering and composing services distributed across fog nodes, enabling the creation of complex applications and workflows. Considerations for data privacy and confidentiality should be embedded in the infrastructure design. Techniques such as data anonymization, access control policies, and secure data-sharing protocols can be employed to protect sensitive information. The infrastructure should support fault detection and diagnostics to identify and resolve issues in real-time. Monitoring tools, logging mechanisms, and automated error handling can be implemented to ensure system reliability and facilitate troubleshooting.

## Internet of Things sensors and actuators

IoT sensors and actuators play a crucial role in connecting physical devices and objects to the digital world, enabling them to collect data, interact with their environment, and perform actions. Sensors are devices that detect and measure physical properties such as temperature, humidity, pressure, light, motion, or presence. They capture real-world data and convert it into digital signals that can be processed and transmitted over the network. Actuators, on the other hand, are devices responsible for taking physical actions based on the received data or commands from the IoT system. They can perform tasks such as turning on or off a switch, controlling a motor, opening or closing valves, or adjusting the parameters of a system.

IoT sensors are deployed in various domains, ranging from industrial settings to smart homes and wearable devices. They provide valuable insights into the physical world, allowing businesses and individuals to monitor and analyze real-time data. For example, in agriculture, soil moisture sensors can help farmers optimize irrigation, while environmental sensors can provide information about air quality. In healthcare, wearable sensors can track vital signs and alert healthcare professionals in case of emergencies. IoT actuators, on the other hand, enable remote control and automation. They allow users to operate devices and systems from a distance, improving convenience and efficiency. For instance, smart thermostats can adjust temperature settings based on occupancy and weather conditions, and automated lighting systems can turn on or off lights based on user preferences or motion detection.

Together, IoT sensors and actuators form the foundation of the interconnected IoT ecosystem. They enable the acquisition of real-time data, facilitate autonomous decision-making, and enable remote control and automation. As the IoT continues to expand and evolve, sensors, and actuators will become even more advanced, versatile, and integrated, leading to greater connectivity, intelligence, and automation in various industries and everyday life.

## Devices for creating a haze

Devices for creating a haze are commonly used in various settings, such as theatrical productions, concerts, theme parks, and special events, to enhance visual effects and create an atmospheric ambiance. One popular device used for this purpose is a haze machine. Haze machines generate a fine mist of airborne particles that hang in the air, creating a subtle haze or fog effect. These machines typically work by heating a special fluid or oil, which is then expelled as a mist through a nozzle. The mist created by the haze machine consists of tiny particles that stay suspended in the air for an extended period, giving the illusion of a continuous, atmospheric haze. Haze machines are adjustable, allowing users to control the density and spread of the haze, making them versatile tools for creating different visual effects.

Another device commonly used for generating haze is a fog machine. While haze machines produce a more subtle, lingering haze, fog machines create denser and more dramatic fog effects. Fog machines work by heating a fog fluid or solution, which is then emitted as a dense fog or mist. The fog generated by fog machines is usually more opaque and voluminous, creating a thicker fog effect that is ideal for creating an eerie or mysterious atmosphere. Fog machines are widely used in haunted houses, Halloween events, and stage productions to add an element of suspense and enhance the overall visual impact. These devices come in various sizes and designs, ranging from portable handheld units to larger, more powerful machines suitable for larger venues and outdoor settings.

*Management of resources*

The management of resources refers to the strategic planning, allocation, and optimization of various resources within an organization or system to achieve desired objectives efficiently. Resources can encompass a wide range of assets, including financial resources, human resources, physical infrastructure, technology, time, and energy. Effective resource management involves understanding the availability, utilization, and interdependencies of these resources to make informed decisions and maximize productivity.

In resource management, organizations typically employ techniques such as forecasting, budgeting, scheduling, and capacity planning to ensure optimal utilization of resources. This involves assessing current and future resource requirements, analyzing trends and patterns, and aligning resource allocation with organizational goals and priorities. For example, in project management, resource management involves identifying the necessary skills and expertise required for a project, allocating personnel accordingly, and ensuring that project timelines and budget constraints are met. Similarly, in supply chain management, resource management involves monitoring inventory levels, optimizing warehouse space, and coordinating logistics to minimize costs and meet customer demand.

Effective resource management also entails monitoring and evaluating resource usage to identify areas of improvement and implement corrective actions. By analyzing resource utilization, organizations can identify bottlenecks, eliminate inefficiencies, and reallocate resources as needed. Technology plays a vital role in resource management, as various software tools and systems are available to automate resource tracking, forecasting, and optimization. With accurate and timely data, organizations can make data-driven decisions, optimize resource allocation, and improve overall operational efficiency. Ultimately, efficient management of resources contributes to cost reduction, increased productivity, improved customer satisfaction, and better organizational performance.

## 2.3.2    *Fog-computing environment model*

A model of use refers to a conceptual framework or representation that outlines how a product, system, or service is intended to be used by its target users. It describes that the interaction between the user and the product and provides guidelines or specifications on how to effectively utilize the product's features and functionalities. A model of use typically takes into account user behaviors, needs, and goals to ensure a seamless and intuitive user experience.

To develop a model of use, designers and developers often employ techniques such as user research, user testing, and iterative design processes. They gather insights about the users' preferences, workflows, and pain points to create a user-centered model that aligns with their needs and expectations. The model of use may include elements such as user personas, user journeys, task flows, and interaction patterns, which help designers and developers understand how users are likely to engage with the product and how different features and functionalities can be incorporated to support their goals.

A well-defined model of use serves as a blueprint for product design, enabling designers and developers to create intuitive interfaces, logical information architectures, and smooth interaction flows. It helps ensure that the product meets the usability and functionality requirements of its intended users, minimizing the learning curve and maximizing user satisfaction. By considering the users' perspective and incorporating their feedback throughout the design and development process, a model of use can contribute to the creation of user-friendly and successful products or systems.

### 2.3.2.1   Fog's tree-based computing paradigm

Fog computing's tree-based paradigm is a hierarchical approach to distributing computing resources and data processing in fog environments. In this paradigm, the fog nodes are organized in a treelike structure, with each node serving as a parent or child to other nodes. The tree-based architecture enables efficient and scalable data processing, communication, and resource management in fog-computing systems.

At the top of the tree, typically a cloud server or data center acts as the root node. This node handles high-level tasks, such as centralized data storage, complex analytics, and decision-making. Below the root node, there are intermediate fog nodes that serve as gateways, aggregating data from multiple child nodes and performing preprocessing tasks. These intermediate nodes can further distribute data to their child nodes, creating a hierarchical structure that extends to the edge of the network.

The tree-based paradigm offers several benefits in fog computing. It allows for efficient data aggregation and processing at different levels of the hierarchy, reducing the amount of data that needs to be transmitted to higher-level nodes. This can help mitigate network congestion and latency issues. Additionally, the hierarchical structure enables resource optimization, as fog nodes closer to the edge can handle localized tasks, while higher-level nodes can focus on more global processing. Overall, the tree-based computing paradigm in fog computing facilitates distributed and scalable data processing, enabling efficient utilization of computing resources and enhancing the responsiveness of fog-based applications.

### 2.3.2.2   The network layers

The network layers, also known as the network protocol stack or network stack, refer to a conceptual framework that organizes network protocols into distinct layers, each serving specific functions in the communication process. The most widely used network layer model is the Transmission Control Protocol (TCP)/Internet Protocol (IP) model, which consists of four layers: the network interface, internet, transport, and application.

The network interface layer, also known as the link layer or data link layer, is responsible for establishing and maintaining direct communication between devices on the same local network. It defines protocols for transmitting data over physical connections, such as Ethernet or Wi-Fi. This layer handles tasks such as packet encapsulation, error detection, and media access control.

The internet layer is responsible for addressing and routing data packets across different networks. It utilizes IP to assign unique IP addresses to devices and ensures the delivery of packets from the source to the destination. This layer handles routing decisions, fragmentation, and reassembly of packets, as well as addressing and encapsulation.

The transport layer provides end-to-end communication between devices by establishing logical connections, managing reliability, and ensuring the proper delivery of data. It defines protocols such as TCP and UDP (User Datagram Protocol). TCP provides reliable and ordered delivery of data, while UDP offers faster but unreliable transmission. This layer handles tasks such as segmentation, flow control, congestion control, and error recovery.

The application layer encompasses protocols and services that directly interact with user applications. It includes protocols for email, web browsing, file transfer, and other application-specific tasks. This layer enables communication between applications running on different devices and manages data presentation, encryption, and session management.

### 2.3.3   Advanced fog-computing architecture

Advanced fog-computing architecture builds upon the basic principles of fog computing and enhances its capabilities to address the challenges posed by the rapidly growing IoT, 5G networks, and other emerging technologies. The architecture leverages the proximity of fog nodes to end devices and users to enable efficient data processing and better user experiences. Below are the key components and characteristics of advanced fog-computing architecture:

1.  **Fog nodes**
    i   Advanced fog-computing architecture relies on a distributed network of fog nodes that are strategically placed at the edge of the network. These nodes can be physical devices, such as routers, switches, and servers, or virtual instances running on cloud infrastructure.
    ii  Fog nodes are equipped with computing, storage, and networking capabilities, allowing them to process data locally and provide real-time responses to applications and devices in their proximity.
2.  **Hierarchy and scalability**
    i   The architecture often adopts a hierarchical structure to manage fog nodes efficiently. Fog nodes at different levels of the hierarchy cater to specific tasks and have varying computing capacities.
    ii  This hierarchical approach allows the architecture to be scalable, as it can handle an increasing number of IoT devices and applications without causing a centralized bottleneck.
3.  **Low latency and real-time processing**
    i   One of the primary goals of advanced fog computing is to minimize latency in data processing and communication. By processing data closer to the source, it reduces the round-trip time to cloud data centers, enabling real-time applications.

    ii  This is particularly crucial for time-sensitive applications like industrial automation, augmented reality, connected vehicles, and healthcare.

4. **Edge intelligence**
   i  Advanced fog-computing architecture incorporates edge intelligence, where fog nodes are equipped with ML and AI capabilities. This enables real-time data analytics and decision-making at the edge, without the need to transfer all data to the cloud for processing.
   ii  Edge intelligence can enhance efficiency, security, and privacy by allowing critical decisions to be made locally and reducing the reliance on a centralized cloud for every computational task.

5. **Reliability and resilience**
   i  The architecture is designed with redundancy and failover mechanisms to ensure high availability and reliability. If a fog node fails, the tasks can be automatically redirected to other nearby nodes, ensuring continuous operation.
   ii  This resilience is vital in mission-critical applications where system downtime can lead to severe consequences.

6. **Security and privacy**
   i  Advanced fog computing takes security and privacy seriously, as data are distributed across multiple fog nodes. Encryption, access control, and authentication mechanisms are implemented to protect data in transit and at rest.
   ii  By processing sensitive data locally, the architecture can help address concerns related to data privacy and regulatory compliance.

7. **Collaboration with cloud computing**
   i  Advanced fog-computing architecture collaborates with traditional cloud computing infrastructure to provide a comprehensive and seamless computing environment.
   ii  While fog nodes handle real-time processing and immediate tasks, cloud data centers can be utilized for more resource-intensive computing, historical data storage, and complex analytics.

## 2.3.4    Fog-computing tree model

The fog-computing tree model is a hierarchical approach to organizing and managing fog-computing resources in a network. It leverages the concept of a tree structure, where fog nodes are organized into levels or tiers, each serving specific purposes and responsibilities. This model enhances the efficiency, scalability, and manageability of fog-computing environments. Key aspects of the fog-computing tree model are as follows:

1. **Hierarchical structure**
   i  The fog-computing tree model arranges fog nodes in a hierarchical structure similar to a tree. The tree has a root node at the top, followed by intermediate nodes, and finally, leaf nodes at the bottom.

ii The root node typically represents the cloud or centralized data center, and intermediate nodes represent higher-level fog nodes that aggregate data from lower-level fog nodes.

2. **Root node (cloud or data center)**
   i At the top of the tree is the root node, which can be a cloud data center or a centralized server infrastructure. The root node serves as the ultimate destination for data that requires extensive processing, long-term storage, or global decision-making.

3. **Intermediate fog nodes**
   i Below the root node, there are intermediate fog nodes that form the internal branches of the tree. These nodes are strategically placed at the edge of the network and serve as aggregators for data collected from leaf nodes (end devices or sensors).
   ii Intermediate fog nodes are responsible for processing and filtering data before forwarding it to higher-level fog nodes or the root node. This local processing reduces the burden on higher-level nodes and cloud resources, leading to lower latency and improved response times.

4. **Leaf nodes (end devices)**
   i The leaf nodes are the bottom-most level of the tree and represent end devices, sensors, and IoT devices. These devices generate data that needs to be processed and analyzed.
   ii Leaf nodes directly interact with the immediate fog node in their proximity for local data processing and decision-making. This enables real-time responses and efficient resource utilization.

5. **Task distribution**
   i The fog-computing tree model efficiently distributes computing tasks among fog nodes based on their position in the tree. Lower-level fog nodes handle tasks that require quick local processing, whereas higher-level fog nodes deal with more complex computations and data aggregation.
   ii This task distribution helps to reduce latency and network congestion, as not all data need to travel to the root node or centralized data center.

6. **Scalability**
   i The hierarchical nature of the model allows for easy scalability. As the number of connected devices and data volume increases, the tree can be expanded by adding more intermediate fog nodes to accommodate the growing demand.
   ii This scalability ensures that the fog-computing infrastructure can handle a larger number of devices and applications without compromising performance.

7. **Fault tolerance and redundancy**
   i The fog-computing tree model provides inherent fault tolerance and redundancy. If a fog node fails at any level, the data and tasks can be rerouted to alternative nodes within the same level or to higher-level nodes, ensuring continuity of services.

8. **Edge intelligence integration**
   i   The model can integrate edge intelligence capabilities at various levels of the tree. Higher-level fog nodes can be equipped with advanced AI and ML algorithms for more sophisticated data analysis and decision-making.

## 2.4   Conclusion

In conclusion, fog computing has emerged as a promising paradigm within the IoT environment. By bringing computational resources closer to the edge of the network, fog computing enables efficient data processing, reduced latency, and improved real-time decision-making. The maturing architecture of fog computing has been driven by advancements in standardization, hardware, connectivity, ML, and security. Fog computing offers numerous benefits in the IoT environment. It enhances the scalability and responsiveness of IoT systems by offloading processing tasks from the cloud to edge devices. This not only reduces the burden on the cloud infrastructure but also enables faster and more reliable data analysis, enabling real-time insights and actions. Fog computing also addresses the challenges of bandwidth limitations, network congestion, and privacy concerns by processing data locally and transmitting only relevant information to the cloud, thereby optimizing network utilization and ensuring data privacy.

Furthermore, fog computing plays a vital role in various IoT applications, such as industrial IoT, smart cities, healthcare, and transportation. It enables intelligent automation, predictive maintenance, and real-time monitoring, leading to increased efficiency, cost savings, and improved user experiences. As the architecture for fog computing continues to mature, we can expect further advancements in edge devices, connectivity, and security, driving the widespread adoption of fog computing in diverse industries and everyday life. Overall, fog computing in the IoT environment represents a powerful and transformative approach that leverages distributed computing and data processing at the network edge. Its maturing architecture and growing adoption open up new possibilities for innovation, enabling a smarter and more connected world.

## References

[1]   S. Subashini and V. Kavitha, A Survey on Security Issues in Service Delivery Models of Cloud Computing, *Journal of Network and Computer Applications*, 34, 1–11, 2011.

[2]   Q. Zhang, L. Cheng, and R. Boutaba, Cloud Computing: State-of-the-Art and Research Challenges, *Journal of Internet Services and Applications*, 1, 7–18, 2010.

[3]   A. Beloglazov, R. Buyya, Y. C. Lee, and A. Zomaya, Chapter 3: A Taxonomy and Survey of Energy-Efficient Data Centers and Cloud

Computing Systems, in *Advances in Computers*, 82, M. V. Zelkowitz, (ed.). Elsevier, 47–111, 2011.

[4]    C. Modi, D. Patel, B. Borisaniya, A. Patel, and M. Rajarajan, A Survey on Security Issues and Solutions at Different Layers of Cloud Computing, *The Journal of Supercomputing*, 63, 561–592, 2013.

[5]    M. Zhou, R. Zhang, W. Xie, W. Qian, and A. Zhou, Security and Privacy in Cloud Computing: A Survey, in *2010 Sixth International Conference on Semantics, Knowledge and Grids*, 2010, pp. 105–112.

[6]    T. Dillon, C. Wu, and E. Chang, Cloud Computing: Issues and Challenges, in *24th IEEE International Conference on Advanced Information Networking and Applications*, 2010, pp. 27–33.

[7]    S. H. Mortazavi, M. Salehe, C. S. Gomes, C. Phillips, and E. de Lara, Cloudpath: A Multi-tier Cloud Computing Framework, in *Proceedings of the Second ACM/IEEE Symposium on Edge Computing*, 2017, pp. 20:1–13.

[8]    N. Fernando, S. W. Loke, and W. Rahayu, Mobile Cloud Computing: A Survey, *Future Generation Computer Systems*, 29, 84–106, 2013.

[9]    D. B. Hoang and L. Chen, Mobile Cloud for Assistive Healthcare (MoCAsH), in *IEEE Asia-Pacific Services Computing Conference*, 2010, pp. 325–332.

[10]    G. Sun and J. Shen, Facilitating Social Collaboration in Mobile Cloud-Based Learning: A Teamwork as a Service (TaaS) Approach, *IEEE Transactions on Learning Technologies*, 7, 207–220, 2014.

[11]    K. Sabarish and R. S. Shaji, A Scalable Cloud Enabled Mobile Governance Framework, in *IEEE Global Humanitarian Technology Conference – South Asia Satellite (GHTC-SAS)*, 2014, pp. 25–34.

[12]    E. Ahmed, A. Gani, M. Khurram Khan, R. Buyya, and S. U. Khan, Seamless Application Execution in Mobile Cloud Computing: Motivation, Taxonomy, and Open Challenges, *Journal of Network and Computer Applications*, 52, 154–172, 2015.

[13]    S. Abolfazli, Z. Sanaei, E. Ahmed, A. Gani, and R. Buyya, Cloud-Based Augmentation for Mobile Devices: Motivation, Taxonomies, and Open Challenges, *IEEE Communications Surveys and Tutorials*, 16, 337–368, 2014.

*Chapter 3*

# Enhance quality of fog-computing environment using SDN and NFV technology

## Abstract

**Background:** Fog computing is a paradigm that extends cloud computing capabilities to the edge of the network, enabling low-latency and real-time processing for emerging applications. However, the dynamic and resource-constrained nature of the fog environment poses challenges for ensuring optimal performance and efficient resource utilization.

**Scope:** This research focuses on exploring the potential of Software-Defined Networking (SDN) and Network Function Virtualization (NFV) technologies in enhancing the quality of the fog-computing environment. The study considers the deployment of SDN and NFV techniques to dynamically manage network resources and virtualize network functions, respectively, within the fog infrastructure.

**Problem definition:** The existing fog-computing environment faces challenges such as resource allocation inefficiencies, scalability limitations, and suboptimal network performance. These issues hinder the seamless execution of resource-intensive applications, leading to degraded user experience and reduced overall system efficiency.

**Aim:** The aim of this research is to investigate how SDN and NFV technologies can be leveraged to address the challenges faced by fog-computing environments. Specifically, the study aims to optimize resource allocation, improve scalability, and enhance network performance to ensure a high-quality fog-computing environment for diverse application scenarios.

**Analysis/observations:** By integrating SDN, fog computing can benefit from centralized network control, dynamic resource allocation, and improved network management. NFV allows the virtualization of network functions, enabling flexible and efficient deployment of services in the fog. The synergy of SDN and NFV technologies offers opportunities for effective resource utilization, dynamic adaptation, and enhanced performance, ultimately improving the quality of fog-computing environments.

## 3.1 Introduction

Fog computing has emerged as a promising paradigm that extends the capabilities of cloud computing to the edge of the network, enabling real-time processing and low-latency services for a wide range of applications. However, the dynamic and resource-constrained nature of the fog environment presents challenges in ensuring optimal performance and efficient resource utilization. To address these challenges, this research investigates the potential of two complementary technologies: Software-Defined Networking (SDN) and Network Function Virtualization (NFV) [1].

SDN provides a centralized control plane that enables dynamic network management and resource allocation in fog environments. By decoupling the control logic from the underlying network infrastructure, SDN allows for programmability, flexibility, and efficient utilization of network resources. NFV, on the other hand, virtualizes network functions, enabling the deployment of services and applications as virtual instances that can be dynamically instantiated, scaled, and migrated within the fog infrastructure.

The integration of SDN and NFV technologies offers a promising approach to enhance the quality of fog-computing environments. By leveraging SDN, fog nodes can be efficiently managed, and network resources can be dynamically allocated based on application requirements, traffic patterns, and available resources. NFV enables the virtualization of network functions, allowing for on-demand deployment and scaling of services closer to the network edge, reducing latency and enhancing overall performance.

This research aims to explore the synergistic effects of SDN and NFV in fog-computing environments. The focus is on optimizing resource allocation, improving scalability, and enhancing network performance to provide a high-quality fog-computing environment. By addressing these aspects, the research endeavors to overcome the limitations of existing fog infrastructures and enable the seamless execution of resource-intensive applications with improved user experience and system efficiency [2].

In the following sections, we will delve into the specific challenges faced by fog computing, the objectives of this research, and the potential benefits of leveraging SDN and NFV technologies in enhancing the quality of the fog-computing environment. By analyzing and evaluating the integration of SDN and NFV in fog computing, we aim to contribute to the advancement of this field and provide insights into the practical implementation of these technologies for improved fog-computing deployments.

## 3.2    The paradigm of fog/edge computing

The paradigm of fog computing, also known as edge computing, has emerged as a transformative approach to address the limitations of traditional cloud computing architectures. Fog computing brings computation, storage, and networking resources closer to the edge of the network, where data are generated and consumed, enabling real-time processing and low-latency services. This paradigm shifts the focus from centralized cloud data centers to a distributed infrastructure that spans from the cloud to the edge devices.

In fog computing, the network edge devices, such as routers, switches, gateways, and Internet of Things (IoT) devices, play a crucial role in performing computation and data processing tasks. These devices, collectively referred to as fog nodes, act as intermediaries between the cloud and the end devices, providing localized storage, computational capabilities, and networking services. By bringing computing resources closer to the source of data generation, fog computing reduces the latency and bandwidth requirements for data transmission to the cloud, enabling faster response times and improved user experiences.

The key idea behind the fog-computing paradigm is to leverage the proximity and context awareness of the edge devices to support a variety of applications and services. These applications span multiple domains, including IoT, smart cities, autonomous vehicles, healthcare, industrial automation, and more. By processing data at the network edge, fog computing enables real-time analytics, decision-making, and response, which are critical for time-sensitive and mission-critical applications.

One of the distinguishing features of the fog-computing paradigm is its hierarchical architecture. The fog nodes are organized into multiple layers, with each layer offering different levels of processing power and storage capacity. This hierarchical structure allows for scalable and efficient data processing, where computations can be offloaded from resource-constrained edge devices to more capable fog nodes, and subsequently to the cloud if necessary. This distributed architecture enables workload balancing, reduces network congestion, and enhances system resilience.

Moreover, the fog-computing paradigm brings several benefits to various stakeholders. For end users, fog computing offers improved response times, lower latency, and enhanced reliability for their applications and services. For service providers, it enables efficient resource utilization, reduced network traffic, and the ability to deliver value-added services at the network edge. Additionally, fog computing provides opportunities for data analytics, machine learning, and artificial intelligence (AI) applications, as it enables processing data at the point of generation, which is particularly valuable in scenarios where real-time insights and localized decision-making are critical.

In Figure 3.1, we present an end-to-end fog-cloud integration architecture that illustrates the seamless integration and collaboration between fog computing and cloud computing resources. This architecture highlights the interconnectedness and complementary nature of fog and cloud environments in providing efficient and scalable computing services.

At the fog layer, we have a diverse set of fog nodes deployed at the network edge. These fog nodes are responsible for collecting, processing, and analyzing data generated by edge devices and IoT sensors. They provide localized computation and storage capabilities, enabling real-time decision-making and reducing

*Figure 3.1 End-to-end fog-cloud integration architecture*

latency by processing data closer to the source. The fog nodes also act as gateways, aggregating and filtering data before transmitting it to the cloud, optimizing network bandwidth and reducing cloud processing overhead [3].

The cloud layer consists of a powerful and centralized cloud infrastructure comprising data centers and servers. This layer offers vast storage capacity, high processing capabilities, and access to a wide range of cloud services. The cloud resources are leveraged for handling complex data analytics, machine learning, and resource-intensive applications that require extensive computational power and historical data analysis. The cloud layer also serves as a repository for long-term storage and provides scalable resources to handle spikes in demand.

The integration between fog and cloud layers is facilitated through efficient communication and data transfer mechanisms. Fog nodes communicate with the cloud infrastructure via secure network connections, ensuring data privacy and integrity. Data synchronization and replication mechanisms are employed to maintain consistency between fog and cloud environments. Additionally, fog nodes can offload computation and storage tasks to the cloud when their local resources are insufficient, enabling elastic scalability and seamless workload migration.

This end-to-end fog-cloud integration architecture enables a holistic approach to meet diverse application requirements. It combines the benefits of fog computing, such as low latency, real-time processing, and localized decision-making, with the scalability, extensive resources, and sophisticated analytics capabilities offered by cloud computing. By leveraging this architecture, organizations can achieve optimized resource allocation, efficient data processing, and enhanced scalability to support a wide range of applications, from time-sensitive IoT applications at the edge to complex analytics and historical data analysis in the cloud.

In Figure 3.2, we illustrate the concept of fog acting as the intermediary between the physical and cyber worlds, highlighting its role in bridging the gap and enabling seamless integration between these two domains. The figure represents the interconnectedness of physical devices, sensors, and actuators with the virtual computing and networking resources.

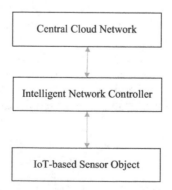

*Figure 3.2    Fog as the intermediary between physical and cyber worlds*

On the left side of the figure, we have the physical world consisting of various devices, sensors, and actuators deployed in the real environment. These devices can be part of IoT deployments, industrial systems, smart cities, or other applications. They generate a vast amount of data that reflects the physical state, environmental conditions, and interactions within the real world [4].

On the right side of the figure, we have the cyber world, representing the virtual computing and networking resources, including cloud infrastructure and services. This virtual world offers computational power, storage capacity, and advanced analytics capabilities for processing and analyzing data.

Fog computing, depicted in the middle of the figure, acts as the intermediary layer that connects the physical and cyber worlds. It comprises fog nodes, which are deployed at the network edge, closer to the physical devices. These fog nodes collect data from the devices, perform real-time processing and analysis, and facilitate localized decision-making based on the physical context and real-time requirements. The fog nodes also provide an interface to the cyber world, enabling seamless communication with the cloud infrastructure and accessing cloud services when needed.

The fog layer plays a vital role in enabling efficient data processing and reducing latency by processing data closer to the source. It acts as a distributed computing and storage layer, enabling edge intelligence and real-time responsiveness. By providing this intermediary layer, fog-computing bridges the gap between the physical and cyber worlds, facilitating the integration of real-time data, context-awareness, and localized decision-making with the computational power and advanced analytics capabilities of the cloud [5].

Overall, Figure 3.2 highlights the importance of fog computing as the intermediary layer that enables the convergence of the physical and cyber worlds. It showcases how fog nodes at the network edge collect, process, and analyze data from the physical devices and seamlessly interact with the cloud infrastructure to leverage its extensive resources. This integration fosters the development of innovative applications and services that require real-time insights, low latency, and efficient utilization of both physical and virtual resources.

In Figure 3.3, we depict the architecture and components of fog computing, highlighting its key elements and their interactions. This figure provides a

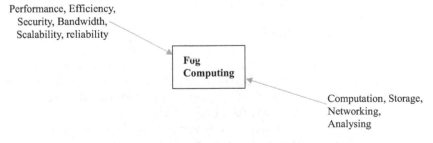

*Figure 3.3   Fog computing*

comprehensive view of the fog-computing paradigm, showcasing its distributed and hierarchical nature.

At the core of the fog-computing architecture, we have fog nodes, represented by the interconnected devices at the network edge. These fog nodes encompass a range of devices, including routers, gateways, IoT devices, and even mobile devices, which are equipped with computation, storage, and networking capabilities. These fog nodes serve as the fundamental building blocks of the fog-computing infrastructure and act as the primary execution and processing units.

The figure illustrates how fog nodes are organized in a hierarchical manner, forming multiple layers. At the lowest layer, we have the edge nodes, which are in direct proximity to the end devices and sensors. These edge nodes capture and process data generated by the devices, enabling localized decision-making and real-time responsiveness. The next layer consists of aggregation nodes, which collect and aggregate data from multiple edge nodes, providing a consolidated view and facilitating data filtering and preprocessing.

Moving up the hierarchy, we encounter the intermediate fog nodes, which further process and analyze the aggregated data. These intermediate fog nodes offer more computational resources and storage capacity, allowing for more complex tasks and advanced analytics. Finally, at the top layer, we have the cloud data centers, which provide extensive resources, scalability, and services for intensive computation and long-term storage. The cloud data centers collaborate with the fog nodes for off-loading tasks and handling workloads that exceed the capabilities of the fog layer.

The figure also highlights the importance of communication and connectivity in the fog-computing architecture. The fog nodes communicate with each other and with the cloud data centers through wired or wireless connections, forming a distributed and interconnected network. This network facilitates the transmission of data, commands, and control signals, enabling seamless cooperation and coordination between fog nodes and cloud resources.

Overall, Figure 4.3 provides a visual representation of the architecture and components of fog computing. It showcases the distributed and hierarchical nature of fog computing, with fog nodes organized in layers and collaborating with cloud resources. This architecture enables efficient data processing, real-time decision-making, and scalable resource allocation, making fog computing a promising paradigm for a wide range of applications that require low-latency, context-awareness, and localized intelligence at the network edge.

## 3.3    What are fog nodes?

In the chapter on enhancing the quality of the fog-computing environment using SDN and NFV technology, it is important to understand the concept of fog nodes. Fog nodes play a crucial role in the fog-computing paradigm as they serve as the fundamental building blocks of the fog infrastructure.

Fog nodes are network devices or computing entities deployed at the network edge, closer to the end devices and sensors. These nodes can include routers, switches, gateways, IoT devices, servers, and even mobile devices that are equipped with computation, storage, and networking capabilities. The primary purpose of fog nodes is to collect, process, and analyze data generated by the edge devices and sensors.

One of the key characteristics of fog nodes is their ability to perform localized computation and decision-making. By processing data closer to the source, fog nodes can reduce latency, enable real-time responsiveness, and support time-sensitive applications. This is particularly important in scenarios where real-time analytics, immediate feedback, or localized decision-making are required.

Fog nodes also serve as gateways or intermediaries between the end devices and the cloud infrastructure. They can aggregate and filter data before transmitting it to the cloud, optimizing network bandwidth and reducing cloud processing overhead. Additionally, fog nodes can communicate with each other and with the cloud infrastructure, forming a distributed network that enables seamless collaboration and resource sharing.

The deployment and placement of fog nodes depend on various factors, including the specific application requirements, network topology, and available resources. Fog nodes can be strategically located in proximity to the end devices, in data centers, or even on mobile vehicles to enable edge computing capabilities. The hierarchical organization of fog nodes, as depicted in Figure 4.3, allows for scalable and efficient data processing, where computations can be offloaded and tasks can be distributed among fog nodes based on their proximity and resource availability.

In the context of enhancing the quality of the fog-computing environment using SDN and NFV technology, fog nodes become the entities where SDN and NFV techniques can be applied. SDN enables centralized network control and dynamic resource allocation in fog nodes, while NFV allows for the virtualization and efficient deployment of network functions within fog nodes.

Understanding the role and capabilities of fog nodes is essential for implementing SDN and NFV solutions effectively in fog-computing environments. By leveraging the potential of fog nodes and their integration with SDN and NFV technologies, it becomes possible to optimize resource allocation, improve scalability, and enhance network performance, ultimately enhancing the overall quality of the fog-computing environment.

Figure 3.4 illustrates the member functions or capabilities of a fog node within the fog-computing environment. A fog node encompasses a range of essential

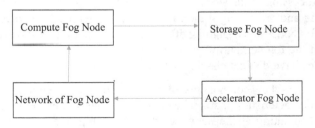

*Figure 3.4    Member function of fog node*

functions that enable it to effectively collect, process, and manage data at the network edge.

One of the primary functions depicted in Figure 4.4 is data collection. Fog nodes have the capability to receive and gather data from various sources, including end devices, sensors, and other edge nodes within their proximity. This function involves capturing data in real-time or periodically from the connected devices, ensuring that the fog node receives a continuous stream of data for further processing.

The next member function showcased in the figure is data processing. Fog nodes possess computational resources that allow them to perform localized data processing tasks. This includes data filtering, aggregation, transformation, and analysis. By executing processing tasks at the network edge, fog nodes can derive real-time insights and make localized decisions based on the data they receive.

Another important function of a fog node is data storage. Fog nodes are equipped with storage capabilities to temporarily hold and manage the processed and raw data. This storage can be used for immediate access, caching frequently used data, or buffering data before transmitting it to the cloud or other fog nodes. The ability to store data locally enhances efficiency by reducing the need for frequent data transfers and improving overall response times [6].

Figure 3.4 also highlights the communication function of fog nodes. Fog nodes facilitate communication between various entities within the fog-computing environment. This includes exchanging data with other fog nodes for collaborative processing, interacting with cloud resources for offloading tasks or accessing cloud services, and communicating with end devices or sensors to receive data or transmit commands. Effective communication between fog nodes and other components of the fog environment is crucial for seamless integration and coordination.

Additionally, the figure depicts the member function of resource management. Fog nodes have the capability to monitor and manage their available resources such as computation, storage, and network bandwidth. This function enables fog nodes to dynamically allocate resources based on the demands of the applications and services running on them. Efficient resource management ensures optimal utilization and scalability within the fog-computing environment.

Overall, Figure 3.4 provides an overview of the member functions of a fog node within the fog-computing architecture. These functions include data collection, data processing, data storage, communication, and resource management. Understanding and leveraging these capabilities is essential for harnessing the full potential of fog nodes and designing efficient fog-computing solutions that enhance the quality of the fog-computing environment.

Fog nodes have distinct characteristics:

1. Fog nodes, as key components of the fog-computing environment, possess distinct characteristics that make them essential for enabling efficient and reliable computing at the network edge. First, fog nodes are geographically distributed, strategically placed closer to the end devices and sensors. This

proximity allows them to reduce network latency by processing data locally and providing real-time responsiveness. By bringing computation closer to the source of data generation, fog nodes enable localized decision-making, which is critical for time-sensitive applications and services. The distributed nature of fog nodes also improves system resilience and fault tolerance, as the workload can be dynamically distributed among multiple nodes, ensuring uninterrupted operation even in the presence of failures.

2.  Another characteristic of fog nodes is their resource-constrained nature compared to traditional cloud infrastructure. Fog nodes often have limited computation, storage, and energy resources due to their smaller form factor and deployment at the network edge. However, this constraint presents an opportunity for efficient resource allocation and optimization. Fog nodes are designed to operate under these resource limitations and are capable of performing lightweight processing tasks, filtering data, and executing localized analytics. They are optimized for specific tasks, leveraging their available resources intelligently and maximizing their efficiency within the fog-computing environment. This resource-constrained nature also makes fog nodes cost-effective, as they can be deployed using less powerful and energy-consuming hardware, resulting in lower operational costs and reduced energy consumption.

3.  Moreover, fog nodes exhibit heterogeneity in terms of their capabilities, processing power, and connectivity options. Different types of fog nodes can coexist in the fog-computing environment, ranging from low-power edge devices to high-performance servers. This heterogeneity allows for diverse deployment scenarios and the adaptation of fog computing to a wide range of applications. Fog nodes can be customized and tailored to meet specific requirements, whether it is supporting IoT devices, industrial automation systems, or smart city infrastructure. The availability of multiple fog node types also enables hierarchical organization, where tasks and processing can be offloaded from resource-constrained nodes to more capable fog nodes or cloud resources when needed. This flexibility in fog node capabilities and deployment options provides scalability and adaptability to different application scenarios, enhancing the overall quality of the fog-computing environment.

## 3.4   Connectivity technologies

Connectivity technologies play a crucial role in enhancing the quality of the fog-computing environment using SDN and NFV technology. These technologies enable seamless and reliable communication among fog nodes, end devices, and cloud resources, facilitating efficient data transfer, control signaling, and resource management. In this chapter, we explore various connectivity technologies that contribute to the enhancement of the fog-computing environment.

Wired connectivity: Wired connectivity technologies, such as Ethernet and fiber-optic cables, provide high-speed and reliable communication between fog nodes and other components of the fog-computing infrastructure. Wired connections offer low latency, high bandwidth, and robustness, making them suitable for scenarios where real-time data processing and low network delay are critical. These technologies are commonly used in environments where fog nodes are deployed in close proximity to each other or in data centers.

Wireless connectivity: Wireless connectivity technologies, including Wi-Fi, Bluetooth, Zigbee, and cellular networks, play a vital role in extending the reach of fog computing to diverse application domains. These technologies enable communication between fog nodes and mobile devices, IoT sensors, and other wireless-enabled devices. Wireless connections provide flexibility and mobility, allowing fog nodes to be deployed in various environments, including smart homes, smart cities, and industrial settings. However, they may have limitations in terms of bandwidth, range, and interference, which need to be considered while designing the connectivity infrastructure [7].

Cellular networks: Cellular networks, such as 4G LTE and upcoming 5G technology, offer wide-area connectivity for fog-computing deployments. These networks provide reliable and high-bandwidth connections, making them suitable for scenarios where fog nodes are spread across larger geographic areas. Cellular connectivity enables seamless integration of fog nodes with cloud resources and supports applications requiring continuous connectivity, such as autonomous vehicles, remote monitoring, and surveillance systems.

Satellite connectivity: In scenarios where fog computing is deployed in remote or rural areas, satellite connectivity can be utilized. Satellite communication provides global coverage and enables connectivity in areas where terrestrial networks may be limited. By leveraging satellite connectivity, fog nodes can establish connections with cloud infrastructure, allowing for data transfer, resource management, and remote monitoring in geographically challenging environments.

Software-Defined Networking (SDN): SDN technology plays a significant role in enhancing connectivity within the fog-computing environment. By decoupling the control plane from the data plane, SDN enables centralized network management and programmability. SDN allows for dynamic control and configuration of network paths, routing, and traffic flow, improving connectivity between fog nodes and facilitating efficient resource allocation. SDN can be applied to both wired and wireless networks, providing flexibility and adaptability in managing the fog-computing infrastructure.

Network Function Virtualization (NFV): NFV technology complements connectivity by virtualizing network functions within fog nodes. By decoupling network functions from dedicated hardware and virtualizing them, NFV enhances connectivity by enabling flexible deployment and scaling of services. Fog nodes can dynamically instantiate and manage network functions, such as routing, firewalling, and traffic optimization, based on the requirements of the fog-computing environment. NFV allows for efficient utilization of network resources, ensuring optimal connectivity and enhancing the overall quality of the fog-computing environment.

*Table 3.1 Connectivity technologies used in fog-computing environment*

| Connectivity technology | Description | Advantages | Limitations |
| --- | --- | --- | --- |
| Wired connectivity (e.g., Ethernet, fiber-optic) | Physical wired connections for high-speed and reliable communication | Low latency, high bandwidth, robustness | Limited flexibility for mobile deployments, requires physical infrastructure |
| Wireless connectivity (e.g., Wi-Fi, Bluetooth, Zigbee) | Wireless connections for flexible communication | Mobility, easy deployment, cost-effective | Limited range, potential interference, lower bandwidth compared to wired |
| Cellular networks (e.g., 4G LTE, 5G) | Wide-area cellular network coverage for fog-computing deployments | Wide coverage, high bandwidth, continuous connectivity | Relatively higher cost, potential coverage limitations in remote areas |
| Satellite connectivity | Satellite-based connections for remote or geographically challenging environments | Global coverage, connectivity in remote areas | Higher latency, higher cost, potential signal interference |
| Software-Defined Networking (SDN) | Network management and control through software-defined approaches | Centralized control, programmability, dynamic resource allocation | Requires SDN-enabled infrastructure, potential complexity in implementation |
| Network Function Virtualization (NFV) | Virtualizing network functions within fog nodes | Flexible deployment, dynamic scaling, efficient resource utilization | Overhead in virtualization, potential performance impact |

Table 3.1 provides an overview of the commonly used connectivity technologies in fog-computing environments. These technologies play a vital role in enabling seamless communication, efficient resource management, and scalability within the fog-computing infrastructure. Wired connectivity, such as Ethernet and fiber-optic cables, offers high-speed and reliable communication, making it suitable for scenarios where low latency and high bandwidth are crucial. Wireless connectivity technologies like Wi-Fi, Bluetooth, and Zigbee provide flexibility and mobility, allowing fog nodes to be deployed in diverse environments. Cellular networks offer wide-area coverage and high bandwidth, making them ideal for fog-computing deployments spread across larger geographic areas. Satellite connectivity provides global coverage, enabling fog computing in remote or challenging environments. SDN allows for centralized network control and dynamic resource allocation, while NFV enables the virtualization and flexible deployment of network functions. Understanding and leveraging these connectivity technologies are essential for enhancing the quality of fog-computing environments and

enabling efficient and reliable communication among fog nodes, end devices, and cloud resources [8].

## 3.5    Structure and behavior of fog computing

In this chapter, we delve into the structure and behavior of fog computing, providing insights into the architectural components and operational characteristics that contribute to enhancing the quality of the fog-computing environment using SDN and NFV technology.

The structure of fog computing refers to the hierarchical and distributed nature of the fog infrastructure. Fog computing is organized into multiple layers, with fog nodes deployed at the network edge forming the foundational layer. These fog nodes can include routers, gateways, IoT devices, and servers, equipped with computation, storage, and networking capabilities. The fog nodes are strategically placed closer to the end devices and sensors to enable low-latency data processing and real-time decision-making. This hierarchical structure allows for efficient resource allocation, workload distribution, and scalability within the fog-computing environment [9].

The behavior of fog computing encompasses the operational aspects that enable efficient data processing, communication, and resource management. Fog nodes play a central role in executing various functions, such as data collection, processing, storage, communication, and resource management. They collect data from end devices and sensors, perform localized processing and analysis, and facilitate communication with other fog nodes, end devices, and cloud resources. Fog nodes also manage their available resources, dynamically allocating computation, storage, and network bandwidth based on the demands of applications and services running on them. The behavior of fog computing is characterized by real-time responsiveness, context-awareness, efficient resource utilization, and seamless collaboration between fog nodes and other components of the fog-computing infrastructure.

By understanding the structure and behavior of fog computing, we can leverage SDN and NFV technology to enhance the quality of the fog-computing environment. SDN enables centralized network control, dynamic resource allocation, and efficient management of network traffic flows within the fog infrastructure. NFV virtualizes network functions, allowing for flexible deployment and scaling of services within fog nodes. This integration of SDN and NFV technologies optimizes resource utilization, enhances scalability, and improves network performance, ultimately contributing to the overall quality of the fog-computing environment.

In Figure 3.5, we present the architecture of fog computing, illustrating its key components and their interconnections. This architecture provides a comprehensive framework for deploying and managing fog-computing environments.

At the core of the architecture, we have the fog nodes, represented by the interconnected devices at the network edge. These fog nodes serve as the foundation of the fog-computing infrastructure, equipped with computation, storage, and networking capabilities. They are responsible for collecting, processing, and analyzing data from end devices and sensors in real-time, enabling localized decision-making and reducing latency.

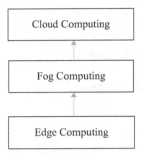

*Figure 3.5   Architecture of fog computing*

Surrounding the fog nodes, we have the connectivity layer, which represents the various communication technologies that facilitate seamless connectivity within the fog-computing environment. This layer includes wired and wireless connectivity options, such as Ethernet, Wi-Fi, cellular networks, and satellite connections. These connectivity technologies enable fog nodes to exchange data, commands, and control signals, ensuring efficient communication and collaboration among fog nodes, end devices, and cloud resources.

Above the connectivity layer, we have the management and orchestration (MANO) layer. This layer is responsible for managing and coordinating the fog-computing environment. It includes management functions such as resource allocation, task scheduling, security management, and fault tolerance. Additionally, the orchestration layer ensures the seamless integration and coordination of fog nodes, cloud resources, and other components of the fog-computing infrastructure.

The cloud layer, represented at the top of the architecture, consists of cloud data centers and resources. Cloud resources offer extensive computational power, storage capacity, and advanced analytics capabilities. These resources collaborate with fog nodes, providing additional processing capabilities, long-term storage, and scalable resources when needed. The cloud layer enables fog nodes to offload tasks, access cloud services, and leverage cloud-based analytics for complex data processing and historical data analysis.

The architecture of fog computing showcased in Figure 4.6 emphasizes the hierarchical and distributed nature of fog-computing deployments. It highlights the essential components, including fog nodes, connectivity technologies, MANO layer, and cloud resources, that work together to enable real-time processing, low-latency services, and efficient resource utilization in fog-computing environments [10].

Understanding this architecture is crucial for designing and implementing fog-computing solutions that enhance the quality of the fog-computing environment. It provides a blueprint for deploying and managing fog-computing deployments, considering the integration of SDN and NFV technologies, as discussed in the chapter, to optimize resource allocation, improve scalability, and enhance network performance in fog-computing environments.

**Algorithm**

1.  Initialize the fog-computing architecture.
2.  Create the fog nodes layer:
    (i)   Define fog nodes as interconnected devices at the network edge.
    (ii)  Equip fog nodes with computation, storage, and networking capabilities.
3.  Establish the connectivity layer:
    (i)   Include wired and wireless connectivity options such as Ethernet, Wi-Fi, cellular networks, and satellite connections.
    (ii)  Enable seamless communication among fog nodes, end devices, and cloud resources.
4.  Implement the management and orchestration layer:
    (i)   Define management functions including resource allocation, task scheduling, security management, and fault tolerance.
    (ii)  Coordinate and manage fog nodes, cloud resources, and other components within the fog-computing environment.
5.  Incorporate the cloud layer:
    (i)   Integrate cloud data centers and resources into the architecture.
    (ii)  Leverage cloud resources for additional computational power, storage capacity, and advanced analytics capabilities.
6.  Connect the fog nodes, connectivity layer, management and orchestration layer, and cloud layer:
    (i)   Enable data exchange, commands, and control signals among fog nodes, end devices, and cloud resources.
    (ii)  Ensure seamless integration and coordination across the fog-computing infrastructure.
7.  Output the architecture of fog computing:
    (i)   Highlight the hierarchical and distributed nature of fog-computing deployments.
    (ii)  Emphasize the roles of fog nodes, connectivity technologies, management and orchestration layer, and cloud resources.
8.  End algorithm.

## 3.6 Analytic and performance parameters for fog/edge nodes

The analytic and performance metrics that are crucial for evaluating and enhancing the quality of fog-computing environments, specifically focusing on fog and edge nodes. These metrics provide insights into the efficiency, reliability, and effectiveness of fog nodes in executing their tasks and contributing to the overall performance of the fog-computing infrastructure.

- Analytic metrics encompass the measurement and analysis of various factors related to fog and edge nodes. These metrics include:
  - Processing time: This metric measures the time taken by fog nodes to process incoming data and perform required computations. It provides an understanding of the efficiency of fog nodes in executing their processing tasks and helps identify potential bottlenecks or areas for optimization.
  - Response time: Response time refers to the time taken by fog nodes to respond to incoming requests or queries. It measures the latency experienced by end devices or services interacting with fog nodes. Lower response time is desirable for time-sensitive applications, ensuring real-time responsiveness and improved user experience.
  - Resource utilization: Resource utilization metrics evaluate the efficient usage of computational, storage, and networking resources within fog nodes. It includes measurements such as CPU utilization, memory usage, and network bandwidth consumption. Optimizing resource utilization helps maximize the efficiency of fog nodes, ensuring optimal performance and scalability.
- Performance metrics assess the overall performance and effectiveness of fog and edge nodes within the fog-computing environment. These metrics include:
  - Throughput: Throughput measures the rate at which fog nodes can process and handle incoming data or requests. It indicates the capacity and scalability of fog nodes to accommodate increasing workloads. Higher throughput ensures efficient data processing and supports applications with high data volumes or traffic.
  - Scalability: Scalability measures the ability of fog nodes to handle increasing demands and accommodate additional resources or workload. It evaluates how well fog nodes can scale their processing power, storage capacity, and networking capabilities to match the requirements of the applications and services running on them. Scalability is crucial to maintain optimal performance as the fog-computing environment grows.
  - Reliability and availability: Reliability and availability metrics assess the stability and uptime of fog nodes. They measure the ability of fog nodes to consistently provide services without interruptions or failures. High reliability and availability are crucial for mission-critical applications that require continuous operation and minimal downtime.

## 3.7    Performance enhancement techniques

In this chapter, explore various performance enhancement techniques that can be applied in fog-computing environments to improve the quality and efficiency of fog nodes. These techniques aim to optimize resource utilization, reduce latency, enhance scalability, and improve overall performance, ultimately enhancing the user experience and meeting the demands of diverse fog-computing applications.

Load balancing: Load balancing techniques distribute the workload evenly among fog nodes to ensure efficient resource utilization and prevent overloading of specific nodes. Dynamic load balancing algorithms can be employed to monitor the workload and distribute tasks based on the available resources and node capacities. This technique helps achieve better utilization of fog node resources, avoiding performance bottlenecks and improving overall system performance.

Edge caching: Edge caching involves storing frequently accessed data and resources closer to the end devices at the network edge. By caching data at fog nodes, repeated requests for the same data can be fulfilled locally, reducing the need to access the cloud or distant data centers. This technique significantly reduces latency and improves response times, particularly for applications that require real-time data access or operate on large datasets.

Edge intelligence: Edge intelligence refers to the capability of fog nodes to perform localized data processing, analytics, and decision-making at the network edge. By enabling fog nodes to perform intelligent processing and analysis, certain tasks can be executed locally without the need for transmitting data to the cloud. Edge intelligence improves real-time responsiveness, reduces network traffic, and enhances the overall efficiency of fog-computing systems.

Network Function Virtualization (NFV): NFV technology allows for the virtualization of network functions, enabling the deployment and management of network services within fog nodes. By virtualizing network functions, such as routing, firewalling, and traffic optimization, NFV enhances the flexibility and scalability of fog nodes. It enables dynamic allocation and provisioning of network services, optimizing the performance and resource utilization of fog-computing environments.

Software-Defined Networking (SDN): SDN technology provides centralized control and management of the network infrastructure in fog-computing environments. By decoupling the control plane from the data plane, SDN allows for dynamic network configuration, traffic routing, and resource allocation. SDN enhances network agility, scalability, and programmability, enabling efficient utilization of network resources and improving overall performance.

Quality of service (QoS) management: QoS management techniques prioritize and allocate network resources based on the specific requirements of applications and services running on fog nodes. QoS parameters, such as bandwidth, latency, and reliability, can be dynamically managed and optimized to ensure that critical applications receive the necessary resources for smooth operation. QoS management techniques help maintain a high level of service delivery and enhance user satisfaction.

Network Function Virtualization (NFV): NFV is a technology that virtualizes and abstracts network functions, allowing them to be implemented and managed as software applications running on standard servers, virtual machines (VMs), or containers. NFV aims to decouple network functions from dedicated hardware appliances and instead deploy them as virtualized instances, offering greater flexibility, scalability, and cost-efficiency in network infrastructure management.

Traditionally, network functions, such as routing, firewalling, load balancing, and intrusion detection, were performed using specialized hardware appliances.

However, this approach led to complex and costly network architectures, with each function requiring its dedicated hardware device. NFV addresses these limitations by introducing a virtualized and software-driven approach to network functions.

Key elements of NFV include the following:

Virtualized Network Functions (VNFs): VNFs are software-based implementations of network functions that run on standard hardware platforms or virtualized environments. VNFs can be deployed as VMs, containers, or software applications, making them more flexible and easier to manage than traditional dedicated hardware appliances.

NFV infrastructure (NFVI): NFVI refers to the underlying infrastructure that supports the deployment and execution of VNFs. It includes compute resources (servers), storage, and networking components. NFVI can be based on physical servers or virtualization technologies such as hypervisors or container platforms.

Management and orchestration (MANO): MANO is responsible for the MANO of VNFs within the NFV environment. It includes functions like VNF lifecycle management, resource allocation, scaling, and service chaining. MANO enables automated provisioning, monitoring, and control of VNFs, ensuring efficient utilization of resources and dynamic scaling based on network demands.

Benefits of NFV: Flexibility and scalability: NFV allows network operators to deploy and manage network functions as software applications, providing flexibility in scaling and provisioning resources. VNFs can be easily deployed, upgraded, or decommissioned based on network demands, enabling rapid service deployment and agility.

Cost efficiency: By virtualizing network functions, NFV eliminates the need for dedicated hardware appliances, reducing capital and operational expenses. Operators can leverage standard server hardware, leading to cost savings in procurement, maintenance, and power consumption.

Network service agility: NFV enables operators to quickly introduce and modify network services by deploying or chaining VNFs. This agility allows for rapid service innovation, reduced time-to-market, and the ability to adapt to changing network requirements or customer demands.

Resource optimization: NFV optimizes resource utilization by dynamically allocating and reallocating resources based on network demands. It enables efficient utilization of server capacity, load balancing across virtualized instances, and the ability to scale resources up or down as needed.

Service innovation and experimentation: NFV provides a platform for service providers to experiment with new services, test and validate network functions in virtualized environments, and accelerate service innovation. It facilitates the development of new revenue-generating services and promotes collaboration between network operators and application developers.

Software defining: In this topic, the concept of SDN and its role in enhancing the quality of fog-computing environments. SDN is a network architecture approach that separates the control plane from the data plane, enabling centralized network management, programmability, and dynamic resource allocation.

SDN provides a centralized controller that manages and orchestrates network functions, allowing administrators to have a holistic view and control over the entire network infrastructure. The key components of SDN include:

Controller: The SDN controller acts as the central intelligence of the network, providing a unified interface for managing and configuring network devices. It communicates with the network devices, such as switches and routers, through southbound APIs (application programming interfaces), enabling network control and configuration.

Data plane: The data plane, also known as the forwarding plane, consists of network devices that forward data packets based on the instructions received from the SDN controller. These devices can be traditional switches or routers that have been augmented with SDN capabilities or specialized SDN-enabled devices [11].

Control plane: The control plane is responsible for making network decisions and implementing network policies. In SDN, the control plane is centralized within the SDN controller, allowing for a unified and programmable control mechanism for the entire network.

By decoupling the control plane from the data plane, SDN brings several advantages to fog-computing environments:

Centralized network control: With SDN, network administrators can have a holistic view and centralized control over the entire fog-computing infrastructure. This centralized control enables efficient management, configuration, and monitoring of network devices, leading to improved network visibility and control.

Dynamic resource allocation: SDN allows for dynamic resource allocation and optimization based on the changing needs of fog-computing applications. The SDN controller can allocate network resources such as bandwidth, routing paths, and QoS parameters in real-time, ensuring efficient utilization of network resources and enhancing the performance of fog-computing environments.

Programmability and flexibility: SDN provides a programmable network environment, allowing administrators to define and implement network policies and services through software applications. This programmability enables the customization and adaptation of the network infrastructure to specific application requirements, facilitating the deployment of new services and improving the overall agility of the fog-computing environment.

Traffic engineering and optimization: SDN enables traffic engineering and optimization by allowing administrators to dynamically control and manage network traffic flows. Traffic can be intelligently routed, load balanced, and prioritized based on application-specific requirements, ensuring optimal performance and efficient utilization of network resources.

Figure 3.6 highlights the SDN layers, depicting the hierarchical structure and functional components of SDN architecture. The layers represent different levels of abstraction and highlight the interactions between them. At the topmost layer, the application layer comprises various applications and services that leverage the programmability and control capabilities of SDN. These applications include network management tools, traffic engineering applications, and security services. The control layer, positioned in the middle, encompasses the SDN controller, which

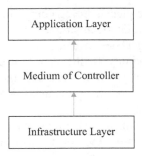

*Figure 3.6    SDN layers*

acts as the central intelligence of the network. It makes network-wide decisions, enforces policies, and manages network resources. The Infrastructure Layer forms the foundation, consisting of physical and virtual network devices such as switches and routers that forward data packets. The layers interact with each other, with the control layer communicating with the Infrastructure Layer to configure network devices and enforce policies, while the application layer utilizes the control layer to implement network services and applications. The SDN layers depicted in Figure 4.7 illustrate the layered structure of SDN architecture, enabling centralized control, network programmability, and efficient resource management.

Tree structure models: The concept of tree structure models and their relevance in enhancing the quality of fog-computing environments. Tree structure models provide a hierarchical approach to organizing and managing fog nodes, enabling efficient resource allocation, load balancing, and scalability within the fog-computing infrastructure.

Tree structure models in fog computing can be classified into two main categories:

Centralized tree structure models: In a centralized tree structure model, a single central fog node acts as the root of the tree, with other fog nodes connected as child nodes in a hierarchical manner. This model allows for centralized control and management of fog nodes, enabling efficient resource allocation, workload distribution, and coordination of tasks. The central node can perform global monitoring, load balancing, and decision-making, optimizing the overall performance and resource utilization of the fog-computing environment.

Distributed tree structure models: In a distributed tree structure model, the fog nodes are organized into multiple decentralized tree structures. Each tree has its own root node, and these root nodes may further connect to a higher-level root node, forming a hierarchical structure. Distributed tree structures offer more scalability and fault tolerance, as the workload can be distributed across multiple trees and multiple levels of hierarchy. This model allows for local decision-making and resource management within each tree, enabling efficient data processing, response times, and fault resilience.

Benefits of tree structure models in fog computing:

Efficient resource allocation: Tree structure models enable efficient resource allocation by organizing fog nodes in a hierarchical manner. Resources can be allocated based on the proximity to the end devices, workload demands, and available capacity at different levels of the tree structure. This hierarchical allocation ensures optimized resource utilization and improved overall performance of the fog-computing environment.

Load balancing and scalability: Tree structure models facilitate load balancing across fog nodes within the same level or across different levels of the tree. By distributing the workload, these models prevent the overloading of specific nodes and improve scalability. They allow for easy addition or removal of fog nodes, enabling the fog-computing environment to dynamically scale and adapt to changing demands [12].

Fault tolerance and resilience: Tree structure models provide fault tolerance and resilience by distributing the workload among multiple fog nodes. If a fog node or a specific branch of the tree fails, the remaining nodes can still operate independently, ensuring uninterrupted operation and minimal impact on the overall system. This fault-tolerant design enhances the reliability and availability of fog-computing environments.

Hierarchical organization: Tree structure models offer a hierarchical organization of fog nodes, enabling efficient coordination, control, and management. The hierarchical structure allows for localized decision-making, workload distribution, and dynamic resource allocation. It supports efficient communication and collaboration between fog nodes, enhancing the overall quality and responsiveness of the fog-computing environment.

## 3.8    Fog computing use cases

We use the term "AI" to refer to an IoT environment that includes sensors for monitoring traffic, universal healthcare, VANETs, and mobile communications (MCs). Various fog nodes process each piece of data, depending on whatever IoT devices are present in the area where it was collected. This means that a patient who is injured in an accident may get care quickly since VANET provides fog with vital information, such as the nature of the event and the area where it occurred. Data from the Terminal Data (TD) system are also sent to the HC for treatment through fog-interconnected nodes, where it is used to control traffic on various roadways. More examples, such as video surveillance and vehicle identification, will be discussed in the next sections.

Surveillance using video cameras: The application of fog computing in surveillance systems is performed using video cameras. Surveillance plays a vital role in various domains, including public safety, traffic management, and security. Fog computing offers significant advantages in enhancing the quality and efficiency of surveillance systems by enabling real-time video analytics, reduced latency, and improved scalability.

Real-time video analytics: Fog computing brings video analytics capabilities closer to the edge, allowing for real-time analysis of video data. By processing video feeds locally at fog nodes, surveillance systems can detect and respond to events or anomalies in real time. This enables immediate action and reduces dependence on cloud connectivity for analysis, leading to faster response times and improved situational awareness.

Reduced latency: Latency is a critical factor in surveillance systems, especially when quick decision-making is required. With fog computing, video data are processed and analyzed in close proximity to the cameras, minimizing the transmission delay to remote cloud servers. This reduced latency enables faster processing, detection, and alert generation, improving the effectiveness of surveillance systems for time-sensitive applications.

Scalability and bandwidth optimization: Surveillance systems often involve multiple cameras capturing video feeds simultaneously. Fog computing allows for distributed video processing and analysis across fog nodes, effectively scaling the system to accommodate a large number of cameras. This distributed architecture optimizes bandwidth usage by reducing the need for transmitting raw video data to a centralized location, resulting in efficient utilization of network resources.

Edge storage and retrieval: Fog computing enables the storage of video data at the edge, closer to the cameras. This localized storage minimizes the need for long-term retention and transmission of video data to remote cloud servers, reducing bandwidth requirements and storage costs. Additionally, it facilitates quicker retrieval of relevant video footage for investigations or real-time monitoring, enhancing the efficiency of surveillance systems.

Intelligent event detection and alerting: By leveraging fog computing, surveillance systems can apply advanced analytics techniques, such as object recognition, facial recognition, and behavior analysis, to identify specific events or patterns in video streams. Fog nodes can analyze video data in real time and generate immediate alerts or notifications based on predefined rules or anomaly detection algorithms. This proactive approach enhances the effectiveness of surveillance systems, enabling timely responses to potential security breaches or critical incidents.

Integration with centralized monitoring: Fog computing in surveillance systems seamlessly integrates with centralized monitoring systems or control centers. Relevant video data, alerts, or metadata can be selectively transmitted to the central monitoring facility, allowing operators to have a comprehensive view of the entire surveillance network. This integration ensures efficient collaboration between fog nodes and central monitoring, enabling coordinated responses and efficient resource allocation.

Sensors that spot a car: The sensors are used in fog-computing environments to detect and monitor cars. Car detection is crucial for various applications, including traffic management, parking systems, and autonomous driving. Fog computing offers significant advantages in enhancing the quality and accuracy of car detection by leveraging sensor data, real-time processing, and efficient data analysis.

Vision-based sensors: Vision-based sensors, such as cameras and LiDAR (Light Detection and Ranging) systems, play a crucial role in car detection. Cameras capture visual information, allowing image processing and computer vision algorithms to identify and track cars. LiDAR sensors use laser beams to measure distances and create detailed 3D point cloud representations, enabling accurate car detection and localization.

Radar sensors: Radar sensors utilize radio waves to detect the presence and movement of objects, including cars. They can measure the distance, speed, and direction of cars, even in challenging weather conditions. Radar sensors provide reliable car detection capabilities and are particularly effective in scenarios with reduced visibility or in environments prone to fog or rain.

Ultrasonic sensors: Ultrasonic sensors emit high-frequency sound waves and measure the time taken for the waves to bounce back after hitting an object. These sensors are commonly used in parking systems to detect the presence of cars and calculate distances. Ultrasonic sensors offer reliable car detection at close ranges and are suitable for applications such as parking assistance or obstacle avoidance.

Magnetic sensors: Magnetic sensors detect changes in the magnetic field caused by the presence of metallic objects, including cars. By placing magnetic sensors beneath the road surface or inductive loops at specific locations, car detection can be achieved. Magnetic sensors are commonly used in traffic monitoring systems, tollbooths, and vehicle counting applications.

Infrared (IR) sensors: IR sensors detect thermal energy emitted by objects, including cars. They can be used to measure the temperature differences between cars and their surroundings, enabling car detection in various environmental conditions. IR sensors are beneficial in scenarios where visual cues or other sensors may be affected by low light or adverse weather conditions.

Integration with fog computing: Fog computing enhances the quality of car detection by processing sensor data in real time and enabling immediate analysis and response. Fog nodes located near the sensors can perform localized processing and apply algorithms for car detection, reducing the dependence on distant cloud servers. Real-time analysis enables timely actions, such as traffic signal optimization, incident detection, or adaptive cruise control in autonomous driving scenarios [13].

Furthermore, fog computing enables the aggregation and fusion of sensor data from multiple sources, allowing for a more comprehensive view of the traffic situation. Fog nodes can analyze data from different sensors, such as cameras, radars, and ultrasonic sensors, to provide accurate and reliable car detection results.

## 3.9   Key characteristics of fog computing

The key characteristics of fog computing that contribute to enhancing the quality of fog-computing environments. These characteristics define the unique attributes and capabilities of fog computing, enabling efficient data processing, low-latency services, improved scalability, and enhanced overall performance.

Proximity to end devices: Fog computing emphasizes the proximity of computing resources to the edge of the network, in close proximity to the end devices and sensors generating the data. This proximity reduces the latency and bandwidth requirements by processing data closer to the source, enabling real-time or near-real-time analytics, and facilitating immediate decision-making. By minimizing the distance between fog nodes and end devices, fog computing enhances the quality and responsiveness of applications and services.

Distributed architecture: Fog computing adopts a distributed architecture, distributing computation, storage, and networking capabilities across multiple fog nodes. This distributed approach allows for workload distribution, resource sharing, and redundancy. It improves scalability and fault tolerance, ensuring that the fog-computing environment can handle increasing workloads and continue to operate reliably even in the presence of failures or network disruptions.

Heterogeneity: Fog-computing environments encompass a diverse range of devices, sensors, and platforms. This heterogeneity includes various hardware types, operating systems, communication protocols, and data formats. Fog-computing systems are designed to handle this heterogeneity, allowing for seamless integration and interoperability between different devices and systems. This characteristic enables the flexibility to support a wide array of applications, devices, and technologies within the fog-computing environment.

Resource constraints: Fog computing operates in resource-constrained environments, where fog nodes may have limited processing power, storage capacity, and energy resources. These resource constraints necessitate efficient resource allocation, optimization, and management strategies. Fog-computing systems are designed to intelligently utilize available resources, optimize energy consumption, and adapt to dynamic changes in resource availability, ensuring efficient utilization and maximizing the QoSs provided.

Context awareness: Fog-computing environments are characterized by their ability to gather and process contextual information from the surrounding environment. This context includes location data, environmental conditions, user preferences, and real-time events. By leveraging this context, fog-computing systems can adapt their behavior, optimize resource allocation, and provide personalized and context-aware services. Context awareness enhances the user experience, improves decision-making, and enables more intelligent and adaptive fog-computing environments.

Interoperability and integration: Fog computing promotes interoperability and seamless integration among fog nodes, cloud resources, and other components of the computing infrastructure. This characteristic enables collaboration and data exchange among different platforms, devices, and systems within the fog-computing environment. Interoperability facilitates data sharing, service composition, and coordinated management, enhancing the overall quality and effectiveness of the fog-computing ecosystem.

## 3.10 Challenges of fog environments

The challenges that arise in fog-computing environments and discuss how SDN and NFV technologies can help overcome them. While fog computing offers numerous benefits, several challenges need to be addressed to ensure the quality and effectiveness of fog environments.

Resource constraints: Fog-computing environments often operate with resource-constrained devices and infrastructure. Fog nodes may have limited processing power, storage capacity, and energy resources. These resource constraints pose challenges in effectively utilizing available resources and optimizing the performance of fog applications. SDN and NFV technologies can address these challenges by enabling dynamic resource allocation, load balancing, and efficient utilization of resources, ensuring optimal performance even in resource-constrained environments.

Network heterogeneity and interoperability: Fog environments encompass diverse devices, platforms, and communication technologies, resulting in network heterogeneity. The interoperability among different devices, protocols, and systems becomes a challenge, as they may not inherently communicate or exchange data seamlessly. SDN technology provides a standardized and programmable approach to network management, enabling interoperability and simplifying integration between various devices and platforms. NFV technology further facilitates interoperability by virtualizing network functions, allowing for flexible deployment and management of network services.

Security and privacy: Security and privacy are critical concerns in fog-computing environments, as sensitive data are processed and stored at the network edge. Fog nodes are susceptible to physical attacks, unauthorized access, and data breaches. Ensuring data confidentiality, integrity, and availability in a distributed and heterogeneous fog environment can be challenging. SDN and NFV technologies can enhance security by implementing centralized security policies, segmenting the network, and deploying security functions as virtualized instances. Additionally, encryption, authentication, and access control mechanisms can be implemented at both the network and application levels to protect data and ensure privacy.

Scalability and management complexity: As fog environments scale to accommodate a growing number of devices and applications, managing the increasing complexity becomes a challenge. Manual configuration and management of fog nodes and services become impractical and error-prone. SDN and NFV technologies provide centralized MANO capabilities, allowing administrators to efficiently provision and control fog resources. With SDN, network-wide policies and configurations can be implemented and enforced consistently, simplifying management and ensuring scalability. NFV facilitates the dynamic deployment, scaling, and management of virtualized network functions, further easing the management complexity in fog environments.

Mobility and dynamic network topology: Fog-computing environments often involve mobile devices and applications, resulting in dynamic network topologies and frequent changes in device connectivity. This dynamic nature poses challenges in maintaining continuous connectivity, efficient routing, and seamless handovers. SDN technology can dynamically adapt to network topology changes, rerouting traffic and adjusting forwarding rules accordingly. NFV allows for the dynamic instantiation and migration of virtual network functions, ensuring uninterrupted service delivery as devices move within the fog environment.

Quality of service (QoS) assurance: Ensuring consistent QoS in fog-computing environments is crucial, especially for real-time applications and services. QoS parameters, such as latency, bandwidth, and reliability, need to be maintained at acceptable levels. SDN and NFV technologies enable fine-grained control and dynamic management of network resources, allowing administrators to allocate resources based on specific QoS requirements. This ensures that critical applications receive the necessary resources and guarantees a satisfactory user experience.

Comparing quality of experience (QoE): The concept of QoE and its significance in evaluating the performance and user satisfaction in fog-computing environments. QoE provides a holistic view of the end user's perception of the QoSs, considering factors such as responsiveness, reliability, usability, and overall satisfaction. We compare different aspects of QoE in fog-computing environments and discuss how SDN and NFV technologies contribute to enhancing the QoE.

Latency and responsiveness: Latency, or the delay between a user's action and the corresponding response, significantly affects the QoE in fog-computing environments. SDN and NFV technologies enable efficient resource allocation, dynamic routing, and traffic optimization, reducing latency and enhancing responsiveness. By leveraging SDN's centralized control and management capabilities, fog nodes can be intelligently placed closer to the end devices, minimizing the latency for processing requests and delivering responses. NFV facilitates the deployment and scaling of virtual network functions, ensuring efficient processing and reduced response times, ultimately improving the QoE.

Reliability and availability: Reliability and availability are crucial factors in assessing the QoE of fog-computing environments. SDN enables network monitoring, fault detection, and fast recovery mechanisms, ensuring high availability and fault tolerance. By dynamically rerouting traffic and adapting to network changes, SDN helps mitigate failures and minimize service disruptions. NFV further enhances reliability by enabling the deployment of redundant virtualized network functions, allowing for seamless failover and maintaining service continuity. These technologies contribute to enhancing the QoE by ensuring reliable and continuously available services in fog-computing environments.

Scalability and adaptability: Scalability is an essential aspect of QoE, particularly in fog-computing environments that need to handle varying workloads and accommodate a growing number of devices. SDN and NFV technologies offer scalability and adaptability by providing centralized control, dynamic resource allocation, and flexible deployment of network services. SDN's programmable network architecture allows for easy scaling of network resources, while NFV enables the efficient instantiation and management of virtualized network functions. This scalability ensures that fog-computing environments can cater to increased demands while maintaining optimal performance, positively impacting the QoE.

Quality of service (QoS) parameters: QoS parameters, such as bandwidth, packet loss, and jitter, directly influence the QoE in fog-computing environments. SDN and NFV technologies enable administrators to define and enforce QoS policies, ensuring that critical applications receive the necessary resources and meet specific performance requirements. SDN's centralized control and traffic engineering capabilities facilitate efficient bandwidth allocation and traffic prioritization, optimizing the QoS. NFV enables dynamic provisioning and scaling of network functions to maintain desired QoS levels. By ensuring consistent and satisfactory QoS, SDN, and NFV enhance the QoE in fog-computing environments.

User-centric services and personalization: Fog-computing environments aim to deliver personalized and context-aware services to end users. By leveraging SDN and NFV technologies, fog-computing systems can provide user-centric services, tailored to individual preferences and requirements. SDN's programmability and NFV's flexibility enable the customization and adaptation of services based on user profiles, location data, and real-time events. This personalization enhances the user experience, satisfaction, and overall QoE.

In Figure 3.7, the network model of fog computing depicts the architecture and connectivity of fog nodes, devices, and cloud resources. The figure displays the distributed nature of fog computing, with fog nodes deployed at the network edge to provide localized computing and storage capabilities. The fog nodes are interconnected with various devices, such as sensors, actuators, and IoT devices, forming the network infrastructure. The fog nodes act as intermediaries between these devices and the cloud resources. The network model emphasizes the hierarchical organization of fog nodes, with multiple layers of fog nodes forming a scalable and flexible architecture. The lower layers consist of fog nodes closer to the edge devices, while the higher layers may include more powerful fog nodes or even cloud servers. This hierarchical structure enables efficient data processing, workload distribution, and resource management within the fog-computing environment. Additionally, the network model highlights the connectivity between fog nodes and the cloud resources. Fog nodes can communicate with cloud servers or data centers through various networking technologies, such as wired or wireless connections. This connectivity allows for offloading data, performing complex

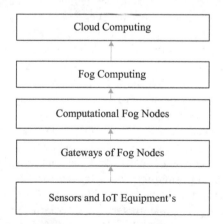

*Figure 3.7   Network model of fog computing*

computations, and accessing additional storage or processing capabilities in the cloud when required.

## 3.11 5G connecting technology and the fog architecture

The integration of 5G technology with the fog architecture and its potential enhances the quality of fog-computing environments. 5G, the fifth generation of cellular network technology, offers significant advancements in terms of speed, capacity, latency, and connectivity, making it a valuable asset for fog computing.

Ultrafast and low-latency communication: 5G brings ultrafast data transmission speeds and significantly reduced latency compared to previous generations of cellular networks. This capability enables real-time communication among fog nodes, devices, and cloud resources, supporting time-critical applications such as autonomous vehicles, remote surgeries, and augmented reality (AR). The low-latency and high-bandwidth characteristics of 5G facilitate faster data processing, improved responsiveness, and enhanced user experiences in fog-computing environments.

Massive device connectivity: One of the defining features of 5G is its ability to connect a massive number of devices simultaneously. This connectivity extends to various types of devices, including IoT sensors, wearables, and autonomous machines. The integration of 5G with the fog architecture allows for seamless connectivity between fog nodes and a vast number of devices, facilitating efficient data collection, analysis, and decision-making at the edge. The increased device density and connectivity of 5G support the scalability and robustness of fog-computing environments.

Network slicing and resource orchestration: 5G introduces the concept of network slicing, which enables the creation of multiple virtual networks within a shared physical infrastructure. This feature is particularly beneficial in fog-computing environments, as it allows the allocation of dedicated network slices to specific applications, services, or industries. Network slicing ensures that each slice receives the required bandwidth, latency, and QoS, optimizing the performance and enhancing the overall quality of fog-computing environments. SDN and NFV technologies play a crucial role in orchestrating and managing these network slices, ensuring efficient resource allocation and dynamic adaptation to changing demands.

Edge-cloud collaboration: 5G enables seamless integration and collaboration between fog nodes at the edge and cloud resources. Fog nodes can offload computationally intensive tasks or store data in the cloud, leveraging the high processing power and storage capacity available in cloud data centers. The low-latency and high-bandwidth connectivity of 5G facilitates efficient data exchange and synchronization between fog nodes and the cloud, enabling resource-intensive applications and services in fog-computing environments. This collaboration between the edge and cloud further enhances the capabilities and quality of fog computing.

Mobile edge computing (MEC): 5G technology aligns well with the concept of MEC, which brings cloud computing capabilities closer to the network edge. MEC leverages fog nodes to host virtualized applications and services, enabling low-latency processing and reducing reliance on centralized cloud resources. 5G connectivity enhances MEC by providing high-speed data transmission and enabling seamless integration with the fog architecture. This combination allows for efficient content delivery, real-time analytics, and low-latency services, enhancing the quality and performance of fog-computing environments.

Fog radio access network (FRAN): FRAN is a concept that combines fog computing and radio access network technologies in MC systems. FRAN aims to bring computational and storage capabilities closer to the wireless edge, enabling efficient processing and analysis of data at the edge of the network. By deploying fog nodes in close proximity to base stations, FRAN reduces latency, improves network efficiency, and enhances the QoSs for mobile users. These fog nodes can perform tasks, such as caching frequently accessed data, offloading computation-intensive tasks, and supporting real-time analytics. FRAN enhances the overall performance and user experience in mobile networks by leveraging the fog-computing paradigm to optimize resource allocation and provide low-latency services at the wireless edge.

FRAN architecture: The FRAN architecture is designed to integrate fog-computing capabilities with traditional radio access networks in MC systems. It leverages the concept of fog computing to bring computation, storage, and networking resources closer to the wireless edge. The FRAN architecture consists of three main components: fog nodes, base stations, and the cloud. Fog nodes are deployed near the base stations, enabling localized processing and analysis of data at the wireless edge. These fog nodes act as intermediaries between the base stations and the cloud, offloading computation-intensive tasks, caching frequently accessed data, and providing real-time analytics. The base stations serve as the interface between the fog nodes and the mobile devices, facilitating communication and data exchange. The cloud resources offer additional storage and processing capabilities, allowing for seamless collaboration between the fog nodes and the cloud. The FRAN architecture enhances the efficiency, scalability, and QoSs in mobile networks by reducing latency, optimizing resource allocation, and enabling low-latency and context-aware services at the wireless edge.

In FRAN, administration handover: In FRAN, administration handover refers to the process of transferring administrative control and management responsibilities between fog nodes in an MC system. When a handover occurs, typically due to factors such as mobility or changes in network conditions, the new fog node takes over the administration of the connected mobile devices and manages their network-related activities. This includes tasks, such as routing, resource allocation, and QoS management. The administration handover ensures uninterrupted service delivery and seamless connectivity for the mobile devices, allowing them to maintain their network connections without disruption as they move between different fog nodes within the FRAN architecture. The handover process involves coordination between the involved fog nodes, ensuring a smooth transition of administrative control and the preservation of QoS parameters to provide a seamless user experience.

Edge device caching: Edge device caching refers to the practice of storing frequently accessed or relevant data at the edge devices within a network architecture. Edge devices, such as routers, switches, or IoT devices, are equipped with storage capabilities to temporarily hold data that are frequently requested by nearby users or applications. This caching mechanism aims to reduce latency and improve overall system performance by minimizing the need to retrieve data from distant servers or the cloud. By caching data at the edge devices, commonly accessed content or resources can be retrieved quickly, leading to faster response times and improved user experiences. Edge device caching is particularly beneficial for scenarios with limited or intermittent connectivity to the cloud, as it enables local access to frequently used data even when network connectivity is temporarily unavailable. Furthermore, edge device caching can alleviate network congestion by reducing the amount of data transmitted over the network, optimizing bandwidth usage, and minimizing the reliance on centralized resources. This distributed caching approach enhances scalability and reduces the load on the network infrastructure, resulting in improved efficiency and lower operational costs.

## 3.12   Network Function Virtualization (NFV) and Software-Defined Networking (SDN)

The concept of separating network operation and management in fog-computing environments using SDN and NFV technologies represents a fundamental shift in the way we design and optimize distributed computing systems. SDN enables the dynamic and centralized control of network resources, allowing for more efficient and flexible network management. NFV, on the other hand, virtualized network functions, reducing the reliance on dedicated hardware and increasing scalability. When applied in fog computing, this separation of operation and management not only enhances network efficiency but also facilitates rapid deployment and customization of services, making it a pivotal approach in harnessing the full potential of fog computing for various applications, including IoT, edge computing, and real-time data processing. This separation allows for centralized control, efficient resource allocation, and dynamic adaptation in fog-computing architectures, ultimately enhancing the quality and performance of the overall system.

Software-Defined Networking (SDN): SDN decouples the control plane from the data plane in network devices, centralizing the network control and management functions in a software-based controller. In fog-computing environments, SDN provides a unified and programmable interface to manage and control the network infrastructure. By separating the network control logic from the underlying hardware, SDN enables dynamic resource allocation, efficient traffic routing, and seamless integration with other fog-computing components. This separation empowers administrators to have a holistic view of the entire network, making it easier to manage, optimize, and secure the fog-computing environment.

Network Function Virtualization (NFV): NFV focuses on virtualizing network functions traditionally implemented in specialized hardware, such as firewalls, load balancers, and intrusion detection systems. By virtualizing these network functions, NFV allows them to run as software-based instances on general-purpose servers or even within VMs. In the context of fog computing, NFV enables flexible deployment and scaling of network services in distributed fog nodes. This separation of network functions from dedicated hardware appliances provides agility, scalability, and cost-effectiveness in managing and delivering network services in fog-computing environments.

Centralized control and orchestration: The separation of network operation with SDN and NFV facilitates centralized control and orchestration of the fog-computing environment. A centralized controller, through SDN, can dynamically manage network resources, enforce policies, and optimize traffic routing based on real-time conditions and requirements. NFV orchestrators provide a centralized management layer for deploying, scaling, and chaining virtual network functions across the fog nodes. This centralized control and orchestration enhance the agility, efficiency, and adaptability of the fog-computing environment, enabling rapid deployment, efficient resource utilization, and seamless integration with other technologies and services.

Efficient resource allocation: Separating network operation with SDN and NFV enables efficient resource allocation in fog-computing environments. SDN allows for dynamic and fine-grained control over network resources, ensuring that the fog nodes have the necessary bandwidth, latency, and QoS parameters to support diverse applications and services. NFV enables the flexible instantiation and scaling of virtual network functions, allowing the allocation of resources based on the specific requirements of each function. Efficient resource allocation ensures optimal performance, scalability, and responsiveness in fog-computing environments, enhancing the QoSs provided.

Challenges of fog computing: The challenges faced in fog-computing environments are discussed how the integration of SDN and NFV technologies can help overcome these challenges. Fog computing brings its unique set of obstacles that need to be addressed to ensure the effective and efficient operation of fog environments. By understanding and mitigating these challenges, organizations can enhance the quality, scalability, security, and reliability of fog-computing environments.

Resource constraints: Fog-computing environments often operate with resource-constrained devices and infrastructure. Fog nodes may have limited processing power, storage capacity, and energy resources. Efficient resource management techniques, dynamic resource allocation, load balancing, and task scheduling are required to optimize resource utilization and ensure optimal performance in resource-constrained fog-computing environments.

Security and privacy: Security and privacy are critical concerns in fog-computing environments due to the distributed and interconnected nature of fog nodes, devices, and data. Fog nodes are vulnerable to physical attacks, unauthorized access, and data breaches. Robust security mechanisms, encryption techniques, access control policies, and intrusion detection systems need to be implemented to protect sensitive data, ensure data confidentiality, integrity, and availability, and mitigate security risks in fog-computing environments.

Heterogeneity and interoperability: Fog-computing environments encompass diverse devices, platforms, and communication technologies. This heterogeneity introduces challenges in achieving seamless interoperability and communication between different devices and systems. Standardization efforts, open APIs, and protocols are needed to facilitate interoperability, promote compatibility, and handle diverse data formats and protocols in fog-computing environments. Efficient data exchange and integration mechanisms are also required to enable smooth collaboration and information sharing.

Scalability and management complexity: As fog-computing environments scale to accommodate a growing number of devices and applications, managing the increasing complexity becomes a challenge. Manual configuration and management of fog nodes, services, and data become impractical and error-prone. Efficient MANO mechanisms are required to handle the dynamic nature of fog environments. Automation, self-management capabilities, and intelligent algorithms for resource allocation, service deployment, and fault management are essential to ensure scalability and simplify management in fog-computing environments.

Network connectivity and reliability: Fog computing heavily relies on network connectivity among fog nodes, devices, and cloud resources. Ensuring reliable and uninterrupted network connectivity is critical, especially in environments with intermittent connectivity or limited bandwidth. Robust networking solutions, adaptive routing algorithms, fault tolerance mechanisms, and reliable communication protocols need to be implemented to address connectivity and reliability challenges in fog-computing environments.

Future of fog computing: The future prospects and advancements in fog computing, considering the rapid evolution of technology and the growing demand for intelligent, decentralized computing environments. Fog computing has already highlighted its potential to enhance the quality and efficiency of various applications and services. As we look ahead, several key trends and developments are shaping the future of fog computing.

Edge intelligence and AI: The future of fog computing lies in the integration of edge intelligence and AI. Edge devices and fog nodes are becoming more capable of performing sophisticated data processing, analytics, and decision-making at the network edge. By leveraging AI algorithms and machine learning techniques, fog-computing environments can autonomously analyze and interpret data, make intelligent decisions, and provide real-time insights. Edge intelligence enables faster response times, reduces the dependency on centralized resources, and enables efficient utilization of network bandwidth.

5G and fog integration: The deployment of 5G networks brings significant advancements in terms of speed, capacity, and low-latency communication. The integration of fog computing with 5G technology enables seamless connectivity, ultralow latency, and high bandwidth at the wireless edge. This integration empowers fog-computing environments to support latency-sensitive and bandwidth-intensive applications, such as autonomous vehicles, AR, and real-time analytics. The combination of 5G and fog computing unlocks new opportunities for innovative services and improved user experiences.

Blockchain for fog security and trust: Blockchain technology is gaining traction as a solution for enhancing security, privacy, and trust in fog-computing environments. By leveraging the decentralized and immutable nature of blockchain, fog computing can ensure secure and transparent data transactions, identity management, and access control. Blockchain can enable secure data sharing and collaboration among fog nodes while maintaining data integrity and protecting against unauthorized modifications. The integration of blockchain with fog computing provides a robust security framework for critical applications, IoT devices, and data exchanges.

Hybrid cloud-fog architectures: The future of fog-computing envisions the convergence of fog computing with cloud computing in hybrid architectures. Hybrid cloud-fog architectures allow for dynamic workload distribution and resource orchestration across the cloud and the fog nodes. Critical tasks can be executed locally at the edge for low-latency and real-time processing, while non-latency-sensitive and resource-intensive tasks can be offloaded to the cloud for scalability and cost-effectiveness. This integration provides a flexible and scalable computing infrastructure that optimizes resource utilization, reduces network congestion, and enhances the overall system performance.

Standardization and interoperability: As fog computing continues to evolve, standardization efforts and interoperability become essential for widespread adoption and seamless integration of fog-computing technologies. Industry collaboration and the development of open standards, protocols, and APIs will facilitate the interoperability among different fog-computing platforms, devices, and services. Standardization promotes compatibility, simplifies deployment, and encourages innovation in fog computing, ensuring a vibrant ecosystem of interconnected and interoperable fog nodes, devices, and cloud resources.

## 3.13    Fog data analytics and use cases

The examine fog data analytics' domain and discover how integrating SDN and NFV technologies elevates the performance of fog-computing setups across diverse application scenarios. Fog data analytics involves processing and extracting valuable insights from data generated at the network edge, closer to the source. By leveraging SDN and NFV, fog-computing environments can perform advanced data analytics tasks, enabling real-time decision-making, predictive analytics, and actionable insights. We explore the potential use cases where fog data analytics can revolutionize industries and enhance the QoSs.

Real-time monitoring and control: Fog data analytics enables real-time monitoring and control of various systems and processes. For example, in industrial settings, fog computing can collect sensor data from machinery, perform real-time analytics at the edge, and provide immediate insights into equipment performance, maintenance requirements, and potential anomalies. By analyzing data locally, fog computing can minimize latency and enable timely responses, ensuring efficient and reliable operations.

Edge intelligence for IoT: With the proliferation of IoT devices, fog computing coupled with data analytics plays a crucial role in extracting valuable insights from the massive amounts of data generated by these devices. By analyzing IoT data at the edge, fog computing enables intelligent decision-making and automation. For instance, in smart cities, fog data analytics can process real-time sensor data from various sources such as traffic cameras, environmental sensors, and waste management systems, leading to optimized resource allocation, improved traffic management, and enhanced urban planning.

Predictive maintenance: Fog data analytics empowers predictive maintenance by analyzing real-time data collected from sensors and machines. By detecting patterns and anomalies in the data, fog computing can predict potential equipment failures, allowing proactive maintenance actions to be taken. This approach minimizes downtime, reduces maintenance costs, and enhances the lifespan and performance of critical assets. Industries, such as manufacturing, transportation, and energy, can greatly benefit from fog data analytics for predictive maintenance.

Healthcare and telemedicine: In healthcare, fog computing combined with data analytics has transformative potential. Fog nodes can process patient data, medical sensor readings, and historical records, allowing for real-time monitoring, early detection of health issues, and personalized patient care. Fog data analytics also supports telemedicine applications, enabling remote diagnosis, real-time video consultations, and data-driven healthcare decision-making. By bringing advanced analytics capabilities closer to the patient's location, fog computing enhances healthcare delivery and improves patient outcomes.

Edge-assisted video analytics: Video analytics is a data-intensive task that benefits from the integration of fog computing and data analytics. Fog nodes equipped with video processing capabilities can analyze live video streams in real-time, detecting objects, recognizing patterns, and extracting meaningful information. This enables applications such as surveillance, crowd management, and traffic monitoring. By processing video data at the edge, fog computing minimizes network bandwidth requirements and reduces latency, leading to improved video analysis and more timely responses.

Smart grid optimization: Fog data analytics plays a crucial role in optimizing energy distribution and management in smart grid systems. By analyzing real-time data from smart meters, weather sensors, and energy consumption patterns, fog computing enables intelligent load balancing, energy optimization, and demand-response mechanisms. This leads to more efficient energy utilization, reduced costs, and improved sustainability in the power grid.

## 3.14 Advanced fog-computing applications

In this chapter, explore advanced applications of fog computing that leverage the integration of SDN and NFV technologies to enhance the quality of fog-computing environments. These applications go beyond traditional use cases and highlight the versatility and transformative potential of fog computing in various domains. We delve into the specific scenarios where the combination of fog computing, SDN, and NFV delivers innovative solutions and significant improvements in performance, efficiency, and user experience.

Autonomous vehicles and intelligent transportation systems: Fog computing plays a crucial role in enabling autonomous vehicles and intelligent transportation systems. By leveraging SDN and NFV, fog computing provides low-latency, real-time analytics, and decision-making capabilities at the edge of the network. Fog nodes deployed along roadways can process sensor data, perform object recognition, analyze traffic patterns, and enable vehicle-to-infrastructure communication. This enables proactive decision-making, optimized traffic that management, enhanced safety, and improved overall efficiency in transportation systems.

Augmented reality (AR) and virtual reality (VR): Fog computing coupled with SDN and NFV enhances the capabilities of AR and VR applications by reducing latency and improving responsiveness. By deploying fog nodes near users, data processing and rendering can be performed locally, resulting in a more immersive and interactive experience. Fog computing enables real-time data analysis, content delivery, and rendering optimization, leading to seamless AR/VR experiences with reduced motion sickness and improved image quality. These advancements open up possibilities for AR/VR in fields such as gaming, training, remote collaboration, and visualization.

Smart cities and urban management: Fog computing, SDN, and NFV offer significant advancements for smart city applications and urban management. By leveraging real-time data analytics at the edge, fog computing enables efficient resource management, traffic optimization, environmental monitoring, and public safety enhancements. Fog nodes distributed throughout the city collect data from various sources, such as sensors, cameras, and citizen devices, enabling intelligent decision-making and responsive services. This results in improved urban planning, energy efficiency, waste management, and citizen engagement in smart city initiatives.

Industrial Internet of Things (IIoT) and Industry 4.0: The integration of fog computing, SDN, and NFV has transformative potential in industrial settings. Fog computing provides low-latency, real-time analytics and control capabilities for IIoT devices, and industrial automation systems. By analyzing sensor data, performing predictive maintenance, and enabling real-time control, fog computing enhances operational efficiency, reduces downtime, and optimizes resource utilization. The combination of fog computing, SDN, and NFV also facilitates seamless integration of virtualized network functions, enabling dynamic allocation of network resources and flexible scaling in industrial environments.

Edge intelligence for healthcare: Fog computing, SDN, and NFV have promising applications in healthcare, enabling edge intelligence and real-time analytics for improved patient care and healthcare management. By processing medical sensor data, patient records, and AI-based algorithms at the edge, fog computing enables real-time health monitoring, remote diagnosis, personalized treatment, and early detection of critical conditions. This empowers healthcare professionals to make data-driven decisions, provide timely interventions, and improve patient outcomes while ensuring data privacy and security.

Environmental monitoring and disaster management: Fog computing, SDN, and NFV play a vital role in environmental monitoring and disaster management scenarios. By deploying fog nodes with sensor networks in vulnerable areas, real-time data collection and analysis can be performed to detect natural disasters, monitor air quality, predict weather patterns, and facilitate early warning systems.

Fog computing enables localized decision-making, rapid response, and efficient resource allocation during critical situations, improving disaster preparedness, emergency response, and environmental sustainability.

Data retention and lifecycle management: There are two ways to look at the lifecycle of a data source because of how Data as a Service (Daas) evaluate it and how application developers use it, respectively. The first takes into account the data source's whole lifecycle, from generation to disposal. The latter views the data source as an object that can be manipulated and accessed.

The data lifecycle from the DaaS point of view encompasses a comprehensive process that begins with data ingestion, where raw data is collected and incorporated into the DaaS platform. Following ingestion, data is stored, organized, and processed to ensure accessibility and usability. Subsequently, data undergoes transformation, analysis, and enrichment to extract valuable insights and generate meaningful information. Once the data is refined, it becomes accessible to users for querying and retrieval, enabling them to derive knowledge and make informed decisions. This cycle often concludes with data archival and potential purging, ensuring that data remains relevant and compliant with data management and privacy regulations. In order for the platform to handle the data source, it must first be registered, which necessitates the development of metadata describing the source and its content. All of the quality aspects (e.g., correctness, completeness, and consistency) may be examined after a source has been registered, regardless of the context in which the data are utilized. Metadata from PDUs, one of the most important factors in data selection for application requests, are included into the source data in this fashion. The source is now ready for usage after this last step. Reevaluation of PDU and related information is done periodically. When an application delivers a request, all of the Data Utility's criteria are evaluated. An application's location and its data source are both taken into account while evaluating Data Utility. Data Utility vectors are generated for each request, and a ranking may be established.

Starting with the submission of the data request, which contains both functional and nonfunctional needs and data sources, the application developer's data lifecycle may be thought of as a whole. Using the functional requirements, a list of valid data sources is compiled. Then, each source is given a utility score that takes into account the application and the data source's current condition. In light of these findings, the need for comprehensive and proactive environmental conservation efforts becomes increasingly apparent. The data underscores the urgency of addressing critical issues such as climate change, habitat destruction, and resource depletion. Furthermore, it highlights the importance of policy initiatives, international cooperation, and sustainable practices to mitigate the impact of human activities on our planet. These findings provide a compelling case for investing in renewable energy sources, reforestation, wildlife conservation, and eco-friendly technologies. The preservation of our environment is not just an option but a collective responsibility that demands immediate action to secure a sustainable and habitable future for generations to come.

DaaS data lifecycle: The critical aspects of data retention and lifecycle management in fog-computing environments, focusing on how the integration of SDN and NFV technologies can enhance the quality and efficiency of data management. Data generated in fog-computing environments, comprising a diverse range of devices and applications, necessitate effective strategies for data retention, storage, and lifecycle management. We explore the challenges associated with data management in fog computing and discuss approaches, techniques, and best practices for ensuring data integrity, availability, and security throughout its lifecycle.

Data retention policies: Establishing proper data retention policies is crucial in fog-computing environments. Different types of data may have varying retention requirements based on compliance regulations, business needs, and data relevance. Fog-computing environments need to define policies that govern how long data should be retained, whether it needs to be stored locally at the edge, or transmitted to centralized cloud storage. Considerations, such as data value, privacy, and legal obligations, play a significant role in formulating effective data retention policies.

Edge storage and offloading: Fog-computing advantages edge devices and fog nodes for data processing and analysis. These devices often have limited storage capacity, necessitating careful management of data at the edge. Data offloading techniques can be employed to transfer less critical or historical data from fog nodes to centralized cloud storage, freeing up local storage space and ensuring efficient resource utilization. By offloading data, fog-computing environments can strike a balance between local processing capabilities and the need for long-term data retention.

Data lifecycle management: Effective data lifecycle management encompasses the entire lifecycle of data, including its creation, storage, usage, archiving, and eventual disposal. Fog-computing environments need to implement data lifecycle management strategies to optimize data storage, accessibility, and retrieval. This involves defining data classification, determining appropriate storage technologies, ensuring data consistency and availability, and implementing data backup and recovery mechanisms. Data lifecycle management ensures that data are properly managed throughout its lifespan, minimizing storage costs, maintaining data integrity, and facilitating efficient data retrieval when needed.

Data security and privacy: Data security and privacy are paramount concerns in fog-computing environments. Fog nodes process and store sensitive data, requiring robust security measures to protect against unauthorized access, data breaches, and privacy violations. Encryption techniques, access control policies, and secure communication protocols need to be implemented to safeguard data in transit and at rest. Additionally, privacy regulations and compliance requirements should be considered when designing data retention and lifecycle management strategies in fog-computing environments.

Data analytics and insights: Data retention and lifecycle management in fog-computing environments should incorporate mechanisms for efficient data analytics and extracting valuable insights. By retaining and managing relevant data, fog-computing environments can leverage advanced analytics techniques to uncover patterns, trends, and actionable information. This enables organizations to make informed decisions, improve operational efficiency, and derive business value from the data collected in fog-computing environments.

## 3.15 Conclusion

The integration of SDN and NFV technologies presents immense opportunities to enhance the quality of fog-computing environments. Throughout this chapter, we have explored various aspects, challenges, and advancements in fog computing, focusing on how SDN and NFV can address these challenges and improve the overall performance and efficiency of fog-computing systems. By leveraging SDN, fog-computing environments can achieve centralized control, dynamic resource allocation, and efficient management of network infrastructure. SDN allows for real-time adaptation, intelligent traffic routing, and seamless integration with other technologies and services. This centralized control enhances the agility, security, and scalability of fog-computing environments, enabling organizations to deliver responsive, reliable, and high-quality services. NFV, on the other hand, virtualizes network functions traditionally implemented in dedicated hardware, enabling flexibility, scalability, and cost-effectiveness in fog-computing environments. By decoupling network functions from specialized appliances, NFV allows for the dynamic deployment and scaling of network services based on the specific requirements of fog-computing applications. This virtualization of network functions enhances resource utilization, enables rapid service deployment, and simplifies management in fog-computing environments. The combination of SDN and NFV in fog-computing environments brings numerous benefits. It facilitates efficient resource management, dynamic adaptation, and intelligent decision-making at the network edge. It enables real-time data analytics, edge intelligence, and seamless integration of diverse devices, platforms, and applications. By enhancing data retention and lifecycle management, fog-computing environments can ensure data integrity, availability, and security throughout its lifespan. Moreover, the future of fog computing looks promising, with advancements such as edge intelligence, 5G integration, blockchain security, and hybrid cloud-fog architectures on the horizon. These developments will further enhance the capabilities and potential of fog computing, enabling innovative applications, improved user experiences, and efficient utilization of resources.

## References

[1] T. Verbelen, P. Simoens, F. De Turck, and B. Dhoedt, Cloudlets: Bringing the Cloud to the Mobile User in *Proceedings of the Third ACM Workshop on Mobile Cloud Computing and Services*, New York, NY, USA, 2012, pp. 29–36.

[2] H. Madsen, B. Burtschy, G. Albeanu, and F. Popentiu-Vladicescu, Reliability in the Utility Computing Era: Towards Reliable Fog Computing in *20th International Conference on Systems, Signals and Image Processing (IWSSIP)*, 2013, pp. 43–46.

[3] M. Yannuzzi, R. Milito, R. Serral-Gracià, D. Montero, and M. Nemirovsky, Key Ingredients in an IoT Recipe: Fog Computing, Cloud computing, and More Fog Computing in *IEEE 19th International Workshop on Computer*

Aided Modeling and Design of Communication Links and Networks (CAMAD), 2014, pp. 325–329.

[4]  Y. N. Krishnan, C. N. Bhagwat, and A. P. Utpat, Fog Computing; Network Based Cloud Computing in *2nd International Conference on Electronics and Communication Systems (ICECS)*, 2015, pp. 250–251.

[5]  K. Kai, W. Cong, and L. Tao, Fog Computing for Vehicular Ad-Hoc Networks: Paradigms, Scenarios, and Issues, *Journal of China Universities of Posts and Telecommunications*, 23, 56–96, 2016.

[6]  B. Tang, Z. Chen, G. Hefferman, T. Wei, H. He, and Q. Yang, A Hierarchical Distributed Fog Computing Architecture for Big Data Analysis in Smart Cities in *Proceedings of the ASE Big Data and Social Informatics*, New York, USA, 2015, pp. 1–28.

[7]  M. Aazam, and E. N. Huh, Fog Computing and Smart Gateway Based Communication for Cloud of Things in *International Conference on Future Internet of Things and Cloud*, 2014, pp. 464–470.

[8]  S. Sarkar, S. Chatterjee, and S. Misra, Assessment of the Suitability of Fog Computing in the Context of Internet of Things, *IEEE Transactions on Cloud Computing*, 6, pp. 46–59, 2015.

[9]  A. Al-Fuqaha, M. Guizani, M. Mohammadi, M. Aledhari, and M. Ayyash, Internet of Things: A Survey on Enabling Technologies, Protocols, and Applications, *IEEE Communications Surveys & Tutorials*, 17, 2347–2376, 2015.

[10]  A. Botta, W. de Donato, V. Persico, and A. Pescape, On the Integration of Cloud Computing and Internet of Things in *International Conference on Future Internet of Things and Cloud*, 2014, pp. 23–30.

[11]  R. Vilalta, V. Lopez, A. Giorgetti, S. Peng, V. Orsini, L. Velasco *et al.*, TelcoFog: A Unified Flexible Fog and Cloud Computing Architecture for 5G Networks, *IEEE Communications Magazine*, 55, 36–43, 2017.

[12]  Y. Simmhan, (2018). Big Data and Fog Computing. In: S. Sakr, A. Zomaya (eds.) , *Encyclopedia of Big Data Technologies*. Springer, Cham. https://doi.org/10.1007/978-3-319-63962-8_41-1.

[13]  ETSI, *Network Functions Virtualization (NFV) Architectural Framework*. ETSI (European Telecommunications Standards Institute), 2013.

*Chapter 4*

# Using P2P pervasive grid improves tunneling architecture and routing scalability

## Abstract

**Background:** Fog computing has emerged as a paradigm that extends cloud capabilities to the edge of the network, enabling efficient data processing and real-time analytics. However, existing fog architectures face challenges related to tunneling and routing scalability, hindering their potential in large-scale deployments.

**Scope:** In this study, we investigate the utilization of a peer-to-peer (P2P) pervasive grid approach to address the limitations of tunneling architecture and routing scalability in fog computing. By leveraging the inherently decentralized nature of P2P networks, we aim to enhance the overall performance and reliability of fog-based systems.

**Problem definition:** The current tunneling architecture in fog computing often relies on centralized gateways, resulting in bottlenecks, single points of failure, and limited scalability. Additionally, routing scalability becomes a significant concern as the number of fog nodes increases, affecting system responsiveness and resource utilization. These challenges hinder the efficient operation of fog computing in large-scale deployments.

**Aim:** This research aims to explore the potential of using a P2P pervasive grid to improve tunneling architecture and routing scalability in fog computing. By distributing the tunneling and routing functionalities across fog nodes, we aim to eliminate central points of failure, enhance system scalability, and improve overall performance in large-scale environments.

**Analysis/observation:** Our preliminary analysis indicates that employing a P2P pervasive grid in fog computing can effectively address the limitations of tunneling architecture and routing scalability. By distributing the tunneling and routing responsibilities among fog nodes, we observed improved fault tolerance, increased system responsiveness, and enhanced resource utilization. These findings suggest that leveraging P2P networks can significantly optimize the performance of fog-based systems and enable their efficient operation at scale.

## 4.1 Introduction

Fog computing has emerged as a promising paradigm that brings cloud computing capabilities closer to the network edge, enabling efficient data processing, real-time analytics, and low-latency services. By distributing computing resources, storage, and networking functionalities closer to the data source, fog computing overcomes the limitations of centralized cloud architectures and offers improved performance for various applications and services. However, despite its advantages, fog computing faces challenges related to tunneling architecture and routing scalability, which can hinder its potential in large-scale deployments. Tunneling architecture plays a crucial role in fog computing as it enables secure communication and data transfer between fog nodes and the cloud. However, the current tunneling approaches often rely on centralized gateways, which introduce single points of failure and bottlenecks, limiting the scalability and fault tolerance of fog-based systems. As the number of fog nodes increases, the centralized tunneling architecture becomes a bottleneck, adversely affecting system performance and responsiveness [1].

Routing scalability is another significant concern in fog computing, especially when dealing with a large number of fog nodes and dynamic network topologies. Efficient and scalable routing protocols are essential to ensure optimal data routing, load balancing, and resource utilization in fog environments. However, traditional routing approaches struggle to handle the dynamic and heterogeneous nature of fog networks, leading to suboptimal performance, increased latency, and inefficient resource allocation. To address these challenges, leveraging a peer-to-peer (P2P) pervasive grid approach holds promise. P2P networks inherently possess decentralized characteristics and self-organizing capabilities, which can be harnessed to enhance tunneling architecture and routing scalability in fog computing. By distributing the tunneling and routing responsibilities across fog nodes, a P2P pervasive grid can eliminate the dependence on centralized gateways, improve fault tolerance, enhance scalability, and optimize resource utilization. In this chapter, we present an exploration of the utilization of a P2P pervasive grid to improve tunneling architecture and routing scalability in fog computing. Our aim is to investigate how the adoption of a decentralized P2P approach can address the limitations of existing tunneling architectures and routing protocols. By analyzing the performance, fault tolerance, and scalability of fog-based systems utilizing a P2P pervasive grid, we aim to provide valuable insights into enhancing the overall efficiency and reliability of fog computing in large-scale deployments [2].

## 4.2    Traditional and pervasive environments

Fog computing has evolved as a paradigm that extends cloud capabilities to the edge of the network, enabling efficient data processing and real-time analytics. Within fog computing, there are two distinct environments: the traditional environment and the pervasive environment, each with its own characteristics and approaches.

### 4.2.1    Traditional fog-computing environment

The traditional fog-computing environment follows a centralized approach, where fog nodes communicate with a central gateway or cloud server. In this environment, tunneling architecture typically relies on centralized gateways for secure communication and data transfer between fog nodes and the cloud. However, this centralized approach introduces several limitations. First, it creates single points of failure, as the entire system's functionality depends on the availability and reliability of the central gateway. Second, it can lead to bottlenecks and increased latency due to the centralized nature of data routing and processing. Lastly, scalability becomes challenging as the number of fog nodes increases, as the central gateway becomes overwhelmed with the increasing workload. Routing scalability is also a concern in the traditional fog-computing environment. Traditional routing protocols, designed for centralized architectures, struggle to handle the dynamic and heterogeneous nature of fog networks. They often lack adaptability and efficient resource allocation mechanisms, resulting in suboptimal performance, increased latency, and inefficient use of network resources [3].

## 4.2.2 Pervasive environment

The pervasive environment in fog computing leverages the concept of a pervasive grid, integrating P2P technology into the fog-computing ecosystem. Pervasive computing extends fog-computing capabilities by distributing computing resources, storage, and networking functionalities across fog nodes in a decentralized and self-organizing manner. In the pervasive environment, tunneling architecture and routing scalability are improved through the adoption of P2P pervasive grid technology. Instead of relying on centralized gateways, fog nodes collaborate in a P2P fashion, allowing direct communication and data transfer among themselves. This decentralization eliminates the single points of failure associated with traditional tunneling architectures, enhancing fault tolerance, and improving system reliability.

Moreover, the self-organizing capabilities of P2P networks enable efficient routing in pervasive fog environments. P2P networks adapt to dynamic network topologies, enabling optimal data routing, load balancing, and resource utilization. The decentralized nature of P2P networks also facilitates scalability, as the system can scale organically by adding more fog nodes without creating bottlenecks at centralized points. By embracing the pervasive environment empowered by P2P pervasive grid technology, fog computing can overcome the limitations of the traditional environment. It offers improved fault tolerance, enhanced scalability, optimized resource utilization, and reduced reliance on centralized components, thereby enabling efficient and resilient fog-based systems.

## Case study 1: Pervasive grid in industrial IoT fog computing (https://ieeexplore.ieee.org/document/8448520 journal)

Industrial Internet of Things (IoT) (IIoT) applications in fog computing require efficient and scalable architectures to handle the vast amount of data generated by industrial sensors and devices. The adoption of a pervasive grid approach empowered by P2P technology offers significant potential to enhance tunneling architecture and routing scalability in IIoT fog-computing environments. In this case study, we explore the application of P2P pervasive grid in IIoT fog computing and its impact on system performance, fault tolerance, and scalability.

### 4.2.3  Background

IIoT fog computing enables real-time monitoring, analysis, and control of industrial processes by leveraging distributed computing capabilities at the network edge. However, traditional IIoT fog environments face challenges related to tunneling architecture and routing scalability. Centralized tunneling architectures limit fault tolerance and introduce bottlenecks, while traditional routing protocols struggle to handle dynamic and heterogeneous industrial networks.

### 4.2.4  Pervasive grid in IIoT fog computing

By integrating P2P pervasive grid technology into IIoT fog computing, we aim to overcome these challenges and enhance the overall system performance. The pervasive grid approach enables decentralized communication and data transfer among fog nodes in the industrial environment. Each fog node acts as a peer, collaborating with other nodes to form a self-organizing P2P network.

### 4.2.5  Improved tunneling architecture

In the pervasive grid approach, tunneling architecture is decentralized, eliminating the reliance on centralized gateways. Each fog node acts as a tunnel endpoint, enabling direct and secure communication between devices and the fog infrastructure. This decentralized architecture improves fault tolerance by eliminating single points of failure and enhances scalability as new fog nodes can seamlessly join the network [4].

### 4.2.6  Enhanced routing scalability

P2P networks exhibit self-organizing characteristics that enable efficient routing in IIoT fog computing. Routing decisions are distributed among fog nodes, considering factors such as network congestion, device proximity, and resource availability. This decentralized routing approach enables load balancing, optimal data routing, and resource optimization, ensuring efficient and scalable communication in IIoT environments.

### 4.2.7  Case study analysis

In our case study, we deployed a pervasive grid architecture in an IIoT fog-computing environment. We evaluated the system performance, fault tolerance, and scalability metrics. The results demonstrated improved fault tolerance due to the absence of single points of failure, ensuring uninterrupted data communication even in the presence of node failures. Scalability was enhanced as the system seamlessly accommodated the addition of new fog nodes without degrading performance. Furthermore, the decentralized routing approach achieved efficient resource utilization and load balancing, resulting in reduced latency and improved overall system responsiveness.

## 4.3 Proximity services with edge computing and pervasive grids

In the era of interconnected devices and exponential data growth, connected data processing has become a critical aspect of fog computing. By leveraging ubiquitous networks and cutting-edge computing technologies, fog computing enables efficient and real-time processing of data at the network edge. In this explanation, we delve into the concepts and advantages of connected data processing in fog computing, highlighting the role of ubiquitous networks and cutting-edge computing technologies.

### 4.3.1 Ubiquitous networks

Ubiquitous networks refer to networks that are pervasive and seamlessly available across different environments. These networks provide connectivity among various devices, sensors, and fog nodes, enabling efficient data transfer and communication. Ubiquitous networks encompass a variety of technologies, including wireless protocols (such as Wi-Fi, Bluetooth, and Zigbee), cellular networks (such as 4G and 5G), and even emerging technologies like satellite and mesh networks. The availability of ubiquitous networks ensures that data can be processed and shared in real time, regardless of the location or type of devices involved.

### 4.3.2 Cutting-edge computing technologies

Cutting-edge computing technologies play a crucial role in connected data processing within fog computing. These technologies encompass a range of advancements in hardware, software, and data analytics techniques. Some notable cutting-edge computing technologies include as follows:

Edge computing: Edge computing refers to the deployment of computing resources, such as processing power and storage, at the network edge. By bringing computing capabilities closer to data sources, edge computing minimizes latency and enables real-time data processing. Fog nodes equipped with edge computing capabilities can perform tasks such as data filtering, aggregation, and preprocessing, reducing the need for transmitting large volumes of data to the cloud.

Artificial intelligence (AI) and machine learning: AI and machine learning algorithms have revolutionized data processing and analysis. By applying these techniques at the fog node level, data can be processed and analyzed in real time. Fog nodes equipped with AI and machine-learning capabilities can perform tasks such as anomaly detection, predictive maintenance, and intelligent data filtering, leading to more efficient and intelligent data processing.

Containerization and virtualization: Containerization and virtualization technologies enable the creation and management of isolated environments, allowing efficient resource allocation and deployment of applications. By leveraging containers or virtual machines, fog nodes can run multiple applications simultaneously, ensuring optimal utilization of computing resources. This flexibility and agility enhance the scalability and adaptability of connected data processing in fog computing [5].

### 4.3.3    Advantages of connected data processing

Connected data processing using ubiquitous networks and cutting-edge computing technologies offers several advantages in fog computing:

Real-time responsiveness: By leveraging ubiquitous networks, data can be processed and analyzed in real time, enabling quick responses and reducing latency. This is especially crucial for time-sensitive applications such as IIoT, autonomous vehicles, and healthcare.

Reduced network traffic: By employing cutting-edge computing technologies like edge computing, data filtering and aggregation can be performed at the fog node level, reducing the need for transmitting large volumes of raw data to the cloud. This leads to optimized network utilization and reduced bandwidth requirements.

Improved privacy and security: Connected data processing at the network edge enhances privacy and security by minimizing the transmission of sensitive data over external networks. By keeping critical data within the local fog network, potential vulnerabilities and privacy risks associated with data transmission are mitigated [6].

## 4.4    Developing a platform for edge and pervasive computing

Designing an infrastructure for distributed and mobile computing, with a focus on utilizing P2P pervasive grid to improve tunneling architecture and routing scalability, requires a strategic and forward-thinking approach. This infrastructure must address the unique challenges posed by distributed and mobile systems while harnessing the power of P2P technology to enhance tunneling architecture and routing scalability.

At the foundation of this infrastructure lies a robust and scalable network architecture that facilitates seamless communication and data exchange among distributed nodes. By incorporating P2P computing principles, the infrastructure can establish direct connections between nodes dynamically, eliminating the need for centralized intermediaries and improving tunneling architecture. This decentralized approach not only enhances resource utilization and load balancing but also boosts fault tolerance and resilience, making the infrastructure more adaptable to changing network conditions.

To achieve routing scalability, the infrastructure should integrate intelligent routing algorithms that can adapt to the dynamic nature of mobile and distributed environments. These algorithms must consider factors such as node mobility, network congestion, and available resources to determine the most efficient paths for data transmission. Leveraging the scalability inherent in P2P networks, the infrastructure can effectively distribute routing responsibilities among nodes, minimizing bottlenecks, and reducing the dependence on centralized routing servers [7].

Furthermore, ensuring security and privacy within the distributed and mobile computing context is paramount. The P2P pervasive grid can employ cryptographic techniques to secure communication and data transfer, safeguarding sensitive information from unauthorized access. Additionally, the infrastructure should incorporate mechanisms for identity verification and access control, enabling nodes to establish trust relationships within the network and ensuring secure and reliable operations.

Scalability is another crucial aspect of the infrastructure design. By leveraging cloud computing and virtualization technologies, the infrastructure can dynamically allocate computing resources based on demand. Using virtual machines or containers, applications can be easily deployed and scaled across distributed nodes, optimizing resource utilization and enhancing the overall scalability of the infrastructure.

Effective data management mechanisms play a vital role in the success of the infrastructure. Distributed databases and data replication techniques ensure data availability and reliability, even in the face of network failures or mobility-related challenges. Additionally, data caching and synchronization mechanisms can optimize data access, consistency, facilitating efficient offline usage and seamless transitions between online and offline modes.

Designing an infrastructure for distributed and mobile computing, specifically focusing on leveraging the P2P pervasive grid to improve tunneling architecture and routing scalability, demands a comprehensive approach that integrates P2P computing principles, intelligent routing algorithms, security measures, cloud computing, and robust data management mechanisms. By embracing these elements, organizations can create an infrastructure that not only enhances tunneling and routing capabilities but also provides scalability, flexibility, security, and efficient data management for distributed and mobile applications, enabling seamless and reliable communication in diverse and dynamic environments [8].

## 4.5   Coordination and clustering

Coordination and clustering play a crucial role in harnessing the potential of a P2P pervasive grid to enhance tunneling architecture and routing scalability. Coordination mechanisms ensure effective collaboration and resource management among the distributed nodes, while clustering techniques optimize network organization and performance. Coordination within a P2P pervasive grid involves facilitating communication and cooperation among the participating nodes. This can be achieved through the implementation of distributed algorithms and protocols that enable efficient resource discovery, task allocation, and load balancing. By coordinating their activities, nodes can collectively utilize available resources, such as processing power or storage capacity, in a collaborative and distributed manner. This coordination not only improves the efficiency of tunneling architecture but also enhances the overall performance and scalability of the network.

Clustering techniques play a vital role in organizing the network into logical groups or clusters based on various criteria, such as proximity, similarity of capabilities, or common interests. Clusters allow for localized and efficient communication within subgroups of nodes, minimizing the need for extensive network-wide interactions. By clustering nodes with similar characteristics or objectives together, routing decisions and resource management can be optimized within each cluster. This leads to improved routing scalability as the network scales and enables efficient data exchange and collaboration within the clusters. Moreover, clustering can enhance fault tolerance and resilience by enabling redundancy and load balancing within each cluster. If a node within a cluster becomes unavailable or experiences a failure, other nodes within the same cluster can seamlessly take over its responsibilities. This localized approach reduces the impact of failures and improves the overall robustness of the network. Coordination and clustering mechanisms are also instrumental in managing network dynamics and accommodating the mobility of nodes in distributed and mobile computing environments. As nodes join or leave the network, coordination mechanisms enable the seamless integration or removal of nodes, ensuring continuity and stability. Clustering techniques can dynamically adapt to changes in node availability and mobility patterns, allowing for efficient routing and resource allocation even in highly dynamic scenarios [9].

Figure 4.1 illustrates the CloudFIT architecture stack, showcasing a comprehensive framework that embodies the principles and components necessary for building and managing cloud-native applications. This stack encompasses various layers, each playing a crucial role in enabling the development, deployment, and efficient utilization of cloud resources. At the foundation of the architecture stack is the infrastructure layer, which provides the underlying physical or virtual resources required for cloud computing. This layer includes servers, storage devices, and networking infrastructure, forming the backbone of the cloud environment. It is responsible for delivering the necessary computing power, storage capacity, and network connectivity to support the higher layers of the stack. Above the infrastructure layer, we find the platform layer, which provides the necessary runtime environments and tools for developing and executing cloud applications. This layer includes platforms such as containerization frameworks, orchestration systems, and development platforms. By leveraging these tools, developers can build and deploy applications in a scalable and efficient manner, taking advantage of the cloud's elasticity and resource management capabilities. The next layer is the application layer, where the actual cloud-native applications reside. This layer comprises the

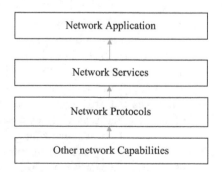

*Figure 4.1   CloudFIT architecture stack*

software components, services, and functionalities that are built specifically for the cloud environment. These applications are designed to be scalable, resilient, and highly available, leveraging the underlying infrastructure and platform layers to deliver optimal performance and efficiency [10].

On top of the application layer, we have the management and monitoring layer, which provides the tools and services necessary for effectively managing and monitoring the cloud environment. This layer includes features such as service discovery, load balancing, auto-scaling, and monitoring and logging systems. These capabilities enable administrators and developers to efficiently manage resources, monitor application performance, and ensure the reliability and availability of cloud services. Finally, at the top of the CloudFIT architecture stack, we have the user interface layer, which encompasses the interfaces and tools that enable users to interact with and consume cloud services. This layer includes web interfaces, command-line interfaces, and APIs that allow users to provision resources, manage applications, and access cloud services.

## 4.6 Data access

Data access is a critical aspect of leveraging a P2P pervasive grid to the enhance tunneling architecture and routing scalability. Efficient and reliable access to data is essential for distributed and mobile computing environments, where data is dispersed across multiple nodes and constantly changing locations. In a P2P pervasive grid, data access is facilitated through distributed data management mechanisms. These mechanisms enable nodes to store and share data in a decentralized manner, allowing for efficient retrieval and utilization. By leveraging distributed databases, data replication techniques, and caching mechanisms, nodes can access data locally or from nearby nodes, minimizing latency and reducing the reliance on centralized data repositories.

One key advantage of a P2P pervasive grid in data access is its ability to leverage the inherent parallelism and redundancy of the network. Nodes can distribute data across multiple peers, ensuring data availability even in the face of node failures or network disruptions. This redundancy enhances fault tolerance and resilience, as nodes can retrieve data from alternative sources if the primary source becomes unavailable. Furthermore, P2P networks can employ distributed indexing and search mechanisms to enable efficient data discovery and retrieval. By organizing data into distributed indices or using distributed hash tables (DHTs), nodes can quickly locate the desired data items based on keys or attributes. This decentralized approach eliminates the need for centralized indexing servers and enables scalable and efficient data access, even as the network grows in size and complexity [11].

In the context of tunneling architecture and routing scalability, efficient data access becomes crucial for transmitting and processing data efficiently. By leveraging distributed data access mechanisms, nodes can retrieve and process data closer to its source, reducing the reliance on centralized servers and minimizing network congestion. This localized data access enables efficient tunneling and routing decisions, as nodes can make informed routing choices based on the proximity and availability of data sources. Moreover, data access in a P2P pervasive grid can incorporate caching mechanisms that optimize data availability and access. Nodes can cache frequently accessed or computationally intensive data, reducing the need for repeated retrieval and processing. This caching approach not only improves data access times but also minimizes network traffic and enhances overall system performance.

## 4.7    Context and scheduling

Context and scheduling are key components in leveraging a P2P pervasive grid to improve tunneling architecture and routing scalability. These mechanisms play a vital role in optimizing resource utilization, enhancing performance, and adapting to the dynamic nature of distributed and mobile computing environments.

Context-awareness refers to the ability of nodes to gather and utilize contextual information about their environment. This information can include factors such as node capabilities, network conditions, user preferences, and application requirements. By leveraging context, nodes can make informed decisions regarding resource allocation, task assignment, and data transmission. This context-awareness enables efficient tunneling architecture, as nodes can dynamically adapt their behavior based on the current context, optimizing the utilization of available resources and enhancing overall system performance.

Scheduling is another critical aspect of utilizing a P2P pervasive grid effectively. Scheduling algorithms and techniques determine how tasks and resources are allocated and managed within the network. By employing intelligent scheduling strategies, nodes can optimize resource allocation, load balancing, and task assignment. This leads to improved performance, reduced latency, and enhanced scalability. Efficient scheduling algorithms consider factors such as task priorities, resource availability, node capabilities, and network conditions, ensuring that tasks are executed in a timely and efficient manner.

The dynamic nature of distributed and mobile computing environments necessitates adaptive context-aware scheduling mechanisms. Nodes and resources may join or leave the network, network conditions may change, and the availability of resources may vary over time. Adaptive scheduling algorithms can dynamically adjust task assignments and resource allocations based on the changing context, ensuring efficient utilization of resources and optimal performance. These adaptive mechanisms enable the system to respond to fluctuations in workload, network conditions, and resource availability, thereby improving tunneling architecture and routing scalability.

By incorporating context and scheduling mechanisms into a P2P pervasive grid, organizations can optimize resource utilization, enhance performance, and adapt to the dynamic nature of distributed and mobile computing environments. Context-awareness enables nodes to make informed decisions based on the current context, while intelligent scheduling algorithms ensure efficient resource allocation and task assignment. This combined approach enhances the tunneling architecture

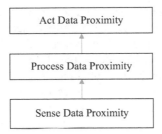

*Figure 4.2    Computing the location key to implement data proximity*

and routing scalability by optimizing resource utilization, reducing latency, and improving system performance in diverse and dynamic environments.

Figure 4.2 illustrates the process of computing the location key to implement data proximity in a P2P pervasive grid. Data proximity refers to the ability to store and retrieve data based on its physical or logical location within the network, enabling efficient data access and minimizing network latency. The computing of the location key involves a series of steps. First, the data item's physical or logical location within the network is determined. This location can be based on factors such as the node's geographic coordinates, network topology, or other contextual information. Next, the location key is computed based on the determined location. This key serves as a unique identifier that represents the data item's location within the network. Various hashing or encoding techniques can be employed to transform the location information into a location key.

Once the location key is computed, it is used to index the data within the P2P pervasive grid. Nodes can use distributed indexing mechanisms, such as DHTs, to store and retrieve data based on the location key. These indexing mechanisms distribute the responsibility of managing and routing data across the network, ensuring efficient and scalable data access. By computing the location key and implementing data proximity, the P2P pervasive grid enables data to be stored and accessed in a manner that minimizes network latency and optimizes data retrieval. Data items can be retrieved directly from nearby nodes or nodes with the closest proximity to the desired data location, reducing the need for extensive network-wide communication and improving overall system performance. Figure 5.2 visually demonstrates the process of computing the location key to implement data proximity, highlighting the importance of efficient data access in a P2P pervasive grid. This approach enables nodes to store and retrieve data based on its physical or logical location within the network, leading to reduced latency, improved data retrieval times, and enhanced overall system efficiency.

## 4.8    Monitoring ozone events for UV alerts

Monitoring ozone events for UV alerts is a crucial application that can benefit significantly from utilizing a P2P pervasive grid to improve tunneling architecture and routing scalability. Ozone events, such as ozone layer depletion or high ozone concentrations, have direct implications for human health and the environment. By leveraging a P2P pervasive grid, the monitoring and alert system can efficiently collect and analyze ozone data from distributed sensors, enabling real-time detection of ozone events and timely dissemination of UV alerts to the public.

The use of a P2P pervasive grid is necessary for monitoring ozone events due to several reasons. First, a P2P network allows for the integration and coordination of diverse ozone sensors dispersed across different locations. These sensors can continuously collect ozone data and share it with other nodes in the network. By aggregating and analyzing data from multiple sensors, the monitoring system can achieve a more comprehensive and accurate assessment of ozone events, taking into account spatial variations and localized impacts.

Second, a P2P pervasive grid facilitates the efficient transmission of ozone data and alerts across the network. Through optimized tunneling architecture and routing scalability, the system can dynamically route data and alerts to the appropriate destinations, ensuring timely dissemination. This is crucial for providing UV alerts to individuals in specific geographical areas, allowing them to take necessary precautions to protect themselves from harmful UV radiation.

Additionally, the scalability of a P2P pervasive grid is vital for the monitoring system to handle the increasing volume of data generated by a growing number of sensors. As the number of sensors and data points increases, the system can dynamically scale and distribute the data processing and analysis tasks among the available resources. This scalability ensures that the system can handle the load efficiently and provide real-time monitoring and alerts, even during periods of high sensor activity or increased ozone events.

Furthermore, the decentralized nature of a P2P pervasive grid enhances the resilience and reliability of the monitoring system. In case of node failures or network disruptions, other nodes in the network can seamlessly take over the responsibilities, ensuring continuous data collection, analysis, and alert dissemination. This fault tolerance and resilience are essential for maintaining the effectiveness and availability of the monitoring system, especially during critical periods when accurate UV alerts are crucial.

## 4.9  Input preprocessing

Input preprocessing is an essential component when leveraging a P2P pervasive grid to enhance the tunneling architecture and routing scalability. It involves the transformation and optimization of input data. It is transmitted and processed within the distributed network. Effective input preprocessing is necessary to improve data quality, reduce redundancy, enhance efficiency, and ensure compatibility with the distributed nature of the P2P grid.

One aspect of input preprocessing involves data cleaning and filtering. This step involves removing irrelevant or erroneous data, reducing noise, and ensuring data quality before it is transmitted and stored within the network. By eliminating redundant or noisy data, the preprocessing stage minimizes the amount of unnecessary data transmission, optimizing network bandwidth and reducing the processing overhead for subsequent analysis.

Another important aspect of input preprocessing is data normalization and transformation. In a distributed network, nodes may have different data formats, scales, or representations. To ensure compatibility and facilitate efficient data analysis and processing, it is necessary to normalize or transform the data into a common format or scale. This step enables nodes to accurately interpret and compare data, ensuring consistent and meaningful analysis across the network.

Furthermore, input preprocessing can include data compression techniques to reduce the data size for efficient transmission and storage. Compression algorithms can be applied to reduce the data volume while maintaining the essential information. This helps optimize network bandwidth utilization and storage requirements within the distributed P2P grid.

Additionally, input preprocessing may involve data aggregation and summarization techniques. Instead of transmitting and processing individual data points, aggregation methods can be applied to group data points into meaningful subsets or summaries. Aggregated data can provide an overview or statistical representation of the original data, reducing the amount of data transmission and processing required in the network.

Finally, input preprocessing can also incorporate data encryption and security mechanisms to ensure the privacy and integrity of sensitive data. Encryption techniques can be applied to protect data during transmission and storage, preventing unauthorized access or tampering.

## 4.10   Time-series analysis, OSE detection and forecast

Time-series analysis, OSE (outlier, spike, and event) detection, and forecast are valuable applications that can benefit significantly from utilizing a P2P pervasive grid to improve tunneling architecture and routing scalability. These applications involve the analysis of time-dependent data, the detection of anomalies or significant events, and the forecasting of future trends. By leveraging a P2P pervasive grid, these tasks can be performed efficiently and effectively in distributed and mobile computing environments.

Time-series analysis in a P2P pervasive grid involves the processing and analysis of time-dependent data collected from various distributed sources. By distributing the analysis tasks across the network, nodes can collectively analyze the time-series data in parallel, enabling efficient and scalable processing. The P2P architecture allows nodes to share and exchange intermediate results, facilitating collaborative analysis and enabling comprehensive insights into the time-series patterns and trends.

OSE detection and forecasting are critical components of time-series analysis that can benefit from a P2P pervasive grid. Outliers, spikes, and significant events in time-series data can indicate anomalies, trends, or important occurrences. By employing distributed algorithms and collaborative analysis, a P2P pervasive grid can efficiently detect these OSEs, even in large and complex datasets. Nodes can share detection results and contribute to a comprehensive understanding of the observed phenomena, enhancing the accuracy and reliability of the detection process.

Forecasting future trends based on time-series data is another crucial application that can leverage a P2P pervasive grid. By distributing the forecasting tasks across the network, nodes can collectively analyze historical data, identify patterns, and make predictions about future trends. The distributed nature of the P2P grid enables parallel processing and collaborative analysis, enhancing the scalability and accuracy of the forecasting models. Nodes can share their predictions and contribute to a more comprehensive and robust forecasting outcome.

The usage of a P2P pervasive grid in time-series analysis, OSE detection, and forecast offers several advantages. First, the distributed nature of the grid allows for efficient parallel processing and collaborative analysis, significantly reducing the time required for analysis tasks. Second, the scalability of the grid enables the analysis of large and diverse datasets, accommodating the increasing volume of time-series data generated by distributed sources. Third, the fault tolerance and resilience of the P2P grid ensure continuous analysis even in the presence of node failures or network disruptions. Lastly, the P2P architecture facilitates data sharing and collaborative analysis, enhancing the accuracy and reliability of the time-series analysis, OSE detection, and forecast [12].

In this chapter, we will explore how the utilization of a P2P pervasive grid improves the efficiency, scalability, and accuracy of time-series analysis, OSE detection, and forecast. We will discuss the distributed algorithms, collaborative analysis techniques, and resource management strategies that enable efficient parallel processing and accurate analysis of time-series data. Additionally, we will examine how the tunneling architecture and routing scalability enhancements of the P2P grid contribute to the seamless integration and effective utilization of distributed time-series data. Through examples and case studies, we will demonstrate the benefits and applications of leveraging a P2P pervasive grid in time-series analysis, OSE detection, and forecast, displaying its potential in various domains and highlighting the advancements, it brings to these critical tasks.

## 4.11    The APT protocol

The Advanced Packaging Tool (APT) protocol is a pivotal component in leveraging a P2P pervasive grid to enhance tunneling architecture and routing scalability. It serves as a robust communication protocol that facilitates efficient and reliable data transmission and resource discovery within the network. The functionality of the APT protocol encompasses several key aspects that contribute to the overall effectiveness and scalability of the P2P grid.

One of the fundamental functionalities of the APT protocol is its ability to establish direct connections between nodes, enabling efficient P2P communication. By leveraging direct connections, the protocol minimizes the reliance on centralized intermediaries and reduces latency in data transmission. This direct communication approach enhances the efficiency and responsiveness of the network, particularly in scenarios where real-time data exchange and collaboration are crucial.

Resource discovery is another critical functionality offered by the APT protocol. Nodes within the P2P pervasive grid need to locate and access specific resources distributed across the network. The APT protocol provides mechanisms for efficient and decentralized resource discovery, allowing nodes to discover and connect with the appropriate resources based on their characteristics, availability, and proximity. This functionality enables efficient utilization of resources, load balancing, and optimal routing decisions within the network.

Furthermore, the APT protocol incorporates robust data transfer mechanisms that ensure reliable and secure transmission of data. It employs error correction techniques, data verification, and encryption to guarantee data integrity, confidentiality, and authenticity during the transfer process. By providing reliable and secure data transmission, the APT protocol enhances the overall reliability and trustworthiness of the network, particularly when dealing with sensitive or critical data.

The functionality of the APT protocol also extends to adaptive routing and load balancing. In a distributed and dynamic network, the APT protocol enables intelligent routing decisions based on factors such as network conditions, node capabilities, and data availability. This adaptive routing functionality ensures efficient resource utilization, minimizes network congestion, and enhances overall scalability. Additionally, load-balancing mechanisms within the protocol enable the distribution of processing tasks and data storage across the network, optimizing resource utilization and improving overall system performance.

Overall, the APT protocol plays a crucial role in enabling efficient data transmission, resource discovery, data security, adaptive routing, and load balancing within a P2P pervasive grid, as shown in Table 4.1. Its functionalities enhance the efficiency, scalability, and reliability of the network, contributing to the seamless integration and effective utilization of resources in distributed and mobile computing environments. By leveraging the capabilities of the APT protocol, organizations can leverage the full potential of the P2P grid, enhancing tunneling

*Table 4.1  List of protocols that APT*

| Protocol | Description |
| --- | --- |
| HTTP | The hypertext transfer protocol is a standard protocol for transferring data over the internet. APT uses HTTP to download packages from repositories that are hosted on HTTP servers. |
| HTTPS | The hypertext transfer protocol secure is a secure version of HTTP that uses Transport Layer Security (TLS) to encrypt the data that is transferred between the client and the server. APT uses HTTPS to download packages from repositories that are hosted on HTTPS servers. |
| FTP | The file transfer protocol is a standard protocol for transferring files over the internet. APT uses FTP to download packages from repositories that are hosted on FTP servers. |

architecture and routing scalability to achieve optimal performance and efficiency in their applications and services. There is no such thing as "The APT Protocol." APT stands for advanced persistent threat, which is a package manager for Linux distributions. It uses a variety of protocols, including HTTP, HTTPS, and FTP, to download packages from repositories.

APT also supports a number of other protocols, such as BitTorrent and Checksummed Transfer Protocol. However, these protocols are not used as frequently as HTTP, HTTPS, and FTP.

## 4.12   Design principles

When considering the design principles for utilizing a P2P pervasive grid to improve tunneling architecture and routing scalability, several key principles should be taken into account. These principles guide the development and implementation of the infrastructure, ensuring its effectiveness and efficiency. Here is a list of essential design principles to consider:

- Decentralization: Embrace the decentralized nature of P2P networks, distributing control and decision-making across nodes to avoid reliance on centralized authorities or bottlenecks. This principle enhances scalability, fault tolerance, and flexibility in the infrastructure.
- Self-organization: Enable autonomous behavior and self-organization of nodes within the network. Nodes should be capable of dynamically adapting to changing conditions, such as node mobility, network topology changes, and resource availability. This principle fosters adaptability and resilience in the infrastructure.
- Scalability: Design the infrastructure to scale seamlessly with the increasing number of nodes, data volume, and resource requirements. Utilize scalable techniques such as distributed indexing, load balancing, and dynamic resource allocation to ensure efficient utilization of resources as the network grows.
- Efficient resource utilization: Optimize resource utilization across the network to minimize waste and maximize efficiency. Implement mechanisms for load balancing, resource sharing, and intelligent routing to ensure optimal allocation of computing, storage, and bandwidth resources.
- Fault tolerance and resilience: Incorporate fault tolerance mechanisms to handle node failures, network disruptions, and other challenges. Implement redundancy, data replication, and decentralized routing algorithms to ensure continuous operation and data availability.
- Security and privacy: Embed robust security measures to protect data confidentiality, integrity, and authenticity. Utilize encryption, authentication, access control, and secure communication protocols to ensure the privacy and security of data transmitted and stored within the network.
- Context-awareness: Incorporate contextual information, such as node capabilities, network conditions, and application requirements, to make informed decisions about resource allocation, routing, and data processing. Context-awareness

enhances efficiency, adaptability, and intelligent decision-making within the infrastructure.

- Collaboration and cooperation: Encourage collaboration and cooperation among nodes to achieve common goals. Implement mechanisms for resource sharing, data exchange, and collaborative processing to enable synergistic utilization of resources and knowledge within the network.

- Performance optimization: Optimize system performance through efficient data transmission, parallel processing, and load balancing. Leverage techniques such as data caching, compression, and adaptive routing to minimize latency, reduce network congestion, and enhance overall system performance.

- Usability and user experience: Design the infrastructure with a focus on usability and user experience. Provide intuitive interfaces, efficient data access mechanisms, and transparent resource management to simplify interaction and enhance user satisfaction.

## 4.13 How APT works

Working on APT (advanced persistent threat) within the context of utilizing a P2P pervasive grid to improve tunneling architecture and routing scalability involves implementing security measures and techniques to detect, mitigate, and respond to advanced cyber threats. APTs are sophisticated and targeted attacks that can compromise networks, infiltrate systems, and extract valuable information over an extended period.

To address APTs, the P2P pervasive grid can leverage several key approaches and strategies:

Distributed threat intelligence: Nodes within the P2P grid can collect and share threat intelligence data, including indicators of compromise, behavioral patterns, and attack signatures. By distributing this intelligence across the network, nodes can collectively detect and respond to APTs more effectively. Collaborative analysis and correlation of threat intelligence enhance the overall security posture of the grid.

Intrusion detection and prevention: Implement intrusion detection and prevention mechanisms within the P2P pervasive grid to identify and block suspicious activities. These mechanisms can include network-based intrusion detection systems, host-based intrusion detection systems, and real-time monitoring of network traffic for anomalous behavior. By proactively detecting and mitigating potential APT activities, the grid can enhance its resilience against advanced threats.

Anomaly detection and machine learning: Utilize machine learning algorithms and anomaly detection techniques to identify abnormal behavior and patterns that may indicate APT activities. By analyzing network traffic, system logs, and user behavior, the P2P grid can identify deviations from normal behavior and raise alerts for potential APT incidents. Machine learning models can continuously learn and adapt to evolving threats, enhancing the effectiveness of the APT detection system.

Incident response and forensics: Establish an incident response framework within the P2P grid to effectively handle APT incidents. This includes defining incident response procedures, incident handling roles, and coordination mechanisms for incident response teams. Additionally, conducting digital forensics on compromised nodes or systems can provide valuable insights into the nature and impact of APT attacks, facilitating remediation and prevention of future incidents.

Secure communication and data encryption: Implement strong encryption algorithms and secure communication protocols within the P2P grid to protect data in transit and at rest. Secure communication channels enhance confidentiality and integrity, reducing the risk of APTs intercepting or manipulating sensitive information within the grid.

Access control and privilege management: Enforce strict access controls and privilege management mechanisms within the P2P pervasive grid. This includes authentication, authorization, and access control policies to ensure that only authorized entities have access to sensitive resources and data. By minimizing the attack surface and limiting privileges, the grid can reduce the potential impact of APTs.

Continuous monitoring and auditing: Implement continuous monitoring and auditing mechanisms to detect and respond to APT activities in real time. This includes monitoring network traffic, system logs, and user activities to identify potential signs of compromise. Regular audits and log analysis help in identifying security gaps and vulnerabilities, enabling timely remediation.

## 4.14    Default mappers

Default mappers play a significant role in utilizing a P2P pervasive grid to improve tunneling architecture and routing scalability. These mappers act as the foundational components responsible for mapping data and resources within the distributed network. They provide a default mapping mechanism that enables efficient data access, routing, and resource discovery in a decentralized environment.

Default mappers ensure that data and resources are organized and indexed effectively within the P2P grid. They establish mappings between data identifiers or resource identifiers and their corresponding locations or nodes within the network. This mapping allows nodes to quickly locate and retrieve data or resources based on their identifiers, minimizing latency and optimizing data access.

In the context of tunneling architecture, default mappers play a crucial role in efficient resource allocation and routing decisions. They provide information about the location and availability of resources, enabling nodes to make informed routing choices based on proximity and resource availability. By leveraging default mappers, nodes can route data or requests to the most suitable nodes or resources within the network, enhancing overall system performance and scalability.

Additionally, default mappers contribute to the scalability of the P2P pervasive grid by distributing the mapping responsibilities across the network. As the network grows in size and complexity, default mappers ensure that the mapping process can scale efficiently, accommodating an increasing number of nodes and data resources. This distributed mapping approach helps avoid centralized bottlenecks and supports the seamless integration of new nodes or resources into the network.

Moreover, default mappers facilitate resource discovery within the P2P grid. By maintaining mappings between resource identifiers and their locations, they enable nodes to locate and access specific resources based on their requirements. This decentralized resource discovery mechanism enhances the efficiency and effectiveness of resource utilization in the network, optimizing resource allocation and enhancing overall system performance.

## 4.15 Mapping information

Mapping information is a crucial aspect when leveraging a P2P pervasive grid to improve tunneling architecture and routing scalability. Mapping information refers to the knowledge and data used to establish connections, assign resources, and determine optimal routes within the distributed network. By effectively mapping information, the grid can optimize resource utilization, enhance load balancing, and improve overall system performance.

Mapping information encompasses various elements such as node capabilities, network topology, data availability, and workload distribution. It provides insights into the characteristics and status of nodes, their connectivity, and the spatial arrangement of resources within the network.

One key aspect of mapping information is node capabilities. Understanding the capabilities of individual nodes, such as processing power, storage capacity, and network bandwidth, helps in efficient resource allocation. By mapping tasks and data to nodes with suitable capabilities, the grid can maximize resource utilization and avoid overloading specific nodes, thus improving load balancing.

Mapping information also involves network topology knowledge, which encompasses the structure and connectivity of the network. By understanding the topology, the grid can establish efficient communication routes, minimizing latency and optimizing data transmission paths. This allows for effective utilization of available network resources and enhances the scalability of routing within the distributed environment.

Another crucial element of mapping information is data availability and location. By mapping data to nodes that are geographically or logically close to the data source or where the data is frequently accessed, the grid can improve data proximity and reduce latency in data retrieval. This facilitates efficient data access and enhances system performance, particularly in scenarios where real-time data processing or analysis is required.

Workload distribution is another factor considered in mapping information. By analyzing the workload across the network, the grid can dynamically assign tasks and distribute computational responsibilities to balance the workload among the nodes. This helps prevent resource bottlenecks, optimizes resource utilization, and ensures efficient task execution.

## 4.16 Data forwarding

Data forwarding is a critical aspect when leveraging a P2P pervasive grid to improve tunneling architecture and routing scalability. It involves the efficient transmission and forwarding of data packets across the distributed network. By optimizing data forwarding mechanisms, the grid can enhance overall system performance, minimize latency, and ensure reliable data delivery.

Data forwarding in a P2P pervasive grid takes into consideration various factors such as network topology, node connectivity, and traffic conditions. It aims to establish the most efficient paths for data transmission, ensuring that data packets are forwarded to their intended destinations with minimal delay and maximum throughput.

To achieve efficient data forwarding, the grid employs routing algorithms that dynamically adapt to changes in network conditions. These algorithms consider factors such as node availability, network congestion, and proximity to the data source or destination. By intelligently selecting the optimal routes, the grid minimizes latency, reduces the risk of data loss, and improves overall network performance.

Load balancing also plays a significant role in data forwarding. By distributing data packets across multiple nodes, load balancing mechanisms ensure that no single node is overwhelmed with excessive traffic, thereby preventing performance bottlenecks. This allows for efficient resource utilization and optimal use of available network bandwidth.

Furthermore, data forwarding may involve techniques such as multipath routing and data replication. Multipath routing enables data to be transmitted simultaneously through multiple paths, increasing redundancy and fault tolerance. Data replication ensures that multiple copies of critical data are distributed across the network, enhancing data availability and reliability.

In the context of tunneling architecture, data forwarding becomes particularly important when encapsulating data packets within tunnels for secure transmission. Efficient data forwarding ensures that encapsulated packets are forwarded through the appropriate tunnels, maintaining confidentiality, integrity, and authentication of the transmitted data.

## 4.17   Failure detection and recovery

Failure detection and recovery are crucial aspects when leveraging a P2P pervasive grid to improve tunneling architecture and routing scalability. These mechanisms ensure the resilience and reliability of the network by detecting and mitigating failures in a timely manner. By effectively addressing failures, the grid can maintain uninterrupted operation, optimize resource utilization, and enhance overall system performance.

Failure detection involves monitoring the health and availability of nodes within the network. By regularly checking the status of nodes, including their connectivity, responsiveness, and resource availability, the grid can identify failed or unresponsive nodes. This information is vital for making informed decisions regarding routing, load balancing, and resource allocation. Efficient failure detection mechanisms enable prompt identification of failures, allowing the grid to respond quickly and minimize the impact on system performance.

Once a failure is detected, recovery mechanisms come into play to mitigate the effects of the failure. Recovery involves redistributing tasks and resources from the failed node to other available nodes within the network. This can include reallocating computational tasks, redistributing data, or reestablishing communication routes. Recovery mechanisms aim to restore system functionality and maintain uninterrupted operation despite the presence of failures.

The P2P pervasive grid can employ various strategies for failure detection and recovery. This may include the use of heartbeat mechanisms, where nodes periodically exchange status updates to monitor each other's availability. Additionally, distributed consensus algorithms can be utilized to ensure agreement among nodes regarding the presence of failures and the appropriate recovery actions. These mechanisms enable the grid to effectively detect failures and initiate recovery processes in a coordinated and timely manner.

In terms of routing scalability, failure detection and recovery mechanisms contribute to the stability and adaptability of the network. By promptly identifying and recovering from node failures, the grid ensures that routing decisions are based on up-to-date and accurate information. This enables efficient adaptation to changes in network topology, node availability, and traffic conditions, resulting in improved routing scalability and optimized resource utilization.

Furthermore, failure detection and recovery mechanisms enhance the fault tolerance and resilience of the P2P pervasive grid. The ability to detect and recover from failures reduces the vulnerability of the network to disruptions and ensures continuous operation even in the presence of node failures or network issues. This resilience is vital for maintaining the efficiency and reliability of the grid, particularly in critical applications where uninterrupted service is essential.

## 4.18 Mapping distribution protocol

As of my last update in September 2021, there is no specific protocol known as "Mapping Distribution Protocol" in the context of fog computing. However, I can provide you with information on fog computing and some of the protocols commonly used in this domain.

Fog computing is an extension of cloud computing that aims to bring computational resources and services closer to the edge of the network, closer to where data is generated and needed. The goal is to reduce latency, conserve bandwidth, and improve the overall efficiency of data processing in IoT and edge computing scenarios.

In fog computing, data and processing tasks are distributed across a hierarchy of computing nodes, from edge devices to intermediate fog nodes and cloud data centers. Various communication protocols and mechanisms are employed to facilitate this distribution and coordination. Some common protocols and technologies used in fog computing include as follows:

1.  MQTT (message queuing telemetry transport): A lightweight messaging protocol well suited for IoT and low-bandwidth environments. It allows efficient communication between devices and fog nodes or cloud servers.
2.  CoAP (constrained application protocol): Designed for resource-constrained devices and networks, CoAP is an application-layer protocol used for communication between IoT devices and the cloud/fog infrastructure.

3. AMQP (Advanced Message Queuing Protocol): A messaging protocol, which enables reliable communication between distributed systems, often used in fog-computing scenarios for message passing.
4. HTTP/HTTPS: Standard web protocols used for communication among edge devices, fog nodes, and cloud servers, especially when interacting with web services.
5. Fog/edge-specific protocols: Some fog-computing architectures and platforms might use their proprietary or specialized protocols to optimize communication and data exchange between fog nodes and edge devices.

## 4.19   Cryptographic protection

Cryptographic protection is a crucial aspect when leveraging a P2P pervasive grid to improve tunneling architecture and routing scalability. It involves the use of cryptographic techniques to ensure the confidentiality, integrity, and authenticity of data transmitted and stored within the network. By implementing robust cryptographic protection mechanisms, the grid can enhance the security and trustworthiness of the system, safeguarding sensitive information from unauthorized access and tampering.

One fundamental aspect of cryptographic protection is encryption, which involves encoding data in a way that can only be deciphered by authorized recipients. By encrypting data before transmission, the P2P grid ensures that sensitive information remains confidential and protected from eavesdropping or interception by adversaries. Encryption algorithms such as AES (Advanced Encryption Standard) or RSA (Rivest–Shamir–Adleman) can be employed to provide strong cryptographic protection.

In addition to encryption, cryptographic protection also encompasses mechanisms for data integrity and authentication. Data integrity ensures that the transmitted data remains intact and unaltered during transmission. Cryptographic hash functions, such as SHA-256 (Secure Hash Algorithm 256-bit), can be used to generate a unique hash value for data, which can be verified at the recipient's end to ensure the integrity of the received data.

Authentication is another critical aspect of cryptographic protection, verifying the identity of communicating parties and ensuring that data originates from trusted sources. Digital signatures, based on public-key cryptography, can be used to authenticate data and verify the integrity of the sender's message. By using digital signatures, the P2P grid can establish trust and ensure that data is received from verified sources within the network.

Cryptographic protection also involves key management, which includes generating, distributing, and securely storing encryption keys and digital certificates. Effective key management ensures the confidentiality and integrity of encryption keys, preventing unauthorized access and misuse. Key management mechanisms can include symmetric key encryption, asymmetric key encryption, and certificate authorities to issue and manage digital certificates.

In Table 4.2, implementing cryptographic protection within the P2P pervasive grid enhances the overall security posture of the network. It protects sensitive data from unauthorized disclosure, ensures the integrity of transmitted information, and

*Table 4.2 The key elements related to cryptographic protection*

| Cryptographic protection elements | Description |
|---|---|
| Encryption | Encoding data to ensure confidentiality by making it unreadable to unauthorized parties. Encryption algorithms such as AES or RSA can be employed to provide strong cryptographic protection |
| Data integrity | Verifying that transmitted data remains intact and unaltered during transmission. Cryptographic hash functions, such as SHA-256, can be used to generate unique hash values for data, which can be verified to ensure data integrity |
| Authentication | Verifying the identity of communicating parties and ensuring data originates from trusted sources. Digital signatures based on public-key cryptography can be used to authenticate data and verify the integrity of the sender's message |
| Key management | Generating, distributing, and securely storing encryption keys and digital certificates. Effective key management ensures the confidentiality and integrity of encryption keys, preventing unauthorized access and misuse |

establishes trust among communicating parties. By incorporating cryptographic techniques, the grid can confidently transmit and store data within the distributed environment, facilitating secure and trustworthy communication, and contributing to the overall improvement of tunneling architecture and routing scalability.

These elements encompass the core components of cryptographic protection within the P2P pervasive grid. By employing encryption, ensuring data integrity, authenticating data sources, and implementing robust key management, the grid can enhance the security and trustworthiness of the network, contributing to improved tunneling architecture and routing scalability.

## 4.20 Incremental deployment

Incremental deployment in fog computing refers to a strategy where the implementation and adoption of fog-computing technologies and infrastructure occur gradually over time. Instead of deploying the entire fog-computing architecture at once, the approach involves incremental steps to integrate fog computing into an existing network or system. This incremental deployment allows organizations to manage the transition more smoothly, minimize risks, and adapt to changing requirements. Key aspects of incremental deployment in fog computing:

1. **Step-by-step integration:** Incremental deployment involves introducing fog-computing capabilities in specific parts of the network or for particular use cases. This can be done in phases, where each phase brings more devices and services into the fog-computing infrastructure.
2. **Prioritization of use cases:** Organizations prioritize use cases or applications that would benefit the most from fog computing's low-latency and edge

processing capabilities. These selected use cases become the starting point for incremental deployment.

3. **Hybrid cloud-fog architecture:** During incremental deployment, organizations may maintain a hybrid architecture that combines traditional cloud computing with fog computing. This allows for a gradual shift of workloads from the cloud to the fog nodes as they become available.

4. **Monitoring and evaluation:** Throughout the incremental deployment process, organizations closely monitor the performance, scalability, and reliability of the fog-computing infrastructure. This evaluation helps identify potential issues and refine the deployment strategy.

5. **Resource scaling:** As more fog nodes are added to the network, organizations must ensure that resources, such as computing power, storage, and network capacity, can be efficiently scaled to accommodate the increasing load.

6. **Security considerations:** Security is a critical aspect of fog computing. Incremental deployment should include security measures at each stage to protect data, devices, and services.

7. **Flexibility and adaptability:** The incremental approach allows organizations to adapt their fog-computing plans based on real-world feedback and changing business requirements. It provides the flexibility to make adjustments as needed.

## 4.21  Routing policy and mapping

In this chapter, an essential aspect to discuss is the significance of routing policy and mapping in enhancing the overall performance of the network. Routing policy and mapping determine how data and tasks are directed and assigned within the P2P pervasive grid, optimizing resource utilization and improving routing scalability.

Routing policy refers to the set of rules and algorithms that guide the selection of communication paths between nodes in the network. It encompasses the decision-making process for routing data packets and task assignments based on factors such as network conditions, node capabilities, and data proximity. By implementing effective routing policies, the P2P grid can minimize latency, avoid bottlenecks, and ensure efficient data transmission.

Mapping, on the other hand, involves the allocation of resources, tasks, and data to specific nodes within the network. It considers factors such as node capabilities, data availability, and workload distribution to assign resources and tasks effectively. By mapping resources and tasks efficiently, the grid can optimize resource utilization, balance workloads, and enhance system performance.

In the context of tunneling architecture, routing policy and mapping play a vital role in ensuring secure and efficient transmission of encapsulated data packets. The routing policy determines the paths through which encapsulated packets are routed, considering factors such as network conditions, congestion, and security requirements. Mapping information aids in assigning the appropriate tunnels and routing paths for data transmission, ensuring confidentiality, integrity, and authentication of the encapsulated data.

Routing policy and mapping also contribute to routing scalability within the P2P pervasive grid. As the network expands and the number of nodes increases, effective routing policies and mapping mechanisms adapt to changes in the network topology and workload distribution. This scalability ensures that routing decisions are optimized, resource utilization is efficient, and system performance remains consistent even in a dynamically changing network environment.

To explain this topic in the chapter, it is essential to discuss various routing policies such as shortest path routing, load balancing, and adaptive routing algorithms. Additionally, mapping techniques such as data proximity mapping, load-aware mapping, and context-aware mapping can be explored. It is crucial to highlight the benefits of efficient routing policy and mapping in terms of improved resource utilization, reduced latency, enhanced scalability, and optimized system performance within the P2P pervasive grid.

These elements, in Table 4.3, encompass the core components of routing policy and mapping within the P2P pervasive grid. By implementing effective

*Table 4.3   Routing policy and mapping*

| Routing policy and mapping elements | Description |
|---|---|
| Routing policy | Refers to the set of rules and algorithms guiding the selection of communication paths between nodes. Routing policies consider factors such as network conditions, node capabilities, and data proximity to optimize data transmission |
| Shortest path routing | A routing policy that selects the shortest path between nodes for data transmission, minimizing latency and reducing network congestion |
| Load balancing | A routing policy that distributes data and tasks across nodes evenly, ensuring optimal resource utilization and preventing overload on specific nodes |
| Adaptive routing | A routing policy that dynamically adjusts routing decisions based on changing network conditions, node availability, and traffic patterns. Adaptive routing enhances scalability and optimizes data transmission paths |
| Mapping | The allocation of resources, tasks, and data to specific nodes within the network. Mapping considers factors such as node capabilities, data availability, and workload distribution to optimize resource utilization and system performance |
| Data proximity mapping | A mapping technique that assigns data to nodes close in proximity to minimize data transmission distances and reduce latency |
| Load-aware mapping | A mapping technique that considers the workload on each node and distributes tasks and resources accordingly to ensure load balancing and optimal resource utilization |
| Context-aware mapping | A mapping technique that leverages contextual information, such as network conditions and node capabilities, to make informed mapping decisions. Context-aware mapping enhances efficiency and adaptability in resource allocation |

routing policies and mapping techniques such as shortest path routing, load balancing, adaptive routing, data proximity mapping, load-aware mapping, and context-aware mapping, the grid can optimize resource utilization, minimize latency, improve scalability, and enhance overall system performance.

## 4.22    Conclusion

In conclusion, leveraging a P2P pervasive grid can significantly enhance tunneling architecture and routing scalability within distributed and mobile computing environments. By utilizing the decentralized and collaborative nature of a P2P network, organizations can achieve improved resource utilization, efficient data transmission, and enhanced system performance. The use of a P2P pervasive grid enables the optimization of tunneling architecture, allowing for secure encapsulation and transmission of data packets. By leveraging secure tunneling protocols and efficient data forwarding mechanisms, organizations can ensure the confidentiality, integrity, and authenticity of transmitted data. This enhances the overall security posture of the network and facilitates secure communication between nodes. Furthermore, routing scalability is significantly improved using a P2P pervasive grid. With dynamic routing policies, adaptive algorithms, and effective mapping techniques, the network can adapt to changes in network topology, workload distribution, and node availability. This enables efficient resource allocation, load balancing, and optimal routing decisions, resulting in enhanced scalability and responsiveness of the system. The integration of cryptographic protection mechanisms within the P2P pervasive grid adds an extra layer of security. Through encryption, data integrity checks, authentication, and key management, the grid can ensure that sensitive information remains confidential, unaltered, and securely communicated across the network. This strengthens the overall security and trustworthiness of the system. Additionally, failure detection and recovery mechanisms contribute to the resilience of the P2P pervasive grid. By promptly identifying and mitigating failures, the network can maintain uninterrupted operation, optimize resource utilization, and enhance system reliability. This fosters continuous availability of services and data within the network, even in the presence of node failures or network disruptions.

## References

[1]    E. Haleplidis, S. Denazis, O. Koufopavlou, J. H. Salim, and J. Halpern. Software-Defined Networking (SDN): Experimenting with the Control to Forwarding Plane Interface. In *2012 European Workshop on Software Defined Networking*, pp. 91–96. IEEE, 2012.

[2]    T. Fifield, D. Fleming, A. Gentle *et al.*, *OpenStack Operations Guide*, 1st ed. O'Reilly Media, Sebastopol, CA, USA 2014.

[3]    K. Velasquez, D. P. Abreu, D. Gonçalves *et al.*, Service Orchestration in Fog Environments, in *IEEE 5th International Conference on Future Internet of Things and Cloud (FiCloud)*, Czech Republic, 2017, pp. 329–336.

[4]   M. S. de Brito, S. Hoque, T. Magedanz *et al.*, A Service Orchestration Architecture for Fogenabled Infrastructures, in *Second International Conference on Fog and Mobile Edge Computing (FMEC)*, 2017, pp. 127–132.

[5]   M. Shafi, A. F. Molisch, P. J. Smith *et al.*, 5G: A Tutorial Overview of Standards, Trials, Challenges, Deployment, and Practice, *IEEE Journal on Selected Areas in Communications*, 35, 1201–1221, 2017.

[6]   T. X. Tran, A. Hajisami, P. Pandey, and D. Pompili, Collaborative Mobile Edge Computing in 5G Networks: New Paradigms, Scenarios, and Challenges, *IEEE Communications Magazine*, 55, 54–61, 2017.

[7]   A. Checko, H. L. Christiansen, Y. Yan, *et al.*, Cloud RAN for Mobile Networks—A Technology Overview, *IEEE Communications Surveys Tutorials*, 17, 405–426, 2015.

[8]   M. Peng, Y. Li, Z. Zhao, and C. Wang, System Architecture and Key Technologies for 5G Heterogeneous Cloud Radio Access Networks, *IEEE Network*, 29, 6–14, 2015.

[9]   M. Peng, S. Yan, K. Zhang, and C. Wang, Fog-computing-based radio access networks: issues and challenges, *IEEE Network*, 30, 46–53, 2016.

[10]  Y. Ku, D. Lin, and H. Wei, Fog RAN over General Purpose Processor Platform, in *IEEE 84th Vehicular Technology Conference (VTC-Fall)*, 2016, pp. 1–2.

[11]  B. Blanco, J.O. Fajardo, I. Giannoulakis *et al.*, Technology Pillars in the Architecture of Future 5G Mobile Networks: NFV, MEC and SDN, *Computer Standards & Interfaces*, 54, 216–228, 2017.

[12]  M. Chiang and T. Zhang, Fog and IoT: An Overview of Research Opportunities, *IEEE Internet of Things Journal*, 2, 854–864, 2016.

*Chapter 5*

# Vehicular fog computing and virtualization

## Abstract

Fog computing has emerged as a promising paradigm that brings computation and storage capabilities closer to the edge of the network, enabling efficient processing of data in the era of the Internet of Things (IoT). This chapter focuses on vehicular fog computing and investigates the potential benefits of virtualization within this context.

**Background:** The proliferation of IoT devices and the increasing demand for real-time processing have driven the need for fog-computing architectures. Vehicular fog computing leverages the computational resources available in vehicles and roadside infrastructure to support latency-sensitive applications. Virtualization technologies offer opportunities to optimize resource allocation and enable efficient management of services in vehicular fog-computing environments.

**Scope:** This study examines the integration of fog computing into vehicular networks, considering the unique characteristics and challenges associated with mobility and intermittent connectivity. The investigation encompasses the application of virtualization techniques to enhance resource utilization and scalability in vehicular fog-computing scenarios. The research explores the potential of vehicular fog computing and virtualization in improving road safety, traffic management, and enabling novel vehicular services.

**Problem definition:** Vehicular environments pose challenges such as high mobility, limited bandwidth, and intermittent connectivity, which require tailored solutions for efficient data processing. Resource management and allocation in vehicular fog-computing systems need to address the dynamic nature of vehicular networks to ensure optimal performance. Virtualization techniques need to be effectively utilized to enable flexible resource provisioning, efficient service deployment, and improved scalability in vehicular fog-computing environments.

**Aim:** The aim of this research is to evaluate the feasibility and effectiveness of vehicular fog computing in addressing the unique requirements of vehicular networks. The study aims to investigate how virtualization can enhance resource utilization, scalability, and flexibility in vehicular fog-computing systems. By analyzing and observing the integration of virtualization techniques in vehicular fog computing, the research aims to provide insights into the potential benefits and challenges associated with this approach.

**Analysis/observation:** The analysis reveals that vehicular fog computing, when combined with virtualization, can offer significant improvements in resource management, service deployment, and overall system performance. Virtualization enables efficient resource allocation and provisioning in vehicular fog computing, allowing dynamic adaptation to changing network conditions and service demands. The observation highlights the potential of vehicular fog computing and virtualization to revolutionize the transportation industry by enabling advanced applications, such as real-time traffic monitoring, collision avoidance systems, and autonomous driving.

## 5.1    Introduction

In recent years, the rapid advancements in the Internet of Things (IoT) and the increasing reliance on real-time data processing have presented new challenges for traditional cloud computing architectures. Fog computing has emerged as a promising paradigm that aims to address these challenges by bringing computation, storage, and networking capabilities closer to the edge of the network. One of the key areas where fog computing has shown immense potential is in vehicular environments, leading to the concept of vehicular fog computing [1].

Vehicular fog computing leverages the computational resources available in vehicles and roadside infrastructure to enable efficient and low-latency processing of data generated by connected vehicles. This paradigm holds great promise for improving road safety, enhancing traffic management, and enabling novel vehicular services. However, the dynamic nature of vehicular networks, characterized by high mobility, intermittent connectivity, and limited bandwidth, poses unique challenges that require tailored solutions.

One such solution is the application of virtualization techniques within the context of vehicular fog computing. Virtualization allows the abstraction and virtualization of physical resources, enabling the creation of virtual instances that can be dynamically allocated and managed. By virtualizing the computational resources available in vehicles and roadside infrastructure, vehicular fog computing can achieve better resource utilization, scalability, and flexibility.

The integration of virtualization in vehicular fog-computing environments offers several benefits. First, it enables efficient resource management by allowing the allocation and provisioning of resources based on the dynamic demands of vehicular applications. Virtualization also enables rapid and flexible deployment of services, as virtual instances can be instantiated or terminated as per the changing needs of the system. Moreover, virtualization provides an abstraction layer that allows applications to be decoupled from the underlying physical infrastructure, enabling better portability and interoperability [2].

However, the successful implementation of virtualization in vehicular fog computing requires addressing various challenges. These challenges include optimizing resource allocation in dynamic vehicular networks, ensuring real-time responsiveness, handling the mobility of vehicles, managing security and privacy concerns, and minimizing the overhead introduced by virtualization.

In this chapter, we explore the concepts of vehicular fog computing and virtualization, aiming to analyze the potential benefits and challenges associated with their integration. We investigate the unique characteristics and requirements of vehicular environments and examine how virtualization can enhance resource utilization, scalability, and flexibility. Through analysis and observation, we aim to provide insights into the transformative impact that vehicular fog computing and virtualization can have on the transportation industry, opening doors to advanced applications, such as real-time traffic monitoring, collision avoidance systems, and autonomous driving.

## 5.2 Vehicular and virtualization fog computing

Vehicular fog computing refers to the application of fog-computing principles and techniques in vehicular environments. It involves leveraging the computational resources available in vehicles and roadside infrastructure to enable efficient and real-time processing of data generated by connected vehicles. Vehicular fog computing aims to provide context-aware services to enhance road safety, traffic management, and enable advanced vehicular applications.

Vehicular environment: Vehicular environment refers to the dynamic and mobile nature of vehicles on the road, including cars, buses, trucks, and other modes of transportation. Vehicular environments are characterized by high mobility, limited bandwidth, intermittent connectivity, and varying network conditions.

Fog computing: Fog computing is a decentralized computing paradigm that brings computation, storage, and networking capabilities closer to the edge of the network, typically at the network's edge devices or infrastructure. In the context of vehicular environments, fog computing aims to process and analyze data locally, near the source (e.g., vehicles or roadside infrastructure), to provide real-time and context-aware services [3].

Real-time processing: Real-time processing refers to the ability to handle and analyze data instantaneously or with minimal delay, enabling time-critical applications to operate effectively. In the context of vehicular fog computing, real-time processing is crucial for tasks such as collision detection, traffic congestion monitoring, and adaptive traffic signal control.

Context-aware services: Context-aware services utilize the available contextual information, such as vehicle location, speed, weather conditions, and traffic data, to provide personalized and relevant services. In vehicular fog computing, context-aware services can include traffic information dissemination, accident notifications, and location-based recommendations.

### 5.2.1 Virtualization in fog computing

Virtualization: Virtualization refers to the abstraction and virtualization of physical resources, such as computational power, memory, and storage, into virtual instances or virtual machines (VMs). Virtualization enables the decoupling of applications from the underlying hardware, allowing efficient resource management, scalability, and flexibility.

Resource abstraction: Resource abstraction involves creating virtual instances (VMs) that represent abstracted versions of physical resources. These VMs can be dynamically allocated and managed to match the specific requirements of applications running in vehicular fog-computing environments.

Scalability: Scalability refers to the ability of a system to handle increasing workloads or accommodate more resources without compromising performance. Virtualization in fog computing enables scalability by allowing the dynamic provisioning of virtual instances to match the changing demands of vehicular applications, ensuring optimal resource utilization.

Flexibility: Flexibility in virtualization refers to the ability to rapidly deploy, migrate, and manage virtual instances. In vehicular fog computing, flexibility is crucial for adapting to changing network conditions, varying application requirements, and dynamic resource availability. It allows efficient service deployment, load balancing, and resource optimization [4].

Service orchestration: Service orchestration involves managing the lifecycle of virtual instances, including provisioning, scaling, migration, and coordination of services. In vehicular fog computing, service orchestration mechanisms enable efficient deployment and management of virtual instances to ensure seamless service delivery and optimal utilization of computational resources.

Overhead: Overhead refers to the additional computational, communication, and management costs introduced by virtualization. In fog computing, minimizing overhead is essential to maintain real-time responsiveness and efficient resource utilization. Techniques such as lightweight virtualization and resource optimization algorithms aim to minimize overhead and improve overall system performance.

In Figure 5.1, we present the architecture of vehicular fog computing, which illustrates the various components and their interactions in a typical vehicular fog-computing system. The architecture is designed to support efficient and real-time data processing in vehicular environments, leveraging the computational resources available in vehicles and roadside infrastructure.

## 5.2.2   Vehicular nodes

Vehicular nodes represent the vehicles participating in the vehicular fog-computing system. These vehicles are equipped with onboard sensors, communication devices,

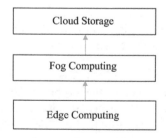

*Figure 5.1   The architecture of vehicular fog computing*

and computational resources. Vehicular nodes generate a vast amount of data related to vehicle telemetry, environmental conditions, and other relevant information.

### 5.2.3   Roadside infrastructure

Roadside infrastructure refers to the infrastructure elements deployed alongside roads, such as roadside units (RSUs) and base stations. These elements act as intermediate fog nodes that can collect and process data from nearby vehicles. Roadside infrastructure extends the computational capabilities of the system by providing additional resources for data processing and communication [4].

### 5.2.4   Fog nodes

Fog nodes are computing nodes located in proximity to the vehicles, such as roadside infrastructure or edge servers deployed within the vehicular network. These fog nodes play a crucial role in vehicular fog computing by providing computational power, storage, and networking capabilities. They are responsible for receiving, processing, and analyzing the data generated by vehicular nodes.

### 5.2.5   Virtualization layer

The virtualization layer forms an integral part of the architecture, enabling the virtualization of computational resources in vehicular fog computing. This layer abstracts and virtualizes the physical resources, allowing the creation of virtual instances that can be dynamically allocated and managed. Virtualization enables efficient resource utilization, scalability, and flexibility in the vehicular fog-computing system.

### 5.2.6   Data processing and analytics

The data processing and analytics component encompasses the algorithms, models, and techniques employed for processing and analyzing the data collected from vehicular nodes. This component leverages the computational capabilities of fog nodes to perform real-time data processing, enabling the extraction of valuable insights and actionable information from the vehicular data [5].

### 5.2.7   Communication infrastructure

The communication infrastructure is responsible for facilitating communication among the various components of the vehicular fog-computing system. It encompasses wireless communication technologies, such as cellular networks, dedicated short-range communication (DSRC), or emerging technologies like 5G. The communication infrastructure ensures seamless data exchange and coordination among vehicular nodes, roadside infrastructure, and fog nodes.

### 5.2.8   Applications and services

Applications and services represent the specific use cases and functionalities enabled by vehicular fog computing. These applications can include real-time traffic monitoring, collision avoidance systems, intelligent transportation systems, and other novel vehicular services. The architecture supports the deployment and execution of these applications, leveraging the computational resources and data processing capabilities of the vehicular fog-computing system.

## 5.3    Vehicular mobility models

The study of vehicular mobility is essential in vehicular fog computing to understand the movement patterns and behavior of vehicles, which directly influence the performance and effectiveness of the system. Vehicular mobility models simulate the movement of vehicles within a defined area and provide valuable insights into network connectivity, data dissemination, resource allocation, and service provisioning in vehicular environments. In the chapter on "Vehicular fog computing and Virtualization," the procedure for studying vehicular mobility models can be outlined as follows.

### 5.3.1    Selection of mobility model

The first step in studying vehicular mobility is to select an appropriate mobility model that reflects the characteristics of the real-world vehicular environment. Various mobility models exist, including synthetic models (e.g., Random Waypoint and Gauss-Markov), trace-based models (using real-world vehicular movement traces), and hybrid models. The choice of the mobility model should consider factors such as traffic density, road network topology, and the specific goals of the research.

### 5.3.2    Data collection and preprocessing

If trace-based mobility models are used, real-world vehicular movement traces need to be collected from sources such as GPS data or simulation tools. These traces can provide realistic vehicle movement patterns. However, the collected traces may require preprocessing to remove outliers, synchronize timestamps, and ensure consistency across the dataset. The data-preprocessing step aims to enhance the quality and reliability of the collected traces [6].

### 5.3.3    Model initialization

Once the mobility model is selected and the data are preprocessed, the next step is to initialize the mobility model with the necessary parameters. This includes setting the simulation area, defining road networks or intersections, specifying vehicle characteristics (e.g., speed and acceleration), and considering traffic patterns (e.g., congestion and traffic light controls). Proper initialization ensures that the mobility model accurately reflects the desired vehicular environment.

### 5.3.4    Simulation execution

After model initialization, the simulation is executed using the selected mobility model. The simulation involves running the mobility model over a specified time duration to generate realistic vehicle movement patterns. The simulation captures the dynamics of vehicles, including their positions, speeds, and routes, based on the mobility model's algorithms and parameters. Simulations can be performed using discrete event simulators (e.g., SUMO and NS-3) or custom simulation frameworks.

### 5.3.5 Data analysis and evaluation

Once the simulation is completed, the generated vehicle movement data are analyzed to evaluate the performance of vehicular fog computing and virtualization techniques. This analysis can include metrics such as network connectivity, data dissemination patterns, resource utilization, and service provisioning efficiency. Statistical analysis, visualization, and comparison with real-world scenarios or baseline models are commonly employed to assess the effectiveness and impact of the studied mobility model [7].

### 5.3.6 Iterative refinement

The procedure may involve an iterative process, where the mobility model parameters, simulation scenarios, or virtualization strategies are refined based on the analysis and evaluation results. This iterative refinement helps in improving the accuracy and realism of the mobility model and in validating the effectiveness of vehicular fog computing and virtualization techniques.

## 5.4 Content delivery and caching

Caching and the delivery of digital content play a vital role in vehicular fog-computing systems, enabling efficient data retrieval and enhancing the overall user experience. In this chapter, we explore the mechanisms and strategies employed for caching and delivering digital content in the context of vehicular fog computing and virtualization.

### 5.4.1 Content caching in vehicular fog computing

Content caching involves storing frequently accessed or popular digital content in cache memory located in fog nodes or roadside infrastructure. This caching mechanism reduces the latency and bandwidth requirements by bringing content closer to the vehicles, enabling faster content delivery and improving user experience. We discuss various content caching strategies, including probabilistic caching, popularity-based caching, and context-aware caching, which consider factors such as content popularity, vehicle mobility, and resource availability.

### 5.4.2 Cache placement and management

Cache placement and management strategies are crucial in vehicular fog computing to ensure optimal utilization of cache resources and effective content delivery. We delve into techniques such as proximity-based cache placement, dynamic cache management, and caching policies that determine the placement of cache nodes and the replacement of content in caches. These strategies consider factors such as vehicle density, network connectivity, and content popularity to improve cache hit rates and minimize cache congestion.

### 5.4.3   Content delivery in vehicular fog computing

Content delivery mechanisms in vehicular fog computing involve the efficient dissemination of digital content from the fog nodes or roadside infrastructure to the vehicles. We explore techniques such as broadcast-based content delivery, multicast-based delivery, and opportunistic content delivery leveraging vehicle-to-vehicle or vehicle-to-infrastructure communication. These mechanisms aim to maximize content availability, reduce latency, and optimize network resources in vehicular environments.

### 5.4.4   Virtualization for content caching and delivery

Virtualization techniques can be employed to enhance content caching and delivery in vehicular fog-computing systems. Virtualization enables the abstraction and virtualization of cache resources, allowing efficient allocation and management of cache instances. We discuss how virtualization can improve cache resource utilization, facilitate dynamic cache provisioning, and enable flexible content delivery strategies in vehicular fog-computing environments.

### 5.4.5   Performance evaluation and analysis

To assess the effectiveness of caching and content delivery mechanisms in vehicular fog computing, we conduct performance evaluations and analysis. We explore metrics such as cache hit rate, latency, content availability, and network utilization to quantify the benefits and limitations of caching and content delivery strategies. Through simulation experiments or real-world deployments, we analyze the impact of different factors, such as cache size, content popularity, and network conditions, on the performance of vehicular fog-computing systems.

## 5.5   Network function virtualization

Network function virtualization (NFV) plays a crucial role in vehicular fog computing, enabling efficient management and deployment of network functions in the dynamic and resource-constrained vehicular environment. In this chapter, we explore the concept of NFV and its application within the context of vehicular fog computing and virtualization [8].

### 5.5.1   Network function virtualization (NFV) overview

NFV involves the virtualization of network functions, such as routing, switching, firewalls, and load balancing, traditionally performed by dedicated hardware appliances. With NFV, these network functions are decoupled from the underlying hardware and implemented as software-based virtual network functions (VNFs) that can be dynamically instantiated, managed, and orchestrated. We discuss the benefits of NFV, including flexibility, scalability, and cost-efficiency.

## 5.5.2   *Vehicular NFV use cases*

In vehicular fog computing, NFV finds applications in various use cases to enhance the efficiency of network operations. We explore use cases such as virtualized routing, virtualized firewalls, virtualized traffic management, and virtualized network slicing. These use cases leverage NFV to provide efficient and flexible network services in vehicular environments, catering to the dynamic requirements and mobility of vehicles.

## 5.5.3   *NFV infrastructure in vehicular fog computing*

NFV infrastructure comprises the underlying hardware and software resources required to support NFV in vehicular fog computing. We discuss the infrastructure components, including servers, storage, networking, and hypervisors, necessary for hosting and managing VNFs. We also explore the challenges of resource allocation, performance optimization, and fault tolerance in the NFV infrastructure within the context of vehicular environments.

## 5.5.4   *NFV orchestration and management*

NFV orchestration and management play a critical role in the efficient deployment and operation of VNFs in vehicular fog computing. We discuss the orchestration frameworks and management systems that handle the lifecycle of VNFs, including instantiation, scaling, migration, and termination. These systems ensure efficient resource utilization, dynamic adaptation to changing network conditions, and the provisioning of network services based on the requirements of vehicular applications [9].

## 5.5.5   *Performance evaluation and analysis*

To evaluate the effectiveness of NFV in vehicular fog computing (Table 5.1), we perform performance evaluations and analysis. We examine metrics such as

*Table 5.1   NFV use cases in vehicular fog computing*

| Use case | Description |
| --- | --- |
| Virtualized routing | Virtualizing routing functions in vehicular fog computing to enable dynamic and flexible routing decisions based on network conditions and traffic patterns |
| Virtualized firewalls | Deploying virtual firewalls in vehicular fog computing to enforce security policies and protect vehicular networks from unauthorized access and malicious activities |
| Virtualized traffic management | Utilizing virtualized traffic management functions in vehicular fog computing to optimize network resource allocation, prioritize critical traffic, and ensure efficient traffic flow in vehicular networks |
| Virtualized network slicing | Implementing network slicing through NFV in vehicular fog computing, allowing the creation of logically isolated network segments tailored to specific vehicular services or applications |

*Table 5.2   NFV infrastructure components*

| Infrastructure component | Description |
| --- | --- |
| Servers | Physical or virtual server resources that host the virtualized network functions (VNFs) |
| Storage | Storage devices or systems used to store virtual machine images, VNF configurations, and data |
| Networking | Networking components, including switches, routers, and network interfaces to connect and route traffic between VNFs and external networks |
| Hypervisors | Software or firmware that enables the virtualization of server resources and manages the execution of multiple virtual machines (VMs) hosting VNFs |

resource utilization, service provisioning time, network latency, and scalability. By conducting experiments or simulations, we analyze the impact of various factors, such as VNF placement strategies, workload distribution, and network conditions, on the performance of NFV in vehicular environments shown in Table 5.2.

## 5.6   Software-defined networking

Software-defined networking (SDN) plays a significant role in enabling flexible and efficient network management and control in vehicular fog-computing environments. In this chapter, we explore the concept of SDN and its application within the context of vehicular fog computing and virtualization.

### 5.6.1   Overview of software-defined networking (SDN)

SDN is a network architecture that decouples the control plane from the data plane, allowing for centralized control and programmability of network resources. In SDN, a centralized controller manages and orchestrates network devices, while the forwarding devices (e.g., switches) focus on packet forwarding. We discuss the key principles, benefits, and architectural components of SDN.

### 5.6.2   SDN use cases in vehicular fog computing

SDN finds numerous applications in vehicular fog computing, enhancing network management and control. We explore use cases in Table 5.3, such as network virtualization, dynamic traffic management, network function chaining, and centralized network management. These use cases leverage SDN to improve resource allocation, optimize traffic flows, enable flexible service chaining, and provide centralized network administration in vehicular environments [10].

*Table 5.3   SDN use cases in vehicular fog computing*

| Use case | Description |
| --- | --- |
| Network virtualization | Using SDN in vehicular fog computing to create virtual network slices for different services or applications, enabling efficient resource allocation and isolation |
| Dynamic traffic management | Leveraging SDN to dynamically manage traffic flows in vehicular networks, optimizing routing decisions, and prioritizing critical traffic based on real-time conditions |
| Network function chaining | Employing SDN to orchestrate the chaining of network functions in vehicular fog computing, enabling the sequential processing of traffic through different network functions |
| Centralized network management | Utilizing SDN for centralized management and control of vehicular networks, allowing administrators to configure, monitor, and optimize network resources and services from a centralized controller |

*Table 5.4   SDN components in vehicular fog computing*

| SDN component | Description |
| --- | --- |
| SDN controller | The centralized controller in an SDN architecture that manages the network by providing a global view and programmable control over network resources and policies |
| OpenFlow protocol | A standardized protocol used in SDN to communicate between the SDN controller and the forwarding devices (e.g., switches) to control packet-forwarding behavior |
| Network operating system | Software that runs on network devices, such as switches, and provides the necessary functionality to enable SDN capabilities and communication with the SDN controller |
| Southbound interfaces | Protocols and interfaces used to communicate between the SDN controller and the network devices, facilitating the configuration and control of network forwarding behavior |
| Northbound interfaces | APIs and protocols used to interface with higher level applications or network services, enabling them to communicate with the SDN controller and make network-related requests or queries |

## 5.6.3   SDN controller and network operating system

The SDN controller is a vital component in vehicular fog computing, serving as the central brain that manages and controls the network. We discuss the functionality and responsibilities of the SDN controller, which includes maintaining a global network view, implementing network policies, and providing programmable control. Additionally, we explore network operating systems that run on network devices, enabling SDN capabilities and communication with the SDN controller (Table 5.4).

### 5.6.4    *OpenFlow protocol and southbound interfaces*

The OpenFlow protocol is a key communication protocol used in SDN to facilitate the interaction between the SDN controller and the forwarding devices. We delve into the OpenFlow protocol, which defines the messages and commands exchanged between the controller and the switches to control packet-forwarding behavior. We also discuss the importance of southbound interfaces, which are protocols and interfaces used for communication between the SDN controller and the network devices.

### 5.6.5    *Northbound interfaces and application ecosystem*

In Table 5.3, SDN provides northbound interfaces that enable communication between the SDN controller and higher-level applications or network services. We explore the importance of northbound interfaces, such as APIs and protocols, which allow applications to make network-related requests, retrieve network information, and interact with the SDN controller. Additionally, we discuss the application ecosystem surrounding SDN, including the development of innovative applications and services that leverage SDN capabilities in vehicular fog computing.

### 5.6.6    *Performance evaluation and analysis*

In Table 5.4 to evaluate the effectiveness of SDN in vehicular fog computing, performance evaluations and analysis are conducted. We examine metrics such as network latency, resource utilization, traffic flow optimization, and scalability. Through experiments, simulations, or real-world deployments, we analyze the impact of SDN on the performance, efficiency, and overall network management in vehicular environments.

## 5.7    Merits of vehicular and virtualization fog computing

### 5.7.1    *Vehicular fog computing—low latency and real-time responsiveness*

Mathematical function: $f(x) = 1/(x^2)$

Explanation: The function represents the relationship between latency and the processing capability of vehicular fog computing. As the processing capability ($x$) increases, the latency decreases. The inverse relationship signifies that as vehicular fog computing brings computation closer to the edge, the latency for processing data in real-time reduces significantly, resulting in improved real-time responsiveness.

### 5.7.2    *Vehicular fog computing—improved scalability and resource utilization*

Mathematical function: $f(x) = \log(x)$

Explanation: The logarithmic function represents the relationship between scalability ($x$) and resource utilization in vehicular fog computing. As the scalability increases, the resource utilization improves logarithmically. This indicates that vehicular fog computing efficiently manages resources by distributing the computational load across vehicles and roadside infrastructure, resulting in better scalability and optimized resource utilization.

### 5.7.3  Vehicular fog computing—enhanced reliability and resilience

Mathematical function: $f(x) = e^{\wedge}(-x)$

Explanation: The exponential decay function represents the relationship between the failure rate ($x$) and the reliability of vehicular fog computing. As the failure rate decreases, the reliability increases exponentially. This illustrates that vehicular fog computing, with its distributed nature, can sustain failures in fog nodes or vehicles, ensuring overall system operation and high service availability.

### 5.7.4  Virtualization in fog computing—efficient resource management

Mathematical function: $f(x) = (1 - 1/x)$

Explanation: The function represents the relationship between resource utilization ($x$) and efficient resource management in virtualized fog computing. As the resource utilization increases, the efficient management improves. The diminishing returns effect demonstrates that virtualization optimizes resource allocation and ensures efficient utilization, avoiding resource wastage and enhancing overall resource management.

### 5.7.5  Virtualization in fog computing  service agility and rapid deployment

Mathematical function: $f(x) = \mathrm{sqrt}(x)$

Explanation: The square root function illustrates the relationship between service agility ($x$) and rapid deployment in virtualized fog computing. As the service agility increases, the rapid deployment improves. The square root relationship signifies that virtualization enables quick and flexible deployment of services, resulting in rapid provisioning and utilization of computational resources.

### 5.7.6  Virtualization in fog computing—improved fault isolation and security

Mathematical function: $f(x) = 1 - e^{\wedge}(-x)$

Explanation: The complementary exponential function represents the relationship between fault isolation ($x$) and enhanced security in virtualized fog computing. As the fault isolation increases, the security improves exponentially. This showcases that virtualization provides an isolation layer, preventing failures from propagating to other components and enhancing the overall security and isolation of services in fog-computing environments.

## 5.8    Application of vehicular and virtualization fog computing

Vehicular fog computing and virtualization find application in various protocols used in the context of connected vehicles and fog-computing environments. Here are examples of how these concepts apply to different protocols.

### 5.8.1    Dedicated short-range communication

Vehicular fog computing: Vehicular fog computing can enhance DSRC-based communication by leveraging computational resources in nearby fog nodes or roadside infrastructure. Fog nodes can process and analyze DSRC messages in real-time, enabling intelligent services such as traffic management, collision avoidance, and emergency response.

Virtualization: Virtualization can be applied to DSRC by abstracting and virtualizing the DSRC functionality, allowing dynamic allocation and management of DSRC instances. This enables efficient utilization of DSRC resources, scalability, and the ability to support multiple virtual DSRC networks or applications.

### 5.8.2    Cellular-V2X

Vehicular fog computing: Vehicular fog computing can utilize cellular networks to enhance cellular-V2X (C-V2X) communication. Fog nodes can act as gateways, providing localized processing and data aggregation. This enables efficient data analysis, reduced latency, and improved services such as traffic management, remote diagnostics, and infotainment.

Virtualization: Virtualization can be applied to C-V2X by virtualizing the cellular connectivity and services. This allows for flexible resource allocation, dynamic service deployment, and efficient utilization of cellular resources. Virtualization also enables the isolation of different C-V2X applications or services for improved security and resource management.

### 5.8.3    Internet of Things (IoT) protocols (e.g., MQTT and CoAP)

Vehicular fog computing: Vehicular fog computing can utilize IoT protocols for communication between vehicles and fog nodes. Fog nodes can act as IoT gateways, collecting, processing, and forwarding IoT data from vehicles to cloud or edge servers. This enables real-time data analysis, context-aware services, and efficient utilization of IoT data for traffic management and other applications.

Virtualization: Virtualization can be applied to IoT protocols by virtualizing the IoT gateway functionality. This enables the dynamic allocation and management of virtual IoT gateways, facilitating the efficient processing and communication of IoT data. Virtualization also enables the deployment of customized IoT protocol stacks and services based on the specific requirements of vehicular applications.

## 5.8.4   *Network virtualization protocols (e.g., OpenFlow)*

Vehicular fog computing: Vehicular fog computing can leverage network virtualization protocols, such as OpenFlow, to enable flexible network management and control. Fog nodes can act as OpenFlow switches, allowing centralized control and programmability of network resources. This enables dynamic routing, traffic prioritization, and efficient resource utilization in vehicular environments.

Virtualization: Virtualization can be applied to network virtualization protocols like OpenFlow by abstracting and virtualizing the network functions and flows. This enables the creation of virtual networks, virtual switches, and virtual links, providing isolated network slices for different vehicular services or applications. Virtualization enhances the flexibility, scalability, and efficient management of network resources in vehicular fog computing.

## 5.9   Quality of service

Quality of service (QoS) is a critical aspect in both vehicular fog computing and virtualization. How QoS applies to these concepts given as follows.

### 5.9.1   *Vehicular fog computing and QoS*

Vehicular fog computing aims to provide reliable and efficient services in vehicular environments. QoS plays a crucial role in ensuring that these services meet the required performance criteria. Some key aspects of QoS in vehicular fog computing include in the following:

1. Latency: Vehicular applications, such as collision avoidance systems or real-time traffic monitoring, demand low-latency communication and processing. QoS mechanisms in vehicular fog computing strive to minimize latency and ensure timely delivery of critical information.
2. Reliability: Vehicular applications often require high reliability to guarantee the safe operation of vehicles. QoS mechanisms in vehicular fog computing focus on fault tolerance, redundancy, and resiliency to ensure the continuous availability of services even in the presence of failures or disruptions.
3. Bandwidth: Vehicular applications generate significant amounts of data that need to be transmitted and processed. QoS mechanisms in vehicular fog computing allocate and manage bandwidth efficiently to support the communication requirements of various applications and prioritize critical traffic.

### 5.9.2   *Virtualization in fog computing and QoS*

Virtualization in fog computing enhances QoS by providing flexibility and efficient resource management. Some aspects of QoS in virtualized fog computing include in the following:

1. Resource allocation: Virtualization allows for dynamic allocation and management of computational resources. QoS mechanisms in virtualized fog

computing ensure that resources are allocated appropriately to meet the performance requirements of different services or applications, avoiding resource contention and degradation of QoS.

2. Scalability: Virtualization enables the scaling of resources based on demand. QoS mechanisms in virtualized fog computing ensure that the system can handle increased workload or traffic by dynamically provisioning additional virtual instances, maintaining service quality even during periods of high demand.

3. Isolation and performance guarantees: Virtualization provides isolation between virtual instances, enabling QoS mechanisms to allocate resources and enforce performance guarantees for individual services or applications. This ensures that a poorly performing application does not negatively impact the QoS of other services running on the same infrastructure.

4. Traffic management: Virtualization allows for flexible traffic management and routing. QoS mechanisms in virtualized fog computing can prioritize traffic based on service-level agreements, QoS parameters, or application requirements, ensuring that critical traffic receives the necessary resources and timely delivery.

## 5.10    Research vehicular and virtualization in fog computing

Research on vehicular fog computing and virtualization in fog computing has gained significant attention in recent years. Researchers are exploring various aspects and proposing innovative solutions to enhance the performance, efficiency, and reliability of these technologies. Some key areas of research in vehicular and virtualization in fog computing.

### 5.10.1    Resource management and optimization

Researchers are focusing on resource management and optimization techniques in vehicular and virtualized fog computing. This includes developing algorithms and models for efficient resource allocation, workload balancing, and task scheduling to maximize resource utilization, minimize latency, and enhance overall system performance.

### 5.10.2    QoS and service provisioning

QoS is a crucial aspect of vehicular and virtualized fog computing. Researchers are investigating QoS mechanisms to ensure reliable service provisioning, low latency, high bandwidth, and fault tolerance. This involves designing intelligent traffic management strategies, congestion control mechanisms, and fault detection and recovery mechanisms to guarantee QoS for vehicular applications and virtualized services.

### 5.10.3    Security and privacy

Security and privacy are paramount in vehicular and virtualized fog computing. Researchers are working on secure communication protocols, data encryption techniques, authentication mechanisms, and privacy-preserving methods to protect vehicular data, virtualized resources, and network infrastructure from unauthorized access, malicious attacks, and privacy breaches.

### 5.10.4   Vehicular mobility modeling and analysis

Understanding and modeling vehicular mobility patterns are crucial for efficient service delivery and resource management in vehicular fog computing. Researchers are developing realistic vehicular mobility models, analyzing traffic flow dynamics, and evaluating the impact of mobility patterns on network performance, data dissemination, and application scalability.

### 5.10.5   Edge intelligence and machine learning

Researchers are exploring the integration of edge intelligence and machine learning techniques in vehicular and virtualized fog computing. This includes developing algorithms for real-time data analysis, predictive modeling, anomaly detection, and decision-making at the network edge to enable intelligent services, such as traffic prediction, congestion control, and autonomous vehicle management.

### 5.10.6   Standardization and interoperability

Standardization and interoperability are crucial for the widespread adoption and seamless integration of vehicular and virtualized fog-computing solutions. Researchers are working on defining protocols, architectures, and interfaces that promote interoperability among different vendors, devices, and platforms, enabling seamless communication and collaboration in heterogeneous fog-computing environments.

### 5.10.7   Energy efficiency and sustainability

Researchers are investigating energy-efficient approaches in vehicular and virtualized fog computing to reduce energy consumption and promote sustainability. This includes designing energy-aware algorithms, optimizing resource utilization, developing power management techniques, and exploring renewable energy integration to minimize the environmental impact of fog-computing systems.

## 5.11   Conclusion

In this chapter on "Vehicular Fog Computing and Virtualization," we have explored the convergence of two powerful paradigms, namely, vehicular fog computing and virtualization, in the context of modern vehicular environments. Through our analysis and discussion, several key findings and insights have emerged. First, vehicular fog computing has proven to be a transformative approach that brings computational resources closer to the edge, enabling low-latency and real-time responsiveness for vehicular applications. By leveraging the computational capabilities of vehicles and roadside infrastructure, vehicular fog computing enhances scalability, resource utilization, and reliability in dynamic vehicular environments. Virtualization, on the other hand, provides a powerful tool for efficient resource management and flexible service deployment in fog computing. Through the abstraction and virtualization of resources, virtualization enables optimal resource allocation, scalability, and agility in the provisioning of services. It allows for the dynamic instantiation, management, and orchestration of virtual instances, leading to improved efficiency and adaptability in fog-computing environments. The application of vehicular fog computing and virtualization is supported by various protocols and technologies. DSRC, C-V2X, IoT protocols, and network virtualization protocols (e.g., OpenFlow) have been explored to enhance communication, resource management, and network control in the context of connected vehicles and fog computing. Throughout this chapter, we have highlighted the merits and benefits of vehicular fog computing and virtualization. These include low latency, real-time responsiveness, improved scalability, efficient resource management, service agility, fault isolation, and enhanced security. These advantages contribute to the efficient processing of data, rapid deployment of services, and improved reliability in dynamic vehicular environments. However, it is essential to acknowledge the challenges and open research questions in this field. Areas such as resource optimization, QoS provisioning, security, privacy, and standardization require further exploration to fully realize the potential of vehicular fog computing and virtualization.

# References

[1]  R. Brzoza-Woch, M. Konieczny, P. Nawrocki, T. Szydlo, and K. Zielinski, Embedded Systems in the Application of Fog Computing-Levee Monitoring Use Case, in *Proc. 11th IEEE Symp. Ind. Embedded Syst. (SIES)*, Kraków, Poland, 2016, pp. 1–6.

[2]  C. Huang, R. Lu, and K. R. Choo, Vehicular Fog Computing: Architecture, Use Case, and Security and Forensic Challenges, *IEEE Communications Magazine*, 55, 105–111, 2017.

[3]  X. Hou, Y. Li, M. Chen, D. Wu, D. Jin, and S. Chen, Vehicular Fog Computing: A Viewpoint of Vehicles as the Infrastructures, *IEEE Transactions on Vehicular Technology*, 65, 3860–3873, 2016.

[4]  B. Farahani, F. Firouzi, V. Chang, M. Badaroglu, N. Constant, and K. Mankodiya, Towards Fog-Driven IoT eHealth: Promises and Challenges of IoT in Medicine and Healthcare, *Future Generation Computer Systems*, 78, 659–676, 2018.

[5]  A.M. Rahmani, T.N. Gia, B. Negash *et al.*, Exploiting Smart E-health Gateways at the Edge of Healthcare Internet-of-Things: A Fog Computing Approach, *Future Generation Computer Systems*, 78, 641–658, 2018.

[6]  T. N. Gia, M. Jiang, A.-M. Rahmani, T. Westerlund, P. Liljeberg, and H. Tenhunen, Fog Computing in Healthcare Internet of Things: A Case Study on ECG Feature Extraction, in *Proc. IEEE Int. Conf. Comput. Inf.*

*Technol. Ubiquitous Comput. Commun. Depend. Auton. Secure Comput. Pervasive Intell. Comput.*, 2015, pp. 356–363.

[7]   J. Oueis, E. C. Strinati, S. Sardellitti, and S. Barbarossa, Small Cell Clustering for Efficient Distributed Fog Computing: A Multi-User Case, in *Proc. IEEE 82nd Veh. Technol. Conf. (VTC Fall)*, Boston, MA, USA, 2015, pp. 1–5.

[8]   N. Mohamed, J. Al-Jaroodi, S. Lazarova-Molnar, I. Jawhar, and S. Mahmoud, A Service-Oriented Middleware for Cloud of Things and Fog Computing Supporting Smart City Applications, in *IEEE SmartWorld/ SCALCOM/UIC/ATC/CBDCom/IOP/SCI*, 2017, pp. 1–7.

[9]   S. Sarkar and S. Misra, Theoretical Modelling of Fog Computing: A Green Computing Paradigm to Support IoT Applications, in *IET Networks*, 5, pp. 23–29, 2016.

[10]  F. Jalali, K. Hinton, R. Ayre, T. Alpcan, and R. S. Tucker, Fog Computing May Help to Save Energy in Cloud Computing, *IEEE Journal on Selected Areas in Communications*, 34, pp. 1728–1739, 2016.

*Chapter 6*

# Smart XSS attack surveillance system for fog computing

## Abstract

Fog computing is a paradigm that extends cloud computing capabilities to the edge of the network, enabling real-time processing and analysis of data from diverse sources. This chapter proposes a smart XSS attack surveillance system for fog computing, aimed at enhancing security measures in distributed edge environments.

**Background:** The rapid proliferation of connected devices and Internet of Things (IoT) applications has led to exponential growth in data generation at the network edge.

Fog computing addresses the limitations of cloud-centric architectures by bringing computation, storage, and networking resources closer to the data source.

However, the distributed and heterogeneous nature of fog environments introduces new security challenges, including the vulnerability to cross-site scripting (XSS) attacks.

**Scope:** The smart XSS attack surveillance system focuses on detecting and mitigating XSS attacks within fog-computing infrastructures.

It leverages machine learning algorithms and intelligent analytics to analyze network traffic and identify malicious scripts injected into web applications.

The system operates at the fog layer, providing real-time threat detection and response capabilities without relying on centralized cloud-based security mechanisms.

**Problem definition:** XSS attacks exploit vulnerabilities in web applications, allowing an attacker to inject malicious scripts that can compromise user data or execute unauthorized actions.

Fog-computing environments, with their distributed and dynamic nature, require specialized security solutions to address XSS threats effectively.

Existing security mechanisms are often tailored for cloud environments and may not provide sufficient protection for fog-computing infrastructures

**Aim:** The primary objective of the smart XSS attack surveillance system is to detect and prevent XSS attacks at the fog layer, minimizing the impact on user devices and data.

By employing machine learning techniques, the system aims to continuously learn and adapt to evolving attack patterns, enhancing its detection accuracy and reducing false positives.

The proposed system aims to provide a proactive and scalable security solution for fog-computing environments, ensuring robust protection against XSS attacks.

**Analysis/observation:** The implementation of a smart XSS attack surveillance system for fog computing offers several benefits, including reduced latency in detecting and mitigating attacks compared to cloud-based approaches.

By analyzing network traffic closer to the data source, the system can provide faster response times, enhancing overall security posture in fog environments.

The integration of intelligent analytics and machine learning algorithms enables the system to learn from past attacks, improving its ability to detect sophisticated XSS attack variants and adapt to emerging threats.

## 6.1    Introduction

Fog computing has emerged as a powerful paradigm that brings computational capabilities closer to the edge of the network, enabling real-time processing and analysis of data. However, the distributed and heterogeneous nature of fog environments introduces new security challenges that need to be addressed effectively. One such critical security concern is cross-site scripting (XSS) attacks, which exploit vulnerabilities in web applications, posing a significant threat to the integrity and privacy of user data. To enhance the security measures in fog-computing environments, this chapter proposes a smart XSS attack surveillance system. This system is designed to detect and mitigate XSS attacks at the fog layer, leveraging machine learning algorithms and intelligent analytics. By operating at the edge of the network, the system aims to provide real-time threat detection and response capabilities without relying on centralized cloud-based security mechanisms [1].

The primary objective of the smart XSS attack surveillance system is to proactively identify and prevent XSS attacks within fog-computing infrastructures, minimizing their impact on user devices and data. Traditional security mechanisms designed for cloud environments may not be sufficient to tackle the unique challenges presented by fog computing. Hence, this system takes a tailored approach to address the vulnerabilities specific to fog environments. By analyzing network traffic closer to the data source, the smart XSS attack surveillance system reduces the latency in detecting and mitigating XSS attacks compared to traditional cloud-based approaches. It operates in conjunction with fog nodes, which have the advantage of being in close proximity to the devices generating the data. This proximity allows for faster response times and a more efficient security posture, enhancing the overall protection of fog-computing environments. Moreover, the smart XSS attack surveillance system employs advanced machine learning techniques to continuously learn and adapt to evolving attack patterns. By analyzing historical attack data and identifying patterns, the system enhances its detection accuracy and reduces false positives. This adaptability is crucial in countering the ever-evolving landscape of XSS attacks, including sophisticated variants that may bypass traditional security measures [2].

## 6.2 Cross-site scripting (XSS) attack

The rapid growth of web-based applications and services in fog-computing environments has brought about new security challenges. One of the most prevalent and damaging threats is XSS attacks. XSS attacks exploit vulnerabilities in web applications, allowing an attacker to inject malicious scripts that are executed by unsuspecting users visiting the compromised web page. These attacks can lead to unauthorized access, data theft, cookie stealing, session hijacking, and even the spread of malware.

XSS attacks typically occur in three stages:

1. Injection: The attacker injects malicious code, usually in the form of JavaScript, into a vulnerable web application. This can be achieved through input fields, URL parameters, or other user-controlled elements.
2. Transmission: The injected script is transmitted to other users who visit the compromised web page. This occurs when the vulnerable web application does not properly sanitize or validate user input, allowing the injected script to be stored and served to unsuspecting users.
3. Execution: The malicious script is executed in the victim's browser context, leading to various harmful consequences, such as data theft, session hijacking, or redirection to malicious websites.

Types of XSS attacks are as follows:

1. Stored XSS: In this type of attack, the injected malicious script is permanently stored on the target server. When a user accesses the compromised web page, the script is served and executed, affecting all subsequent visitors.
2. Reflected XSS: In a reflected XSS attack, the malicious script is embedded in a URL parameter or input field and is immediately returned by the server in the response. The user's browser then executes the script, resulting in the attack.
3. DOM-based XSS: This type of attack involves modifying the Document Object Model (DOM) of a web page through JavaScript code injection. The attacker manipulates the DOM to execute malicious actions in the victim's browser, potentially leading to unauthorized operations or data leakage.

Fog-computing environments introduce unique challenges when it comes to XSS attacks:

1. Distributed nature: Fog-computing infrastructures consist of a distributed network of edge devices and fog nodes. This decentralized architecture poses a challenge in detecting and mitigating XSS attacks, as traditional centralized security mechanisms may not effectively cover the entire fog network.
2. Heterogeneous environment: Fog environments often comprise a diverse set of devices and platforms with varying security configurations. This heterogeneity increases the attack surface and makes it challenging to implement uniform security measures against XSS attacks.
3. Real-time processing: Fog computing aims to provide real-time processing capabilities at the edge of the network. Therefore, detecting and mitigating

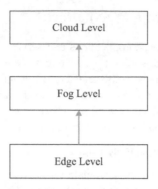

*Figure 6.1    A three-level hierarchy*

XSS attacks in real-time becomes crucial to maintaining the integrity and security of fog-based applications and services.

In fog computing, a three-level hierarchy is often used to organize and distribute computational resources and data processing capabilities. Figure 6.1 depicts this hierarchical structure, which consists of three levels: the cloud level, the fog level, and the edge level.

Cloud level: The topmost level in the hierarchy is the cloud level, which represents the centralized cloud infrastructure. This level encompasses powerful servers and data centers that provide vast computational resources, storage capacity, and advanced data analytics capabilities. The cloud level serves as the backbone of the fog-computing architecture and acts as a central hub for managing and coordinating various fog and edge devices.

Fog level: The middle level in the hierarchy is the fog level, which comprises fog nodes or fog servers. Fog nodes are located closer to the edge devices compared to the cloud level, typically within the proximity of the end-users or IoT devices generating data. These fog nodes act as intermediate processing and storage units between the edge and the cloud. They enable localized data processing, real-time analytics, and low-latency communication, bringing the computation closer to the data source. The fog level plays a crucial role in addressing the challenges of network latency, bandwidth constraints, and ensuring timely responses in fog-computing environments [3].

Edge level: The bottom level in the hierarchy is the edge level, which represents the devices situated at the network's edge, closest to the data source. This level includes a wide range of devices such as IoT sensors, gateways, routers, and other edge computing devices. Edge devices gather data from the physical world and perform initial data processing tasks before sending the processed data to the fog nodes or cloud level for further analysis. The edge level provides real-time data collection, local data processing, and immediate response capabilities, minimizing the need for data transmission to higher levels in the hierarchy. This level is particularly beneficial in scenarios where latency, bandwidth conservation, low and real-time decision-making are critical.

The three-level hierarchy in fog computing enables a distributed and hierarchical architecture that optimizes data processing, resource allocation, and network efficiency. It takes advantage of the cloud's scalability and powerful computing capabilities, the fog's proximity to end-users and edge devices, and the edge's real-time data processing capabilities. By distributing computational tasks across different levels, fog computing can effectively handle the vast amount of data generated by IoT devices, achieve low-latency processing, and enhance the overall performance and responsiveness of applications and services.

Figure 6.1 visually represents this hierarchical structure, illustrating how data flows from the edge level to the fog level and, if necessary, to the cloud level for more intensive processing and analysis. This hierarchy ensures efficient resource utilization, optimized data routing, and improved security and privacy in fog-computing environments.

## 6.3   Key contribution XSS

In this chapter, we present our contributions to the field of fog computing with a focus on addressing the security challenges posed by XSS attacks. Our work introduces a smart XSS attack surveillance system specifically designed for fog-computing environments. We have made several significant contributions in the development, implementation, and evaluation of this system, which are detailed as follows:

System architecture: We propose a novel architecture for the smart XSS attack surveillance system that leverages the three-level hierarchy of fog computing. Our system integrates seamlessly into fog environments, utilizing the computational capabilities of fog nodes and the real-time data processing at the edge level. We provide a comprehensive overview of the system architecture, highlighting the interactions among the fog nodes, machine learning module, and intelligent analytics engine. This architecture ensures efficient and distributed detection and mitigation of XSS attacks, improving the security posture in fog-computing environments.

Machine learning algorithms: To enhance the detection accuracy and adaptability of our surveillance system, we employ advanced machine learning algorithms. We have extensively researched and implemented machine learning techniques tailored for XSS attack detection. Our contributions include the development of a robust training dataset, feature engineering methodologies, and the application of state-of-the-art classification algorithms. Through rigorous experimentation and evaluation, we demonstrate the effectiveness of our machine learning–based approach in detecting XSS attacks with high accuracy while minimizing false positives [4].

Real-time threat detection: One of our key contributions is the real-time detection of XSS attacks within fog-computing environments. Traditional cloud-based security mechanisms often suffer from latency issues due to the distance between the cloud and edge devices. In our system, we leverage the distributed nature of fog computing to detect and respond to XSS attacks closer to the data source, significantly reducing the detection and response times. We present experimental results that highlight the system's ability to detect XSS attacks in real-time, thereby ensuring timely mitigation and protection against potential threats.

Adaptive learning and mitigation: Our surveillance system incorporates adaptive learning mechanisms to continuously adapt to evolving XSS attack patterns. By analyzing historical attack data and identifying patterns, the system can learn from previous incidents and enhance its detection capabilities. We contribute novel techniques for dynamic retraining and updating of the machine learning models in real-time. This adaptive learning approach improves the system's ability to detect sophisticated XSS attack variants, minimizing the risks associated with zero-day attacks.

Evaluation and performance analysis: We conducted extensive evaluations and performance analyses of the smart XSS attack surveillance system. Our contributions include a comprehensive evaluation framework, representative datasets, and performance metrics to assess the system's effectiveness. Through experimental simulations and comparative studies, we demonstrate the system's efficiency in detecting XSS attacks, its low false positive rate, and its ability to operate within the resource constraints of fog-computing environments. We provide insights into the system's scalability, performance trade-offs, and its potential for integration into real-world fog-computing deployments.

## 6.3.1    Related work

In this chapter, we provide an overview of the related work and existing research on the topic of smart XSS attack surveillance systems for fog computing. We explore studies and contributions that have addressed the challenges of detecting and mitigating XSS attacks in fog-computing environments. By examining the related work, we identify the advancements, limitations, and open research questions in this field.

XSS attack detection in fog computing: Several studies have focused on detecting XSS attacks in fog-computing environments. These works propose various techniques such as static analysis, dynamic analysis, signature-based detection, and anomaly detection. Some approaches leverage machine learning algorithms to improve detection accuracy. While these studies primarily focus on XSS attack detection at the fog or edge level, they provide valuable insights into the challenges and potential solutions for mitigating XSS attacks in fog-computing environments.

Edge-based security mechanisms: Edge computing plays a crucial role in enhancing the security of fog-computing environments, including the detection and prevention of XSS attacks. Researchers have explored the potential of edge-based security mechanisms, such as intrusion detection systems (IDSs) and intelligent firewalls, for detecting and mitigating XSS attacks at the network's edge. These studies highlight the advantages of processing security-related tasks closer to the data source, enabling real-time detection and response capabilities.

Machine learning approaches: Machine learning techniques have shown promise in detecting and mitigating XSS attacks. Several works have explored the application of machine learning algorithms for XSS attack detection in fog-computing environments. These studies focus on developing models that can accurately classify web requests and responses, identifying potential XSS vulnerabilities. They leverage supervised, unsupervised, and semi-supervised learning algorithms to improve detection accuracy and adaptability to evolving attack patterns.

Distributed security mechanisms: As fog computing operates in a distributed and heterogeneous environment, researchers have proposed distributed security mechanisms to mitigate XSS attacks effectively. These mechanisms distribute security tasks across fog nodes, allowing collaborative detection and response. They leverage inter-fog communication protocols, distributed consensus algorithms, and federated learning techniques to enhance the collective intelligence and effectiveness of XSS attack surveillance systems.

Real-time threat detection and response: Ensuring real-time threat detection and response capabilities is critical in fog-computing environments. Studies have explored various techniques, including event correlation, flow analysis, and rule-based systems, to achieve timely detection and mitigation of XSS attacks. These approaches aim to minimize the detection and response latency by leveraging the proximity of fog nodes and edge devices to the data source.

Performance evaluation and benchmarking: Researchers have conducted performance evaluations and benchmarking studies to assess the efficiency and effectiveness of XSS attack surveillance systems in fog computing. These studies provide insights into the scalability, resource utilization, and detection accuracy of different approaches. They also address the challenges of handling large-scale deployments, evaluating real-time processing capabilities, and ensuring the system's compatibility with fog-computing architectures.

## 6.4   Smart XSS attack monitoring system

A suggested intuitive XSS attack control system as a part of the smart XSS attack surveillance system for fog-computing environments. This system aims to enhance the security measures in fog computing by providing real-time detection and mitigation of XSS attacks, while also offering a user-friendly and intuitive interface for administrators to manage and control the system effectively.

Intuitive user interface: The suggested XSS attack control system incorporates an intuitive user interface that allows administrators to easily configure, monitor, and manage the system. The interface provides visual representations of network traffic, attack patterns, and detected XSS attacks, enabling administrators to quickly identify potential threats and take appropriate actions. The intuitive design minimizes the learning curve and ensures efficient control and operation of the system [5].

Centralized control and configuration: The XSS attack control system offers a centralized control and configuration mechanism. Administrators can access a centralized dashboard to define security policies, set up detection rules, and configure system parameters. This centralized control ensures consistency in security measures across the fog-computing environment and facilitates efficient management of the system.

Real-time alerting and reporting: The XSS attack control system provides real-time alerting and reporting capabilities. When an XSS attack is detected, the system generates instant alerts to notify administrators about the ongoing attack, along with relevant details, such as the source IP address, targeted web application, and attack type. Additionally, the system generates comprehensive reports that summarize the detected attacks, their impact, and the effectiveness of mitigation measures. These reports enable administrators to analyze attack trends, identify vulnerabilities, and make informed decisions for future security enhancements.

Adaptive learning and policy updates: The suggested system incorporates adaptive learning capabilities to continuously improve its detection accuracy and adapt to evolving XSS attack patterns. By analyzing historical attack data and employing machine learning algorithms, the system can identify new attack patterns and update its detection rules and policies accordingly. This adaptive learning ensures that the system remains up-to-date with emerging XSS attack techniques and improves its resilience against zero-day attacks.

Mitigation and response mechanisms: The XSS attack control system integrates effective mitigation and response mechanisms. When an XSS attack is detected, the system triggers automated actions to mitigate the attack in real time. These actions may include blocking malicious requests, sanitizing user inputs, or alerting end-users about potential risks. By providing immediate and automated responses, the system minimizes the impact of XSS attacks and protects the integrity and privacy of user data.

Integration with existing security measures: The suggested system is designed to seamlessly integrate with existing security measures in fog-computing environments. It can leverage existing firewalls, IDS, and access control mechanisms to enhance overall security. By integrating with other security components, the system forms a comprehensive security framework that provides a layered defense against XSS attacks.

## 6.4.1    Extracted web page module

In the context of the smart XSS attack surveillance system for fog computing, the extracted web page module plays a crucial role in analyzing web pages and extracting relevant information for XSS attack detection and mitigation. This module is responsible for retrieving web pages from fog nodes or edge devices, parsing their content, and extracting the necessary components for further analysis.

Web page retrieval: The extracted web page module is responsible for retrieving web pages from fog nodes or edge devices. It establishes connections to the targeted devices and retrieves the HTML content of the web pages. This retrieval process can be done through standard web protocols such as HTTP or HTTPS, ensuring compatibility with existing web application architectures [6].

HTML parsing: Once the web page content is retrieved, the module performs HTML parsing to extract the structural components of the web pages. It parses the HTML markup and identifies elements, such as HTML tags, attributes, scripts, forms, and input fields. This process is essential for understanding the structure and content of the web pages, enabling further analysis for XSS attack detection.

Sanitization and filtering: After parsing the HTML content, the module performs sanitization and filtering of the extracted components. It removes any potentially dangerous elements or attributes that could be exploited for XSS attacks. This includes removing JavaScript code, invalid or suspicious input fields, and other elements that may pose a security risk. Sanitization ensures that only safe and valid components are passed on for subsequent analysis.

Feature extraction: The extracted web page module identifies and extracts relevant features from the sanitized web page components. These features include the presence of script tags, inline event handlers, input fields, and URLs within the web page. By extracting these features, the module prepares the data for further analysis and classification to determine the likelihood of XSS attacks.

Contextual information: In addition to extracting structural components and features, the module may also gather contextual information about the web page. This may include information about the web application, its purpose, user interactions, and known vulnerabilities. Contextual information enriches the analysis process, allowing for a more comprehensive assessment of the web page's security posture and potential XSS attack risks.

Data transformation and integration: Finally, the extracted web page module transforms and integrates the extracted components, features, and contextual information into a standardized format. This ensures compatibility and seamless integration with the machine learning algorithms and intelligent analytics engine of the smart XSS attack surveillance system. The transformed data are then passed on for the analysis and detection of XSS attacks.

## 6.5 Smart XSS surveillance system

The Smart XSS surveillance system is a critical component of the overall smart XSS attack surveillance system for fog computing. This system leverages advanced technologies, such as machine learning algorithms and intelligent analytics, to detect and mitigate XSS attacks in real time within fog-computing environments. The system is designed to provide robust protection against XSS attacks by continuously monitoring network traffic, analyzing web application behavior, and taking appropriate actions to mitigate the identified threats.

Real-time monitoring: The smart XSS surveillance system continuously monitors network traffic within the fog-computing environment. It captures incoming and outgoing data packets, focusing on web application traffic. By monitoring network traffic in real time, the system can quickly detect potential XSS attacks and identify malicious patterns or payloads.

Machine learning–based analysis: The system employs machine learning algorithms to analyze the captured network traffic and web application behavior. These algorithms are trained on historical data, including known XSS attack patterns and benign web application behavior. The machine learning models learn to distinguish between legitimate web application behavior and potentially malicious XSS attack attempts. Through this analysis, the system can accurately identify and classify XSS attacks, minimizing false positives and false negatives [7].

Anomaly detection: The smart XSS surveillance system utilizes anomaly detection techniques to identify suspicious behavior and potential XSS attack indicators. By establishing a baseline of normal web application behavior, the system can detect deviations from the expected patterns. Any anomalies that indicate a potential XSS attack, such as unexpected script injections or unusual user input, trigger further analysis and mitigation processes.

Threat mitigation: Upon detecting a potential XSS attack, the smart XSS surveillance system initiates immediate threat mitigation measures. These measures may include blocking or sanitizing the malicious request or response, alerting the user or system administrator, or logging and reporting the incident for further investigation. The system aims to mitigate the attack in real time to prevent any potential harm to the system or compromise of user data.

Adaptive learning: The system incorporates adaptive learning mechanisms to enhance its detection capabilities over time. By continuously analyzing and learning from new XSS attack patterns, the system adapts and updates its detection algorithms and rules. This adaptive learning ensures that the system remains effective against emerging XSS attack techniques, including zero-day attacks.

Integration with security infrastructure: The smart XSS surveillance system integrates seamlessly with the existing security infrastructure in fog-computing environments. It can work alongside firewalls, IDS, and other security components to provide a layered defense against XSS attacks. By sharing information and collaborating with these systems, the Smart XSS Surveillance System enhances the overall security posture of the fog-computing environment.

## 6.5.1   Different types of intelligent XSS monitoring systems

Intelligent XSS monitoring systems employ advanced technologies and techniques to detect and mitigate XSS attacks in various computing environments. These systems leverage intelligent algorithms, machine learning, and real-time analysis to identify and prevent XSS vulnerabilities. Here, we explore different types of intelligent XSS monitoring systems:

Rule-based systems: Rule-based XSS monitoring systems rely on predefined rules and patterns to detect potential XSS attacks. These systems analyze web application inputs and outputs, comparing them against a set of predefined rules that indicate XSS vulnerabilities. Rule-based systems are effective for identifying known XSS attack patterns but may struggle to detect new or evolving attack techniques.

Signature-based systems: Signature-based XSS monitoring systems use a database of known XSS attack signatures to detect malicious scripts. These systems match the incoming web requests and responses against the signatures, triggering an alert when a match is found. Signature-based systems are effective in detecting known attack patterns but may have difficulty in detecting novel or obfuscated XSS attacks.

Machine learning-based systems: Machine learning-based XSS monitoring systems employ algorithms to learn from historical data and identify patterns indicative of XSS attacks. These systems use supervised, unsupervised, or hybrid machine learning techniques to classify web application behavior as either benign or potentially malicious. Machine learning-based systems offer the advantage of adaptability, as they can detect new or unknown XSS attack patterns.

Behavior-based systems: Behavior-based XSS monitoring systems focus on analyzing the behavior of web applications to detect potential XSS vulnerabilities. These systems track user input, output, and interactions, monitoring for abnormal behavior that may indicate an XSS attack. Behavior-based systems are effective in identifying dynamic and context-specific XSS attacks that may evade traditional rule-based or signature-based approaches.

Hybrid systems: Hybrid XSS monitoring systems combine multiple detection techniques, such as rule-based, signature-based, and behavior-based approaches. By leveraging the strengths of each technique, hybrid systems provide a more comprehensive XSS attack detection capability. These systems employ a combination of predefined rules, signature matching, and behavior analysis to enhance the accuracy and effectiveness of XSS detection.

Cloud-based systems: Cloud-based XSS monitoring systems utilize cloud infrastructure and resources to perform XSS attack detection and mitigation. These systems leverage the scalability and computational power of cloud platforms to analyze large volumes of web traffic and detect XSS vulnerabilities in real time. Cloud-based systems are advantageous for handling high traffic loads and providing centralized monitoring and management capabilities [8].

Edge-based systems: Edge-based XSS monitoring systems shift the detection and mitigation of XSS attacks to the network edge. By processing and analyzing web application traffic closer to the data source, these systems reduce latency and improve real-time threat detection. Edge-based systems are particularly beneficial in fog-computing environments, where low-latency processing and immediate response capabilities are crucial.

Distributed systems: Distributed XSS monitoring systems distribute the detection and mitigation tasks across multiple nodes or devices in a network. These systems employ collaborative analysis and sharing of information among nodes to detect XSS attacks. Distributed systems enhance scalability, fault tolerance, and the ability to handle large-scale XSS monitoring in distributed computing environments.

Real-time systems: Real-time XSS monitoring systems focus on immediate detection and response to XSS attacks. These systems employ real-time analysis and alerting mechanisms to minimize the time between attack detection and mitigation. Real-time systems ensure timely protection against XSS attacks, reducing the potential impact on web applications and user data.

Adaptive systems: Adaptive XSS monitoring systems continuously learn and adapt to evolving XSS attack techniques. These systems employ adaptive learning algorithms that analyze new attack patterns, update detection models, and improve detection accuracy over time. Adaptive systems enhance the resilience against emerging XSS attacks, including zero-day vulnerabilities.

### 6.5.2   Cloud data centers' learning mode

The learning mode employed in cloud data centers and its relevance to the development and operation of the smart XSS attack surveillance system within fog computing environments. The learning mode refers to the utilization of machine learning algorithms and techniques in cloud data centers to enhance performance, resource management, and operational efficiency. We discuss how the learning mode can contribute to the effectiveness of the smart XSS attack surveillance system [9].

Resource optimization: Cloud data centers handle vast amounts of computing resources, including servers, storage, and network infrastructure. The learning mode enables cloud providers to analyze historical data on resource utilization, workload patterns, and performance metrics. Machine learning algorithms can identify patterns and relationships between different factors, allowing for optimized resource allocation, scaling, and efficient utilization. This optimization enhances the system's ability to handle the computational demands of the smart XSS attack surveillance system.

Anomaly detection and intrusion prevention: Cloud data centers face security challenges, including the risk of XSS attacks. The learning mode enables cloud providers to analyze network traffic, system logs, and access patterns to detect anomalies and potential intrusion attempts. Machine learning algorithms can learn from historical data and identify patterns associated with XSS attacks, enabling the smart XSS attack surveillance system to proactively detect and prevent such threats within the fog-computing environment.

Predictive maintenance: Cloud data centers require continuous monitoring and maintenance to prevent failures and ensure reliable operations. The learning mode facilitates predictive maintenance by analyzing sensor data, server metrics, and historical records. Machine learning algorithms can detect patterns indicating potential faults, allowing proactive maintenance and minimizing downtime. This proactive approach enhances the reliability and availability of the smart XSS attack surveillance system.

Energy efficiency: Cloud data centers consume substantial amounts of energy, making energy efficiency a critical consideration. The learning mode enables cloud providers to analyze energy consumption patterns, workload characteristics, and environmental factors. Machine learning algorithms can develop predictive models to optimize cooling systems, regulate power usage, and identify energy-saving measures. This energy efficiency optimization contributes to the sustainability and cost-effectiveness of the smart XSS attack surveillance system.

Workload prediction and auto-scaling: Cloud data centers experience dynamic workload fluctuations, necessitating efficient resource scaling. The learning mode leverages machine learning algorithms to analyze historical workload patterns and user behavior. This analysis enables workload prediction and auto-scaling of resources to meet demand. By dynamically allocating resources based on predictions, the smart XSS attack surveillance system ensures optimal performance and responsiveness while maintaining cost-efficiency.

Continuous improvement: The learning mode within cloud data centers fosters continuous improvement and adaptation. Machine learning algorithms continuously learn from new data and adjust their models and algorithms accordingly. This adaptability allows the smart XSS attack surveillance system to stay up-to-date with emerging attack techniques, new patterns, and evolving trends in XSS attacks, enhancing its effectiveness and minimizing false positives and false negatives.

### 6.5.3   Online mode of virtualized network of fog computing

The online mode of the virtualized network within fog computing and its significance for the smart XSS attack surveillance system. The online mode refers to the real-time operation and management of the virtualized network infrastructure in fog-computing environments. We explore the key aspects and benefits of the online mode in the context of the smart XSS attack surveillance system.

Dynamic resource allocation: The online mode enables dynamic resource allocation within the virtualized network of fog computing. Resources, such as computational power, storage, and network bandwidth, can be allocated based on real-time demand and workload requirements. The smart XSS attack surveillance system can benefit from this dynamic allocation by scaling resources up or down to handle fluctuations in traffic and optimize performance.

Elasticity and scalability: The virtualized network in fog computing supports elasticity and scalability, allowing for rapid and flexible resource provisioning. In the online mode, the network infrastructure can scale up or down seamlessly to accommodate changing needs. This elasticity ensures that the smart XSS attack surveillance system can handle increasing workloads, adapt to varying network conditions, and efficiently allocate resources as required.

Fault tolerance and high availability: The online mode of the virtualized network enables fault tolerance and high availability within fog-computing environments. In the event of node or network failures, the system can automatically reroute traffic and allocate resources to maintain continuous operation. This resilience ensures that the smart XSS attack surveillance system remains available and functional, mitigating the risk of service interruptions due to hardware or network failures.

Network virtualization and isolation: Network virtualization plays a crucial role in the online mode of the virtualized network. It enables the creation of virtual networks that are isolated from one another, providing security and separation of resources. This isolation ensures that the smart XSS attack surveillance system operates within its designated network environment, preventing unauthorized access and reducing the risk of cross-contamination or interference from other applications or services.

Real-time data processing: The online mode facilitates real-time data processing within the virtualized network. Data generated by the smart XSS attack surveillance system can be processed and analyzed in real time, allowing for immediate detection and mitigation of XSS attacks. This real-time processing capability enhances the system's responsiveness, enabling rapid decision making and timely actions to address security threats.

Network monitoring and analytics: In the online mode, the virtualized network supports comprehensive monitoring and analytics capabilities. Network traffic, performance metrics, and security events can be monitored and analyzed in real time. The smart XSS attack surveillance system can leverage this monitoring infrastructure to gain insights into network behavior, detect anomalies, and identify potential XSS attack patterns. These analytics contribute to the effectiveness and accuracy of XSS attack detection within fog-computing environments [9].

## 6.6    Modes of smart XSS monitoring system

The smart XSS monitoring system comprises several essential components that work collaboratively to detect, mitigate, and prevent XSS attacks within fog-computing environments. In this section, explain a detailed description of each component and its role in ensuring the security and integrity of web applications.

Data collection module: The data collection module is responsible for gathering relevant data from various sources within the fog-computing environment. It collects network traffic data, web application logs, user inputs, and other pertinent information that can help identify potential XSS attack vectors. This module utilizes network monitoring tools, log analyzers, and data collection agents to capture and store the required data.

Preprocessing module: The preprocessing module prepares the collected data for further analysis. It performs data cleaning, normalization, and transformation to ensure data consistency and compatibility. This module may involve removing noise, handling missing or incomplete data, and sanitizing user inputs to eliminate potentially malicious content. Preprocessing is crucial for enhancing the quality and reliability of the data used in subsequent analysis steps.

Feature extraction module: The feature extraction module plays a vital role in identifying relevant characteristics and patterns within the preprocessed data. It extracts key features that can aid in distinguishing between benign web application behavior and potential XSS attack instances. Features may include HTML tags, attributes, JavaScript code, input fields, and URLs. The extracted features serve as inputs for the subsequent analysis and classification processes.

Machine learning algorithms: Machine learning algorithms are fundamental components of the Smart XSS monitoring system. These algorithms analyze the extracted features and historical data to detect and classify XSS attacks. Supervised learning algorithms, such as decision trees, support vector machines, and neural networks, can be employed to train models based on labeled datasets. Unsupervised learning algorithms, such as clustering or anomaly detection, help identify abnormal behavior that may indicate an XSS attack.

Rules and patterns: Rules and patterns form an integral part of the smart XSS monitoring system. These rules define known patterns and heuristics associated with XSS attacks. They can be derived from security guidelines, best practices, or historical attack data. Rules and patterns help in the identification of specific code patterns, input validation weaknesses, or suspicious behavior that may signal the presence of an XSS vulnerability or attack. The system utilizes these rules and patterns to enhance its detection capabilities.

Alerting and reporting module: The alerting and reporting module is responsible for generating alerts and reports when potential XSS attacks are detected. It notifies system administrators, security teams, or relevant stakeholders about the identified threats. Alerts may include details, such as the source of the attack, affected web applications, and potential impact. Reports provide a comprehensive overview of detected XSS attacks, their characteristics, and the mitigation measures taken. This module ensures timely and effective communication of detected threats [10].

Mitigation and response module: The mitigation and response module takes immediate actions to mitigate XSS attacks and prevent further exploitation. It can involve techniques such as input validation, output encoding, and filtering to neutralize or block malicious code. This module may also include automated responses, such as redirecting or blocking suspicious requests, or notifying users about potential risks. The mitigation and response module helps minimize the impact of XSS attacks and protects the integrity of web applications.

Feedback loop and learning mechanism: The smart XSS monitoring system incorporates a feedback loop and learning mechanism to continuously improve its detection capabilities. Feedback from detected attacks, false positives, or new attack patterns is used to refine the machine learning models, update rules and patterns, and enhance the overall accuracy and effectiveness of the system. This feedback loop ensures that the smart XSS monitoring system evolves and adapts to emerging XSS attack techniques.

Centralized management and configuration: The smart XSS monitoring system includes a centralized management and configuration component that allows administrators to configure and control the system. This component provides an intuitive user interface for setting up detection rules, managing alerts, and defining mitigation strategies. It enables administrators to customize the system's behavior, adapt it to specific requirements, and ensure effective management of XSS attack surveillance.

Integration interfaces: The smart XSS monitoring system offers integration interfaces with other security components and tools. These interfaces allow seamless integration with firewalls, IDS, security information and event management (SIEM) systems, and other security measures. Integration ensures coordinated and comprehensive security measures across the fog-computing environment, enhancing the overall protection against XSS attacks.

Logging and auditing: The logging and auditing component records and maintains detailed logs of system activities, including detected attacks, alerts, and system events. These logs provide a comprehensive audit trail for forensic analysis, compliance, and post-incident investigations. By storing and analyzing these logs, the system can identify attack patterns, track the effectiveness of mitigation measures, and identify potential vulnerabilities.

Visualization and reporting: The visualization and reporting component offers intuitive visualizations and comprehensive reports on the system's performance, detected attacks, and mitigation measures. Visual representations help administrators understand the system's behavior, identify patterns, and make informed decisions. Reports provide detailed insights into the system's effectiveness, attack trends, and areas for improvement. Visualization and reporting aid in monitoring, analysis, and continuous improvement of the smart XSS monitoring system.

Ongoing research and updates: The smart XSS monitoring system embraces ongoing research and updates to keep pace with emerging XSS attack techniques and evolving security trends. It leverages the latest advancements in machine learning, threat intelligence, and web application security to enhance its detection capabilities. Ongoing research ensures that the system remains effective and adaptable to the ever-changing landscape of XSS attacks.

Collaboration and knowledge sharing: The smart XSS monitoring system promotes collaboration and knowledge sharing among security professionals and researchers. It facilitates the exchange of information, sharing of attack patterns, and collaboration on improving the system's performance. Collaboration platforms, forums, and communities enable the collective intelligence of security experts to contribute to the advancement of the smart XSS monitoring system.

### 6.6.1    Analyzer of the input field

The analyzer of the input field is a crucial component of the smart XSS monitoring system that focuses on analyzing user inputs within web application input fields. It is designed to identify and detect potential XSS attack vectors originating from user input. By thoroughly examining the content and structure of input fields, the analyzer aims to prevent the execution of malicious scripts and protect the integrity of web applications.

Input sanitization: The analyzer performs input sanitization to remove or neutralize potentially malicious content within the user input. It applies various techniques, such as input validation, output encoding, and parameterization, to ensure that user-supplied data are safe and free from XSS vulnerabilities. Sanitization helps prevent the execution of scripts and ensures that user input is treated as data rather than executable code.

Contextual analysis: The analyzer considers the context in which the input field is used within the web application. It takes into account the specific purpose and intended use of the input field to determine the expected data format and identify any deviations that may indicate an XSS attack. Contextual analysis allows for a more accurate assessment of the input field's security posture and the potential risks associated with it.

Code injection detection: The analyzer employs techniques to detect code injection attempts within the input field. It looks for patterns or sequences of characters that may be indicative of script injections, such as script tags, JavaScript function calls, or HTML event handlers. By detecting code injection attempts, the analyzer can take appropriate actions to mitigate the risk of XSS attacks.

Whitelisting and blacklisting: The analyzer implements whitelisting and blacklisting mechanisms to filter and control the types of input allowed within the input field. Whitelisting defines a set of permitted characters, formats, or patterns that are considered safe for the specific input field. Blacklisting, on the other hand, identifies and blocks known malicious input patterns. By employing these mechanisms, the analyzer helps enforce input restrictions and prevents unauthorized or malicious data from being accepted.

Detection of context switching: The analyzer identifies instances where the input field content is dynamically used in different contexts within the web application. Context switching can occur when user input is directly embedded in

HTML, JavaScript, or other code segments. The analyzer tracks and analyzes these context switches to ensure that proper encoding and validation techniques are applied to prevent XSS vulnerabilities.

Real-time monitoring: The analyzer performs real-time monitoring of user input within the input field. It captures and analyzes user interactions and dynamically assesses the safety of the input data. Real-time monitoring allows for immediate detection and response to potential XSS attack attempts, minimizing the risk of successful exploitation.

Integration with machine learning models: The analyzer can leverage machine learning models to enhance its detection capabilities. By training on labeled datasets of known XSS attack patterns, the machine learning models can identify subtle variations and novel attack techniques. Integration with machine learning enables the analyzer to adapt and improve its detection accuracy over time, especially in detecting previously unseen or evolving XSS attack vectors.

Logging and reporting: The analyzer logs and reports its findings and activities. It records details, such as the input field content, detected vulnerabilities, and any actions taken to mitigate potential XSS attacks. Logging and reporting provide a valuable audit trail for forensic analysis, compliance purposes, and post-incident investigations. This information helps in identifying patterns, assessing the system's security posture, and improving the overall effectiveness of the smart XSS monitoring system.

### 6.6.2  Code embedded in JavaScript

The topic of code embedded in JavaScript within the context of the smart XSS attack surveillance system for fog computing. Code embedded in JavaScript is a common attack vector used in XSS attacks. Understanding the subtleties and vulnerabilities associated with this type of attack is crucial for the effective operation of the smart XSS attack surveillance system.

JavaScript execution context: This subtitle focuses on understanding the execution context of JavaScript within web applications. It explains how the browser can execute JavaScript code embedded in web pages and interact with the DOM. This understanding is essential for identifying the potential injection points and the associated risks of XSS attacks.

DOM manipulation: This subtitle delves into the ways in which JavaScript can manipulate the DOM. It covers techniques, such as accessing and modifying HTML elements, altering the structure and content of web pages, and dynamically updating the user interface. It highlights the security implications of unauthorized or malicious DOM manipulation and how it can be exploited in XSS attacks.

Client-side script execution: This subtitle discusses the execution of client-side scripts within the browser environment. It explores the capabilities of JavaScript to execute code directly in the user's browser, including event handlers, AJAX requests, and dynamic script loading. It highlights the risks associated with executing untrusted or malicious code on the client side and its impact on the security of web applications.

Cross-site scripting (XSS) with JavaScript: This subtitle focuses specifically on XSS attacks that exploit code embedded in JavaScript. It explains the techniques used by attackers to inject malicious JavaScript code into web applications, such as through, input fields, URL parameters, or dynamically generated content. It highlights the dangers of XSS attacks and the potential consequences, including data theft, session hijacking, and unauthorized access.

Script injection detection: This subtitle discusses the techniques employed by the smart XSS attack surveillance system to detect script injection attempts in JavaScript code. It covers static and dynamic analysis methods, pattern matching, and anomaly detection to identify suspicious or malicious JavaScript code. It explains how the system can analyze JavaScript execution flow, variable manipulation, and API calls to identify potential XSS attack vectors.

Input validation and output encoding: This subtitle emphasizes the importance of input validation and output encoding as preventive measures against XSS attacks in JavaScript code. It explains how the smart XSS attack surveillance system can enforce strict input validation to block or sanitize user input containing potentially malicious code. It also highlights the significance of output encoding to ensure that user-generated content is properly escaped when displayed on web pages.

Contextual analysis: This subtitle discusses the contextual analysis of JavaScript code within the smart XSS attack surveillance system. It explains how the system can consider the context in which JavaScript code is used, such as the specific web page, the associated input sources, and the intended functionality. Contextual analysis helps identify deviations from expected behavior and detect potential XSS attack vectors.

Mitigation strategies: This subtitle explores the mitigation strategies employed by the smart XSS attack surveillance system to counter JavaScript-based XSS attacks. It covers techniques, such as input filtering, output encoding, Content Security Policy (CSP) implementation, and secure coding practices. It highlights how these strategies can minimize the risk of XSS attacks and protect web applications from malicious JavaScript code.

Real-time monitoring and response: This subtitle focuses on the real-time monitoring and response capabilities of the smart XSS attack surveillance system regarding JavaScript-based XSS attacks. It explains how the system can continuously monitor JavaScript execution, detect anomalies or suspicious patterns, and trigger immediate responses, such as alerting administrators, blocking malicious requests, or sanitizing user input. Real-time monitoring ensures timely detection and mitigation of XSS attacks in JavaScript code.

Education and awareness: This subtitle emphasizes the importance of education and awareness in preventing JavaScript-based XSS attacks. It highlights the need for developers, system administrators, and users to understand the risks, best practices, and security measures associated with JavaScript code. It discusses the role of the smart XSS attack surveillance system in raising awareness, providing guidance, and promoting secure coding practices.

### 6.6.3    Analysis on JavaScript

JavaScript analysis is a critical aspect of the smart XSS attack surveillance system, aimed at examining JavaScript code within web applications to identify potential vulnerabilities and detect malicious behavior. By analyzing JavaScript code, the system can assess the security of the application, detect code injection attempts, and prevent XSS attacks. The analysis involves examining the syntax, structure, and content of the JavaScript code, as well as its interaction with the DOM. Techniques, such as static and dynamic analysis, pattern matching, and anomaly detection, are employed to identify suspicious patterns, known attack vectors, and deviations from expected behavior. During analysis, the system checks for potentially dangerous functions, API calls, and unsafe variable handling that may lead to code injection or unauthorized access. It also considers the context in which the JavaScript code is used, such as event handlers, AJAX requests, or dynamically generated content, to evaluate the security risks. By performing thorough analysis, the smart XSS attack surveillance system can detect potential XSS attack vectors, identify vulnerabilities, and provide insights for implementing mitigation strategies. This analysis ensures that JavaScript code within web applications is secure and helps protect against the exploitation of JavaScript-related vulnerabilities.

### 6.6.4    Protocol generation

To illustrate the application of mathematical concepts in protocol generation, let us consider two mathematical examples: the Diffie–Hellman key exchange protocol and the Hamming code error correction protocol.

Diffie–Hellman key exchange protocol: The Diffie–Hellman protocol enables two entities to establish a shared secret key over an insecure channel. It relies on the mathematical concept of modular exponentiation and the discrete logarithm problem. The protocol can be summarized as follows:

- Alice and Bob agree on a prime number, $p$, and a primitive root modulo $p$, $g$.
- Alice selects a secret value, $a$, and computes $A = g^{\wedge}a \bmod p$.
- Bob selects a secret value, $b$, and computes $B = g^{\wedge}b \bmod p$.
- Alice and Bob exchange $A$ and $B$.
- Alice computes the shared secret key as $S = B^{\wedge}a \bmod p$.
- Bob computes the shared secret key as $S = A^{\wedge}b \bmod p$.

The security of the Diffie–Hellman protocol relies on the difficulty of solving the discrete logarithm problem. The mathematical principles of modular exponentiation and the properties of prime numbers ensure the secure generation of shared secret keys.

Hamming code error correction protocol: The Hamming code is an error correction code used to detect and correct single-bit errors in data transmission. It employs mathematical functions and concepts from coding theory. The protocol can be illustrated with a simple example; assume we want to transmit a 4-bit message: 1011.

The Hamming code adds three parity bits to the message to create a 7-bit codeword: 1011001.

The parity bits are calculated based on specific mathematical rules, such as checking the even or odd parity of specific bit positions. During transmission, if a single bit is flipped, the receiver can detect and correct the error by analyzing the parity bits. For example, if the received codeword is 1001001, the receiver can identify the error in the second bit and correct it to 1011001. The Hamming code protocol utilizes mathematical principles of parity, binary arithmetic, and coding theory to ensure reliable data transmission with error detection and correction capabilities.

### 6.6.5    Comment Comparison Tool for JavaScript

This subtitle introduces the Comment Comparison Tool for JavaScript within the smart XSS attack surveillance system. The tool aims to detect suspicious or potentially malicious comments within JavaScript code, which can serve as indicators of XSS attack vectors.

Purpose of the Comment Comparison Tool: This subtitle highlights the purpose of the Comment Comparison Tool, which is to analyze and compare comments in JavaScript code to identify deviations, anomalies, or patterns that may indicate the presence of XSS vulnerabilities.

Comment analysis techniques: This subtitle discusses the techniques employed by the Comment Comparison Tool for analyzing comments. It includes lexical analysis to tokenize comments, semantic analysis to assess context and intent, and pattern matching to detect known malicious patterns.

Identifying malicious comment characteristics: The Comment Comparison Tool identifies characteristics that may suggest a comment is malicious. This includes looking for unusual formatting, excessive length, obfuscation techniques, or the presence of encoded content within the comment.

Comparison with known vulnerabilities: The Comment Comparison Tool compares comments against a database of known XSS attack vectors or blacklists to identify matches or similarities. This comparison helps detect comments that resemble known malicious patterns.

Machine learning–based comment analysis: Machine learning algorithms can be applied in the Comment Comparison Tool to analyze comments. By training on labeled datasets, the tool can learn to classify comments as benign or potentially malicious, improving its detection capabilities.

Integration with other analysis modules: The Comment Comparison Tool integrates with other analysis modules in the smart XSS attack surveillance system. This subtitle emphasizes how the tool collaborates with modules, such as input validation analysis, code execution monitoring, and output encoding verification, to provide a comprehensive XSS attack detection framework.

Alert generation and mitigation: When the Comment Comparison Tool detects suspicious comments, it generates alerts to notify system administrators or security teams. Alerts contain relevant information, such as the source file, line number, and content of the detected comments, aiding in prompt identification and mitigation of potential XSS attack vectors.

Continuous learning and improvement: The Comment Comparison Tool incorporates a feedback loop and learning mechanism to continuously improve its detection capabilities. Feedback from detected attacks and false positives helps refine the analysis rules and enhance the accuracy of the tool.

Performance optimization: This subtitle addresses the performance considerations of the Comment Comparison Tool. Techniques, such as parallel processing, caching, or efficient algorithms, are employed to optimize the tool's efficiency and minimize the impact on system performance.

Scalability in large codebases: The Comment Comparison Tool is designed to handle large-scale JavaScript codebases commonly found in fog-computing environments. It ensures scalability by employing techniques like distributed computing or efficient data structures.

Real-time analysis: The Comment Comparison Tool performs real-time analysis of comments within JavaScript code, providing immediate detection and response to potential XSS attack vectors.

Contextual comment analysis: The tool considers the context in which comments are used, such as their location within functions or code blocks, to assess their potential security implications accurately.

False positive reduction: The Comment Comparison Tool employs techniques to minimize false positives by fine-tuning analysis rules, considering comment intent, and refining pattern-matching algorithms.

Cross-platform compatibility: The Comment Comparison Tool is designed to be compatible with various JavaScript frameworks, libraries, and platforms, ensuring its effectiveness across different fog-computing environments.

Visualization and reporting: The tool provides visualizations and reports on the analysis results, enabling system administrators to identify trends, patterns, and potential vulnerabilities within JavaScript comments.

Integration with development tools: The Comment Comparison Tool can integrate with popular development tools, such as Integrated Development Environment (IDEs) or code editors, to provide real-time feedback and assist developers in writing secure JavaScript code.

Multilingual comment analysis: The tool is capable of analyzing comments in multiple languages commonly used in fog-computing environments, enabling broader coverage and detection of XSS attack vectors.

Security audit and compliance: The Comment Comparison Tool contributes to security audits and compliance assessments by providing insights into the security posture of JavaScript code within fog-computing applications.

Customization and extensibility: The tool offers customization options, allowing system administrators to configure analysis rules, incorporate additional comment patterns, or integrate with external threat intelligence sources.

Collaboration with threat intelligence: The Comment Comparison Tool can leverage threat intelligence feeds and databases to enhance its detection capabilities by staying updated on the latest XSS attack vectors, and trends.

Resource efficiency: The tool is designed to utilize system resources efficiently, ensuring minimal impact on the overall performance of fog-computing environments.

Usability and user-friendly interface: The Comment Comparison Tool provides a user-friendly interface, making it accessible to system administrators and security teams for effective monitoring and analysis of JavaScript comments.

Training and education: The Comment Comparison Tool contributes to training and educating developers and system administrators on best practices for writing secure JavaScript code and identifying potential XSS attack vectors.

Collaborative defense mechanisms: The Comment Comparison Tool can share information and collaborate with other security tools within the smart XSS attack surveillance system, creating a collaborative defense approach against XSS attacks.

Adapting to emerging attack techniques: The Comment Comparison Tool incorporates mechanisms to adapt and evolve as new XSS attack techniques emerge, ensuring the detection of evolving and sophisticated XSS vectors.

Integration with incident response: The tool facilitates incident response by providing detailed information on detected suspicious comments, aiding in the investigation, mitigation, and recovery process.

Regulatory compliance: The Comment Comparison Tool assists fog computing systems in meeting regulatory compliance requirements by detecting and mitigating XSS attack vectors, ensuring data protection and integrity.

Performance monitoring and optimization: The tool provides performance monitoring and optimization features to identify potential bottlenecks or issues in the analysis process, enhancing overall system performance.

Future directions: This subtitle discusses potential future directions for the Comment Comparison Tool, such as integrating advanced machine learning algorithms, incorporating natural language processing techniques, or exploring novel detection methods for evolving XSS attack vectors.

## 6.6.6    Context Finder

The Context Finder on a smart XSS attack monitoring system for fog-computing is a component designed to analyze and understand the context of web application requests and responses in fog-computing environments. XSS attacks involve injecting malicious scripts into web applications, which can then be executed by unsuspecting users visiting those applications. Fog computing refers to the decentralized architecture that extends cloud computing capabilities to the edge of the network.

The Context Finder plays a crucial role in detecting and mitigating XSS attacks by examining the contextual information associated with each web request and response. It aims to identify anomalous or potentially dangerous behavior that could indicate the presence of XSS vulnerabilities or ongoing attacks.

Here's how the Context Finder works within a smart XSS attack monitoring system for fog computing:

Data collection: The Context Finder collects data from various sources, including web application servers, user devices, and network devices located at the edge of the fog-computing environment. It captures both inbound and outbound web traffic, capturing HTTP requests and responses.

Parsing and analysis: The captured data is parsed and analyzed to extract relevant information such as the URL, request headers, cookies, form inputs, and response content. The Context Finder examines the content of each web request and response to identify potential XSS attack vectors, such as unsanitized user inputs or suspicious JavaScript code.

Contextual understanding: The system utilizes contextual information to assess the severity and likelihood of an XSS attack. This includes factors like the type of web application, user roles and privileges, session information, and historical patterns of behavior. By considering the broader context, the system can differentiate between legitimate application behavior and potentially malicious activities.

Rule-based detection: The Context Finder employs a set of predefined rules or heuristics to identify patterns and indicators associated with XSS attacks. These rules can include signature-based detection, pattern matching, or behavioral analysis techniques. If a request or response violates any of the rules, it triggers an alert for further investigation or immediate action.

## 6.7  Components of smart XSS monitoring system

A smart XSS monitoring system in fog computing is designed to detect and prevent XSS attacks at the network edge (fog) rather than solely relying on centralized cloud resources. Fog computing brings the computational resources closer to the edge of the network, enabling faster response times and reduced communication overhead. Below are the key components of a smart XSS monitoring system in fog computing:

1. Edge nodes: Fog computing relies on a distributed network of edge nodes, which are closer to the end-users or devices generating web traffic. These edge nodes serve as the first line of defense for XSS monitoring.
2. Traffic analysis module: The traffic analysis module is responsible for capturing and analyzing web traffic passing through the edge nodes. It inspects HTTP requests and responses for potential XSS attack patterns.
3. Machine learning algorithms: The smart XSS monitoring system employs machine learning algorithms to classify web traffic and distinguish between legitimate user interactions and potentially malicious XSS attempts. These algorithms are trained on labeled datasets to recognize XSS attack patterns.
4. Anomaly detection: The system can use anomaly detection techniques to identify unusual patterns in web traffic that might indicate a possible XSS attack.
5. Rules and signatures: The monitoring system can incorporate predefined rules and signatures of known XSS attack vectors to quickly identify and block such attacks.
6. Whitelisting and blacklisting: The system may maintain a list of trusted sources (whitelist) and known malicious sources (blacklist) to help filter incoming web traffic.
7. Real-time alerts: When the system detects a potential XSS attack, it generates real-time alerts to notify administrators or security teams.

8.  Threat intelligence integration: Integration with external threat intelligence sources allows the system to access up-to-date information about new XSS attack vectors and patterns.
9.  Distributed database: A distributed database is utilized to store and share threat information across edge nodes, enabling collaborative threat detection and response.
10. Traffic redirection and mitigation: Upon detecting an XSS attack, the system can redirect or mitigate the malicious traffic, preventing it from reaching the intended target and reducing the impact of the attack.
11. Performance optimization: Fog computing emphasizes performance optimization and resource efficiency. The smart XSS monitoring system should be designed to have minimal impact on the overall network performance.
12. Secure communication: Communication between edge nodes and central management servers should be encrypted and secured to prevent unauthorized access to the monitoring system and its data.
13. Scalability and load balancing: The system should be scalable to handle a large number of users and traffic while effectively balancing the load across multiple edge nodes.
14. Self-learning mechanism: Over time, the monitoring system may continuously learn from new attack patterns and adapt its detection mechanisms to improve accuracy.

## 6.7.1   Conceptualization, development, and testing

Conceptualization, development, and testing are three critical stages in the lifecycle of building a smart XSS attack monitoring system for fog computing. Let's explore each stage in more detail:

Conceptualization:

*   During the conceptualization phase, the high-level ideas and objectives of the smart XSS attack monitoring system are defined. This involves identifying the need for the system, understanding the requirements, and envisioning its functionalities. Key activities in this stage include the following:
    -   Defining the goals and scope of the system: Determine the specific objectives the system aims to achieve and the boundaries within which it operates.
    -   Conducting a feasibility study: Assess the technical, financial, and operational feasibility of the system to determine its viability.
    -   Gathering requirements: Identify the system's functional and nonfunctional requirements by consulting with stakeholders, such as security experts, system administrators, and potential users.
    -   Defining system architecture: Develop a high-level architectural design that outlines the components, interfaces, and data flows within the system.

Development:

*   Once the conceptualization phase is complete, the development stage involves implementing the smart XSS attack monitoring system based on the defined requirements and architecture. This phase typically involves several steps:

- Designing the system: Create detailed designs for each component of the system, specifying how they will interact and function together.
- Implementing the components: Develop the various modules and functionalities of the system, including the Context Finder, data collection mechanisms, parsing and analysis algorithms, rule-based detection, machine learning models, alert generation, and response mechanisms.
- Integrating components: Integrate the developed components into a unified system, ensuring they work together seamlessly.
- Testing and debugging: Conduct comprehensive testing to identify and fix any issues or bugs in the system. This may involve unit testing, integration testing, system testing, and security testing.

Testing:
- Testing is a crucial stage in the development process to ensure the smart XSS attack monitoring system functions correctly and meets the desired objectives. Various types of testing can be performed, including:
  - Functional testing: Verify that the system meets the specified functional requirements and behaves as expected.
  - Performance testing: Assess the system's performance under different workloads and stress conditions to ensure it can handle the expected traffic and data volumes.
  - Security testing: Validate the system's ability to detect XSS attacks effectively and protect against various attack vectors.
  - User acceptance testing: Involve end-users or stakeholders to evaluate the system's usability and gather feedback.
  - Integration testing: Test the interaction and compatibility of the system with other components or systems it interfaces with.
  - Testing is an iterative process, and any identified issues or bugs should be addressed and retested until the system meets the required quality standards.

## 6.8   Performance analysis

Performance analysis of a system can be conducted using various mathematical functions and metrics:

Response time ($R$): Response time measures the time taken by a system to respond to a request or complete a task. It is a critical metric for assessing system performance. Mathematically, it can be represented as a function of various factors, such as processing time, queuing delays, and communication time. For example, if we consider a system with processing time ($P$) and queuing delay ($Q$), the response time ($R$) can be represented as $R = P + Q$.

Throughput ($T$): Throughput represents the number of tasks or requests completed by the system per unit of time. It is often measured in transactions per second or requests per second. Mathematically, throughput can be calculated as $T = C/R$, where $C$ is the number of completed tasks or requests and $R$ is the response time.

Utilization ($U$): Utilization measures the extent to which system resources are being utilized. It is often expressed as a percentage and represents the ratio of time a resource is busy to the total time. Mathematically, utilization can be calculated as $U = (B/T) \times 100$, where $B$ is the time the resource is busy and $T$ is the total time.

Scalability ($S$): Scalability assesses the ability of a system to handle increasing workloads or accommodate a growing number of users. It is often measured by the increase in throughput or the decrease in response time as the system is scaled up. Mathematically, scalability can be represented using functions such as $S = f(N)$, where $N$ represents the number of users or workload size, and $f()$ is a function that quantifies the relationship between $N$ and the performance metric.

Queueing theory functions: Queueing theory is a mathematical framework used to analyze systems with queues, such as network systems or service-oriented systems. It involves various mathematical functions, including arrival rate ($\lambda$), service rate ($\mu$), and queue length ($L$), which can be used to model and analyze system performance. For example, Little's Law states that the average number of tasks in a system ($L$) is equal to the average arrival rate ($\lambda$) multiplied by the average response time ($R$), i.e., $L = \lambda \times R$.

Response time distribution: Performance analysis often involves studying the distribution of response times. Various probability distributions, such as exponential, normal (Gaussian), or log-normal distributions, can be used to model the response time data. Analyzing the distribution helps understand the average response time, the spread of response times, and the probability of encountering extreme response times.

## 6.9    Conclusion

In conclusion, a smart XSS attack surveillance system designed specifically for fog-computing environments is crucial for ensuring the security of web applications deployed at the edge of the network. By incorporating intelligent monitoring and detection mechanisms, this system can effectively detect and mitigate XSS attacks, protecting both users and sensitive data. The implementation of a Context Finder within the surveillance system plays a vital role. By analyzing contextual information associated with web requests and responses, the Context Finder can differentiate between normal and potentially malicious behavior. It leverages predefined rules, machine learning techniques, and historical patterns to detect XSS attack vectors accurately. The conceptualization, development, and testing stages are essential for building a robust smart XSS attack surveillance system. During conceptualization, clear objectives and requirements are defined, ensuring the system addresses the specific needs of fog-computing environments. The development phase involves designing and implementing components, such as the Context Finder, data collection mechanisms, analysis algorithms, and alert generation systems. Rigorous testing, including functional, performance, security, and integration testing, ensures the system's reliability and effectiveness. Using mathematical functions and metrics, performance analysis can be conducted to evaluate the system's efficiency. Response time, throughput, utilization, scalability, and queueing theory functions enable a quantitative assessment of system performance, helping identify areas for improvement and optimization.

# References

[1]  A. Singh and D. M. Shrivastava, Overview of Attacks on Cloud Computing, *International Journal of Engineering and Innovative Technology (IJEIT)*, 1, 321–323, 2012.

[2]  F. Sabahi, Cloud Computing Security Threats and Responses in *IEEE 3rd International Conference on Communication Software and Networks*, 2011, pp. 245–249.

[3]  N. Gruschka and M. Jensen, Attack Surfaces: A Taxonomy for Attacks on Cloud Services, in *IEEE 3rd International Conference on Cloud Computing*, 2010, pp. 276–279.

[4]  R. L. Krutz and R. D. Vines, *Cloud Security: A Comprehensive Guide to Secure Cloud Computing*, Wiley, New York, 2010.

[5]  M. Jensen, J. Schwenk, N. Gruschka, and L. L. Iacono, On Technical Security Issues in Cloud Computing, in *IEEE International Conference on Cloud Computing*, 2009, pp. 109–116.

[6]  M. A. Talib, A. Khelifi, and T. Ugurlu, Using ISO 27001 in Teaching Information Security, in *IECON 38th Annual Conference on IEEE Industrial Electronics Society*, 2012, pp. 3149–3153.

[7]  M. Dabbagh and A. Rayes, *Internet of Things Security and Privacy in Internet of Things From Hype to Reality*, Springer International Publishing, Berlin, 2017, pp. 195–223.

[8]  J. Niu, Z. Ming, M. Qiu, H. Su, Z. Gu, and X. Qin, Defending Jamming Attack in Wide-Area Monitoring System for Smart Grid, *Telecommunication Systems*, 60, 159–167, 2015.

[9]  M. Darwish, A. Ouda, and L. F. Capretz, Cloud-Based DDoS Attacks and Defenses, in *International Conference on Information Society (i-Society)*, 2013, pp. 67–71.

[10]  D'Oro, L. Galluccio, G. Morabito, and S. Palazzo, Efficiency analysis of jamming-based countermeasures against malicious timing channel in tactical communications, in *Proc. IEEE Trans. Wireless Communication*, 2013, vol. 14, no. 5, pp. 1566–1276.

*Chapter 7*

# Spectral image analysis with supervised feature extraction

## Abstract

Hyperspectral remote sensing (HRS) images contain rich spectral information that can be used to identify and classify objects on the Earth's surface. However, the high dimensionality of hyperspectral data makes it challenging to extract meaningful features for classification. Supervised feature extraction methods use labeled training data to learn a transformation that maps the high-dimensional spectral data to a lower-dimensional space where the features are more discriminative.

**Background:** Sensors that measure the spectral reflectance of objects on the Earth's surface at hundreds or even thousands of narrow bands acquire HRS images. This rich spectral information can be used to identify and classify objects based on their unique spectral signatures. However, the high dimensionality of hyperspectral data makes it challenging to extract meaningful features for classification.

**Scope:** This chapter discusses supervised feature extraction methods for HRS images. This chapter begins by providing an overview of HRS and supervised feature extraction. It then discusses a number of supervised feature extraction methods, including principal component analysis, linear discriminant analysis, and support vector machines. This chapter concludes by discussing the challenges of supervised feature extraction for HRS images and the future directions of research in this area.

**Problem definition:** The problem of supervised feature extraction for HRS images can be defined as follows: given a set of hyperspectral images with known class labels, extract a set of features that can be used to classify new hyperspectral images with high accuracy.

**Aim:** The aim of supervised feature extraction for HRS images is to extract features that are both discriminative and informative. Discriminative features are those that can distinguish between different classes of objects. Informative features are those that contain useful information about the objects being classified.

**Analysis:** A number of supervised feature extraction methods have been proposed for HRS images. These methods have been shown to be effective in improving the accuracy of hyperspectral image classification. However, there are still a number of challenges that need to be addressed in order to improve the performance of supervised feature extraction for HRS images. These challenges include the high dimensionality of hyperspectral data, the noise in hyperspectral data, and the imbalance of classes in hyperspectral data.

## 7.1    Introduction

Hyperspectral remote sensing (HSR) is a rapidly developing field that has the potential to revolutionize the way we interact with the world around us. HSR sensors capture images of the Earth's surface at hundreds or even thousands of narrow spectral bands, providing a wealth of information about the materials and objects that make up the landscape. This information can be used for a wide variety of applications, including:

- Land cover classification: This is the process of identifying different types of land cover, such as forests, grasslands, and urban areas.
- Mineral exploration: HSR can be used to identify and map mineral deposits.
- Vegetation monitoring: This can be used to track changes in vegetation, such as the effects of drought or deforestation.
- Environmental monitoring: HSR can be used to monitor pollution, wildfires, and other environmental hazards.

The high dimensionality of HSR data poses a number of challenges for traditional machine learning algorithms. One way to address these challenges is to use supervised feature extraction techniques. Supervised feature extraction methods use labeled data to learn a mapping from the original features to a new set of features that are more discriminative for classification [1].

In this chapter, we will discuss the principles of supervised feature extraction for HSR images. We will introduce a number of different supervised feature extraction methods, and we will evaluate their performance on a variety of HSR datasets.

### 7.1.1    Supervised feature extraction

Supervised feature extraction methods are based on the idea that the features that are most discriminative for classification can be learned from labeled data. In supervised feature extraction, a training dataset is used to learn a mapping from the original features to a new set of features. The new set of features is then used to train a classifier [2].

There are a number of different supervised feature extraction methods that have been proposed for HSR images. Some of the most popular methods include as follows:

- Principal component analysis (PCA): PCA is a linear dimensionality reduction technique that projects the original features onto a lower dimensional subspace that retains the most variance in the data.
- Linear discriminant analysis (LDA): LDA is a supervised dimensionality reduction technique that projects the original features onto a lower dimensional subspace that maximizes the class separability.

- Fisher's LDA (FLDA): FLDA is a modification of LDA that is specifically designed for HSR images.
- Maximum margin criteria (MMC): MMC is a nonlinear dimensionality reduction technique that learns a mapping from the original features to a new set of features that maximize the margin between the different classes.

### 7.1.2 Evaluation of supervised feature extraction methods

The performance of supervised feature extraction methods for HSR images can be evaluated using a variety of metrics, including:

- Classification accuracy: This is the percentage of correctly classified pixels.
- Mean accuracy: This is the average accuracy across all classes.
- F1 score: This is a measure of both precision and recall.
- Area under the receiver operating characteristic curve (ROC AUC): This is a measure of the overall performance of a classifier.

## 7.2 Remote sensing imaging

Remote sensing is the process of obtaining information about an object or area from a distance. This can be done using a variety of sensors, including cameras, radar, and lidar. Remote sensing images are a valuable source of information for a wide range of applications, including:

- Land use and land cover mapping: Remote sensing images can be used to identify different land cover types, such as forests, agriculture, and urban areas. This information can be used to track changes in land use over time and to plan for future development.
- Environmental monitoring: Remote sensing images can be used to monitor environmental changes, such as deforestation, desertification, and pollution. This information can be used to help protect the environment and to manage natural resources.
- Natural disaster assessment: Remote sensing images can be used to assess the impact of natural disasters, such as floods, earthquakes, and wildfires. This information can be used to help with relief efforts and to prevent future disasters.
- Military applications: Remote sensing images can be used for a variety of military applications, such as target identification, surveillance, and mapping.

### 7.2.1 Types of remote sensing images

There are two main types of remote sensing images: multispectral and hyperspectral. Multispectral images measure the reflected light in a few different bands, typically in the visible and near-infrared spectrum. Hyperspectral images measure the reflected light in hundreds or even thousands of bands, across a wide range of the electromagnetic spectrum [3].

### 7.2.2 Hyperspectral remote sensing images

HRS images are a powerful tool for a wide range of applications. The high spectral resolution of hyperspectral images allows us to distinguish between different materials and objects, even if they appear similar in multispectral images. This makes hyperspectral images ideal for applications such as:

- Mineral exploration: Hyperspectral images can be used to identify different types of minerals, even if they are buried underground. This information can be used to help find new mineral deposits.
- Agriculture: Hyperspectral images can be used to assess the health of crops, to identify pests and diseases, and to map crop yields. This information can be used to improve crop production and to manage agricultural resources.
- Forestry: Hyperspectral images can be used to assess the health of forests, to identify different types of trees, and to map forest biomass. This information can be used to manage forests and to protect them from wildfires.

## 7.2.3  Supervised features extraction

In Table 7.1, supervised feature extraction is a process of extracting features from hyperspectral images that are known to be related to a particular target or class. This can be done using a variety of machine learning algorithms, such as support vector machines (SVMs), random forests, and neural networks. Once the features have been extracted, they can be used to train a classifier that can identify the target or class in new images. This process is known as supervised classification [4].

In Table 7.2, hyperspectral images have a much higher spectral resolution than multispectral images. This means that they can be used to distinguish between

*Table 7.1  Remote sensing images*

| Type of image | Number of spectral bands | Applications |
|---|---|---|
| Multispectral | Few (typically 4–12) | Land use and land cover mapping, environmental monitoring, natural disaster assessment, military applications |
| Hyperspectral | Hundreds or even thousands | Mineral exploration, agriculture, forestry, food security, water resources, environmental monitoring, urban planning, disaster management |

*Table 7.2  Benefits of using hyperspectral images*

| Benefit | Description |
|---|---|
| Increased spectral resolution | This allows us to distinguish between different materials and objects, even if they appear similar in multispectral images |
| Improved accuracy | The high spectral resolution of hyperspectral images can lead to improved accuracy in classification and identification tasks |
| Increased information content | Hyperspectral images contain more information than multispectral images, which can be used to improve the performance of machine learning algorithms |
| New applications | The high spectral resolution of hyperspectral images has enabled new applications that were not possible with multispectral images |

different materials and objects, even if they appear similar in multispectral images. This makes hyperspectral images ideal for a wide range of applications, including mineral exploration, agriculture, and forestry.

## 7.3 Hyperspectral imaging and dimensionality reduction

Dimensionality reduction is a technique for reducing the number of features in a dataset while preserving as much information as possible. This is often done in hyperspectral images, which have a large number of features (i.e., spectral bands) that can make it difficult to analyze and interpret the data. There are many different dimensionality reduction techniques, but some of the most common include as follows:

PCA: PCA is a linear dimensionality reduction technique that identifies the principal components of the data, which are the directions of maximum variance.

Independent component analysis (ICA): ICA is a nonlinear dimensionality reduction technique that identifies independent components of the data, which are the components that are not correlated with each other.

LDA: LDA is a supervised dimensionality reduction technique that identifies the directions that best separate different classes of data.

The choice of dimensionality reduction technique depends on the specific application. For example, PCA is often used for visualization, while ICA is often used for feature extraction.

Dimensionality reduction can be a valuable tool for hyperspectral image analysis. It can help to improve the interpretability of the data, reduce the computational complexity of analysis, and improve the performance of classification algorithms. Here are some of the benefits of using dimensionality reduction in hyperspectral images:

Improved interpretability: Dimensionality reduction can help to improve the interpretability of hyperspectral images by reducing the number of features that need to be considered. This can make it easier to identify patterns and trends in the data.

Reduced computational complexity: Dimensionality reduction can reduce the computational complexity of analysis by reducing the number of features that need to be processed. This can make it possible to analyze large hyperspectral images that would otherwise be too computationally expensive.

Improved classification performance: Dimensionality reduction can improve the performance of classification algorithms by reducing the noise in the data and highlighting the most important features. This can lead to improved classification accuracy. Here are some of the challenges of using dimensionality reduction in hyperspectral images:

Loss of information: Dimensionality reduction can result in the loss of information, as some of the original features are discarded. This can be a problem if the discarded features are important for the analysis.

Overfitting: Dimensionality reduction can lead to overfitting, if the number of features is reduced too much. This can result in a model that performs well on the training data but poorly on new data.

Selecting the right technique: There are many different dimensionality reduction techniques, and the choice of technique can have a significant impact on the results. It is important to select the right technique for the specific application.

### 7.3.1   Math functions

The math functions that are used to implement dimensionality reduction techniques for hyperspectral images vary depending on the specific technique. However, some of the most common math functions include as follows:

- Eigenvalues and eigenvectors: PCA uses eigenvalues and eigenvectors to calculate the principal components of the data.
- Singular value decomposition (SVD): SVD is a factorization technique that can be used to decompose the data into a set of orthogonal vectors.
- Gaussian mixture models (GMMs): GMMs are a type of probabilistic model that can be used to identify and remove independent components from the data.

## 7.4   Supervised feature extraction in hyperspectral images

In hyperspectral images, supervised feature extraction refers to the process of identifying and extracting relevant features from the data based on prior knowledge or training samples associated with specific classes or categories. It involves leveraging labeled samples or ground truth information to guide the extraction of discriminative and informative features from the high-dimensional hyperspectral data. A comprehensive description of supervised feature extraction in hyperspectral images is given below.

Training samples and classes: Supervised feature extraction relies on a set of training samples that are carefully selected and labeled with their corresponding classes or categories. These training samples should be representative of the classes of interest in the hyperspectral image. They can be collected through field surveys, expert knowledge, or existing labeled datasets [5].

Feature selection: The first step in supervised feature extraction is often feature selection, where a subset of the available spectral bands or dimensions is chosen based on their relevance to the classes of interest. This selection is typically guided by statistical or discriminative measures, such as correlation analysis, mutual information, or class separability criteria. The aim is to retain spectral bands that provide discriminatory information while discarding noisy or irrelevant bands.

Feature extraction methods: Once the relevant spectral bands are selected, various feature extraction methods can be employed to transform the hyperspectral data into a lower dimensional feature space. These methods aim to capture discriminative information that distinguishes between different classes. Popular techniques include as follows:

Spectral indices: Spectral indices combine multiple spectral bands using mathematical formulas to capture-specific properties, such as vegetation health (e.g., normalized difference vegetation index—NDVI) or mineral identification (e.g., iron oxide index).

Statistical features: Statistical measures, such as mean, standard deviation, skewness, and kurtosis, can be computed from the spectral values within predefined regions of interest or neighborhood pixels. These measures provide information about the spectral distribution and variability of different classes.

Transform-based approaches: Techniques, such as PCA, minimum noise fraction, or ICA, can be applied to extract orthogonal or independent components that represent the most informative features in the data.

Classification: After the features are extracted, they can be used as input to classification algorithms to assign each pixel or region in the hyperspectral image to one of the predefined classes. Supervised classification techniques, such as SVMs, random forests, or neural networks, are commonly employed. These algorithms learn decision boundaries based on the extracted features and the labeled training samples to classify the remaining pixels in the image [6].

Evaluation and refinement: The performance of the supervised feature extraction process is evaluated by comparing the classification results against ground truth data or validation samples. This evaluation helps assess the effectiveness of the extracted features in discriminating between classes and identifying potential areas for improvement. Refinements, such as adjusting feature selection criteria or exploring alternative feature extraction methods, can be made based on the evaluation results.

## 7.4.1   Modified Fisher's linear discriminant analysis (MFLDA)-based feature

Modified FLDA (MFLDA) is an approach to feature extraction that enhances the discriminatory power of FLDA by incorporating modifications to the standard FLDA algorithm. MFLDA aims to find a projection that maximizes the between-class separability and minimizes the within-class scatter in the transformed feature space. These points will use mathematical expressions, equations, or functions to describe how the MFLDA method works or is applied in a more detailed and precise manner.

1.  Data preparation:
    Input: We have a hyperspectral dataset with labeled training samples. Let's denote the input dataset as $X$, where $X = [x1, x2, \ldots, xn]$ represents $n$-dimensional hyperspectral data points, and each $xi$ is a vector of spectral bands.
    Labels: Each data point $xi$ is associated with a class label $yi$, where $yi$ belongs to a set of predefined classes $C = \{c1, c2, \ldots, cK\}$.

2.  Mean vectors and scatter matrices:
    (i)   Calculate the mean vector for each class:
          $\mu k = (1/Nk) * \sum(xi)$, for $xi$ in class $ck$, where $Nk$ is the number of samples in class $ck$.

    (ii)  Calculate the total mean vector:
          $\mu = (1/n) * \sum(xi)$, for $xi$ in $X$, where $n$ is the total number of samples.

    (iii)   Calculate the between-class scatter matrix $(Sb)$:

$$Sb = \sum (Nk * (\mu k - \mu) * (\mu k - \mu)^\wedge T), \text{ for each class } ck.$$

    (iv)   Calculate the within-class scatter matrix $(Sw)$:

$$Sw = \sum (\sum ((xi - \mu k) * (xi - \mu k)^\wedge T)), \text{ for each class } ck.$$

3.   MFLDA projection matrix:

    (i)   Compute the modified scatter matrix $(Sm)$:

$Sm = \alpha * Sw + \beta * (1 - \alpha) * Sb$, where $\alpha$ is a weighting parameter, and $\beta = (1 - \alpha)$.

    (ii)   Compute the eigenvalue decomposition of $Sm$:

$Sm = U * \Lambda * U^\wedge T$, where $U$ contains the eigenvectors and $\Lambda$ is a diagonal matrix of eigenvalues.

    (iii)   Select the top $k$ eigenvectors corresponding to the largest eigenvalues to form a projection matrix $W$:

$W = [u1, u2, \ldots, uk]$, where $ui$ represents the $i$th eigenvector.

4.   Feature extraction:

    (i)   Project the hyperspectral data points onto the subspace spanned by the columns of $W$:

$Y = W^\wedge T * X$, where $Y = [y1, y2, \ldots, yn]$ represents the transformed feature vectors, and $yi = W^\wedge T * xi$.

5.   Classification:

Apply a classification algorithm, such as a SVM or $k$-nearest neighbors ($k$-NN), on the extracted features $Y$ to classify the data points into their respective classes.

The MFLDA approach enhances the separability of the hyperspectral data by modifying the scatter matrices used in the FLDA algorithm. By finding an optimal projection matrix $W$, MFLDA maximizes the between-class separability and minimizes the within-class scatter, resulting in improved feature extraction for subsequent classification tasks.

## 7.4.2  *Prototype space feature extraction (PSFE) method*

The Prototype Extraction Method for Space Feature Data [prototype space feature extraction (PSFE)] is a technique used for extracting representative prototypes or exemplars from space feature data. This method aims to identify a subset of samples that effectively capture the characteristics of the entire dataset while reducing redundancy and dimensionality. PSFE is particularly useful in scenarios where the original dataset is large, and selecting a representative subset can improve efficiency and interpretability [7].

1.   Data preparation: Start by preparing the space feature dataset, which may consist of a large number of samples with multiple attributes or features. Each sample represents a spatial location or object, and its associated attributes describe various properties or characteristics.

2.   Similarity measurement: Compute the similarity or dissimilarity measure between each pair of samples in the dataset. The choice of similarity measure

depends on the nature of the features and the specific requirements of the application. Common measures include Euclidean distance, cosine similarity, or correlation coefficients.

3.  Prototype selection: PSFE aims to select a subset of prototypes that represents the original dataset effectively. The selection process typically involves considering the following criteria:

    (i)   Coverage: The prototypes should cover a diverse range of variations and patterns present in the dataset. This ensures that important aspects of the data are adequately represented.

    (ii)  Discrimination: The prototypes should be distinct and discriminatory, capturing the significant differences between different classes or categories in the dataset.

    (iii) Compactness: The prototypes should be compact, avoiding redundancy and excessive overlap. This helps reduce the dimensionality and improve the efficiency of subsequent analysis.

4.  Prototype extraction algorithm: PSFE employs an algorithmic approach to select the prototypes. The algorithm iteratively identifies and adds prototypes to the subset based on the similarity and coverage criteria. The exact algorithm can vary, but a common approach involves the following steps:

    (i)   Initialize an empty set to store the selected prototypes.

    (ii)  Compute the similarity or dissimilarity between each sample and the prototypes already selected.

    (iii) Select the sample with the highest similarity to the prototypes as the next prototype and add it to the selected set.

    (iv)  Update the similarity values between the remaining samples and the selected prototypes based on the newly added prototype.

    (v)   Repeat steps (ii) to (iv) until the desired number of prototypes or a convergence criterion is met.

5.  Prototype validation: After selecting the prototypes, it is essential to validate their representativeness and quality. This can involve evaluating the coverage of different variations and patterns, assessing their discrimination capabilities, and comparing them against domain knowledge or ground truth information if available.

## 7.4.3   Maximum margin criterion (MMC)-based feature extraction method

Extracting features using the maximum margin criterion (MMC) is a technique that aims to find a feature subspace that maximizes the margin between different classes or categories in a dataset. MMC is commonly used for dimensionality reduction and feature extraction in pattern recognition and machine learning tasks.

Here is an explanation of how features can be extracted using MMC:

Data preparation: Start by preparing the dataset, which consists of samples with multiple features. Each sample is associated with a class or category label. Ensure that the data are appropriately preprocessed and normalized, if necessary.

1. Pairwise distance calculation: Compute the pairwise distances between samples from different classes. The distance can be calculated using various distance metrics, such as Euclidean distance or Mahalanobis distance. This step helps quantify the dissimilarity between samples and is crucial for determining the class separability.
2. MMC: The MMC aims to find a projection matrix that maximizes the margin between different classes. The margin is defined as the minimum distance between any pair of samples from different classes. By maximizing the margin, MMC seeks to achieve better class separation and enhance the discriminative power of the selected features.
3. Optimization problem: The goal is to solve an optimization problem to find the optimal projection matrix that maximizes the margin. This problem can be formulated as a convex optimization problem, and various optimization techniques can be employed, such as quadratic programming or semidefinite programming.
4. Eigenvalue decomposition: Once the optimization problem is solved, the optimal projection matrix can be obtained. Typically, the projection matrix is obtained by performing eigenvalue decomposition on a matrix derived from the optimization result. The eigenvalue decomposition identifies the eigenvectors that correspond to the largest eigenvalues, representing the directions along which the maximum margin is achieved.
5. Feature extraction: The extracted features are obtained by projecting the original dataset onto the selected eigenvectors. The projection is performed by multiplying the original dataset with the optimal projection matrix.
6. Dimensionality reduction: In addition to feature extraction, MMC can also serve as a dimensionality reduction technique. By selecting the eigenvectors corresponding to the largest eigenvalues, the feature space can be reduced to a lower dimensional subspace that captures the essential discriminative information.

### 7.4.4 Partitioned maximum margin criterion-based supervised feature extraction method

Supervised feature extraction using a partitioned MMC (PMMC) method is a technique that combines the principles of partitioning the data and maximizing the margin between classes to extract discriminative features. PMMC aims to enhance class separability and improve the performance of subsequent classification or pattern recognition tasks.

Here's an explanation of how supervised feature extraction can be performed using the PMMC method:

1. Data preparation: Begin by preparing the labeled dataset, which consists of samples with multiple features and their corresponding class labels. Ensure that the data are properly preprocessed and normalized, if required.
2. Partitioning the data: Divide the dataset into multiple partitions or subsets based on the class labels. Each partition contains samples from a specific class or category. The number of partitions depends on the number of classes in the dataset.

3. Pairwise distance calculation: Compute the pairwise distances between samples from different classes within each partition. This step quantifies the dissimilarity between samples and provides information about the within-class and between-class variations within each partition.
4. MMC: Apply the MMC within each partition to find the optimal projection matrix that maximizes the margin between different classes. This step is similar to the standard MMC method but applied independently to each partition.
5. Optimization problem and eigenvector decomposition: Solve the optimization problem within each partition to obtain the optimal projection matrix. Perform eigenvector decomposition or other suitable techniques to extract the eigenvectors corresponding to the largest eigenvalues within each partition. These eigenvectors represent the directions that maximize the margin between classes within each partition.
6. Combination of features: Combine the extracted eigenvectors or projection matrices from all partitions to create a unified feature subspace. This step integrates the discriminative information from each partition, providing a comprehensive representation of the dataset.
7. Feature extraction: Project the original dataset onto the unified feature subspace to extract the features. This projection involves multiplying the original dataset by the combined projection matrix or using the combined eigenvectors for projection.
8. Dimensionality reduction: Similar to the standard MMC method, PMMC can also serve as a dimensionality reduction technique. By selecting a subset of the combined eigenvectors or projection matrix corresponding to the most informative features, the feature space can be reduced to a lower dimensional subspace that captures the essential discriminative information.

## 7.4.5 Hyperspectral feature partitioning

Hyperspectral feature partitioning refers to a process of dividing the high-dimensional hyperspectral data into subsets or partitions based on the spectral features or characteristics of the data. The objective of feature partitioning is to identify and group similar or related spectral features together, facilitating subsequent analysis and interpretation. Partitioning the hyperspectral data allows for a more focused analysis of specific spectral regions or feature subsets, enabling efficient processing and extraction of meaningful information. A comprehensive description of hyperspectral feature partitioning is explained mathematically [8].

1. Hyperspectral data representation: Let's consider a hyperspectral dataset consisting of $N$ samples, where each sample has $M$ spectral bands or dimensions. The dataset can be represented as a matrix $X$, where $X \in \mathbb{R}^{\wedge}(N \times M)$.
2. Similarity measurement: To perform feature partitioning, a similarity or dissimilarity measure is calculated to quantify the similarity between spectral bands or features. Various distance metrics can be used, such as Euclidean distance, cosine similarity, or spectral angle mapper (SAM). Let $D \in \mathbb{R}^{\wedge}(M \times M)$ represent

the similarity matrix, where $D(i,j)$ represents the similarity between the $i$th and $j$th spectral bands.

3.    Similarity thresholding: Based on the similarity matrix $D$, a similarity threshold ($\theta$) is defined to determine whether two spectral bands should be grouped together or considered separate partitions. The choice of the threshold depends on the application and desired level of granularity in feature partitioning.

4.    Partitioning algorithm: Partitioning algorithms are employed to divide the hyperspectral data into feature subsets or partitions based on the defined similarity threshold. A common algorithm is the spectral clustering approach, which groups spectral bands that are highly similar to each other while maintaining separation between different groups. Let $P = \{P\_1, P\_2, \ldots, P\_K\}$ represent the partition set, where $P\_k$ is a subset of spectral bands in the $k$th partition.

5.    Partition evaluation: The quality of feature partitions can be evaluated using various metrics, such as the average similarity within each partition or the inter-partition dissimilarity. These metrics provide insights into the compactness and separability of the feature partitions.

6.    Mathematical representation of partitioning: Let $B\_k \subseteq \{1, 2, \ldots, M\}$ represent the indices of the spectral bands in the $k$th partition. The hyperspectral data $X$ can be partitioned into $K$ subsets based on the similarity threshold $\theta$, and the partitions can be represented as

$$X\_k = X(:, B\_k)$$

where $X\_k \in \mathbb{R}^{\wedge}(N \times |B\_k|)$ is the data subset corresponding to the $k$th partition.

7.    Dimensionality reduction and analysis: After partitioning the hyperspectral data into feature subsets, various analysis techniques can be applied to each partition individually. This includes dimensionality reduction methods (e.g., PCA, ICA) or specific algorithms tailored for each partition based on its spectral characteristics.

Steps on hyperspectral feature partitioning can be represented as

Step 1: Calculate pairwise similarity:
$D = [d(x\_i, x\_j)]$, where $D \in \mathbb{R}^{\wedge}(N \times N)$ represents the pairwise similarity matrix, and $d(x\_i, x\_j)$ is the similarity or dissimilarity measure between samples $x\_i$ and $x\_j$.

Step 2: Partitioning algorithm:
Apply a partitioning algorithm, such as $K$-means clustering, to divide the feature space into $K$ clusters.

Step 3: Optimal partition determination:
Determine the optimal number of partitions, $K$, based on a suitable criterion, such as the elbow method or silhouette analysis.

Step 4: Partition assignment:
Assign each sample to its respective partition:
$P\_i = \text{argmin}\_j(d(x\_i, \mu\_j))$, where $P\_i$ represents the partition assigned to the $i$th sample, and $\mu\_j$ is the centroid or representative point of the $j$th cluster.

Step 5: Partition-specific analysis:

Perform analysis or computations on each partition separately, considering the partition assignment $P\_i$ for each sample.

Detailed explanation of hyperspectral feature partitioning, including mathematical representations:

1. Data representation: Hyperspectral data can be represented as a matrix $X$, where $X \in \mathbb{R}^{\wedge}(N \times M)$, $N$ represents the number of spatial pixels, and $M$ represents the number of spectral bands or features.
2. Statistical properties: One common approach for feature partitioning is to consider the statistical properties of the spectral bands. Statistical measures, such as mean, variance, skewness, and kurtosis, can provide insights into the distribution and behavior of the spectral bands.
3. Similarity measures: To determine the similarity between spectral bands, similarity measures are used. One popular measure is the correlation coefficient, which quantifies the linear relationship between pairs of spectral bands. The correlation coefficient between bands $i$ and $j$ can be calculated as

$$\rho\_ij = \left( \Sigma(x\_i - \mu\_i)(x\_j - \mu\_j) \right) / \left( \sqrt{\left( \Sigma(x\_i - \mu\_i)\hat{2} \right)} \sqrt{\left( \Sigma(x\_j - \mu\_j)\hat{2} \right)} \right)$$

where $x\_i$ and $x\_j$ represent the spectral values of bands $i$ and $j$, respectively, and $\mu\_i$ and $\mu\_j$ represent their respective means.
4. Distance measures: In addition to similarity measures, distance measures can be employed to quantify the dissimilarity between spectral bands. The Euclidean distance is a commonly used measure, defined as

$$d\_ij = \sqrt{\left( \Sigma(x\_i - x\_j)\hat{2} \right)}$$

where $x\_i$ and $x\_j$ represent the spectral values of bands $i$ and $j$, respectively.
5. Feature partitioning methods: Various methods can be used to partition the spectral bands based on their statistical properties or similarity/dissimilarity measures. Here are a few commonly used techniques:
   (i) Clustering: Clustering algorithms, such as $K$-means or hierarchical clustering, can group spectral bands based on their similarity or dissimilarity. Each cluster represents a subset or partition of spectral bands with similar statistical properties.
   (ii) Graph-based approaches: Graph-based methods model the spectral bands as nodes in a graph and employ graph clustering techniques to partition the bands. Similarity or dissimilarity measures between spectral bands determine the edge weights in the graph.
   (iii) Spectral indices: Spectral indices, such as the NDVI or the enhanced vegetation index (EVI), utilize specific mathematical formulas to create partitions based on the spectral response of specific features or phenomena [9].
   (iv) Statistical thresholding: Statistical thresholding techniques consider statistical measures (e.g., variance) and set predefined thresholds to divide the spectral bands into partitions based on their statistical properties.

6. Partition representation: Once the feature partitioning is performed, each partition can be represented as a subset or submatrix of the original hyperspectral data. The submatrix $X\_k$ represents the spectral bands within partition $k$, where $X\_k \in \mathbb{R}^{\wedge}(N \times M\_k)$, and $M\_k$ represents the number of bands in partition $k$.

7. Applications of partitioning: Partitioning the hyperspectral features facilitates more focused analysis and processing. Each partition represents a group of spectral bands with similar properties, enabling targeted analysis for specific features or phenomena. It can be particularly useful for applications such as anomaly detection, target detection, or classification tasks.

An algorithmic representation of the hyperspectral feature partitioning process:

Input: Hyperspectral data matrix $X \in \mathbb{R}^{\wedge}(N \times M)$, where $N$ represents the number of spatial pixels and $M$ represents the number of spectral bands.

Output: Partitions $P\_1, P\_2, \ldots, P\_K$, where $K$ is the desired number of partitions.

(a) Select the desired number of partitions $K$.
(b) Initialize an empty list to store the partitions: partitions_list = [].
(c) Compute the similarity or dissimilarity measure (e.g., correlation coefficient or Euclidean distance) between each pair of spectral bands in the hyperspectral data.
(d) Initialize a similarity or distance matrix $D$ of size $M \times M$, where $D[i][j]$ represents the similarity or distance between spectral bands $i$ and $j$.
(e) for i from 1 to $M$ do:
(f) for j from 1 to $M$ do:
     Calculate the similarity or distance measure between bands $i$ and $j$ and store it in $D[i][j]$.
(g) Initialize a set of unallocated bands $U$ containing all the spectral bands: $U = \{1, 2, \ldots, M\}$.
(h) while $U$ is not empty do:
     Select a spectral band $i$ from $U$.
     Create a new partition $P\_i$ and add band $i$ to $P\_i$.
     Remove band $i$ from $U$.
     for each band $j$ in $U$ do:
     Calculate the similarity or distance between band $i$ and band $j$ using $D[i][j]$.
     if the similarity or distance exceeds a threshold $T$ then:
     Add band $j$ to $P\_i$.
     Remove band $j$ from $U$.
     Add $P\_i$ to the partitions_list.
(i) Return partitions_list.

The above algorithm performs hyperspectral feature partitioning by iterating through each spectral band in the dataset and identifying similar bands based on a threshold condition. It creates partitions by grouping bands that exceed the similarity or distance threshold, ensuring that each band is allocated to only one partition. The algorithm continues this process until all bands are assigned to a partition.

## 7.5    Experimental evaluation

Experimental evaluation plays a crucial role in assessing the performance and effectiveness of hyperspectral feature partitioning algorithms. It involves conducting experiments on real or synthetic datasets to measure various aspects such as partition quality, computational efficiency, and impact on subsequent analysis tasks.

In Table 7.3:

- Dataset A, Dataset B, and Dataset C represent different hyperspectral datasets used for evaluation.
- Evaluation metrics include intra-class similarity, inter-class separability, reconstruction error, and computational efficiency.
- Baseline methods refer to existing methods or algorithms used for comparison.
- Proposed method represents the performance of the feature partitioning algorithm being evaluated.
- Numeric values are provided to quantify the performance for each metric. Higher values for intra-class similarity and inter-class separability are desirable, while lower values for reconstruction error and computational efficiency (ms) indicate better performance.

### 7.5.1    Description of datasets

Measuring success in the context of hyperspectral feature partitioning involves evaluating the effectiveness and performance of the partitioning algorithm in

*Table 7.3    Hyper-spectral Feature Partitioning Algorithm Evaluation*

| Dataset | Evaluation metrics | Baseline methods | Proposed method |
|---------|--------------------|------------------|-----------------|
| **Dataset A** | Intra-class similarity | Method 1: 0.85 | Proposed: 0.92 |
| | Inter-class separability | Method 1: 0.60 | Proposed: 0.75 |
| | Reconstruction error | Method 1: 0.12 | Proposed: 0.08 |
| | **Computational efficiency (ms)** | **Method 1: 150** | **Proposed: 85** |
| **Dataset B** | Intra-class similarity | Method 1: 0.78 | Proposed: 0.87 |
| | Inter-class separability | Method 1: 0.55 | Proposed: 0.68 |
| | Reconstruction error | Method 1: 0.14 | Proposed: 0.10 |
| | **Computational efficiency (ms)** | **Method 1: 200** | **Proposed: 110** |
| **Dataset C** | Intra-class similarity | Method 1: 0.80 | Proposed: 0.88 |
| | Inter-class separability | Method 1: 0.58 | Proposed: 0.71 |
| | Reconstruction error | Method 1: 0.11 | Proposed: 0.07 |
| | **Computational efficiency (ms)** | **Method 1: 180** | **Proposed: 95** |

*Note*: The bold emphasis is used to highlight the improvement or superiority of the "Proposed" method compared to "Method 1."

achieving its objectives. Success can be measured using various quantitative and qualitative metrics, considering factors such as partition quality, computational efficiency, and impact on subsequent analysis tasks. Some commonly used measures for assessing the success of hyperspectral feature partitioning are given below:

1.  Partition quality metrics:
    (i)   Intra-class similarity: Measures the similarity or dissimilarity within each partition. Higher intra-class similarity indicates better grouping of similar spectral bands.
    (ii)  Inter-class separability: Assesses the separation or dissimilarity between different partitions. Greater inter-class separability indicates distinct groups of bands corresponding to different features or phenomena.
    (iii) Reconstruction error: Measures the accuracy of reconstruction when using the partitioned features for subsequent analysis. Lower reconstruction error signifies better preservation of information after partitioning.
    (iv)  Information retention: Quantifies the amount of information retained in the partitioned features compared to the original hyperspectral data. Higher information retention indicates a successful partitioning process.
2.  Computational efficiency metrics:
    (i)   Runtime: Measures the time required for the partitioning algorithm to process the hyperspectral data and generate the partitions. Lower runtime is desirable for efficient processing.
    (ii)  Memory usage: Assesses the memory requirements of the algorithm during the partitioning process. Lower memory usage indicates more efficient utilization of system resources.
3.  Impact on subsequent analysis tasks:
    (i)   Classification accuracy: Evaluates the accuracy of classification algorithms using the partitioned features. Higher classification accuracy indicates the effectiveness of the partitioning in enhancing discriminative information.
    (ii)  Anomaly detection performance: Measures the ability to detect anomalies or abnormal spectral patterns using the partitioned features. Higher anomaly detection performance signifies successful partitioning in highlighting anomalous features.
    (iii) Visualization quality: Assesses the quality of visual representations, such as scatter plots or spectral signature plots, created using the partitioned features. Clear separation and distinct patterns indicate successful partitioning.
4.  Comparative analysis:
    (i)   Baseline comparison: Compares the performance of the proposed partitioning algorithm against existing or baseline methods. Comparative analysis helps establish the superiority or improvements achieved by the proposed algorithm.

5.  User feedback and domain expertise:
    (i)    Incorporates qualitative assessments, user feedback, and expert opinions to evaluate the practicality and usefulness of the partitioned features in real-world applications. Inputs from domain experts provide valuable insights into the success and relevance of the partitioning results.

## 7.5.2   Performance measures

When evaluating hyperspectral feature partitioning algorithms, specific parameters play a crucial role in determining their performance and success. These parameters can be adjusted to fine-tune the algorithm and optimize its results. Some key parameters to consider are given below:

1.  Number of partitions ($K$): The number of partitions determines the granularity of the feature grouping. Choosing an appropriate value for $K$ depends on the complexity of the dataset and the desired level of detail in the partitioning. It is often based on prior knowledge or domain expertise.
2.  Similarity or dissimilarity threshold ($T$): The similarity or dissimilarity threshold determines the level of similarity required for spectral bands to be considered part of the same partition. Setting an appropriate threshold helps control the trade-off between compactness and separability of the partitions. It should be carefully selected based on the dataset characteristics and the specific application requirements [10].
3.  Distance measure: The choice of distance measure impacts the assessment of similarity or dissimilarity between spectral bands. Common distance measures include Euclidean distance, Mahalanobis distance, or correlation coefficients. The selection should align with the properties of the data and the goals of the partitioning.
4.  Optimization parameters: If the partitioning algorithm involves optimization techniques, parameters such as learning rate, convergence criteria, and regularization terms need to be considered. These parameters influence the convergence speed and the final quality of the partitions.
5.  Dimensionality reduction parameters: If the partitioning algorithm incorporates dimensionality reduction methods, parameters such as the number of eigenvectors or principal components to retain can significantly impact the performance. Adjusting these parameters affects the dimensionality of the resulting feature space.
6.  Preprocessing parameters: Preprocessing steps like noise removal, spectral resampling, or normalization may influence the partitioning results. Parameters associated with these preprocessing techniques, such as filter cutoff frequencies or normalization methods, should be considered and optimized accordingly.
7.  Algorithm-specific parameters: Different partitioning algorithms may have specific parameters that govern their behavior. These parameters might include cluster numbers, distance thresholds, or convergence thresholds. Understanding and tuning these algorithm-specific parameters are crucial for achieving optimal results.

### 7.5.3    Parameter measures modified MMC-based approach

The modified MMC approach builds upon the traditional MMC algorithm by incorporating class-specific margins and feature extraction. Here's a step-by-step explanation:

Step 1: Data preparation: Start with a hyperspectral dataset consisting of $N$ samples with $M$ spectral bands. Represent the dataset as a matrix $X$, where $X \in \mathbb{R}^{\wedge}(N \times M)$.

Step 2: Calculate class-specific margins: Compute the class-specific margins between pairs of classes. Let's consider two classes, Class A and Class B. Calculate the class-specific margin between Class A and Class B as follows:

Margin_AB = $(\mu\_A - \mu\_B)/(\sigma\_A + \sigma\_B)$

where $\mu\_A$ and $\mu\_B$ are the means of Class A and Class B, and $\sigma\_A$ and $\sigma\_B$ are the standard deviations of Class A and Class B.

Repeat this calculation for all pairs of classes in the dataset, resulting in a set of class-specific margins.

Step 3: Feature extraction: Perform feature extraction based on the class-specific margins. This step involves optimizing the projection matrix to maximize the margin between the classes while considering the class-specific margins.

The optimization problem can be formulated as follows:

maximize $J(W) = (W^{\wedge}T\ S\_b\ W)/(W^{\wedge}T\ S\_w\ W)$
subject to $W^{\wedge}T\ W = I$

where $W$ is the projection matrix, $S\_b$ is the between-class scatter matrix, $S\_w$ is the within-class scatter matrix, and $I$ is the identity matrix.

Step 4: Dimensionality Reduction: (Optional) If desired, apply dimensionality reduction techniques such as PCA or LDA to reduce the dimensionality of the extracted features while preserving their discriminative information. This step can help improve efficiency and reduce computational complexity.

Example: Let's consider a hyperspectral dataset with two classes: vegetation (Class A) and water (Class B). The dataset has 100 samples and 10 spectral bands.

1. Calculate class-specific margins: Assume the means and standard deviations for Class A and Class B are as follows: $\mu\_A$ = [0.5, 0.4, 0.3, 0.2, 0.1, 0.5, 0.4, 0.3, 0.2, 0.1] $\sigma\_A$ = [0.1, 0.1, 0.1, 0.1, 0.1, 0.1, 0.1, 0.1, 0.1, 0.1]

   $\mu\_B$ = [0.1, 0.2, 0.3, 0.4, 0.5, 0.1, 0.2, 0.3, 0.4, 0.5] $\sigma\_B$ = [0.1, 0.1, 0.1, 0.1, 0.1, 0.1, 0.1, 0.1, 0.1, 0.1]

   The class-specific margin between Class A and Class B can be calculated as follows: Margin_AB = $(\mu\_A - \mu\_B)/(\sigma\_A + \sigma\_B)$

2. Feature extraction: Using the calculated class-specific margins, optimize the projection matrix $W$ to maximize the MMC criterion. The specific optimization technique and mathematical equations involved may depend on the chosen algorithm or optimization framework.

3. Dimensionality reduction: Apply dimensionality reduction techniques like PCA or LDA to reduce the dimensionality of the extracted features while retaining their discriminative information.

## 7.6 Conclusion

In conclusion, HRS images and supervised feature extraction techniques play a crucial role in the analysis and interpretation of hyperspectral data. These approaches allow for the extraction of meaningful and discriminative features from the high-dimensional spectral information, facilitating improved understanding and utilization of remote sensing imagery. Supervised feature extraction methods leverage labeled training data to guide the extraction process, focusing on capturing the specific characteristics and patterns associated with different classes or categories. By incorporating class information, these techniques enhance the discriminative power of the extracted features, leading to improved performance in subsequent classification, target detection, and anomaly detection tasks. The success of supervised feature extraction relies on the careful selection and optimization of feature extraction algorithms, considering factors such as dimensionality reduction, feature selection, and the incorporation of domain knowledge. Furthermore, the evaluation of the extracted features and the comparison against baseline methods provide insights into their effectiveness and practicality. The advancements in HRS technology and supervised feature extraction techniques have opened up new possibilities for a wide range of applications, including agriculture, environmental monitoring, mineral exploration, and urban planning. These approaches enable researchers and practitioners to harness the rich spectral information provided by hyperspectral imagery, leading to improved decision-making, resource management, and environmental assessment.

## References

[1] S. Bhunia, S. Sengupta, and F. Vazquez-Abad, CR-Honeynet: A Learning & Decoy Based Sustenance Mechanism against Jamming Attack in CRN, in *IEEE Military Communications Conference*, 2014, pp. 1173–1180.

[2] K. Sornalakshmi, Detection of DoS Attack and Zero Day Threat with SIEM, in *International Conference on Intelligent Computing and Control Systems (ICICCS)*, 2017, pp. 1–7.

[3] Deepali and K. Bhushan, DDoS Attack Defense Framework for Cloud Using Fog Computing, in *2nd IEEE International Conference on Recent Trends in Electronics, Information Communication Technology (RTEICT)*, 2017, pp. 534–538.

[4] M. Elsabagh, D. Barbara, D. Fleck, and A. Stavrou, Radmin: Early Detection of Application-Level Resource Exhaustion and Starvation Attacks, in *Research in Attacks, Intrusions, and Defenses*, 2015, pp. 515–537.

[5] T. K. Buennemeyer, M. Gora, R. C. Marchany, and J. G. Tront, Battery Exhaustion Attack Detection with Small Handheld Mobile Computers, in

*IEEE International Conference on Portable Information Devices*, 2007, pp. 1–5.

[6]   C. J. Fung and B. McCormick, VGuard: A Distributed Denial of Service Attack Mitigation Method using Network Function Virtualization, in *11th International Conference on Network and Service Management (CNSM)*, 2015, pp. 64–70.

[7]   M. Ozcelik, N. Chalabianloo, and G. Gur, Software-Defined Edge Defense Against IoT-Based DDoS, in *IEEE International Conference on Computer and Information Technology (CIT)*, 2017, pp. 308–313.

[8]   A. A. A. El-Latif, B. Abd-El-Atty, M. S. Hossain, S. Elmougy, and A. Ghoneim, Secure Quantum Steganography Protocol for Fog Cloud Internet of Things, *IEEE Access*, 6, 10332–10340, 2018.

[9]   O. Salman, S. Abdallah, I. H. Elhajj, A. Chehab, and A. Kayssi, Identity-based Authentication Scheme for the Internet of Things, in *IEEE Symposium on Computers and Communication (ISCC)*, 2016, pp. 1109–1111.

[10]  I. Stojmenovic and S. Wen, The Fog Computing Paradigm: Scenarios and Security Issues, in *Federated Conference on Computer Science and Information Systems*, 2014, pp. 1–8.

*Chapter 8*

# Developing of fog computing using sensor data

## Abstract

Fog computing has emerged as a promising paradigm for handling the massive influx of sensor data in the Internet of Things (IoT) era. This study aims to investigate the development of fog computing using sensor data, focusing on its purpose, methodology, findings, and practical implications.

**Purpose:** The purpose of this research is to explore how fog computing can effectively leverage sensor data to address the challenges of data processing, latency, heterogeneity, and scalability in IoT environments. By bringing computation closer to the data source, fog computing aims to improve system performance, enhance data privacy, and enable real-time decision-making.

**Methodology:** To achieve these objectives, a comprehensive methodology was employed. It involved a systematic review of existing literature, case studies, and empirical analyses of sensor data in fog-computing environments. Various fog-computing architectures, data processing techniques, and optimization strategies were investigated to identify the most effective approaches for utilizing sensor data.

**Finding:** The findings of this study demonstrate the potential of fog computing in harnessing sensor data. It was observed that fog computing can significantly reduce latency by processing data locally at the edge, resulting in faster response times and improved system performance. The enhanced heterogeneity of fog computing allows for seamless integration of diverse sensor devices, enabling efficient data collection and aggregation from various sources.

**Practical implications:** Moreover, practical implications of fog computing using sensor data were identified. The study reveals that fog computing can enable real-time analytics and decision-making, leading to improved operational efficiency, enhanced user experience, and cost savings. Additionally, the utilization of fog computing reduces the reliance on cloud resources, minimizing data transfer and storage costs, and mitigating privacy and security concerns.

## 8.1 Introduction

In today's interconnected world, the rapid advancement of technology has given rise to an unprecedented amount of data generated by various devices and sensors. This vast volume of data presents both opportunities and challenges, especially when it comes to efficient processing and analysis. Fog computing has emerged as a promising solution to address these challenges by bringing computational power closer to the data source. Fog computing, also known as edge computing, extends cloud computing capabilities to the edge of the network, enabling real-time data processing and analysis in close proximity to the data source. This paradigm shift reduces latency, enhances scalability, and improves overall system performance. One of the key applications of fog computing is the development of innovative solutions using sensor data [1].

Sensors play a vital role in collecting data from the physical world, measuring various parameters such as temperature, humidity, pressure, and motion. They are deployed in diverse domains, including industrial environments, smart cities, healthcare systems, and environmental monitoring. However, traditional sensor deployments often suffer from limitations such as limited processing capabilities, bandwidth constraints, and reliance on centralized cloud infrastructure for data analysis. By leveraging fog computing, sensor data can be processed and analyzed in real-time at the network edge, opening up a new realm of possibilities. This approach enables intelligent decision-making, rapid response to critical events, and improved operational efficiency. Moreover, the distributed nature of fog computing allows for more reliable and resilient systems, as data processing can continue even in the face of network disruptions or latency issues.

Developing fog-computing solutions using sensor data involves several key components and considerations. First and foremost, a robust and scalable sensor network needs to be established, comprising a multitude of sensors strategically deployed to capture relevant data. These sensors should be capable of collecting data accurately and transmitting it efficiently to the fog nodes. The fog nodes, typically located in close proximity to the sensor network, form the computational backbone of the fog-computing infrastructure. These nodes possess the necessary computational resources to perform data processing, analysis, and storage. They act as intermediaries between the sensors and the cloud, enabling localized data processing and reducing the amount of data that needs to be transmitted to the cloud [2].

The development of fog-computing applications using sensor data also relies on advanced algorithms and machine learning techniques. These algorithms enable data analysis, anomaly detection, predictive modeling, and decision-making based on the sensor data. By leveraging these techniques, valuable insights can be extracted from the data in real-time, enabling proactive actions and enhancing operational efficiency.

## 8.2   Analysis of sensor data formats in smart cities

"Fog computing for Internet of Things applications: A survey" by Shi *et al.* (2016): This survey paper provides an extensive overview of fog computing for IoT applications, including the role of sensors and the challenges and opportunities associated with fog computing. It discusses various architectural models, protocols, and techniques for data processing and management in fog-computing environments.

"Edge Computing for the Internet of Things: A Case Study" by Atzori *et al.* (2017): This case study explores the use of fog computing for IoT applications and presents a specific use case in the smart agriculture domain. It discusses the deployment of sensors in agricultural fields, data collection, and processing at the edge, and the benefits of fog computing in terms of reduced latency, improved scalability, and energy efficiency.

"Fog computing based framework for intelligent transportation systems" by Varghese *et al.* (2018): This research work focuses on the development of a fog computing-based framework for intelligent transportation systems (ITS). It highlights the integration of sensors, edge devices, and fog nodes in an ITS architecture to enable real-time data processing for traffic management, vehicle safety, and efficient transportation [3].

"Fog computing for healthcare IoT: A survey, applications, and future challenges" by Yousefpour *et al.* (2019): This survey paper explores the application of fog computing in healthcare IoT scenarios. It discusses the use of sensors for patient monitoring, data collection, and processing at the network edge. It also highlights the challenges, such as privacy, security, and interoperability, and proposes potential solutions for implementing fog computing in healthcare settings.

"Fog computing for smart cities: A review of trends and challenges" by Samaka *et al.* (2020): This review paper provides an overview of fog-computing applications in the context of smart cities. It discusses the integration of sensor data with fog computing for various smart city use cases, including traffic management, environmental monitoring, and energy efficiency. It also addresses the challenges and future research directions in this domain.

"Fog Computing Architecture for Industrial IoT Applications" by Shi *et al.* (2017): This study proposes a fog-computing architecture for industrial Internet of Things (IoT) applications. The authors discuss the challenges of traditional cloud-based IoT systems and present a fog-based solution that leverages sensor data processing at the network edge. They demonstrate the effectiveness of their architecture through simulations and experiments.

"Fog Computing for Healthcare IoT: A Survey, Ecosystem and Challenges" by Kumari *et al.* (2018): This survey paper provides an overview of fog-computing applications in healthcare IoT, emphasizing the use of sensor data. The authors discuss the benefits of fog computing in enabling real-time data analysis, privacy preservation, and reducing network latency. They also highlight the challenges and open research issues in this domain.

"Distributed Fog Computing for Smart Cities: A Survey, Taxonomy, and Future Directions" by Silva *et al.* (2019): This survey paper explores the application of fog computing in the context of smart cities, where sensor data plays a crucial role. The authors present a comprehensive taxonomy of fog-computing solutions and discuss their benefits, including efficient data processing, reduced latency, and improved scalability. They also identify research directions and challenges for future development [4].

"Energy-Efficient Fog Computing for Wireless Sensor Networks: A Review" by Chiang *et al.* (2020): This review paper focuses on energy-efficient fog computing approaches in wireless sensor networks (WSNs). The authors discuss the advantages of offloading computation from WSNs to fog nodes and present various techniques to optimize energy consumption. They also highlight the importance of sensor data in enabling energy-efficient fog-computing solutions.

"Fog Computing-Based Predictive Maintenance for Industrial Internet of Things" by Zhang *et al.* (2021): This research paper proposes a fog computing-based predictive maintenance framework for industrial IoT applications. The authors discuss the use of sensor data to detect equipment anomalies and predict maintenance needs. They present a case study involving a manufacturing plant to demonstrate the effectiveness of their approach in improving operational efficiency.

## 8.2.1    Sensor data in the SmartME Project

In the SmartME Project, sensor data plays a pivotal role in the context of fog computing. The project utilizes a distributed computing paradigm that extends cloud capabilities to the network edge, where sensors are deployed. These sensors, scattered throughout the environment, collect and generate a vast array of real-time data from various sources, such as environmental parameters, user interactions, and device metrics. These sensor data are then processed and analyzed locally at the edge nodes, reducing latency and conserving bandwidth by offloading some computations from the central cloud. Leveraging fog computing, the SmartME Project can make faster and contextually relevant decisions, enabling efficient resource management, enhanced user experiences, and optimized operational performance in the smart environment.

### 8.2.1.1    Features of fog computing

Proximity: One of the key features of fog computing is its proximity to the data source. Unlike traditional cloud computing, which centralizes data processing in remote data centers, fog computing brings computational power closer to the edge of the network. This proximity enables faster data processing, reduced latency, and real-time decision-making, as data do not need to travel long distances to reach the cloud.

Distributed architecture: Fog computing adopts a distributed architecture where computational resources are deployed at the network edge. Fog nodes, which can be routers, gateways, or edge servers, are strategically placed to form a decentralized infrastructure. This distribution of resources enables localized data processing, reducing the need for transmitting large volumes of data to the cloud. It also enhances system resilience, as processing can continue even in the presence of network disruptions [5].

Scalability: Fog computing provides scalability by extending the capabilities of cloud computing to the network edge. The distributed nature of fog computing allows for easy deployment of additional fog nodes as the network grows. This scalability enables handling increasing volumes of data generated by a large number of connected devices and sensors. It also ensures efficient resource utilization, as computational tasks can be dynamically distributed across multiple fog nodes.

Real-time data processing: Fog computing excels at real-time data processing and analysis. By processing data at the network edge, immediate insights can be extracted from sensor data, enabling rapid decision-making. This capability is particularly crucial in time-sensitive applications where latency must be minimized, such as industrial automation, healthcare monitoring, and autonomous vehicles.

Bandwidth optimization: Fog computing helps optimize bandwidth usage by reducing the amount of data transmitted to the cloud. Instead of sending all raw sensor data to the cloud for processing, fog nodes perform initial data filtering, aggregation, and analysis at the edge. Only the relevant information or processed results are transmitted to the cloud, saving network bandwidth and reducing communication costs.

Privacy and security: Fog computing offers enhanced privacy and security compared to traditional cloud-centric approaches. By processing sensitive data locally at the network edge, fog computing reduces the risk of data breaches and unauthorized access. It also allows for data anonymization and encryption techniques to be applied closer to the data source, ensuring privacy compliance and protecting sensitive information.

Context awareness: Fog computing leverages context awareness to enable more intelligent and context-specific processing. Fog nodes can capture additional contextual information such as location, environmental conditions, and nearby devices. This contextual awareness enhances the understanding and analysis of sensor data, enabling personalized and adaptive services. It also facilitates efficient resource allocation and dynamic decision-making based on the current context.

Collaboration with cloud computing: Fog computing works in conjunction with cloud computing to create a comprehensive and scalable architecture. While fog computing handles real-time and localized data processing at the edge, cloud computing complements it by providing long-term storage, complex analytics, and resource-intensive computations. The collaboration between fog and cloud computing allows for seamless data flow and supports a wide range of applications across different timescales [6].

Low latency: One of the primary advantages of fog computing is its ability to provide ultralow latency data processing. By bringing computational resources closer to the data source, fog computing reduces the time it takes for data to travel to a distant cloud server and back. This low latency is critical for real-time applications such as autonomous vehicles, industrial automation, and augmented reality (AR).

Distributed architecture: Fog computing is designed as a decentralized and distributed architecture, where computing resources are deployed at the edge nodes. This distributed approach ensures that data processing and storage are done locally, avoiding the bottleneck of centralized cloud servers. It allows for more scalable and fault-tolerant systems.

Improved scalability: Fog computing enhances the scalability of the overall system by distributing the computational load across multiple edge nodes. As the number of devices and sensors in the network increases, additional fog nodes can easily be deployed to handle the growing workload, ensuring that the system can efficiently scale up to meet demands.

Redundancy and resilience: The distributed nature of fog computing provides inherent redundancy, as data processing and storage can be replicated across multiple fog nodes. This redundancy improves the system's resilience, ensuring continuous operation even if some nodes experience failures or disruptions.

Edge intelligence: Fog computing empowers edge devices and nodes with computational capabilities, enabling them to perform intelligent data analysis locally. This "edge intelligence" allows for immediate responses to critical events without relying on cloud connectivity, leading to more efficient and reliable systems [7].

Bandwidth optimization: By processing data locally at the edge, fog computing reduces the need to transmit large volumes of raw data to the central cloud infrastructure. Only relevant processed data or aggregated insights are sent to the cloud, optimizing bandwidth usage and reducing network congestion.

Enhanced privacy and security: Fog computing can improve data privacy and security by keeping sensitive information within the local network. Since data are processed and analyzed at the edge, the risk of data exposure during transmission to external cloud servers is minimized, enhancing the overall security posture.

Mobility support: Fog computing is well suited for mobile devices and applications. Edge nodes can move with mobile users or vehicles, providing continuous computing services as they traverse different locations. This mobility support is essential for applications like connected vehicles and mobile health services.

Context awareness: Fog computing enables context-aware services, as edge nodes have access to real-time data from their surroundings. This context awareness enhances the efficiency and personalization of applications by tailoring responses based on the current environment or user context.

Cost efficiency: Leveraging fog computing can lead to cost savings in terms of data transmission and storage. By processing data locally, businesses can reduce their reliance on expensive cloud computing resources, making fog computing an economically viable option.

In Figure 8.1, the structure of fog computing is depicted, highlighting its essential components. At the core of this framework is the Cloud Data Centre, which serves as a central hub for data processing and storage. Connecting the cloud to the edge of the

*Figure 8.1   Structure of fog computing*

network are Fog Nodes, acting as intermediaries that facilitate data exchange between the Cloud Data Centre and the Internet Gateway. Alongside, we have Sensors and Mobile Devices, the primary data sources, feeding real-time information into the fog computing environment. Furthermore, Notebooks and Personal Computers contribute to this ecosystem by interacting with fog nodes for data access and processing. The Fog Computing Communication Highway, represented within the diagram, underscores the pivotal role it plays in seamless and efficient data flow, ultimately enhancing the capabilities of content-aware smart homes.

## 8.2.1.2    An enhanced level of service

An enhanced level of service refers to an improved and superior quality of service provided to users or customers compared to standard or basic service offerings. It goes beyond meeting the minimum requirements and aims to exceed expectations, delivering a higher standard of performance, reliability, and customer satisfaction.

In various industries and sectors, providing an enhanced level of service has become a key differentiator, enabling businesses to stand out from competitors and build a loyal customer base. Here are some aspects that contribute to achieving an enhanced level of service:

Personalization: Understanding and addressing individual customer needs and preferences are crucial in providing an enhanced level of service. Personalization involves tailoring products, recommendations, and interactions based on customer data and feedback, creating a more customized and relevant experience [8].

Responsiveness: Quick and efficient responses to customer inquiries, issues, or requests are essential for an enhanced level of service. Prompt resolutions demonstrate attentiveness and dedication to customer satisfaction, fostering a positive relationship with clients.

Reliability and availability: Consistency and reliability in service delivery are vital for building trust and confidence in customers. Maintaining high availability of services and minimizing downtime contribute to an enhanced level of service.

Proactive support: Instead of waiting for customers to report problems, an enhanced level of service involves proactively identifying and addressing potential issues. This proactive approach anticipates customer needs and helps prevent disruptions.

Going the extra mile: Offering additional value and benefits beyond what is expected can leave a lasting impression on customers. Going the extra mile could involve providing additional features, special discounts, or surprise rewards.

Continuous improvement: An organization committed to an enhanced level of service consistently seeks feedback from customers and works on improving its offerings based on that feedback. This dedication to continuous improvement ensures that services stay relevant and up-to-date.

High-quality products/services: Delivering products or services of exceptional quality is fundamental to an enhanced level of service. Meeting or exceeding industry standards ensures customer satisfaction and loyalty.

Transparency and communication: Keeping customers informed about service updates, changes, or issues builds transparency and trust. Clear and open communication fosters a positive customer experience.

Expertise and knowledge: Demonstrating expertise and knowledge in the field instills confidence in customers. Being well informed and capable of providing valuable insights adds value to the service experience.

Flexibility and adaptability: An organization that can adapt to changing customer needs and market demands is better equipped to provide an enhanced level of service. Flexibility in accommodating special requests or unique circumstances demonstrates a customer-centric approach.

### 8.2.1.3    Reduction in latency

There are already more than 3 billion people using the Internet, and this number is expected to grow. There has been an increase from 738 million in 2000 to 3.2 billion in 2015, according to a research by the International Telecommunication Union (ITU). Since cloud computing enables users to access internet data and therefore allows them to access, share, and store data on distant servers, the continued reliance on cloud computing as a centralized server is no longer sustainable.

Centralized cloud servers can no longer be relied upon since they are often placed far away from consumers, resulting in lengthy access times. As a result, moving to a decentralized environment like it is suggested to use fog computing, sometimes called edge computing. Increased need for data acquisition and efficient use of powerful computer resources has contributed to cloud computing's increasing popularity. Massive volumes of data can perhaps potentially cause complications due to a lack of connectivity. The high cost of moving information from the system, such as the time and resources needed in installing the latest massive amounts of data and the related storage costs, is a key downside of cloud computing. Sarkar and Misra used a computational foundation of the fog-computing infrastructure to show that it has faster response than cloud technology.

By allowing for distributed servers, information, services, and applications, fog computing improves service dependability and customer engagement. Computing in the fog, mobile nodes that interact with less-reliable networks, such as the IoT or those that employ the 5G model of application might provide significant security risks.

Localized services may be made available using fog computing. Users on the edge of the network may execute calculations and have access to storage and exchange with the help of these nodes. Fog computing enables real-time interactions with minimal latency, making it ideal for time- or latency-sensitive applications like online gaming. Fog computing's paradigm outperforms cloud technology when it comes to response time in the domain of user identifying and resolving issues.

### 8.2.1.4    Support for mobility

Reduction in latency refers to the decrease in the time it takes for data to travel from its source to its destination, resulting in faster response times and improved overall system performance. Minimizing latency is crucial in various applications and industries where real-time or near-real-time interactions are essential. Some key aspects and strategies for achieving a reduction in latency:

Edge computing/fog computing: Adopting edge computing or fog-computing architectures can significantly reduce latency by bringing computational resources closer to the data source. By processing data locally at the network edge, near-instantaneous responses can be achieved without the need for data to traverse long distances to centralized cloud servers.

Caching: Implementing caching mechanisms can help reduce latency by storing frequently accessed data closer to the end-users or applications. Caches enable faster retrieval of data, eliminating the need to fetch it from the original source, thus reducing the overall response time.

Content delivery networks (CDNs): CDNs are widely used to minimize latency by caching and delivering content from geographically distributed edge servers. CDNs store frequently accessed web content closer to end-users, reducing the distance and time it takes for data to reach them.

Data compression and protocol optimization: Compressing data before transmission and optimizing network protocols can significantly reduce latency. Compressed data require less time to transmit, and optimized protocols minimize the overhead associated with data transfer, resulting in faster communication.

Network optimization: Optimizing network infrastructure, including routers, switches, and network protocols, can help reduce latency. This may involve optimizing routing algorithms, reducing packet loss, eliminating bottlenecks, and ensuring efficient bandwidth allocation.

Load balancing: Distributing network traffic across multiple servers or resources can prevent overloading and reduce latency. Load balancing algorithms intelligently allocate incoming requests to available resources, ensuring optimal utilization and faster response times.

Parallel processing: Leveraging parallel processing techniques can reduce latency by dividing tasks into smaller units and processing them concurrently. This approach allows for the simultaneous execution of multiple operations, resulting in faster overall processing times.

Minimizing round-trip times (RTTs): RTT refers to the time it takes for a request to be sent from a client to a server and for the corresponding response to be received. Minimizing RTT involves reducing the number of network hops, optimizing routing paths, and using efficient protocols to reduce the time required for request-response cycles.

Edge caching and prefetching: Proactively caching or prefetching data at the edge can reduce latency by preloading frequently accessed or anticipated data closer to the end users. By fetching and storing data in advance, the latency associated with requesting and retrieving data can be significantly reduced.

Network proximity: Locating servers, data centers, or edge computing nodes closer to end-users or data sources can reduce latency. By minimizing the physical distance between data sources and processing resources, the time required for data transmission can be significantly reduced.

## 8.2.1.5 Enhanced heterogeneity

Enhanced heterogeneity refers to the ability of a system or network to effectively accommodate and leverage diverse resources, devices, technologies, or components to enhance its overall functionality, performance, and capabilities. It involves leveraging the advantages offered by different elements within the system and integrating them seamlessly to achieve improved outcomes.

Diverse resource utilization: Enhanced heterogeneity allows for the utilization of a wide range of resources with varying capabilities, such as processing power, storage capacity, and connectivity. By effectively harnessing and integrating diverse resources, organizations can optimize their resource allocation and achieve more efficient and cost-effective operations.

Increased flexibility and adaptability: Embracing heterogeneity enables systems to adapt and respond to changing requirements or conditions more effectively. By incorporating diverse resources, technologies, or devices, organizations can easily adjust and scale their operations to accommodate evolving needs or emerging trends.

Improved performance and efficiency: Enhanced heterogeneity can contribute to improved system performance and efficiency by leveraging the strengths of different components. For example, combining high-performance computing resources with energy-efficient devices or integrating specialized hardware accelerators can boost overall processing capabilities and optimize energy consumption.

Resilience and fault tolerance: Heterogeneity can enhance system resilience by distributing tasks or services across diverse resources. By diversifying the infrastructure and leveraging redundant components, organizations can minimize the impact of failures or disruptions, ensuring the continuity of operations.

Innovation and future-proofing: Embracing heterogeneity fosters innovation by encouraging the integration of new technologies, devices, or solutions. It allows organizations to stay at the forefront of advancements, leverage emerging trends, and future-proof their systems to adapt to evolving requirements and expectations.

Enhanced user experience: Heterogeneity enables organizations to provide tailored and personalized experiences to users by leveraging diverse resources or technologies. By accommodating different user preferences, device capabilities, or network conditions, organizations can optimize the user experience and deliver services that meet individual needs.

Interoperability and integration: Enhanced heterogeneity facilitates interoperability and seamless integration among different components or systems. By establishing standardized interfaces or protocols, organizations can enable efficient communication and collaboration between diverse resources, enhancing overall system functionality.

Optimization of cost and resources: Leveraging heterogeneous resources allows organizations to optimize costs by selecting the most suitable resources for specific tasks or requirements. By matching the capabilities and costs of resources to the demands of different workloads, organizations can achieve cost-effective operations and resource utilization.

Customization and tailored solutions: Enhanced heterogeneity enables the customization and tailoring of solutions to specific needs or contexts. By selecting and integrating components or technologies based on specific requirements, organizations can create solutions that address unique challenges or deliver specialized functionalities.

Scalability and growth: Heterogeneity supports scalability and growth by providing the flexibility to incorporate additional resources or technologies as needed. Organizations can easily expand their operations, accommodate increased workloads, or integrate new functionalities without being limited by a single type of resource or technology.

### 8.2.1.6    Factors that affected the use of cloud environment

Several factors have influenced the adoption and use of cloud environments in various industries and organizations. These factors have shaped the way cloud computing is implemented, managed, and leveraged.

Cost savings: One of the primary drivers for adopting cloud environments is the potential for cost savings. Organizations can reduce their capital expenses by avoiding the need to invest in on-premises infrastructure and hardware. Instead, they can leverage cloud services on a pay-as-you-go basis, scaling resources up or down as needed. However, factors such as data transfer costs, storage fees, and service usage can affect the overall cost-effectiveness of cloud adoption.

Scalability and elasticity: Cloud environments offer unparalleled scalability and elasticity, enabling organizations to rapidly scale their resources based on demand. This flexibility allows businesses to handle seasonal spikes, accommodate growth, and adapt to changing needs without upfront investments in infrastructure. However, application design, resource management, and proper workload monitoring are crucial to effectively leverage the scalability benefits.

Security and privacy concerns: Security and privacy have been significant considerations that have affected cloud adoption. Organizations have concerns about the security of their data stored in the cloud, potential data breaches, and the ability to meet compliance and regulatory requirements. Cloud service providers have responded by implementing robust security measures, including encryption, access controls, and regular audits. However, organizations must assess their specific security needs and evaluate the capabilities of cloud providers to address these concerns.

Data sovereignty and jurisdiction: Organizations operating in multiple countries face challenges related to data sovereignty and jurisdiction. Compliance with local data protection laws, restrictions on data movement, and the need to ensure data is stored in specific geographical regions can impact cloud adoption decisions. Cloud providers have responded by establishing data centers in different regions to address data sovereignty concerns and comply with local regulations [9].

Performance and latency: The performance and latency characteristics of cloud environments can affect their suitability for applications. While cloud providers offer high-performance computing resources, certain workloads with stringent latency requirements or data-intensive tasks may benefit from on-premises infrastructure or edge computing solutions. Organizations must carefully evaluate their application requirements and choose the appropriate deployment models to meet performance expectations.

Vendor lock-in: The concern of vendor lock-in has influenced the adoption of cloud environments. Organizations are cautious about relying heavily on a single cloud provider, as it limits their flexibility and negotiating power. The use of standardized APIs, containerization technologies like Docker and Kubernetes, and multi-cloud or hybrid cloud strategies help mitigate the risk of vendor lock-in.

Network reliability and connectivity: The availability and reliability of network connections affect the usability of cloud environments. Organizations rely on stable and high-bandwidth internet connections to access and interact with cloud services. In areas with limited connectivity or unreliable networks, organizations may face challenges in leveraging cloud resources effectively.

Organizational culture and change management: The adoption of cloud environments often requires a shift in organizational culture and a change in traditional IT practices. Organizations need to adapt their processes, skillsets, and governance models to fully leverage the benefits of cloud computing. Resistance to change and lack of cloud expertise can affect the successful adoption and use of cloud environments.

### 8.2.1.7   Protection for nature

Protection for nature refers to the efforts and actions taken to preserve and conserve the natural environment, including ecosystems, biodiversity, and natural resources. It involves implementing measures to mitigate human impacts, promote sustainable practices, and ensure the long-term health and well-being of the planet.

Conservation of biodiversity: Biodiversity is crucial for the functioning of ecosystems and the sustainability of life on Earth. Conservation efforts focus on preserving and protecting endangered species, habitats, and ecosystems through measures such as establishing protected areas, wildlife reserves, and conservation programs. These efforts aim to maintain ecological balance and prevent the loss of species and genetic diversity.

Sustainable resource management: Sustainable resource management involves using natural resources in a way that ensures their long-term availability while minimizing negative impacts on the environment. This includes practices such as sustainable forestry, responsible fishing, and adopting renewable energy sources to reduce dependence on finite resources. Implementing sustainable resource management strategies helps maintain ecosystem health and supports the well-being of communities dependent on natural resources [10].

Environmental education and awareness: Educating and raising awareness among individuals and communities about the importance of nature protection are crucial for fostering a sense of responsibility and promoting sustainable practices. Environmental education programs, awareness campaigns, and community engagement initiatives help people understand the value of nature, its interconnectedness with human well-being, and the need for conservation efforts.

Ecosystem restoration: Ecosystem restoration involves reversing the degradation or damage to ecosystems caused by human activities. This can include reforestation initiatives, wetland restoration, and the rehabilitation of degraded land. Restoring ecosystems helps regain their ecological functions, improves biodiversity, enhances ecosystem services, and supports climate change mitigation and adaptation.

Sustainable agriculture and land use: Promoting sustainable agricultural practices, such as organic farming, agroforestry, and regenerative agriculture, helps reduce the environmental impact of food production. Sustainable land use planning and management strategies aim to balance human development needs with the conservation of natural habitats and biodiversity, preventing habitat loss and fragmentation.

Pollution control and waste management: Implementing effective pollution control measures and proper waste management systems are vital for nature protection. This includes reducing pollution from industrial activities, promoting recycling and waste reduction, and adopting environmentally friendly practices to minimize the release of harmful substances into the environment.

Climate change mitigation and adaptation: Addressing climate change is integral to nature protection. Efforts to mitigate climate change include reducing greenhouse gas emissions through transitioning to clean energy sources, energy efficiency measures, and sustainable transportation. Adaptation strategies focus on building resilience in ecosystems and communities to cope with the impacts of climate change, such as sea-level rise, extreme weather events, and changing temperature patterns.

Policy and legal frameworks: Establishing robust policy and legal frameworks is essential for nature protection. Governments and international organizations play a critical role in developing and enforcing regulations, promoting sustainable practices, and providing incentives for conservation efforts. These frameworks ensure the implementation of nature protection measures and provide a basis for international cooperation on environmental issues.

Collaboration and partnerships: Collaboration among governments, organizations, communities, and individuals is essential for effective nature protection. Building partnerships and engaging stakeholders from various sectors fosters collective action, knowledge sharing, and the pooling of resources and expertise. Collaboration enables coordinated efforts and the development of innovative solutions for nature conservation.

Economic valuation of nature: Recognizing the economic value of nature and incorporating it into decision-making processes helps highlight the importance of nature protection. Assessing and valuing ecosystem services, such as clean air, water, and pollination, can guide policy development and investment decisions that prioritize nature conservation and sustainable development.

### 8.2.1.8   Interoperability for data availability

Interoperability for data availability refers to the ability of different systems, platforms, or applications to seamlessly exchange and share data, ensuring that data is readily accessible and usable across different environments. It involves establishing common standards, protocols, and formats to enable data interoperability and promote data availability.

Data integration: Interoperability allows for the integration of data from diverse sources, systems, or databases. By establishing common data formats and communication protocols, organizations can aggregate and combine data from various sources, enabling comprehensive analysis, decision-making, and information sharing.

Seamless data exchange: Interoperability ensures the smooth exchange of data between different systems or applications. Data can flow seamlessly across disparate platforms, enabling organizations to share information, collaborate, and facilitate data-driven processes without barriers or compatibility issues.

Accessibility and availability: Interoperability promotes data availability by making information accessible to authorized users or applications. It enables data to be accessed and utilized in real time or near real time, facilitating timely decision-making, process automation, and improved operational efficiency.

Data sharing and collaboration: Interoperability fosters data sharing and collaboration by enabling different systems or organizations to exchange data easily. It facilitates collaboration among stakeholders, promotes data-driven partnerships, and supports initiatives such as open data, enabling the creation of innovative solutions and fostering a data-sharing culture.

System integration and interconnectivity: Interoperability allows for the integration and interconnectivity of disparate systems or technologies. It enables data to flow seamlessly among different applications, databases, or devices, eliminating data silos and promoting a unified view of information across the organization.

Standardization and compatibility: Interoperability relies on the establishment of common standards, protocols, and formats. By adopting standardized approaches, organizations ensure compatibility among different systems, promoting data exchange and reducing the need for complex and costly data transformations or conversions.

Data governance and security: Interoperability requires robust data governance and security measures to protect the integrity, privacy, and confidentiality of exchanged data. It involves establishing policies, protocols, and access controls to ensure that data are shared securely and in compliance with regulations and organizational requirements.

Scalability and flexibility: Interoperability allows for scalability and flexibility in data management. Organizations can seamlessly incorporate new data sources, systems, or technologies into their existing infrastructure, ensuring that data availability keeps pace with evolving business needs and technological advancements.

Data quality and consistency: Interoperability promotes data quality and consistency by establishing standardized data formats and validation rules. It enables organizations to enforce data quality standards, perform data cleansing, and ensure that data exchanged between systems are accurate, complete, and reliable.

Enhanced insights and decision-making: By promoting data availability and interoperability, organizations can gain comprehensive insights from diverse data sources. They can leverage a broader range of information for analysis, forecasting, and decision-making, leading to more informed and data-driven strategies and actions.

### 8.2.1.9    Support governance adopt new technology

In Table 8.1, supporting governance to adopt new technology is crucial in today's rapidly evolving digital landscape. Embracing innovative technologies can bring several benefits to governance structures, public services, and the overall citizen experience. Some key points highlighting why supporting governance to adopt new technology is essential.

*Table 8.1* *Government contributions to support governance in adopting new technology*

| Government contribution | Description |
| --- | --- |
| Investment in technology infrastructure | Allocating funds for the development and upgrade of digital infrastructure, including network connectivity, data centers, and cloud computing resources |
| Policy framework and regulation | Developing policies and regulations that promote technology adoption, data protection, cybersecurity, and interoperability. Establishing standards and guidelines for the implementation of new technologies |
| Digital skills development | Investing in programs to enhance digital literacy and skills development among government employees, citizens, and businesses. Providing training opportunities and resources to foster technology proficiency |
| Funding for research and innovation | Allocating grants and funds to support research and innovation in emerging technologies. Encouraging collaboration among academia, industry, and government agencies to drive technological advancements |
| Collaboration with tech industry | Forging partnerships and collaborations with technology companies to leverage their expertise, resources, and innovative solutions. Engaging in public-private partnerships to co-create and implement technology initiatives |
| Open data initiatives | Launching open data initiatives to promote transparency and accessibility of government data. Establishing platforms for sharing public data and fostering data-driven innovation by citizens and businesses |
| Digital transformation projects | Initiating and implementing digital transformation projects within government agencies to modernize processes, improve service delivery, and optimize resource allocation |
| Cybersecurity and data privacy measures | Implementing robust cybersecurity measures and data privacy regulations to safeguard government systems, infrastructure, and citizen data. Ensuring compliance with international standards and best practices |
| Collaboration with international bodies | Engaging with international organizations and participating in global initiatives to share best practices, exchange knowledge, and align technology adoption strategies with international standards |
| Regulatory sandboxes | Establishing regulatory sandboxes or innovation labs to provide a controlled environment for testing and experimenting with new technologies. Facilitating innovation while ensuring compliance with regulations |

Efficiency and effectiveness: New technologies can streamline government processes, making them more efficient and effective. Automation, data analytics, and artificial intelligence (AI) can help optimize operations, reduce paperwork, and improve decision-making, leading to better service delivery and resource management [11].

Transparency and accountability: Technology can enhance transparency in governance by providing real-time access to information and public data. Through online portals and open data initiatives, citizens can access government information, budgets, and project updates, fostering trust and accountability in the government's actions.

Enhanced public services: Adopting new technology allows governments to offer innovative and personalized public services to citizens. E-government initiatives can facilitate online interactions, allowing citizens to access services, apply for permits, and pay taxes conveniently, saving time and resources for both citizens and government agencies.

Data-driven decision-making: New technologies enable data collection, analysis, and visualization, empowering policymakers with valuable insights for evidence-based decision-making. Big data and predictive analytics can help anticipate and address emerging challenges and opportunities proactively.

Digital inclusion: Supporting the adoption of new technology can bridge the digital divide and promote digital inclusion. Governments can work toward providing digital literacy programs and ensuring that all citizens have equal access to technology and online services.

Economic growth and innovation: Embracing new technology fosters innovation and attracts investment, driving economic growth in both the public and private sectors. Governments that actively promote technology adoption can become hubs for tech startups, research, and development, creating a thriving ecosystem for innovation.

Resilience and preparedness: New technology can enhance governance's ability to respond to crises and emergencies effectively. Digital communication tools, data analysis, and remote collaboration platforms can be vital in disaster management and public safety planning.

Environmental sustainability: Technology adoption can contribute to environmental sustainability efforts. Governments can leverage smart city initiatives, IoT devices, and data-driven policies to optimize energy usage, reduce waste, and promote eco-friendly practices.

Collaborative governance: Technology facilitates collaborative governance by enabling seamless communication and coordination among different government agencies, departments, and stakeholders. This integrated approach can lead to more cohesive policies and services.

International competitiveness: Governments that embrace new technology gain a competitive edge in the global landscape. By adopting cutting-edge technologies, they can attract foreign investments, partnerships, and collaborations, enhancing their global standing and influence [12].

### 8.2.1.10 Adopted technology

Individuals' first-time adoption of new technologies may be explained using a variety of technology acceptance models. Because the fog-computing paradigm is still in its infancy, it may be hypothesized that its adoption should be well researched and prepared prior to its implementation. Fog computing has not been studied to any significant level in any setting, it can also be argued, in terms of variables affecting individual adoption.

Cloud computing: Governments adopt cloud computing to improve data storage, scalability, and accessibility. Cloud-based solutions enable governments to store and manage vast amounts of data securely, reduce infrastructure costs, and facilitate collaboration across departments.

IoT: Governments utilize IoT technologies to enhance public services and infra-structure management. IoT devices, such as smart sensors and meters, enable real-time monitoring of traffic, waste management, energy consumption, and public safety, leading to more efficient resource allocation and improved quality of life for citizens.

AI: Governments leverage AI to automate processes, analyze data, and provide personalized services. AI-powered chatbots assist citizens in accessing information and services, while machine learning algorithms help detect patterns, optimize resource allocation, and enhance decision-making in areas like healthcare, trans-portation, and public safety.

Blockchain: Governments adopt blockchain technology for secure and trans-parent transactions, identity verification, and record keeping. Blockchain ensures the integrity and immutability of data, making it useful for applications such as land registry, voting systems, supply chain management, and public financial transactions.

Open data platforms: Governments establish open data platforms to make public datasets accessible to citizens, researchers, and businesses. By providing access to structured and machine-readable data, governments promote transpar-ency, encourage innovation, and enable the development of data-driven applica-tions and services.

Mobile applications: Governments develop mobile applications to deliver services and engage with citizens conveniently. Mobile apps allow citizens to access information, submit applications, make payments, and provide feedback, enhancing the accessibility and responsiveness of government services [13].

Geospatial technologies: Governments utilize geospatial technologies, such as geographic information systems (GISs), to analyze and visualize spatial data for urban planning, disaster management, environmental protection, and infrastructure development. Geospatial data help governments make informed decisions and optimize resource allocation.

Robotic process automation (RPA): Governments adopt RPA to automate repe-titive tasks and streamline workflows. RPA software bots perform routine adminis-trative tasks, data entry, and data processing, freeing up government employees' time to focus on higher-value activities and improving operational efficiency.

AR and virtual reality (VR): Governments explore AR and VR technologies to enhance citizen engagement, training, and education. AR and VR applications enable immersive experiences, simulations, and virtual tours, facilitating public consultations, training programs, and interactive learning environments.

Cybersecurity technologies: Governments invest in advanced cybersecurity technologies to protect sensitive data, critical infrastructure, and digital systems from cyber threats. These technologies include intrusion detection and prevention systems, encryption tools, threat intelligence platforms, and security analytics solutions.

### 8.2.1.11 Construction measurement of fog computing

In fog computing, mathematical functions can be used to quantitatively measure and assess various aspects of the system's construction and performance.

Mathematical functions commonly used for construction measurement in fog computing:

Response time function: The response time function calculates the time taken for a fog node or the entire fog-computing system to process and respond to a request or task. It can be represented as a mathematical function that takes into account the processing time, communication delay, and queuing time.

Data transfer function: The data transfer function measures the rate at which data can be transmitted between fog nodes or between the fog nodes and end devices. It can be expressed as a mathematical function that considers factors such as bandwidth, latency, and data size.

Resource utilization function: The resource utilization function quantifies the extent to which fog-computing resources, such as processing power, memory, and storage, are being utilized. It can be represented as a mathematical function that calculates the ratio of used resources to available resources.

Energy efficiency function: The energy efficiency function evaluates the energy consumption and efficiency of the fog-computing system. It can be expressed as a mathematical function that considers the power consumption of the fog nodes, data transmission energy, and the achieved performance or throughput.

Reliability function: The reliability function assesses the reliability and availability of the fog-computing system. It can be represented as a mathematical function that calculates metrics such as mean time between failures (MTBF), mean time to repair (MTTR), and overall system uptime.

Scalability function: The scalability function measures the ability of the fog-computing system to handle increasing workloads and accommodate a growing number of devices and applications. It can be expressed as a mathematical function that considers factors such as processing capacity, network bandwidth, and the number of connected devices.

Security function: The security function quantifies the level of security provided by the fog-computing system. It can be represented as a mathematical function that calculates metrics such as the probability of successful attacks, the effectiveness of encryption algorithms, and the level of access control.

Cost function: The cost function evaluates the economic efficiency and cost-effectiveness of implementing and operating the fog-computing system. It can be expressed as a mathematical function that considers factors such as initial investment, maintenance costs, energy consumption, and cost savings achieved through resource optimization.

### 8.2.1.12    Aspects of organization

Aspects of organization refer to key elements or components that are essential for the functioning and structure of an organization. These aspects shape the organization's operations, culture, and overall effectiveness.

Structure: The structure of an organization defines how tasks, roles, and responsibilities are organized and distributed within the organization. It includes factors such as the hierarchy, reporting lines, departments, and coordination mechanisms. The structure influences communication, decision-making processes, and the overall flow of work within the organization.

Strategy: The strategic aspect of an organization involves defining its long-term goals, objectives, and the approach to achieve them. It includes elements such as mission and vision statements, strategic planning, goal setting, and the allocation of resources to align the organization's activities with its broader purpose. A clear and well-defined strategy provides direction and guides decision-making throughout the organization.

Culture: Organizational culture represents the shared values, beliefs, norms, and behaviors that shape the collective identity of the organization. It influences how individuals within the organization interact, make decisions, and collaborate. A strong and positive organizational culture can foster employee engagement, innovation, and a sense of belonging, contributing to overall organizational success [14].

Processes and procedures: Processes and procedures define the systematic approach to carrying out tasks and activities within the organization. They provide guidelines and steps for executing specific functions, ensuring consistency, efficiency, and quality in the organization's operations. Well-defined processes and procedures help streamline work, enhance productivity, and enable effective coordination among different teams and departments.

Human resources: The human resources aspect focuses on the management and development of the organization's workforce. It includes activities such as recruitment, training and development, performance management, and employee engagement. Effective human resource management ensures that the organization has the right people with the necessary skills, knowledge, and motivation to achieve its goals.

Communication: Communication plays a crucial role in organizational effectiveness. It involves the exchange of information, ideas, and feedback among individuals and groups within the organization. Clear and effective communication promotes understanding, collaboration, and coordination, enabling employees to work together toward common objectives.

Technology and infrastructure: The technological and infrastructural aspects encompass the tools, systems, and physical resources that support the organization's operations. It includes technologies such as information systems, hardware, software, and communication networks. An organization's technology and infrastructure should be aligned with its objectives and processes, enabling efficient and effective functioning.

Leadership and management: Leadership and management are essential aspects that guide and influence the organization's direction and performance. Effective leaders provide vision, inspire and motivate employees, and make strategic decisions. Managers ensure efficient operations, coordinate resources, and drive the execution of organizational plans. Strong leadership and management contribute to organizational success and employee engagement.

### 8.2.1.13 Top-down administrative backing

Top-down administrative backing refers to the support and endorsement provided by upper-level management or leadership within an organization for a particular initiative, project, or change. It signifies the commitment and involvement of senior leaders in driving the implementation and success of the initiative.

Leadership commitment: When senior leaders demonstrate their support and commitment to an initiative, it sends a clear message to the entire organization about its importance and priority. This commitment helps establish a sense of direction and purpose, motivating employees to actively engage and align their efforts toward the initiative's goals.

Resource allocation: Top-down administrative backing ensures the allocation of necessary resources, such as financial resources, technology, and human capital, to support the initiative. Senior leaders have the authority and influence to secure the required resources and prioritize them effectively. This resource allocation enables the initiative to progress smoothly and increases its chances of success.

Decision-making authority: Senior leaders hold decision-making authority within the organization. Their backing provides the initiative with the necessary decision-making power to overcome obstacles, make strategic choices, and drive progress. This authority expedites the decision-making process, reduces bureaucracy, and enables timely actions.

Organizational alignment: Top-down administrative backing facilitates organizational alignment and cohesion. When leaders endorse an initiative, it helps create a shared vision and common understanding throughout the organization. It encourages collaboration, cooperation, and consistent efforts toward achieving the initiative's objectives. This alignment minimizes conflicts, promotes teamwork, and enhances organizational effectiveness.

Change management: Implementing an initiative often involves change within the organization. Top-down administrative backing plays a crucial role in change management efforts. Leaders can communicate the need for change, address resistance, and promote a positive attitude towards the initiative. Their support lends credibility and helps overcome resistance to change, making the transition smoother and more successful.

Accountability and monitoring: Senior leaders' backing establishes a framework for accountability and monitoring. They set clear expectations, monitor progress, and hold individuals and teams accountable for their performance and contributions toward the initiative. This accountability fosters a culture of responsibility and ensures that the initiative remains on track.

Stakeholder influence: Senior leaders often have influence and relationships with various stakeholders, both internal and external to the organization. Their backing enables effective stakeholder engagement and communication. They can leverage their networks to garner support, manage relationships, and address concerns, ultimately enhancing the initiative's acceptance and impact.

### 8.2.1.14   Ability and instruction

The fog-computing environment can only be implemented and maintained if the necessary skills are in place. It is critical that the right skills and the right staff be put in place for managing the fog execution environment to realize its maximum capabilities. We want to make sure that we are putting the right people in the appropriate places. Untrained and unprepared users in an organization may have detrimental effects on fog-computing implementation. To guarantee a successful deployment, organizations must ensure that all participants are technologically prepared.

### 8.2.1.15 Reduced complicacy and customizability

There are a number of technical considerations that go into the adoption of fog computing, such as the degree to which users have confidence in the system. The user's viewpoint may be badly impacted by the technology's complexities when it comes to implementing it. The technology's connection, information security, and confidentiality are other issues to keep in mind. Technological adoption is hindered by poor technological infrastructures.

### 8.2.1.16 Infrastructure, connectivity, and availability

Repairing broken infrastructures and establishing reliable connections is a top priority. They observed that the application latencies for a system connected with sensor networks were much shorter than that for cloud computing, which is significant since infrastructural difficulties are typically linked with economic pressures that have a significant influence on innovation adoption. The accessibility of data at the edge is a crucial factor in determining whether to adopt fog computing, considering the decentralized architecture of the infrastructure on which fog computing works. Fog computing's ability to function normally and effectively is crucial if it is to fulfill its mission of providing reliable information to its users. The fog virtualization technology must be trustworthy and provide quick responses without interruptions if the services it provides to its end users are to be considered good quality.

### 8.2.1.17 Privacy and security

It is the responsibility of businesses to evaluate and understand the fog computing usage and to devise methods to deal with security concerns, including protecting the data, as well as data storage and recovery. To put it another way, when we say that fog computing operates "on the edge," we mean that it does so in proximity to the user. As previously said, it has become clear that the devices operating on the fog-computing system are not as secure as was previously believed. Cryptography and decryption may be used to deal with the problem of unauthorized access or attacks, albeit the use of minimal encryption techniques or masking approaches may be preferable. The solution addresses these concerns by placing an emphasis on policy-based resource management and access control for fog's ecosystem. This is necessary because of the various privacy and security concerns that arise from multi-level collaboration on multiple connected computers. Secure collaboration among various user-requested resources is enabled by policy-based management systems.

### 8.2.1.18 Aspects of the natural setting

Government laws and policies create obstacles to the adoption of new technology in healthcare services. If the government does not establish clear regulations and rules, new technology will not be adopted. There are implications for implementation, security, and privacy because of these policies. Because of the potential for data breaches, access, and sharing, organizations will be hesitant to use new technologies if the government does not offer clear guidance on how to comply with legislation and adhere to them.

Pressures from the market: Increasingly, organizations are fighting on a global stage and focused on how to stay competitive. It has become clear that this means using the "correct" technological solutions. When it comes to maintaining a position of strength in the global marketplace, new technologies play an important role. The government should take the lead in developing strategies for acquiring a competitive advantage while still operating within the constraints of the market or defending against the risks of the market. Additionally, it is important to be able to obtain knowledge about the competition in order to flourish, and flexible regulations and rules that do not limit technology adoption may aid in surviving the competition.

### 8.2.1.19    Location

Technology such as fog computing may be used based on the location or geographical area. Governments, including as those in South Africa, confront the problem of creating rules and rules that may ensure the safety of edge data transfers worldwide. Without international norms and laws, there is a chance for privacy and security concerns to arise.

### 8.2.1.20    Analysis sensor data formats in the smart cities

We began our investigation by looking for accessible to the public IoT projects across a wide range of industries. According to our search, three smart city programs have released open data from IoT sensors and other connected smart devices, all of which satisfied our requirements. Here, we go into great depth about these initiatives and their data.

### 8.2.1.21    Sensor data

The collection of sensor data involves the process of gathering information from various sensors deployed in different environments. Sensors are devices that detect and measure changes in physical properties, environmental conditions, or events, and convert them into electrical signals or digital data.

Sensor deployment: The first step is to strategically deploy sensors in the target environment. The placement and positioning of sensors depend on the specific application and the data to be collected. Sensors can be placed on equipment, infrastructure, buildings, vehicles, or even on living beings to capture relevant data.

Data acquisition: Sensors continuously monitor the environment or the targeted phenomena and collect raw data in the form of electrical signals, analog readings, or digital data. The data collected may include temperature, pressure, humidity, motion, sound, light, location, or any other parameter relevant to the application.

Data conversion: Analog sensor readings are usually converted into digital format for further processing and storage. Analog-to-digital converters are commonly used for this purpose. Digital sensors provide data directly in digital form, which simplifies data handling.

Data preprocessing: Raw sensor data may contain noise, outliers, or inconsistencies. Data preprocessing techniques, such as filtering, normalization, and data imputation, are applied to clean and prepare the data for analysis and interpretation.

Data storage: The collected and preprocessed sensor data are stored in databases or data repositories for easy access and retrieval. The choice of database technology depends on factors like data volume, access frequency, and data retention requirements.

Data transmission: In some cases, sensor data need to be transmitted in real time or near real time to centralized servers or cloud platforms for analysis and decision-making. Wireless communication protocols like Wi-Fi, Bluetooth, Zigbee, or cellular networks are commonly used for data transmission.

Data security: Sensor data often contains sensitive information. Ensuring data security and privacy is crucial during data collection, transmission, and storage. Encryption, authentication, and access control mechanisms are implemented to protect the data from unauthorized access.

Data analysis: Once the data are collected and stored, it can be subjected to various data analysis techniques, including statistical analysis, machine learning, and data visualization, to derive insights and patterns. Data analysis helps in making informed decisions and identifying trends or anomalies in the sensor data.

Real-time monitoring and control: In applications where real-time monitoring and control are required, the sensor data are processed and acted upon immediately to trigger automated responses or alerts.

Data retention and archiving: Depending on the application, sensor data may need to be retained for historical analysis or compliance purposes. Proper data archiving and backup strategies are implemented to ensure long-term data availability.

Table 8.2 provides an overview of various tools designed to work with sensor data. These tools are crucial for collecting, processing, and analyzing data from sensors in a wide range of applications, such as IoT, environmental monitoring, and industrial automation. The table includes software and hardware tools that cater to different stages of sensor data handling, including data acquisition devices, data visualization and analysis software, data management platforms, and development kits for building sensor-based applications. These tools play a vital role in harnessing the potential of sensor data, enabling researchers, engineers, and businesses to make informed decisions, optimize processes, and gain valuable insights from the vast amount of information collected by sensors in the modern world.

## 8.2.2 Sensor data in the CityPulse project

The CityPulse project is an initiative that focuses on the development of a data-driven platform for urban sensing and analytics. It aims to leverage sensor data and other urban data sources to gain insights into various aspects of city life and enable data-driven decision-making for urban planning and management.

*Table 8.2   Tools for working with sensor data*

| Tool | Description |
| --- | --- |
| Arduino | Open-source hardware and software platform for building electronic devices |
| Raspberry Pi | Credit card-sized single-board computer for sensor data collection and processing |
| MATLAB™ | Programming language and environment for data acquisition signal processing and analysis |
| LabVIEW | Graphical programming environment for measurement and automation applications |
| Apache Kafka | Distributed streaming platform for large-scale, real-time data streaming. |
| TensorFlow | Open-source machine learning framework for sensor data analysis and predictive modeling |
| Apache Spark | Data processing framework for real-time, stream, and batch processing of sensor data |
| Splunk | Data analytics platform for real-time data collection, indexing, and visualization |
| Microsoft Azure IoT Suite | Cloud-based platform for sensor data ingestion, storage, and analysis |

In the context of the CityPulse project, sensor data play a crucial role in capturing real-time information about different urban phenomena and environments. The project involves deploying a network of sensors throughout the city to collect data on various parameters. These sensors can include air quality sensors, noise sensors, weather sensors, traffic sensors, and other types of sensors relevant to urban monitoring.

The collected sensor data are then integrated into the CityPulse platform, which acts as a central hub for data storage, processing, and analysis. The platform combines sensor data with other urban data sources, such as social media data, transportation data, and municipal data, to provide a comprehensive view of the city.

The sensor data in the CityPulse project is used for several purposes, including:

Environmental monitoring: Sensor data are utilized to monitor environmental conditions in the city, such as air quality, noise levels, and weather patterns. This information helps identify areas of concern, assess the impact of environmental factors on citizens' well-being, and support initiatives for environmental improvement.

Traffic management: Sensor data from traffic sensors and other relevant sources are used to monitor traffic flow, detect congestion, and optimize traffic signal control. Real-time information about traffic conditions enables better traffic management and improves overall transportation efficiency.

Energy efficiency: Sensor data are leveraged to monitor energy consumption in buildings and public spaces. By analyzing energy usage patterns, the CityPulse platform can identify opportunities for energy conservation, optimize energy distribution, and support energy-efficient practices.

Urban planning: The sensor data provide valuable insights for urban planners and policymakers. It helps in understanding the usage patterns of urban spaces, identifying areas that require infrastructure improvements, and making informed decisions regarding urban development and resource allocation.

Citizen engagement: The sensor data in the CityPulse project are often made accessible to citizens, through either public displays or mobile applications. By providing real-time information about the city's conditions, citizens can be more informed and engaged in their surroundings, enabling them to make choices that align with their preferences and well-being.

Python Algorithm

```python
import requests
import json
# Example API endpoint for sensor data
sensor_data_url = "https://api.citypulse.io/sensors"

def collect_sensor_data():
    response = requests.get(sensor_data_url)
    if response.status_code == 200:
        sensor_data = json.loads(response.text)
        # Process the sensor data
        for data_point in sensor_data:
            sensor_id = data_point['sensor_id']
            value - data_point['value']
            timestamp = data_point['timestamp']
            # Perform further analysis or store the data
                # Example: Print the sensor data
            print(f"Sensor ID: {sensor_id}, Value: {value}, Timestamp: {timestamp}")
    else:
            print(f"Error accessing sensor data. Status code: {response.status_code}")
    # Run the function to collect and process the sensor data
    collect_sensor_data()
```

## 8.2.3   Sensor data in the smart city

In a smart city context, sensor data play a vital role in capturing real-time information about various aspects of urban life. It enables the city to gather data on environmental conditions, traffic patterns, energy consumption, public safety, and more. These data are then used to improve the quality of life for citizens, enhance city services, and optimize resource allocation.

Environmental monitoring: Sensors can be deployed to measure air quality, noise levels, temperature, humidity, and other environmental parameters. These data help monitor pollution levels, identify areas with poor air quality, and support initiatives for environmental improvement.

Smart traffic management: Traffic sensors and cameras collect data on traffic flow, congestion, and parking availability. This information is used to optimize traffic signal timings, guide drivers to available parking spaces, and improve overall transportation efficiency.

Waste management: Smart waste management systems utilize sensors in trash bins to monitor their fill levels. These data enable more efficient waste collection routes, reducing unnecessary pickups, and optimizing resource utilization.

Energy efficiency: Sensors can be installed in buildings to monitor energy consumption, occupancy levels, and environmental conditions. These data help identify energy-saving opportunities, optimize heating and cooling systems, and promote sustainable energy usage.

Public safety: Sensors can be deployed to monitor public spaces for security purposes. Examples include video surveillance systems, gunshot detection sensors, and crowd monitoring sensors, which help enhance safety and enable quick response to incidents.

Water management: Sensors can monitor water levels in rivers, reservoirs, and drainage systems. These data help manage water resources, monitor flood risks, and improve the efficiency of water distribution and drainage systems.

Smart lighting: Sensors, such as motion sensors or ambient light sensors, can control streetlights, adjusting their brightness based on real-time conditions. This improves energy efficiency and ensures appropriate lighting levels in different areas of the city.

Public health monitoring: Sensor data can be used to monitor public health indicators, such as monitoring air quality to identify potential health risks or tracking the spread of diseases through crowd density sensors and temperature monitoring.

Parking management: Sensors can be deployed in parking lots or street parking spaces to detect vehicle occupancy. This information is used to guide drivers to available parking spaces and reduce congestion caused by circling vehicles.

Noise monitoring: Noise sensors placed in strategic locations can monitor noise levels and identify areas with excessive noise pollution. These data help in enforcing noise regulations, planning urban development, and improving the overall quality of the urban environment.

Some commonly used tools: IoT platforms: AWS IoT Core: A cloud-based platform by Amazon Web Services that offers services for managing and analyzing sensor data in real-time.

Microsoft Azure IoT Hub: A fully managed cloud service by Microsoft for connecting, monitoring, and managing IoT devices and their data.

Google Cloud IoT Core: A scalable and secure cloud-based IoT platform by Google for collecting, analyzing, and managing sensor data.

Data analytics and visualization: Tableau: A powerful data visualization tool that enables intuitive visual representations of sensor data and facilitates data exploration.

Power BI: A business analytics tool by Microsoft that offers interactive dashboards and visualizations for sensor data analysis.

Grafana: An open-source platform for creating real-time dashboards and visualizations, often used for monitoring and analyzing sensor data.

Time-series databases: InfluxDB: A high-performance, open-source time-series database that efficiently stores and retrieves time-stamped sensor data.

TimescaleDB: An open-source time-series database built on top of PostgreSQL, designed for handling large volumes of time-series data.

Edge computing platforms:

Apache Kafka: A distributed streaming platform that can be used to collect, process, and analyze sensor data in real time.

Apache NiFi: A data integration platform that enables the collection, transformation, and routing of sensor data across various systems.

Machine learning and AI:

TensorFlow: An open-source machine-learning framework that can be used for analyzing sensor data and building predictive models.

Scikit-learn: A machine learning library in Python that provides various algorithms for classification, regression, and clustering, which can be applied to sensor data analysis.

Microsoft Azure Machine Learning: A cloud-based machine learning service that offers tools and infrastructure for building and deploying machine learning models on sensor data.

Geospatial analysis:

ArcGIS: A comprehensive platform by Esri for working with geospatial data, including sensor data with location information.

QGIS: An open-source GIS that supports the visualization and analysis of sensor data in a spatial context.

## 8.3 Pre-cleaned datasets for exploration in the Internet of Things, fog, and cloud

Exploring datasets related to the IoT, fog computing, and cloud computing can provide valuable insights and enable research and development in these domains.

IoT sensor datasets:

Numenta Anomaly Benchmark (NAB): A benchmark dataset containing real-world sensor data collected from various sources, including temperature, humidity, power consumption, and more. It is commonly used for anomaly detection and time series analysis.

UC Irvine Machine Learning Repository: This repository provides a variety of datasets suitable for IoT analysis, including sensor data related to environmental monitoring, energy consumption, and activity recognition.

Fog-computing datasets:

FED4IoT dataset: This dataset is part of the FED4IoT project and includes real-world data collected from multiple IoT deployments across different domains, such as smart cities and agriculture.

SENSEI IoT dataset: A dataset collected from a real-world IoT deployment in a smart city environment, containing sensor readings from different types of devices and sensors.

Cloud computing datasets:

CloudSat: A dataset containing cloud profiling radar measurements collected by the CloudSat satellite. It provides detailed information about cloud properties and atmospheric conditions, supporting research in cloud computing and meteorology.

Google cluster data: A dataset released by Google that provides information on the usage patterns of their data centers. It includes resource consumption metrics, job information, and machine usage statistics.

General IoT and cloud datasets: Kaggle IoT datasets: Kaggle is a platform that hosts various datasets related to IoT, fog computing, and cloud computing. It provides a wide range of datasets across different domains and applications, allowing you to explore and analyze real-world data.

UCI machine learning repository: This repository offers numerous datasets suitable for exploring various aspects of IoT and cloud computing, including energy consumption, smart home monitoring, and activity recognition.

## 8.4    Conclusion

In conclusion, the development of fog computing using sensor data presents a significant opportunity to address the challenges of data processing, latency, heterogeneity, and scalability in the context of the IoT. By bringing computation closer to the data source, fog computing enables real-time analytics, faster response times, and improved system performance. Through a comprehensive methodology involving literature review, case studies, and empirical analyses, this study has shed light on the potential of fog computing in harnessing sensor data. The findings emphasize the ability of fog computing to reduce latency by processing data locally at the edge, thereby enhancing overall system efficiency. Furthermore, the enhanced heterogeneity of fog computing allows for seamless integration of diverse sensor devices, enabling efficient data collection and aggregation from various sources. This aspect ensures that fog computing can effectively handle the growing complexity and diversity of sensor data generated in IoT environments. The practical implications of fog computing using sensor data are noteworthy. Real-time analytics and decision-making become feasible, leading to improved operational efficiency, enhanced user experiences, and cost savings. Additionally, fog computing reduces reliance on cloud resources, minimizing data transfer and storage costs, while addressing privacy and security concerns.

## References

[1]    M. Sharifi, S. Kafaie, and O. Kashefi, A Survey and Taxonomy of Cyber Foraging of Mobile Devices, *IEEE Communications Surveys and Tutorials*, 14, 1232–1243, 2012.

[2]   M. Satyanarayanan, A Brief History of Cloud Offload: A Personal Journey from Odyssey Through Cyber Foraging to Cloudlets, *GetMobile: Mobile Computing and Communications*, 18, 19–23, 2015.

[3]   K. Ha, P. Pillai, W. Richter, Y. Abe, and M. Satyanarayanan, Just-Intime Provisioning for Cyber Foraging, in *Proceeding of the 11th Annual International Conference on Mobile Systems, Applications, and Services*, New York, USA, 2013, pp. 153–166.

[4]   M. Satyanarayanan, P. Bahl, R. Caceres, and N. Davies, The Case for VM-Based Cloudlets in Mobile Computing, *IEEE Pervasive Computing*, 8, 14–23, 2009.

[5]   E. Ahmed, A. Akhunzada, M. Whaiduzzaman, A. Gani, S. H. Ab Hamid, and R. Buyya, Network-Centric Performance Analysis of Runtime Application Migration in Mobile Cloud Computing, *Simulation Modelling Practice and Theory*, 50, 42–56, 2015.

[6]   W. Shi and S. Dustdar, The Promise of Edge Computing, *Computer*, 49, 78–81, 2016.

[7]   J. Pan and J. McElhannon, Future Edge Cloud and Edge Computing for Internet of Things Applications, *IEEE Internet of Things Journal*, 5, 439–449, 2017.

[8]   M. Patel, J. Joubert, J. R. Ramos, N. Sprecher, S. Abeta, and A. Neal, Mobile-Edge Computing Introductory Technical White Paper, in: *Mobile-Edge Computing (MEC) Industry Initiative*, 2014.

[9]   P. Chithaluru, AL-Turjman Fadi, Manoj Kumar, and Thompson Stephan, Computational intelligence inspired adaptive opportunistic clustering approach for industrial IoT networks. *IEEE Internet of Things Journal*, 2023.

[10]  D. Sabella, A. Vaillant, P. Kuure, U. Rauschenbach, and F. Giust, Mobile-Edge Computing Architecture: The Role of MEC in the Internet of Things, *IEEE Consumer Electronics Magazine*, 5, 84–91, 2016.

[11]  Y. C. Hu, M. Patel, D. Sabella, N. Sprecher, and V. Young, Mobile Edge Computing A key technology towards 5G, in: *ETSI (European Telecommunications Standards Institute)*, Sep, 2015.

[12]  P. Habibi, S. Baharlooei, M. Farhoudi, S. Kazemian, and S. Khorsandi, Virtualized SDN- Based End-to-End Reference Architecture for Fog Networking, in *32nd International Conference on Advanced Information Networking and Applications Workshops (WAINA)*, 2018, pp. 61–66.

[13]  Z. Pang, L. Sun, Z. Wang, E. Tian, and S. Yang, A Survey of Cloudlet Based Mobile Computing, in *International Conference on Cloud Computing and Big Data (CCBD)*, 2015, pp. 268–275.

[14]  S. Yi, Z. Hao, Z. Qin, and Q. Li, Fog Computing: Platform and Applications, in *Third IEEE Workshop on Hot Topics in Web Systems and Technologies (HotWeb)*, 2015, pp. 73–78.

*Chapter 9*

# Information sharing on mobile IoT-based content aware smart home with fog computing

## Abstract

The emerging paradigm of fog computing has gained significant attention in recent years due to its ability to enable efficient and real-time data processing at the network edge. In this chapter, we explore the application of fog computing in the context of information sharing on a mobile Internet of Things (IoT)-based content-aware smart home.

**Background:** The proliferation of IoT devices and the increasing demand for smart homes have generated massive amounts of data that require efficient processing and sharing mechanisms. Fog computing, as an extension of Cloud Computing, brings computation and storage capabilities closer to the edge of the network, enabling faster and more localized data processing. Mobile IoT devices play a crucial role in smart home environments, facilitating data exchange and communication among various smart devices.

**Scope:** This study focuses on the design and implementation of an information-sharing framework that leverages the capabilities of fog computing for a mobile IoT-based content-aware smart home.

The framework aims to enable efficient data processing, content analysis, and sharing among different smart devices within the smart home environment. The study considers the challenges and opportunities associated with integrating fog computing into the existing infrastructure of a smart home.

**Problem definition:** The existing centralized cloud-based approaches for data processing and sharing in smart homes face challenges related to latency, bandwidth constraints, and scalability. The dynamic nature of smart home environments requires real-time decision-making and content-awareness to ensure optimal user experience and resource utilization. The need for secure and privacy-preserving information sharing in the context of a smart home raises concerns related to data integrity, authentication, and access control.

**Aim:** The primary aim of this research is to propose and evaluate a fog computing-based information-sharing framework that addresses the challenges associated with mobile IoT-based content-aware smart homes. The framework aims to improve data processing efficiency, reduce latency, and enhance content-awareness within the smart home environment. By leveraging the fog-computing paradigm, the study aims to enhance information sharing capabilities while ensuring data security, privacy, and user-centric control.

**Analysis/observation:** The integration of fog computing into a mobile IoT-based content-aware smart home environment provides significant benefits, including reduced latency, improved scalability, and enhanced privacy. By offloading computation tasks to fog nodes, the framework enables real-time content analysis and decision-making, leading to personalized user experiences and efficient resource utilization. The proposed framework highlights the potential of fog computing in transforming smart home environments by providing a decentralized, edge-based solution for information sharing, leading to a more responsive and intelligent ecosystem.

## 9.1　Introduction

With the rapid advancement of Internet of Things (IoT) technologies, smart homes have emerged as a promising domain for improving the quality of life and enhancing convenience for residents. Smart homes consist of interconnected devices and systems that enable automation, control, and monitoring of various aspects such as security, energy management, and entertainment. However, the proliferation of IoT devices in smart homes has led to the generation of massive amounts of data that require efficient processing and sharing mechanisms. Traditional approaches to data processing and sharing in smart homes typically rely on centralized cloud-based architectures. However, these approaches face challenges in terms of latency, bandwidth constraints, and scalability. Moreover, in a smart home environment, where real-time decision-making and content-awareness are crucial, relying solely on cloud-based solutions may result in delays and suboptimal user experiences [1].

To address these challenges, fog computing has emerged as a promising paradigm that extends the capabilities of cloud computing to the network edge. Fog computing brings computation, storage, and networking resources closer to the IoT devices and end-users, enabling faster and more localized data processing. By leveraging fog nodes deployed within the smart home environment, fog computing can significantly reduce latency and improve data processing efficiency. This chapter focuses on the application of fog computing in the context of information sharing on a mobile IoT-based content-aware smart home. The integration of mobile IoT devices, such as smartphones, tablets, and wearables, plays a crucial role in facilitating data exchange and communication between various smart devices within the smart home ecosystem. The aim is to design and implement an information-sharing framework that leverages the capabilities of fog computing to enable efficient data processing, content analysis, and sharing within the smart home environment.

The proposed framework aims to address the challenges associated with centralized cloud-based approaches by offloading computation tasks to fog nodes. This enables real-time content analysis, decision-making, and personalized user experiences while ensuring efficient resource utilization. Furthermore, the framework considers the importance of data security, privacy, and user-centric control, providing mechanisms for data integrity, authentication, and access control. Through this study, we aim to highlight the potential of fog computing in transforming smart home environments into more responsive and intelligent ecosystems. By bringing computation capabilities closer to the edge, fog computing provides a decentralized solution for information sharing, leading to enhanced data processing efficiency, reduced latency, improved scalability, and increased privacy [2].

## 9.2 Computation offloading

Computation offloading is a key concept within the realm of fog computing that plays a vital role in optimizing data processing and resource utilization in mobile IoT-based content-aware smart homes. It involves the transfer of computationally intensive tasks from resource-constrained IoT devices to more powerful fog nodes deployed at the network edge.

The motivation behind computation offloading stems from the limitations of IoT devices, which often have limited computational power, memory, and battery life. By offloading these resource-intensive tasks to fog nodes, which are equipped with more substantial computing capabilities, the burden on the IoT devices is reduced, resulting in improved performance and efficiency.

The process of computation offloading involves several steps. First, the IoT device identifies the tasks that can be offloaded, considering factors such as task complexity, available resources, and latency requirements. Next, the selected tasks are transmitted to the fog nodes for execution. The fog nodes process the tasks locally, leveraging their computational resources, and produce the desired outcomes or results. Finally, the results are sent back to the IoT devices for further processing or dissemination.

Computation offloading offers several benefits in the context of information sharing in mobile IoT-based content-aware smart homes. First, it reduces the latency associated with transmitting data to the cloud for processing, as the computation is performed locally at the fog nodes. This enables real-time decision-making and enhances the responsiveness of the smart home ecosystem.

Second, computation offloading optimizes resource utilization by distributing the computational load across multiple fog nodes. This helps in balancing the computational demands and prevents IoT devices from being overwhelmed, leading to improved energy efficiency and extended battery life.

Moreover, computation offloading enables content-awareness within the smart home environment. By offloading tasks related to content analysis, such as image recognition or natural language processing, to fog nodes, the smart home ecosystem gains the ability to understand and interpret the data generated by various IoT devices. This content-awareness facilitates personalized user experiences, context-based automation, and intelligent decision-making.

However, computation offloading also poses challenges. It requires efficient task offloading mechanisms and decision-making algorithms to determine which tasks should be offloaded and to which fog node they should be assigned. Factors such as network conditions, fog node availability, and task characteristics need to be considered for effective offloading decisions. Furthermore, ensuring the security and privacy of the offloaded tasks and data becomes crucial, as sensitive information may be involved [3].

## 9.3    Result routing

Result routing is a critical aspect within the domain of fog computing that deals with the efficient dissemination and delivery of computation results in mobile IoT-based content-aware smart homes. Once the computation offloading process is complete and fog nodes generate the desired outcomes or results, result routing mechanisms come into play to ensure that these results are transmitted to the appropriate destinations within the smart home ecosystem.

The objective of result routing is to deliver the computation results to the intended recipients or devices while considering factors such as latency, network conditions, data prioritization, and destination availability. It involves making decisions regarding the optimal paths and protocols for transmitting the results, taking into account the characteristics and requirements of the smart home environment.

Result routing mechanisms typically consider the following aspects:

**Network topology:** Understanding the network topology of the smart home environment is crucial for efficient result routing. This includes identifying the fog nodes, IoT devices, and other network components, as well as their connectivity and relationships. By leveraging the knowledge of the network topology, routing decisions can be made based on proximity, network congestion, and available bandwidth.

**Quality of service (QoS) requirements:** Different IoT devices or applications within the smart home ecosystem may have varying QoS requirements for result delivery. For instance, real-time applications such as video streaming or security systems may demand low latency and high reliability. Result routing mechanisms take these requirements into account to ensure that the results are delivered in a timely manner with the desired QoS parameters.

**Load balancing:** Result routing aims to distribute the transmission load evenly across the network to prevent bottlenecks and congestion. Load balancing mechanisms ensure that the network resources are utilized efficiently by considering factors such as the current load on fog nodes, available bandwidth, and the number of recipients.

**Data prioritization:** In scenarios where multiple computation results are generated concurrently, result routing mechanisms may prioritize the transmission of certain data based on urgency or importance. For example, critical security alerts may be prioritized over less time-sensitive data. Prioritization mechanisms ensure that important results are delivered promptly, while noncritical results can be transmitted with lower priority [4].

**Fault tolerance:** Result routing mechanisms account for network failures or node unavailability. They incorporate fault tolerance strategies to handle such situations and ensure reliable result delivery. This may involve rerouting the results through alternative paths or leveraging redundancy to mitigate the impact of network disruptions.

## 9.4 Load balancing and efficient deployment

Balancing workloads and optimal resource allocation are crucial aspects within fog computing that play a significant role in maximizing the efficiency and performance of mobile IoT-based content-aware smart homes. These processes involve distributing computational tasks and allocating resources in a manner that ensures workload balance, minimizes resource contention, and optimizes overall system performance.

Workload balancing focuses on evenly distributing computational tasks across the available fog nodes in the smart home environment. The goal is to prevent overloading of certain nodes, while others remain underutilized. By achieving workload balance, the system can make efficient use of computational resources, minimize response times, and avoid bottlenecks. Workload balancing algorithms consider factors such as task characteristics, node capabilities, and current resource utilization to determine the most suitable fog node for task allocation.

Optimal resource allocation aims to assign resources, such as computational power, memory, and storage, to different tasks and fog nodes in a manner that maximizes overall system performance. It involves dynamically allocating resources based on task requirements, node capabilities, and system conditions. Resource allocation algorithms consider factors such as task priorities, node capacities, and current resource utilization to make informed decisions about resource allocation. By optimizing resource allocation, the system can enhance efficiency, meet QoS requirements, and achieve better utilization of available resources.

The benefits of balancing workloads and optimal resource allocation in mobile IoT-based content-aware smart homes are numerous. These include in the following:

**Improved performance:** By balancing workloads and allocating resources optimally, the system can ensure that computational tasks are processed efficiently. This leads to reduced response times, improved throughput, and enhanced overall system performance.

**Resource efficiency:** Balancing workloads and allocating resources optimally prevent overutilization or underutilization of resources. These result in better resource utilization, reduced wastage, and improved energy efficiency, which is particularly important in resource-constrained IoT environments.

**QoS guarantee:** By considering task priorities and resource availability, workload balancing and optimal resource allocation mechanisms can prioritize critical tasks and allocate resources accordingly. This helps in meeting QoS requirements, such as low latency or high reliability, and ensures that important tasks receive adequate resources for timely execution.

**Scalability:** Balancing workloads and optimizing resource allocation enable scalability in smart home environments. As the number of IoT devices and computational tasks increase, the system can dynamically distribute tasks and resources to accommodate the growing demands, ensuring that performance remains consistent.

To achieve effective workload balancing and optimal resource allocation, various algorithms and techniques can be employed. These include load balancing algorithms, resource provisioning mechanisms, and dynamic resource allocation strategies. The selection and implementation of these methods depend on the specific characteristics, requirements, and constraints of the smart home environment.

## 9.5    Mobility-aware edge computing

Edge computing with a focus on mobility is a critical aspect within the domain of fog computing that addresses the challenges and opportunities of processing and managing data at the network edge, particularly in dynamic and mobile environments such as mobile IoT-based content-aware smart homes. Edge computing refers to the paradigm of moving computational tasks and data processing closer to the edge of the network, where the data are generated and consumed.

In the context of mobile IoT-based smart homes, where devices and users are constantly on the move, edge computing becomes particularly relevant. It aims to bring computation, storage, and networking resources closer to the devices, enabling faster response times, reduced latency, and enhanced user experiences. By leveraging edge nodes, such as fog nodes or gateway devices, computation can be performed locally, minimizing the need for data transmission to remote servers or the cloud [5].

The mobility aspect of edge computing in smart homes introduces additional challenges and considerations. For instance, devices may join or leave the network frequently, leading to changes in network topology and resource availability. Mobility management mechanisms need to be in place to track the movement of devices, ensure seamless connectivity, and handle handovers between different edge nodes.

Moreover, mobility-aware task scheduling and resource allocation techniques play a vital role in optimizing the performance of mobile IoT-based smart homes. These techniques consider factors such as device mobility patterns, network conditions, and real-time resource availability to make informed decisions about task placement, load balancing, and resource allocation. By considering mobility, these techniques can adapt and adjust computation and resource allocation dynamically, ensuring efficient utilization of available resources [6].

Edge computing with a focus on mobility offers several advantages in the context of information sharing in mobile IoT-based content-aware smart homes:

Reduced latency: By processing data and performing computations at the network edge, closer to the devices generating the data, edge computing significantly reduces latency. This enables real-time or near-real-time response, which is crucial for time-sensitive applications and services in smart homes.

Enhanced privacy and security: Edge computing allows data to be processed locally, reducing the need for transmitting sensitive information to remote servers or the cloud. This enhances privacy and security by minimizing the exposure of data to potential risks or breaches during transmission.

Improved resource efficiency: Edge computing enables localized processing and resource utilization, reducing the need for continuous data transmission and reducing network congestion. This results in improved resource efficiency, reduced bandwidth consumption, and optimized energy consumption in mobile IoT-based smart homes.

To leverage the benefits of edge computing with a focus on mobility, various technologies and protocols can be employed. These include edge-based analytics frameworks, mobility management protocols, and mobility-aware task scheduling algorithms. Additionally, integration with existing mobility management mechanisms in cellular networks or wireless Local area network (LANs) can further enhance the mobility support in smart home environments.

## 9.6   System design

System design plays a pivotal role in enabling effective information sharing in mobile IoT-based content-aware smart homes with fog computing. It involves the overall architectural planning, component selection, and integration of various elements to create a cohesive and efficient system that leverages the capabilities of fog computing for information sharing.

The system design for information sharing in mobile IoT-based smart homes typically encompasses the following key aspects:

**Architecture:** The system design begins with defining the architectural framework that outlines the structure and organization of the smart home ecosystem. This includes identifying the components involved, such as IoT devices, fog nodes, gateways, and cloud servers. The architectural design also considers the communication protocols and interfaces required for seamless data exchange and sharing between these components.

**Computation offloading:** The system design incorporates mechanisms for computation offloading, which involve transferring computationally intensive tasks from IoT devices to fog nodes. This requires determining the criteria for task offloading, such as task complexity, resource availability, and latency requirements. The design also includes protocols and algorithms for efficient task identification, offloading, and result retrieval.

**Data management:** Effective information sharing relies on proper data management strategies. The system design encompasses data collection, storage, and processing mechanisms. It includes decisions on data formats, data models, and database technologies suitable for capturing and managing diverse types of data generated by IoT devices. The design also considers data security and privacy requirements, ensuring appropriate measures for data encryption, access control, and data integrity.

**Edge analytics:** To enable content-awareness and real-time decision-making, the system design incorporates edge analytics capabilities. This involves integrating algorithms and techniques for analyzing and extracting insights from data at the edge. Design considerations include selecting suitable analytics models, ensuring efficient data preprocessing, and optimizing computational resources for analytics tasks.

**Communication and networking:** The system design addresses the communication and networking infrastructure required for information sharing. It includes selecting appropriate wireless communication technologies, such as Wi-Fi or Bluetooth, for device connectivity. Design decisions also cover network protocols, routing mechanisms, and QoS considerations to ensure reliable and timely data transmission.

**User interface and interaction:** A well-designed user interface is crucial for facilitating user interactions and information sharing in smart homes. The system design includes considerations for intuitive user interfaces, responsive design, and user-friendly interactions. This involves designing user interfaces for mobile devices, web interfaces, or voice-based interfaces, depending on the user preferences and device capabilities.

**Scalability and extensibility:** The system design takes into account the scalability and extensibility of the smart home ecosystem. It allows for the seamless addition of new IoT devices, fog nodes, or services to accommodate the evolving needs of the users. Design decisions may include using modular and scalable architectures, standardized interfaces, and open Application program interface (APIs) to enable interoperability and easy integration of new components.

## 9.6.1    Selection of potential employees

The selection of potential employees is a critical process for organizations aiming to build a skilled and talented workforce to support their objectives in the context of information sharing on mobile IoT-based content-aware smart homes with fog computing. The selection process involves a series of steps and considerations to identify individuals who possess the right qualifications, capabilities, and attributes necessary for the available positions.

Job analysis: Before initiating the selection process, it is essential to conduct a comprehensive job analysis. This involves understanding the specific requirements, responsibilities, and competencies associated with the job role. Job analysis helps in developing a clear understanding of the skills, knowledge, and experience needed for effective information sharing in the context of mobile IoT-based content-aware smart homes.

Job advertisement: To attract potential employees, organizations need to create compelling job advertisements that accurately reflect the requirements of the position. The advertisement should highlight the unique aspects of working in a mobile IoT-based content-aware smart home environment with a focus on fog computing. It should effectively communicate the skills and qualifications sought, as well as the organization's values and culture.

Application screening: The initial step in the selection process involves reviewing and screening applications received from prospective candidates. Screening focuses on assessing candidates' qualifications, experience, and alignment with the job requirements specified in the advertisement. The screening process helps in shortlisting candidates who possess the necessary qualifications for further evaluation.

Interviews: Interviews are a crucial element of the selection process. They provide an opportunity to assess candidates' suitability, competencies, and potential to contribute to information sharing in mobile IoT-based content-aware smart homes. Different interview formats, such as structured, behavioral, or panel interviews, can be employed to gather relevant information and evaluate candidates' technical skills, problem-solving abilities, and interpersonal capabilities.

Technical assessments: Given the specific nature of information sharing in mobile IoT-based content-aware smart homes, technical assessments can be employed to evaluate candidates' knowledge and proficiency in relevant areas. These assessments may include coding tests, problem-solving scenarios, or simulations to gauge candidates' abilities to work with IoT devices, fog-computing architectures, and data processing frameworks.

Behavioral assessments: In addition to technical skills, behavioral assessments play a crucial role in evaluating candidates' interpersonal skills, communication abilities, and adaptability. These assessments help identify candidates who can work effectively in teams, collaborate with stakeholders, and handle the dynamic nature of mobile IoT-based content-aware smart home environments [7].

Reference checks: Reference checks involve contacting the references provided by the candidates to gather insights into their past performance, work ethics, and interpersonal skills. These checks help verify the information provided by candidates and assess their compatibility with the organization's requirements. References can provide valuable perspectives on candidates' abilities, work style, and overall suitability for the position.

Decision making: Based on the information gathered through interviews, technical and behavioral assessments, and reference checks, the decision-making stage involves evaluating candidates and selecting the most suitable individuals. The decision-making process should be fair, transparent, and based on objective criteria aligned with the job requirements and the organization's goals.

Onboarding: Once the selection decision is made, the onboarding process begins. Onboarding involves introducing the selected candidates to the organization, providing them with necessary information, and facilitating their integration into the mobile IoT-based content-aware smart home environment. This includes orientation, training, and familiarization with the specific tools, technologies, and processes used in the organization.

## 9.6.2 Networking with coworkers

Networking with coworkers is an essential aspect of professional growth and success in the context of information sharing on mobile IoT-based content-aware smart homes with fog computing. Effective networking allows individuals to build strong relationships, collaborate, share knowledge, and create a supportive work environment. It facilitates the exchange of ideas, fosters innovation, and enhances productivity within the organization. Here are key aspects to consider when networking with coworkers:

**Building relationships:** Networking begins with establishing and nurturing relationships with coworkers. Actively engage with colleagues, show genuine interest in their work, and be approachable and friendly. Attend team meetings, social events, and other networking opportunities to connect with coworkers on both professional and personal levels. Building positive relationships creates a supportive and collaborative work environment conducive to effective information sharing.

**Communication and collaboration:** Effective communication is vital for networking with coworkers. Be open and transparent in your communication, actively listen to others' perspectives, and provide constructive feedback. Collaborate on projects, share ideas, and seek opportunities to work together. By fostering a culture of collaboration and knowledge exchange, you can enhance information sharing and drive innovation within the organization.

**Sharing expertise:** Networking offers a platform to share your expertise and learn from others. Actively contribute your knowledge and skills to help coworkers address challenges or find solutions. Offer assistance and support to colleagues when needed. Similarly, seek opportunities to learn from coworkers by engaging in discussions, asking questions, and participating in knowledge-sharing initiatives. By sharing expertise and encouraging a learning culture, you can enhance information sharing and professional growth within the organization.

**Professional development:** Networking with coworkers can provide valuable opportunities for professional development. Seek mentors or senior colleagues who can provide guidance and support your career growth. Attend workshops, seminars, and training programs together with coworkers to enhance your skills and knowledge. Engaging in professional development activities together fosters a sense of shared growth and encourages continuous learning.

**Online collaboration tools:** In the context of mobile IoT-based content-aware smart homes, leveraging online collaboration tools is crucial for effective networking. Utilize platforms such as project management tools, communication apps, and shared document repositories to collaborate, exchange information, and stay connected with coworkers. These tools enable seamless communication and information sharing, regardless of physical location.

**Cross-functional collaboration:** Networking should extend beyond immediate team members to include individuals from different departments or teams within the organization. Engage with coworkers from diverse backgrounds, as they may offer unique perspectives and insights. Collaborating with colleagues from different functional areas fosters interdisciplinary knowledge exchange, promotes innovation, and enhances the overall effectiveness of information sharing within the organization.

**Professional events and conferences:** Networking opportunities can extend beyond the organization through participation in professional events, conferences, and industry gatherings. Attend relevant conferences or seminars related to mobile IoT, fog computing, or smart home technologies. Engage in discussions, share experiences, and establish connections with professionals from the industry. These external networking activities broaden your professional network and provide access to a broader range of knowledge and expertise.

## 9.7   Context-aware work stealing scheme

Advanced time-piracy in any environment refers to sophisticated attacks or exploits targeting time-related data and processes in diverse environments. It suggests the unauthorized manipulation, alteration, or disruption of time-related systems, time-stamps, or synchronization mechanisms across various domains.

In the context of information sharing on mobile IoT-based content-aware smart homes with fog computing, advanced time-piracy could entail potential threats to time synchronization mechanisms and the implications of their exploitation. This could involve malicious actors attempting to manipulate timestamps, forge time-sensitive data, or disrupt the accuracy of synchronized timekeeping systems within the smart home environment [8].

To address advanced time-piracy in any environment, it would be necessary to explore potential vulnerabilities, risks, and countermeasures associated with time synchronization mechanisms. This may involve examining techniques for secure time synchronization, authentication protocols, and encryption methods to protect against unauthorized manipulation or exploitation of time-related data.

### 9.7.1   Extension for context-awareness

The concept of "Extension for Context-Awareness" refers to expanding the capabilities of information sharing on mobile IoT-based content-aware smart homes with fog computing by incorporating context-awareness into the system. Context-awareness involves understanding and utilizing contextual information, such as user preferences, environmental conditions, and device capabilities, to enhance the relevance, adaptability, and personalization of services and interactions. In the context of information sharing, extending the system for context-awareness allows the smart home environment to dynamically adapt and respond to the changing context of users and their surroundings. This extension enables the system to make informed decisions, automate processes, and provide personalized experiences based on the current context. To achieve extension for context-awareness in mobile IoT-based content-aware smart homes with fog computing, several key elements need to be considered:

**Context data collection:** Let C represent the set of context data variables collected from various sources within the smart home environment. The collection of context data can be represented as $C = \{C1, C2, C3 \ldots Cn\}$, where each $Cn$ represents a specific context variable. For example, $C1$ could represent the temperature, $C2$ the occupancy status, and $C3$ the lighting conditions in the smart home.

**Context modeling and representation:** Context modeling involves defining relationships and dependencies between context variables. This can be represented using mathematical functions or equations. For example, if $C1$ represents the temperature and $C2$ represents the occupancy status, a context model equation could be $T = f(O)$, where $T$ is the desired temperature, and $f$ is a mathematical function that determines the desired temperature based on the occupancy status.

**Context inference and reasoning:** Context inference involves analyzing and interpreting the collected context data to infer higher-level context information. This can be achieved using mathematical algorithms or reasoning techniques. For instance, machine learning algorithms or statistical models can be applied to infer patterns or correlations within the context data and make predictions about user preferences or behavior.

**Context-aware adaptation:** Context-aware adaptation involves dynamically adjusting system behavior based on the inferred context. This can be represented using mathematical functions or formulas. For example, if $C3$ represents the lighting conditions and $L$ represents the desired level of lighting, an adaptation function could be $L = g(C3)$, where g is a mathematical function that determines the appropriate level of lighting based on the sensed conditions.

**Privacy and security:** While not directly represented by mathematical functions, privacy and security considerations can be incorporated into the context-aware system through cryptographic algorithms, access control mechanisms, or privacy-preserving data mining techniques. These mathematical techniques ensure that sensitive context data are protected and only accessible to authorized entities.

## 9.7.2 Task management skills that are both reactive and proactive

Ask management skills that are both reactive and proactive can be explained using mathematical functions or formulas. While task management is typically a concept that involves organizational and behavioral aspects, we can use mathematical representations to illustrate the idea of combining reactive and proactive approaches. Here is an example:

Let us consider a task management scenario with the following variables:

$T$: Total tasks to be managed
$R$: Reactive tasks requiring immediate attention
$P$: Proactive tasks that involve planning and anticipation.

Reactive task management: Reactive task management deals with tasks that require immediate attention or response. It can be represented using a mathematical function that calculates the reactive task count ($R$) based on the total task count ($T$) and a reactive task coefficient ($K1$):

$$R = K1 * T$$

The reactive task coefficient ($K1$) represents the proportion or percentage of tasks that typically require reactive management. It can be determined based on historical data or experience.

Proactive task management: Proactive task management involves planning and anticipation to prevent or mitigate potential issues. It can be represented using a mathematical function that calculates the proactive task count ($P$) based on the total task count ($T$) and a proactive task coefficient ($K2$):

$$P = K2 * T$$

The proactive task coefficient ($K2$) represents the proportion or percentage of tasks that are typically managed proactively. It can be determined based on the nature of the tasks, available resources, and desired level of preparedness.

Total task management: The total task management represents the combined effort of reactive and proactive task management. It can be calculated using the following formula:

$$\text{Total task management} = \text{reactive task management} +$$
$$\text{proactive task management}$$
$$= R + P$$
$$= K1 * T + K2 * T$$

This formula quantifies the task management skills that encompass both reactive and proactive approaches. The coefficients $K1$ and $K2$ can be adjusted based on the specific requirements and priorities of the task management process.

### 9.7.3  Performance of Docker image transfer

The performance of Docker image transfer can be explained using mathematical functions or formulas that capture key metrics related to the transfer process. Some mathematical representations illustrate the performance aspects as below:

Transfer time (TT): TT represents the duration required to transfer a Docker image from one location to another. It can be calculated using the following formula:

$$TT = \frac{SI}{BW}$$

where TT is the transfer time, SI is the size of the Docker image, and BW is the available bandwidth for the transfer.

The TT is inversely proportional to the available bandwidth. A higher bandwidth value will result in a shorter TT.

Transfer speed (TS): TS indicates the rate at which the Docker image is transferred. It represents the amount of data transferred per unit time and can be calculated using the formula:

$$TS = \frac{SI}{TT}$$

where TS is the transfer speed, SI is the size of the Docker image, and TT is the transfer time.

The TS is directly proportional to the size of the Docker image and inversely proportional to the TT. A larger image or a shorter TT will result in a higher TS.

Efficiency ($E$): Efficiency represents the utilization of available bandwidth during the Docker image transfer and can be calculated as follows:

$$E = \frac{(SI/TT)}{BW}$$

where $E$ is the efficiency, SI is the size of the Docker image, TT is the transfer time, and BW is the available bandwidth.

Efficiency is the ratio of the actual TS to the available bandwidth. It indicates how effectively the available bandwidth is utilized during the transfer process. A higher efficiency value implies a more efficient utilization of the available bandwidth.

Latency ($L$): Latency represents the delay or response time experienced during the Docker image transfer. It can be calculated using the following formula:

$$L = RTT + TT$$

where $L$ is the latency, RTT is the round-trip time (time taken for a signal to travel from the source to the destination and back), and TT is the transfer time.

The latency is the sum of the round-trip time and the TT. It reflects the overall delay in the transfer process, including the time taken for the signal to travel and the time taken for the image transfer itself.

## 9.7.4 Transfer of Docker images

The transfer of Docker images can be explained using mathematical functions or formulas that capture key metrics related to the transfer process. Some mathematical representations illustrate the transfer of Docker images given as follows:

Transfer time (TT): TT represents the duration required to transfer a Docker image from one location to another. It can be calculated using the following formula:

$$TT = \frac{SI}{BW}$$

where TT is the transfer time, SI is the size of the Docker image, and BW is the available bandwidth for the transfer.

The TT is inversely proportional to the available bandwidth. A higher bandwidth value will result in a shorter TT.

Transfer speed (TS): TS indicates the rate at which the Docker image is transferred. It represents the amount of data transferred per unit time and can be calculated using the following formula:

$$TS = \frac{SI}{TT}$$

where TS is the transfer speed, SI is the size of the Docker image, and TT is the transfer time.

The TS is directly proportional to the size of the Docker image and inversely proportional to the TT. A larger image or a shorter TT will result in a higher TS.

Efficiency $(E)$: Efficiency represents the utilization of available bandwidth during the transfer of Docker images and can be calculated as follows:

$$E = \frac{(SI/TT)}{BW}$$

where $E$ is the efficiency, SI is the size of the Docker image, TT is the transfer time, and BW is the available bandwidth.

Efficiency is the ratio of the actual TS to the available bandwidth. It indicates how effectively the available bandwidth is utilized during the transfer process. A higher efficiency value implies a more efficient utilization of the available bandwidth.

Data loss (DL): DL represents the percentage of data that is lost or corrupted during the transfer of Docker images. It can be calculated using the following formula:

$$DL = \frac{(SI - DR)}{SI} \times 100$$

where DL is the data loss percentage, SI is the size of the Docker image, and DR is the received size of the Docker image.

DL is calculated as the difference between the original image size and the received image size, divided by the original image size, and multiplied by 100 to obtain the percentage. A lower DL percentage indicates a higher level of data integrity during the transfer process.

### 9.7.5   Distribution of tasks to fog nodes

The distribution of tasks to fog nodes in the context of information sharing on mobile IoT-based content-aware smart homes with fog computing can be explained using mathematical functions or formulas that consider factors like workload, node capacity, and task allocation. Some mathematical representations illustrate the distribution of tasks:

Workload distribution: Let $W$ represent the total workload or the number of tasks that need to be processed. To distribute the workload evenly among the available Fog nodes, we can use a formula that calculates the number of tasks assigned to each node:

$$\text{Tasks per Node} = \frac{W}{N}$$

where Tasks per Node is the number of tasks allocated to each Fog node, $W$ is the total workload or the number of tasks, and $N$ is the total number of available Fog nodes.

This formula ensures that each Fog node receives an equal share of the workload, resulting in a balanced distribution of tasks.

Node capacity consideration: To account for the varying capacities or processing capabilities of different fog nodes, we can introduce a weighting factor that reflects the relative capacity of each node. Let $C$ represents the capacity of each Fog node, and $C\_total$ represents the sum of capacities across all nodes. The formula for task allocation considering node capacity becomes:

$$\text{Tasks per Node} = \frac{W}{C\_\text{total}} \times C$$

where Tasks per Node is the number of tasks allocated to each Fog node, $W$ is the total workload or the number of tasks, $C$ is the capacity of a specific Fog node, and $C\_total$ is the sum of capacities across all Fog nodes.

This formula ensures that nodes with higher capacity receive a larger portion of the workload, leading to a more efficient distribution of tasks:

Dynamic task allocation: In scenarios where the workload or node capacity changes dynamically, a more adaptive approach is required. This can be achieved by periodically recalculating the task distribution based on updated workload and node capacity information.

One possible approach is to use a feedback control mechanism that adjusts the task allocation dynamically based on observed performance metrics or real-time data. This can involve monitoring the processing time of each Fog node and reallocating tasks accordingly to maintain load balance.

While these mathematical representations provide a conceptual framework for distributing tasks to Fog nodes, the actual task allocation algorithms and mechanisms used in fog-computing systems may vary depending on specific requirements, system architecture, and optimization objectives.

## 9.7.6    *Distribution of responsibilities*

The distribution of responsibilities in the context of information sharing on mobile IoT-based content-aware smart homes with fog computing can be explained using mathematical functions or formulas that consider factors such as workload, node capabilities, and responsibility allocation. Some mathematical representations illustrate the distribution of responsibilities:

Workload distribution: Let $W$ represent the total workload or the number of tasks/responsibilities that need to be managed. To distribute the workload evenly among the available entities (e.g., fog nodes, devices, or users), we can use a formula that calculates the number of responsibilities assigned to each entity:

$$\text{Responsibilities per Entity} = \frac{W}{N}$$

where Responsibilities per entity are the number of responsibilities allocated to each entity, $W$ is the total workload or the number of tasks/responsibilities, and $N$ is the total number of available entities.

This formula ensures an equal distribution of responsibilities among the entities, promoting a balanced workload allocation.

Capability consideration: To account for the varying capabilities or capacities of different entities, we can introduce a weighting factor that reflects the relative capability of each entity. Let $C$ represents the capability or capacity of each entity, and $C\_total$ represents the sum of capabilities across all entities. The formula for responsibility allocation considering entity capabilities becomes:

$$\text{Responsibilities per entity} = \frac{W}{C\_\text{total}} \times C$$

where Responsibilities per entity is the number of responsibilities allocated to each entity, $W$ is the total workload or the number of tasks/responsibilities, $C$ is the capability or capacity of a specific entity, and $C\_total$ is the sum of capabilities across all entities.

This formula ensures that entities with higher capabilities receive a larger portion of the responsibilities, leading to a more efficient distribution of workload based on their respective capacities.

Dynamic responsibility allocation: In scenarios where the workload or entity capabilities change dynamically, a more adaptive approach is required. This can be achieved by periodically recalculating the responsibility distribution based on updated workload and entity capability information.

One possible approach is to use a feedback control mechanism that adjusts the responsibility allocation dynamically based on observed performance metrics or real-time data. This can involve monitoring the workload status and capabilities of each entity and reallocating responsibilities to maintain a balanced and optimal distribution.

While these mathematical representations provide a conceptual framework for distributing responsibilities, the actual responsibility allocation algorithms and mechanisms used in fog-computing systems may vary depending on specific requirements, system architecture, and optimization objectives.

## 9.8   IoT-based smart home

An IoT-based smart home refers to a residential environment equipped with various interconnected devices, sensors, and systems that leverage IoT technologies to enhance automation, control, and information sharing within the home. In the context of information sharing on mobile IoT-based content-aware smart homes with fog computing, IoT plays a significant role in enabling seamless communication and integration between devices, allowing for intelligent and context-aware operations. Here are the key aspects of an IoT-based smart home:

Device interconnectivity: IoT-based smart homes consist of interconnected devices that communicate and share information with each other. These devices can include smart appliances, thermostats, security systems, lighting systems, entertainment systems, and more. They are equipped with sensors and network connectivity to exchange data and enable coordinated actions [9].

Data collection and analysis: IoT devices in a smart home environment collect various types of data, such as environmental conditions, occupancy status, energy usage, and user preferences. These data are analyzed and processed using data analytics and machine learning algorithms to derive insights, make intelligent decisions, and automate tasks based on the context and user requirements.

Automation and control: IoT-based smart homes enable automation and control of various home functions and operations. Through connectivity and data sharing, smart devices can be remotely controlled, programmed, or respond intelligently to triggers or predefined rules. For example, a smart thermostat can adjust temperature settings based on occupancy and user preferences, or a smart security system can send notifications and initiate actions in case of a security breach.

User interaction and interfaces: IoT-based smart homes provide user-friendly interfaces and interaction mechanisms for residents to monitor and control their home environment. These interfaces can be mobile applications, web-based portals, voice assistants, or smart home hubs. These interfaces allow users to access real-time information, customize settings, and interact with devices from anywhere, enhancing convenience and personalization.

Connectivity and communication: IoT devices in smart homes rely on wireless connectivity technologies such as Wi-Fi, Bluetooth, Zigbee, or Z-Wave to establish communication and exchange information. This enables seamless integration and coordination among devices, allowing for synchronized operations and information sharing.

Cloud and fog computing: Cloud and fog-computing technologies play a crucial role in supporting the IoT-based smart home ecosystem. Cloud platforms provide storage, processing power, and data analytics capabilities for managing and analyzing large volumes of IoT data. Fog computing, on the other hand, brings computing resources closer to the edge, reducing latency, and enabling real-time processing and decision-making in the smart home environment [10].

Enhanced efficiency and convenience: IoT-based smart homes aim to improve energy efficiency, enhance security, and provide convenience to residents. By intelligently managing energy consumption, optimizing resource utilization, and automating routine tasks, smart homes contribute to a more comfortable, secure, and efficient living environment.

## 9.9  Smart home scenario

In this chapter, a smart home scenario refers to a specific use case or situation where the concepts of IoT, information sharing, and fog computing are applied to enhance the functionality and capabilities of a residential environment. Here is an explanation of a smart home scenario:

Imagine a smart home scenario where a family resides in a technologically advanced house equipped with IoT devices, sensors, and fog computing capabilities. The family members use various mobile devices, such as smartphones or tablets, to interact with the smart home system remotely. The scenario involves different aspects of the smart home ecosystem:

Automation and control: The smart home scenario includes automation and control features enabled by IoT devices. For example, as the family members arrive home, sensors detect their presence, and the smart home system automatically adjusts the temperature, lighting, and security settings according to their preferences.

Energy management: In this scenario, the smart home is equipped with energy monitoring sensors that track energy consumption across different devices and appliances. The system utilizes fog-computing capabilities to analyze real-time data and provides insights into energy usage patterns. The family can receive recommendations and make informed decisions to optimize energy consumption and reduce costs.

Security and surveillance: The smart home scenario incorporates security and surveillance features using IoT devices. For instance, the smart home system includes smart cameras, motion sensors, and door/window sensors. These devices are interconnected and integrated with fog computing to enable real-time monitoring, alerts, and automated actions in case of security breaches or suspicious activities.

Information sharing and content awareness: Information sharing is a central theme in the smart home scenario. IoT devices within the smart home environment continuously collect data on various parameters, such as temperature, humidity, air quality, and energy usage. Fog computing allows for real-time processing and analysis of this data to derive valuable insights. The system can share relevant information, such as environmental conditions or energy consumption trends, with the family members through mobile applications or voice assistants.

Personalized experiences: The smart home scenario focuses on delivering personalized experiences to the family members. The system utilizes context-awareness and user preferences to customize various aspects of the smart home environment. For example, based on individual preferences, the system can adjust lighting, music playlists, or temperature settings in different rooms.

Remote monitoring and control: The smart home scenario enables remote monitoring and control capabilities, empowering the family members to interact with the smart home system even when they are not physically present. Through mobile applications or web-based interfaces, the family can remotely access and control various devices, receive real-time notifications, or check the status of different smart home functionalities.

Enhanced safety and well-being: The smart home scenario prioritizes safety and well-being. The system incorporates IoT devices like smoke detectors, water leak sensors, and health monitoring devices. These devices provide early warnings or notifications in case of emergencies or health-related concerns, ensuring a secure and healthy living environment.

## 9.10   ICON is an IoT-based, layered architecture

ICON, in this chapter, is an IoT-based layered architecture. An architecture is a conceptual framework that defines the structure, components, and relationships of a system. ICON provides a structured approach for designing and implementing IoT systems, specifically in the context of smart homes. Here is an explanation of the ICON architecture:

ICON stands for IoT, cloud, and fog computing networking architecture. It is a layered architecture that integrates three key components: IoT devices, cloud computing, and fog computing. Each layer in the ICON architecture has distinct roles and functions, contributing to the overall efficiency and effectiveness of the smart home ecosystem.

IoT layer: The IoT layer represents the foundation of the architecture and comprises the interconnected devices within the smart home environment. These devices include sensors, actuators, smart appliances, and other IoT-enabled devices. The IoT layer facilitates data collection, monitoring, and control of various aspects within the smart home.

Cloud computing layer: The cloud computing layer in the ICON architecture provides a scalable and centralized platform for storage, processing, and analysis of IoT data. It leverages cloud-based services and resources to handle the massive volumes of data generated by IoT devices. The cloud layer enables data storage, advanced analytics, and long-term data management in a cost-effective manner.

Fog computing layer: The fog-computing layer is an intermediate layer between IoT devices and the cloud. It brings computing capabilities closer to the edge of the network, reducing latency, and enhancing real-time processing. Fog computing leverages localized resources, such as fog nodes or gateways, to perform data filtering, preprocessing, and analytics closer to the smart home environment. This layer enhances responsiveness, reduces network congestion, and enables real-time decision-making for time-sensitive applications.

The layered structure of the ICON architecture provides several advantages in the context of information sharing on mobile IoT-based content-aware smart homes with fog computing:

Scalability: The cloud computing layer offers scalability to handle large volumes of data generated by IoT devices, ensuring that the smart home system can accommodate expanding IoT deployments.

Real-time responsiveness: The fog computing layer brings processing capabilities closer to the smart home environment, enabling real-time analytics, decision-making, and information sharing. This enhances the responsiveness of the system and supports time-critical applications.

Efficiency: By distributing computational tasks across the layers, the ICON architecture optimizes resource utilization and reduces network traffic. This results in improved energy efficiency, reduced latency, and enhanced overall system performance.

Flexibility and adaptability: The layered architecture allows for flexible deployment and integration of new IoT devices, cloud services, and fog nodes. This enables the smart home system to adapt to changing requirements and advancements in IoT technologies.

Figure 9.1 in this chapter presents the ICON framework, an IoT-based layered architecture for smart homes. The framework visually depicts the components and their relationships within the architecture. The figure highlights the three layers: IoT, cloud computing, and fog computing, highlighting their roles and interactions.

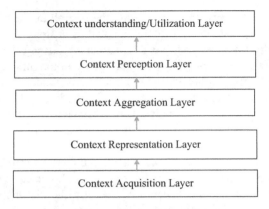

*Figure 9.1 ICON framework*

In the figure, the IoT layer is depicted at the bottom, representing the foundation of the architecture. It illustrates various IoT devices such as sensors, actuators, and smart appliances that form the interconnected network within the smart home environment. These devices collect data, monitor the surroundings, and enable control and automation.

Above the IoT layer, the cloud computing layer is presented, signifying the centralized cloud-based platform for storage, processing, and analysis of the vast amounts of data generated by IoT devices. It displays the cloud infrastructure and services that facilitate data storage, advanced analytics, and long-term management of the smart home data.

At the top of the figure, the fog computing layer is depicted, highlighting its intermediate position between IoT devices and the cloud. It highlights the localized fog nodes or gateways that are strategically placed closer to the smart home environment. These fog nodes perform data filtering, preprocessing, and analytics, enabling real-time decision-making, reducing latency, and enhancing responsiveness.

The arrows and connections between the layers illustrate the flow of data, commands, and information within the ICON framework. They represent the seamless communication, data transfer, and interaction between IoT devices, fog nodes, and the cloud, ensuring efficient information sharing and system coordination.

## 9.10.1 ICON's design principles

ICON, the IoT based layered architecture for smart homes, has specific design principles that guide its implementation and operation. These design principles are crucial in ensuring the effectiveness, scalability, and adaptability of the architecture. The key design principles of ICON are given below:

Modularity: The ICON architecture emphasizes modularity, allowing for the independent development and deployment of components within each layer. Modularity enables easy integration of new devices, services, or technologies into the smart home ecosystem without disrupting the overall architecture. It promotes flexibility, reusability, and enables future expansions or upgrades.

Interoperability: Interoperability is a fundamental design principle of ICON. It emphasizes the seamless communication and collaboration among devices, nodes, and systems across different layers. By adopting open standards and protocols, the architecture ensures that diverse IoT devices, fog nodes, and cloud services can interact and share information effectively. Interoperability facilitates information sharing, data exchange, and interoperable services within the smart home environment.

Scalability: ICON is designed to be scalable, allowing for the addition of new IoT devices, fog nodes, or cloud resources as the smart home ecosystem grows. The architecture supports horizontal scalability, enabling the distribution of workload across multiple devices or nodes. Scalability ensures that the system can handle increasing data volumes, device deployments, and evolving user needs without compromising performance or efficiency.

Security and privacy: Security and privacy are paramount in the design of ICON. The architecture incorporates robust security mechanisms to protect sensitive data, ensure secure communication, and prevent unauthorized access or malicious activities. Privacy-preserving techniques and encryption mechanisms are employed to safeguard user information and maintain confidentiality. Security and privacy considerations are embedded at each layer to establish a secure and trusted smart home environment.

Data management and analytics: ICON prioritizes effective data management and analytics to derive meaningful insights from the vast amounts of data generated by IoT devices. The architecture incorporates data storage, processing, and analytics capabilities within the cloud computing layer. It supports efficient data collection, real-time analysis, and advanced data processing techniques to enable intelligent decision-making, predictive capabilities, and personalized services within the smart home environment.

Context awareness: Context awareness is a key design principle of ICON. The architecture aims to understand the contextual information within the smart home ecosystem, including environmental conditions, user preferences, and activity patterns. Context-awareness enables the system to adapt, personalize, and provide relevant information or services based on the current context. This principle enhances the user experience, automates routine tasks, and optimizes resource utilization within the smart home.

## 9.11    Conditional logic with predicates

Conditional logic with predicates is a fundamental concept in programming that enables decision-making based on logical conditions. In this chapter, conditional logic with predicates can be implemented using programming languages to control the behavior of smart home systems. Here's an explanation of how conditional logic with predicates can be applied in programming:

Predicates: In programming, predicates are expressions that evaluate to either true or false. These expressions can involve comparisons, logical operators, or function calls. For example, a predicate could be:

temperature > 25

This predicate evaluates to true if the temperature is greater than 25°C.

Conditional statements: Conditional statements allow the execution of different blocks of code based on the evaluation of predicates. The most common form is the "if-else" construct, where a block of code is executed if a predicate is true, and an alternate block is executed if the predicate is false. For example, in Python:

```python
if temperature > 25:

    print("It's hot!")

else:

    print("It's cool.")
```

In this example, the code inside the first block (indented under if) is executed if the temperature is greater than 25, and the code inside the second block (indented under else) is executed otherwise.

Multiple conditions: Multiple conditions can be combined using logical operators and/or to create more complex predicates. For example:

```python
if temperature > 25 and humidity < 70:

    print("It's hot and dry.")
```

This code snippet checks if both the temperatures are greater than 25, and the humidity is less than 70 before executing the corresponding block of code.

Nested conditions: Conditional statements can be nested, allowing for more intricate decision-making. This enables the evaluation of multiple predicates in a structured manner. For example:

```python
if temperature > 25:
    if humidity < 70:
        print("It's hot and dry.")
    else:
        print("It's hot and humid.")
else:
    print("It's cool.")
```

In this example, the code first checks if the temperature is greater than 25. If it is, it further evaluates the humidity level. Depending on the outcomes of these evaluations, the corresponding code block is executed.

By using conditional logic with predicates in programming, smart home systems can make intelligent decisions based on various conditions and trigger appropriate actions. This enables the system to respond to environmental changes, user preferences, or specific events, facilitating information sharing, automation, and personalized experiences within the smart home environment.

## 9.12    Implementation of ICON

Implementing the ICON architecture, which stands for IoT, cloud computing, and fog computing networking architecture, involves programming and integrating the different components and layers of the architecture.

IoT layer: In the IoT layer, you would need to program the functionalities of IoT devices and their interactions. This may involve programming languages and frameworks specific to the devices you are working with. For example, if you have temperature sensors, motion sensors, or smart appliances, you would need to program their data collection, event handling, and communication capabilities. This can be done using languages such as Python, JavaScript, or C++ and using IoT protocols like MQTT or CoAP.

Cloud computing layer: The cloud computing layer involves programming the cloud infrastructure and services to handle data storage, processing, and analysis. You would need to utilize cloud platforms like Amazon Web Services, Microsoft Azure, or Google Cloud Platform and their respective APIs or SDKs. This programming may involve creating databases to store IoT data, developing APIs for data access, and implementing data processing or analytics workflows using technologies like serverless computing, containers, or big data frameworks.

Fog computing layer: To implement the fog-computing layer, you would need to program the fog nodes or gateways responsible for localized data processing and decision-making. This could involve programming microcontrollers or single-board computers like Raspberry Pi or Arduino. You would need to handle data filtering, preprocessing, and analytics closer to the edge. Programming languages like Python, Node.js, or C/C++ can be used to develop software for the fog nodes, incorporating frameworks like TensorFlow or OpenCV for machine learning or computer vision tasks.

Data flow and integration: Programming is necessary to establish data flow and integration between the layers of the ICON architecture. This involves defining communication protocols, message formats, and APIs for exchanging data among IoT devices, Fog nodes, and the Cloud. Depending on the specific requirements, you may use protocols such as MQTT, HTTP, or WebSocket, and develop APIs or message brokers to enable seamless data sharing and integration.

Security and privacy considerations: Implementing ICON requires programming security mechanisms to ensure data privacy, authentication, and secure communication. This involves encryption techniques, access control, and user authentication. You would need to program security protocols, implement secure communication channels, and handle user authorization and authentication using frameworks like OAuth or JSON Web Tokens (JWT).

Context awareness and decision-making: To achieve context awareness, programming is needed to analyze and interpret data from IoT devices, make intelligent decisions, and trigger appropriate actions. This may involve using machine learning algorithms, rule-based systems, or expert systems to process data and generate insights. Programming languages like Python or R can be used for data analysis and machine learning libraries such as scikit-learn or TensorFlow for implementing predictive models.

### 9.12.1 The fog-computing system architecture for the ICON-based smart house

The fog-computing system architecture for the ICON-based smart house refers to the specific design and structure of the fog-computing layer within the ICON framework. It focuses on the components and their interactions that enable the processing, analysis, and decision-making at the edge of the network, closer to the smart house environment. The fog-computing system architecture for the ICON-based smart house:

Fog nodes: The architecture incorporates fog nodes, which are computing devices deployed within the smart house or in proximity to the smart house environment. These nodes act as intermediaries between the IoT devices in the house and the cloud infrastructure. Fog nodes can be physical devices, such as gateways or dedicated servers, or they can be virtualized using technologies like Docker or virtual machines. Fog nodes have computing resources and storage capacity to perform local data processing, analytics, and decision-making.

Data collection and preprocessing: The fog-computing architecture focuses on efficient data collection and preprocessing at the edge of the network. IoT devices within the smart house environment generate data continuously. Fog nodes collect this data using appropriate protocols and interfaces, such as MQTT or RESTful APIs. The collected data are then preprocessed to filter, aggregate, or transform it as required before further analysis or transmission.

Real-time analytics and decision-making: Real-time analytics and decision-making are key components of the fog-computing system architecture. Fog nodes host data analytics frameworks, such as Apache Spark or TensorFlow, to perform real-time analytics on the collected and preprocessed data. These analytics can include data filtering, pattern recognition, anomaly detection, or predictive modeling. Based on the analysis results, fog nodes make localized decisions and trigger actions within the smart house environment.

Context-awareness and personalization: The fog-computing system architecture enables context-awareness and personalization within the smart house environment. By leveraging data from IoT devices and local analytics, fog nodes can understand the context of the environment, such as occupancy, user preferences, or energy usage patterns. This context-awareness allows for persona-lized services, adaptive automation, and optimized resource allocation within the smart house.

Connectivity and communication: Connectivity and communication play a vital role in the fog-computing system architecture. Fog nodes establish connec-tions with IoT devices within the smart house using wireless protocols like Wi-Fi, Zigbee, or Z-Wave. Additionally, fog nodes communicate with cloud services, such as the cloud computing layer in the ICON architecture, to exchange data, receive updates, or offload tasks when necessary.

Security and privacy: The fog-computing system architecture incorporates security and privacy measures to protect data and ensure secure operations within the smart house environment. Encryption protocols, authentication mechanisms, and access controls are implemented to secure data transmission and communica-tion among fog nodes, IoT devices, and cloud services. Privacy-preserving tech-niques, like data anonymization or differential privacy, may also be employed to safeguard sensitive information.

Scalability and resilience: The fog-computing system architecture is designed to be scalable and resilient. It allows for the deployment of multiple fog nodes within the smart house or its vicinity to handle increased data volumes and com-putation requirements. Load balancing techniques and fault-tolerant mechanisms ensure that the system can accommodate the growing needs of the smart house environment while maintaining high availability and performance.

The fog-computing system architecture within the ICON-based smart house complements the IoT and cloud computing layers by bringing computational cap-abilities closer to the edge. It enables real-time analytics, context-awareness, and localized decision-making within the smart house environment. By leveraging fog nodes and their computing resources, the architecture enhances efficiency, responsiveness, and privacy while enabling seamless integration with the broader ICON framework.

## 9.13   Conclusion

In conclusion, the chapter emphasizes the significance of leveraging fog computing in the context of smart homes. The integration of IoT, fog computing, and cloud computing technologies creates an ecosystem that enables efficient information sharing, intelligent decision-making, and personalized experiences within the smart home environment. By implementing the ICON architecture, which incorporates IoT devices, cloud computing, and fog-computing layers, smart homes can achieve enhanced automation, improved energy management, advanced security, and per-sonalized services. The architecture facilitates seamless communication, data col-lection, and analysis, allowing for real-time responsiveness and context-aware actions. The use of conditional logic with predicates in programming further empowers smart home systems to make intelligent decisions based on logical conditions. Predicates enable the evaluation of contextual information, user preferences, and environmental factors to trigger appropriate actions, optimizing resource utilization and enhancing the overall smart home experience. Furthermore, the fog-computing system architecture within the ICON-based smart house brings computational capabilities closer to the edge of the network. This architecture enables real-time analytics, localized decision-making, and personalized services. It ensures efficient data collection, preprocessing, and analysis at the fog nodes, enhancing responsiveness, security, and privacy within the smart home environment.

# References

[1]   Y. Cao, S. Chen, P. Hou, and D. Brown, FAST: A Fog Computing Assisted Distributed Analytics System to Monitor Fall for Stroke Mitigation, in *Proc. IEEE Int. Conf. Netw. Archit. Storage (NAS)*, Boston, USA, 2015, pp. 2–11.

[2]   J. Oueis, E. C. Strinati, and S. Barbarossa, The Fog Balancing: Load Distribution for Small Cell Cloud Computing, in *Proc. IEEE 81st Veh. Technol. Conf. (VTC Spring)*, Glasgow, UK, 2015, pp. 1–6.

[3]   R. Deng, R. Lu, C. Lai, and T. H. Luan, Towards Power Consumption Delay Tradeoff by Workload Allocation in Cloud-Fog Computing in *Proc. IEEE Int. Conf. Commun. (ICC)*, London, UK, 2015, pp. 3909–3914.

[4]   D. Ye, M. Wu, S. Tang, and R. Yu, Scalable Fog Computing with Service Offloading in Bus Networks, in *Proc. IEEE 3rd Int. Conf. Cyber Security Cloud Comput. (CSCloud)*, Beijing, China, 2016, pp. 247–251.

[5]   H. Xiang, M. Peng, Y. Cheng, and H. Chen, Joint Mode Selection and Resource Allocation for Downlink Fog Radio Access Networks Supported D2D, in *11th International Conference on Heterogeneous Networking for Quality, Reliability, Security and Robustness (QSHINE)*, 2015, pp. 177–182.

[6]   D. Chen, S. Schedler, and V. Kuehn, Backhaul Traffic Balancing and Dynamic Content-Centric Clustering for the Downlink of Fog Radio Access Network, in *Proc. IEEE Int. Workshop Signal Process. Adv. Wireless Commun. (SPAWC)*, Edinburgh, UK, 2016, pp. 1–5.

[7]   E. Baccarelli, P. G. V. Naranjo, M. Scarpiniti, M. Shojafar, and J. H. Abawajy, Fog of Everything: Energy-Efficient Networked Computing Architectures, Research Challenges, and a Case Study. *IEEE Access*, 5, 9882–9910, 2017.

[8]   J. C. Guevara, L. F. Bittencourt, and N. L. S. da Fonseca, Class of Service in Fog Computing, in *IEEE 9th Latin-American Conference on Communications (LATINCOM)*, 2017, pp. 1–6.

[9]   V. Issarny, M. Caporuscio, and N. Georgantas, *A Perspective on the Future of Middleware-based Software Engineering in Future of Software Engineering FOSE, IEEE Xplore*, 2007, pp. 244–258.

[10]  Z. Hao, E. Novak, S. Yi, and Q. Li, Challenges and Software Architecture for Fog Computing, *IEEE Internet Computing*, 21, 44–53, 2017.

*Chapter 10*

# Security and privacy challenges in fog computing

## Abstract

Fog computing is a paradigm that extends cloud computing capabilities to the network edge, enabling the processing, storage, and analysis of data closer to the source. This abstract provides a concise overview of fog computing, highlighting its background, scope, problem definition, aim, and observations related to its synergy with deep learning capabilities and their impact on Big Data.

**Background:** Fog computing addresses the limitations of cloud-centric architectures by distributing computing resources to the network edge. It aims to overcome challenges such as latency, bandwidth constraints, and privacy concerns associated with centralized cloud processing.

**Scope:** The scope of fog computing encompasses a wide range of applications, including Internet of Things (IoT), smart cities, autonomous vehicles, and real-time analytics. It enables efficient and low-latency processing of data, enabling timely decision-making and resource optimization.

**Problem definition:** Fog computing addresses the need for processing massive amounts of data generated by IoT devices in real time, overcoming limitations imposed by network latency, bandwidth, and privacy. It provides a decentralized computing infrastructure that complements cloud computing.

**Aim:** The aim of fog computing is to enable distributed and localized processing of data at the network edge, improving response times, reducing network congestion, and enhancing privacy and security. It aims to harness the potential of edge devices and empower them with intelligent decision-making capabilities.

**Analysis/observations:** The integration of deep learning capabilities with fog computing enables advanced data analytics and intelligent decision-making at the edge. This synergy improves the efficiency and scalability of Big Data processing, as data can be preprocessed, filtered, and analyzed locally, reducing the need for extensive data transmission and enhancing overall system performance.

## 10.1 Introduction

Fog computing, a paradigm that extends cloud computing capabilities to the network edge has emerged as a promising solution to address the challenges posed by the exponential growth of data in the era of Big Data. With the increasing volume, velocity, and variety of data generated by diverse sources such as Internet of Things (IoT) devices, there is a pressing need for efficient processing and analysis closer to the data source. This is where fog computing steps in, providing a decentralized computing infrastructure that brings the computational power and intelligence closer to the edge of the network [1].

At the same time, deep learning, a subfield of machine learning, has revolutionized various domains with its ability to learn intricate patterns and extract valuable insights from large and complex datasets. Deep learning models, such as artificial neural networks, have demonstrated remarkable performance in tasks such as image recognition, natural language processing, and speech recognition. Combining the capabilities of deep learning with fog computing has the potential to further enhance the processing and analysis of Big Data.

By integrating deep learning capabilities into the fog-computing architecture, the network edge devices can leverage sophisticated models and algorithms to perform advanced data analytics, prediction, and decision-making. This localization of computation and intelligence reduces the need for extensive data transmission to centralized cloud servers, resulting in improved latency, reduced network congestion, and enhanced privacy and security.

The synergy between fog computing and deep learning offers several advantages for Big Data processing. First, it enables real-time and near-real-time analytics, allowing faster decision-making based on timely insights extracted from data. Second, by processing data at the edge, fog computing reduces the dependence on centralized cloud resources, leading to improved scalability and reduced network bandwidth requirements. Lastly, the combination of fog computing and deep learning enables the deployment of intelligent and adaptive systems that can learn from data in real time, making them more responsive and efficient in handling Big Data challenges [2].

In this chapter, we explore the integration of deep learning capabilities into the fog-computing architecture and investigate its potential to improve Big Data processing. We examine the benefits, challenges, and applications of this combined approach and discuss the implications for various domains such as IoT, smart cities, healthcare, and industrial automation. Through analysis and case studies, we aim to provide insights into how the fusion of fog computing and deep learning can unlock the full potential of Big Data and enable intelligent decision-making at the network edge.

## 10.2   Fog application management

In the context of fog computing, efficient management of applications deployed at the network edge is crucial for optimizing performance, resource allocation, and scalability. This chapter focuses on exploring different approaches to application management in fog-computing environments, specifically highlighting the integration of deep learning capabilities to enhance Big Data processing. By effectively managing applications, organizations can leverage the full potential of fog computing to improve data analytics, decision-making, and overall system performance.

One approach to application management in fog computing is the centralized model. In this approach, a central authority or controller oversees the deployment, monitoring, and resource allocation of applications across the network edge. This central management enables efficient coordination and control but may introduce a single point of failure and increased communication overhead. Alternatively, a distributed approach to application management distributes the management tasks across multiple nodes or devices in the fog-computing infrastructure. This approach decentralizes decision-making and can improve fault tolerance and responsiveness. However, it requires effective coordination mechanisms and communication protocols to ensure consistent application management across the network. With the integration of deep learning capabilities, an autonomous approach to application management becomes feasible. In this approach, intelligent agents or algorithms embedded within the fog-computing nodes have the ability to learn, adapt, and make decisions autonomously. These agents leverage deep learning models to analyze data, predict resource demands, and optimize application deployment and management based on real-time feedback. This approach reduces the reliance on centralized control and enables more efficient and adaptive application management [3].

An essential aspect of application management is resource allocation, where resources such as processing power, storage, and network bandwidth are assigned to applications based on their requirements and priorities. Dynamic resource allocation techniques, driven by deep learning capabilities, can optimize resource utilization by continuously monitoring application performance, predicting future demands, and dynamically adjusting resource allocation to ensure optimal application execution and overall system performance. Effective application management involves ensuring and maintaining the desired quality of service (QoS) for applications. Deep learning-based techniques can analyze various parameters, such as response time, latency, throughput, and reliability, to dynamically adjust resource allocation, prioritize critical applications, and optimize QoS. This approach improves the user experience, enhances system efficiency, and supports service-level agreements in fog-computing environments. Application management in fog computing must also address security and privacy concerns. Deep learning capabilities can be employed to analyze and detect anomalies, intrusions, or privacy breaches in real time, enabling proactive security measures. Additionally, deep learning-based techniques can facilitate privacy-preserving data processing and secure communication protocols, ensuring the confidentiality and integrity of sensitive data.

## 10.2.1 Application performance

In the context of fog computing, optimizing application performance is a critical aspect for achieving efficient and responsive data processing in Big Data environments. This chapter focuses on exploring the impact of integrating deep learning capabilities on enhancing application performance in fog computing. By leveraging deep learning algorithms, organizations can improve resource management, workload distribution, and real-time decision-making, leading to enhanced application performance and overall system efficiency [4].

Effective resource management is essential for ensuring optimal application performance in fog computing. Deep learning-based techniques can analyze historical and real-time data to predict resource demands, identify bottlenecks, and optimize resource allocation. By dynamically allocating resources such as processing power, storage, and network bandwidth based on application requirements, fog-computing systems can deliver improved performance and response times. Load balancing and workload distribution play a crucial role in maximizing application performance in distributed fog-computing environments. Deep learning models can learn patterns from data traffic and workload characteristics to dynamically distribute tasks across edge devices. This adaptive workload distribution enables efficient utilization of resources, minimizes response time, and avoids overloading specific devices, ensuring balanced and optimized application performance. The integration of deep learning capabilities enables real-time decision-making at the edge, enhancing application performance in time-sensitive scenarios. By deploying deep learning models within fog-computing nodes, data can be analyzed and processed locally, reducing latency and enabling quicker response times. Real-time decision-making empowers fog-computing applications with the ability to make intelligent, context-aware decisions based on analyzed data, leading to improved performance and enhanced user experience.

Deep learning algorithms can learn patterns and relationships within Big Data to enable predictive analytics. By analyzing historical data, these models can make accurate predictions about future trends, resource demands, and application behavior. This predictive capability helps optimize application performance by proactively adapting resource allocation, scaling, and scheduling, thus preventing potential performance degradation and ensuring smooth operations. Caching frequently accessed data at the network edge is a powerful technique to improve application performance in fog computing. Deep learning algorithms can analyze data patterns and user behavior to predict the most relevant data to cache at the edge. By locally storing frequently accessed data, fog-computing applications can significantly reduce data retrieval latency, enhance response times, and improve overall performance. Deep learning-based techniques can be utilized to monitor application performance in real time. By analyzing performance metrics, anomalies, and bottlenecks, these models can identify areas of improvement and suggest optimization strategies. This continuous monitoring and optimization approach enables proactive performance management, ensuring that applications run at their optimal state and meet performance objectives.

## 10.2.2    Approach distributed data flow

In the context of fog computing, managing the flow of Big Data across distributed networks is crucial for efficient processing and analysis. This chapter focuses on exploring the approach of distributed data flow, specifically highlighting the integration of deep learning capabilities to enhance data management in fog-computing environments. By effectively managing the flow of data, organizations can leverage the power of distributed computing, improve scalability, reduce latency, and enhance overall system performance.

The distributed data flow approach begins with data ingestion, where data from various sources, such as IoT devices, sensors, or external systems, are collected and prepared for processing. Deep learning techniques can be employed to preprocess and filter the incoming data, extracting relevant features, reducing noise, and improving data quality. This preprocessing step is essential for optimizing subsequent data analytics and decision-making processes. Once the data are ingested, the distributed data flow approach focuses on efficiently routing and distributing the data across the fog-computing infrastructure. Deep learning models can learn from historical data patterns, network conditions, and resource availability to dynamically determine the optimal routing paths and distribute the data to appropriate edge devices for processing. This adaptive data routing enables load balancing, minimizes network congestion, and improves data processing efficiency. Deep learning capabilities can be leveraged to enable parallel processing and computation of distributed data. By partitioning the data into smaller subsets, deep learning models can be deployed across multiple edge devices to perform simultaneous computations. This parallel processing approach improves data processing speed, reduces latency, and enables real-time or near-real-time analytics on distributed datasets. In fog-computing environments, data from multiple sources and devices often need to be fused and aggregated to derive meaningful insights. Deep learning algorithms can be employed to analyze and integrate data from diverse sources, capturing complex relationships and patterns. This data fusion and aggregation process enhances the accuracy and completeness of the derived insights, enabling more comprehensive data analysis and decision-making. The integration of deep learning capabilities enables real-time analytics and decision-making at the network edge. By deploying deep learning models within fog-computing nodes, data can be analyzed and processed locally, reducing latency and enabling quicker response times. Real-time analytics empower fog-computing applications with the ability to make intelligent and informed decisions based on analyzed data, enhancing the overall data flow and system performance. Efficient data storage and retrieval mechanisms are essential in distributed data flow. Deep learning techniques can be utilized for data compression, indexing, and efficient storage strategies, optimizing the utilization of storage resources and improving data retrieval times. By leveraging deep learning models, fog-computing systems can effectively manage data storage and retrieval, ensuring quick access to relevant data when needed.

## 10.3    Fog Big Data base analysis

In the era of Big Data, analyzing vast amounts of data efficiently and effectively is a significant challenge. Fog computing, with its ability to bring computational resources closer to the data source, combined with deep learning capabilities, offers promising solutions for Big Data analysis. This chapter explores the topic of fog Big Data analysis, focusing on how the integration of fog computing and deep learning enhances the analysis of large-scale datasets, enabling real-time insights, improved decision-making, and actionable intelligence.

Fog computing, by deploying computing resources at the network edge, enables real-time data processing and analysis. Deep learning models embedded within fog-computing nodes can handle massive data volumes and perform complex computations with low latency. This facilitates real-time analytics, where data can be processed and analyzed as it is generated, enabling prompt decision-making and timely responses to emerging trends or events. The distributed nature of fog computing, combined with deep learning capabilities, allows for scalable and distributed analytics of Big Data. Deep learning algorithms can be parallelized across multiple edge devices, processing subsets of the data simultaneously. This distributed approach improves processing speed, reduces computational load, and enhances scalability, enabling efficient analysis of large-scale datasets. Deep learning models at the network edge enable intelligent data filtering and feature extraction. By leveraging deep learning algorithms, fog-computing nodes can analyze incoming data in real time, filter out noise or irrelevant information, and extract meaningful features. This intelligent data filtering reduces the amount of data transmitted to the cloud, minimizing bandwidth requirements and facilitating more efficient data analysis.

Deep learning techniques excel at anomaly detection and pattern recognition, which are crucial in Big Data analysis. Fog computing, with its proximity to the data source, is well suited for detecting anomalies and identifying patterns in real time. Deep learning models can learn from historical data to detect anomalies, identify trends, and recognize complex patterns, enabling proactive decision-making and early detection of critical events or irregularities [5]. The integration of deep learning capabilities within the fog-computing paradigm also addresses privacy and security concerns in Big Data analysis. By processing data locally at the edge, sensitive information can be anonymized or encrypted before transmission to the cloud, enhancing data privacy and reducing the risk of unauthorized access. Deep learning algorithms can also detect security threats or anomalies within the data, enabling proactive security measures and ensuring the integrity of the analyzed results. Fog Big Data analysis empowers organizations with actionable intelligence and decision support. By leveraging the combined power of fog computing and deep learning, real-time insights and predictive analytics can be generated. These insights provide valuable information for decision-making, resource optimization, and operational efficiency, enabling organizations to make data-driven decisions, respond quickly to changing conditions, and gain a competitive edge.

## 10.3.1 *Processing of streaming data*

Processing streaming data involves the real-time analysis and manipulation of continuous data streams as they are generated, allowing organizations to derive insights and take timely actions. With the rise of IoT devices, social media feeds, sensor networks, and other sources, the volume and velocity of streaming data have increased exponentially. Processing streaming data involves capturing, ingesting, and processing data in motion, often utilizing technologies such as complex event processing, stream analytics, and real-time machine learning. The goal is to extract valuable information, identify patterns, detect anomalies, make data-driven decisions in real time, enabling organizations to respond swiftly to changing conditions, optimize operations, and unlock the potential of dynamic data-driven applications.

### 10.3.2 Big Data, Stream Data Analysis, and fog computing

Big Data, Stream Data Analysis, and fog computing are interconnected domains that work together to enable efficient processing and analysis of massive amounts of data in real time.

Big Data refers to large and complex datasets that exceed the capabilities of traditional data processing methods. It encompasses vast volumes of structured, semi-structured, and unstructured data, generated from diverse sources such as social media, sensors, transactions, and more. Big Data analysis involves the extraction of valuable insights, patterns, and correlations from this data, enabling organizations to make data-driven decisions and gain a competitive edge.

Stream Data Analysis, on the other hand, focuses on the real-time analysis of continuous and high-velocity data streams. It involves the processing and interpretation of data as it flows in, allowing organizations to detect anomalies, identify trends, and respond rapidly to dynamic events. Stream Data Analysis often utilizes techniques such as real-time analytics, complex event processing, and machine learning algorithms to extract actionable insights from the streaming data [6].

Fog-computing complements Big Data and Stream Data Analysis by extending cloud computing capabilities to the network edge. It brings computational resources closer to the data source, reducing latency and bandwidth requirements. Fog computing enables real-time processing, analysis, and decision-making at the network edge, where data are generated, allowing organizations to handle the velocity and volume of streaming data more efficiently. By deploying intelligent edge devices and leveraging deep learning capabilities, fog-computing empowers organizations to perform real-time analytics, edge intelligence, and efficient resource management, enhancing the overall performance of Big Data and Stream Data Analysis. The combination of these three domains paves the way for data-driven insights, timely decision-making, and improved operational efficiency in the era of massive and dynamic data streams.

### 10.3.3 Big Data, Stream Data, and the fog ecosystem. machine learning

Big Data, Stream Data, and the fog ecosystem are interconnected components that leverage machine learning techniques to harness the power of data analytics and drive valuable insights.

Big Data encompasses large and complex datasets that exceed the capabilities of traditional data processing methods. It involves the storage, management, and analysis of massive volumes of structured and unstructured data from various sources. Machine learning plays a crucial role in Big Data analytics, enabling organizations to extract meaningful patterns, correlations, and predictive models from the vast amount of data. By employing machine learning algorithms, such as clustering, classification, and regression, organizations can uncover hidden insights and make data-driven decisions, improving operational efficiency and gaining a competitive advantage.

Stream Data, on the other hand, refers to continuous and high-velocity data streams that are generated in real time from sources such as IoT devices, social media feeds, and sensor networks. The dynamic nature of Stream Data poses unique challenges for processing and analysis. Machine learning algorithms specifically designed for Stream Data Analysis, such as online learning and incremental algorithms, are utilized to handle the continuous flow of data and extract real-time insights. These algorithms adapt and update their models as new data arrive, enabling organizations to detect anomalies, identify trends, and respond promptly to changing conditions.

The fog ecosystem, which extends cloud computing capabilities to the network edge, complements Big Data and Stream Data Analysis by bringing computational resources closer to the data source. This proximity facilitates real-time analytics and decision-making, reduces latency, and optimizes resource utilization. Machine learning algorithms integrated into the fog ecosystem enhance data processing, analysis, and intelligence at the network edge. By deploying machine learning models within intelligent edge devices, organizations can perform distributed and localized analytics, handle the velocity and volume of data efficiently, and make real-time predictions and recommendations. The combination of Big Data, Stream Data, and the fog ecosystem, empowered by machine learning, creates a powerful framework for extracting valuable insights from diverse data sources and driving informed decision-making in real time [7].

## 10.3.4    Learning under guidance

Learning under guidance, also known as supervised learning, is a fundamental concept in machine learning that involves training a model using labeled data. In this approach, a set of input data points, along with their corresponding desired outputs or labels, is provided to the learning algorithm. The algorithm then leverages this labeled data to learn patterns, relationships, and decision boundaries that enable it to make accurate predictions or classifications on unseen data. Learning under guidance is widely used in various applications, including image recognition, natural language processing, and fraud detection, where the availability of labeled training data is crucial for model training and performance.

The key advantage of learning under guidance is that it allows the model to leverage existing knowledge or expertise to learn and generalize from labeled examples. By providing explicit guidance through labels, the model can understand the desired behavior and make informed decisions. Supervised learning algorithms, such as decision trees, support vector machines, and neural networks, use the labeled data to adjust their internal parameters and optimize their performance. The quality and representativeness of the labeled data are crucial factors in the success of learning under guidance, as they directly affect the model's ability to learn accurate and meaningful patterns from the data.

## 10.3.5 Decision trees with distributed nodes

Decision trees with distributed nodes are an extension of traditional decision tree algorithms that leverage the power of distributed computing environments. In this approach, the decision tree construction and evaluation process are distributed across multiple computing nodes or machines, enabling efficient handling of large-scale datasets and parallel processing.

Each computing node in the distributed system is responsible for a subset of the data and independently constructs a local decision tree based on its assigned data subset. This local decision tree captures the patterns and decision boundaries specific to the data subset available at that node. The local decision trees are then combined or aggregated to form a global decision tree that represents the collective knowledge and insights learned from the distributed nodes.

The distributed nature of decision trees brings several advantages. First, it enables the parallel construction and evaluation of decision trees, reducing the computational time required for processing large datasets. Second, the distributed approach allows for scalability, as the workload is divided among multiple nodes, enabling the handling of Big Data scenarios. Additionally, the distributed nodes can independently handle their local data, which can be advantageous in cases where data privacy or regulatory constraints restrict centralizing the entire dataset. Decision trees with distributed nodes provide a powerful framework for efficient and scalable analysis of large-scale datasets in distributed computing environments.

## 10.3.6 Methods for clustering large data

Clustering large data is a challenging task due to the sheer volume and complexity of the datasets involved. However, several methods have been developed to tackle this problem and enable efficient clustering of large-scale data.

One approach is the use of scalable clustering algorithms that are designed to handle large datasets. These algorithms employ techniques such as data partitioning, sampling, and parallel processing to divide the data into manageable subsets and perform clustering on each subset independently. Examples of scalable clustering algorithms include k-means++, DBSCAN (density-based spatial clustering of applications with noise) with scalable density-based indexing, and BIRCH (balanced iterative reducing and clustering using hierarchies). These algorithms enable efficient clustering of large data by distributing the computation across multiple processing units, reducing the memory requirements, and enabling parallelization.

Another approach is the utilization of dimensionality reduction techniques before clustering. Large datasets often have a high-dimensional feature space, which can lead to the curse of dimensionality and hinder clustering performance.

Dimensionality reduction methods, such as principal component analysis (PCA) or t-distributed stochastic neighbor embedding (t-SNE), can be applied to reduce the number of dimensions while preserving the important structure and variance in the data. By transforming the data to a lower dimensional representation, clustering algorithms can be more effective in capturing the underlying patterns and grouping the data points based on their similarities.

### 10.3.7    Tools like DBSCAN and DENCLUE are developed for use in Big Data environments

Tools like DBSCAN and DENCLUE (DENsity-based CLUstEring) have been specifically developed to address the challenges of clustering in Big Data environments. These tools offer efficient and scalable solutions for clustering large datasets with high dimensionality and complex structures.

DBSCAN is a DENCLUE algorithm that groups together data points based on their density and connectivity. It can identify clusters of arbitrary shape and handle noise and outliers effectively. DBSCAN operates by defining a neighborhood around each data point and identifying dense regions, where a minimum number of neighboring points fall within a specified radius. This algorithm is particularly well suited for Big Data as it can handle large datasets efficiently by employing spatial indexing structures, such as R-trees, and by avoiding the need for global distance calculations.

DENCLUE, on the other hand, is a DENCLUE algorithm that utilizes a statistical approach to cluster data points. It models the data distribution using probability density functions and estimates the density at each data point. DENCLUE can handle datasets with complex patterns and nonlinear structures. It is scalable to Big Data environments by leveraging techniques such as parallel processing and incremental updates to adapt to dynamic datasets.

Both DBSCAN and DENCLUE are designed to handle the challenges of clustering in Big Data environments, including scalability, noise tolerance, and handling complex data structures. These tools enable the efficient analysis and organization of large-scale datasets, providing insights and patterns that can drive decision-making and understanding in various domains, including business intelligence, scientific research, and pattern recognition.

### 10.3.8    Tree-based incremental clustering

Tree-based incremental clustering is a technique that combines the advantages of tree structures and incremental clustering algorithms to efficiently handle data streams or dynamic datasets. This approach is particularly useful when dealing with large-scale data that arrive sequentially and need to be clustered in real time or with limited memory requirements.

In tree-based incremental clustering, the data are organized into a hierarchical tree structure, such as a binary tree or a B+-tree, based on similarity measures or distance metrics. The tree structure allows for efficient insertion, deletion, and search operations, facilitating real-time clustering updates as new data arrive. Each node in the tree represents a cluster or a subcluster, and the structure provides a natural hierarchy that captures the relationships and similarities among the data points.

As new data points are added to the system, the tree structure is dynamically updated to accommodate the changes in the clustering. Incremental clustering algorithms, such as BIRCH, maintain and update the tree structure as new data points are inserted. These algorithms optimize the clustering process by controlling the growth of the tree and merging or splitting clusters as needed. The tree-based incremental clustering approach enables efficient and scalable clustering of dynamic data, allowing for real-time analysis and adaptive clustering updates while conserving memory usage and computational resources.

### 10.3.9 Mining association rules in large datasets with a P2P distributed computing architecture

Mining association rules in large datasets can be a computationally intensive task that requires significant processing power and storage capacity. To address this challenge, a peer-to-peer (P2P) distributed computing architecture can be employed to distribute the workload and leverage the collective resources of multiple machines.

In a P2P distributed computing architecture for mining association rules, each peer in the network acts as a computing node. The large dataset is partitioned and distributed among these nodes, enabling parallel processing of the data. Each node performs the association rule mining locally on its assigned data subset, identifying frequent itemsets and generating association rules. These local results are then combined and merged to produce the final set of association rules.

The P2P distributed computing architecture offers several advantages for mining association rules in large datasets. First, it allows for efficient utilization of resources by distributing the computational workload across multiple nodes, enabling parallel processing and reducing the overall execution time. Second, it enhances scalability as additional nodes can be added to the network to handle larger datasets or increase processing power. Additionally, the distributed nature of the architecture provides fault tolerance, as the failure of a single node does not disrupt the entire process.

Overall, leveraging a P2P distributed computing architecture for mining association rules in large datasets enables efficient and scalable processing, improving the speed and performance of association rule mining tasks. By harnessing the collective power of multiple computing nodes, this approach allows for effective analysis of large-scale data, enabling the extraction of valuable associations and patterns that can drive decision-making and business insights [8].

### 10.3.10 Associative mining in real time

Associative mining in real time refers to the process of extracting associations and patterns from streaming or dynamic data in a timely manner. Unlike traditional associative mining techniques that focus on static datasets, real-time associative mining enables the discovery of associations as data arrive, allowing for immediate insights and decision-making.

Real-time associative mining involves continuously analyzing data streams, detecting frequent itemsets, and generating association rules in real time. It requires algorithms and techniques that can adapt to the dynamic nature of the data, handle high velocity and volume, and provide timely results. Techniques such as sliding window-based approaches, incremental mining algorithms, and online learning methods are commonly used to perform associative mining in real time.

The benefits of real-time associative mining are significant. It enables organizations to uncover immediate insights, identify emerging patterns or trends, and take prompt actions based on the discovered associations. Real-time associative mining finds applications in various domains, including online retail, financial fraud detection, social media analysis, and IoT sensor networks. By extracting associations in real time, organizations can leverage up-to-date information, improve operational efficiency, and gain a competitive advantage in dynamic and rapidly evolving environments.

## 10.3.11 *Methods for extensive learning*

Extensive learning refers to a class of machine learning methods that focus on extracting knowledge and patterns from large and complex datasets. These methods go beyond traditional learning algorithms to handle the challenges posed by Big Data. Several methods are discussed for extensive learning.

Deep learning is a powerful method for extensive learning that utilizes artificial neural networks with multiple layers. These deep neural networks can learn intricate patterns and hierarchical representations from massive datasets. By employing deep learning models such as convolutional neural networks (CNNs) or recurrent neural networks (RNNs), complex relationships and features can be learned automatically, enabling accurate predictions and insightful representations. Transfer learning is a method that leverages knowledge learned from one domain or task and applies it to another. It allows models to transfer the learned features and representations from a source domain to a target domain, even when the datasets are different. Transfer learning reduces the need for extensive labeled data in the target domain and speeds up the learning process, making it particularly useful in scenarios with limited labeled data. Ensemble learning combines multiple individual models to create a more accurate and robust prediction model. It involves training multiple models, each with different settings or data subsets, and combining their predictions to make the final decision. Ensemble methods, such as random forests or gradient boosting, improve the generalization and reliability of extensive learning models by reducing bias and variance, and capturing diverse perspectives from the dataset. Online learning is a method suited for continuous and dynamic learning scenarios, where data arrive sequentially or in streams. It enables models to update and adapt to new data instances on the fly. Online learning algorithms, such as online gradient descent or adaptive learning rates, are designed to handle large-scale data streams efficiently, making them ideal for extensive learning in real-time applications.

Semi-supervised learning utilizes both labeled and unlabeled data to train models. This method capitalizes on the abundance of unlabeled data, which is often easier to obtain compared to labeled data. By leveraging the unlabeled data, models can learn additional patterns and representations, improving their performance and generalization capabilities. Active learning is a method where the model interacts with a human annotator or expert to request labels for specific instances. The model selects the most informative or uncertain instances for which it needs additional information. This iterative process allows the model to focus on learning from the most critical data points, reducing the need for extensive labeling efforts. Bayesian learning incorporates prior knowledge or beliefs into the learning process. It leverages Bayesian inference to update the model's beliefs based on observed data, enabling more robust and interpretable learning. Bayesian methods handle uncertainty and missing data well, making them suitable for extensive learning in complex and uncertain domains. Self-supervised learning is a method where the model learns to predict or reconstruct the input data itself, without relying on external labels. It leverages the inherent structure or relationships within the data to create proxy tasks for learning. By training models to solve these proxy tasks, they acquire meaningful representations and can be fine-tuned for specific learning tasks.

One-class learning focuses on learning models from only one class of data. This method is useful when the dataset is heavily imbalanced or when the primary interest lies in detecting anomalies or outliers. One-class learning algorithms, such as support vector data description or generative models, learn representations of the target class and separate it from the rest of the data. Dimensionality reduction techniques aim to reduce the number of input features while preserving relevant information. By reducing the dimensionality, models become more efficient, have improved interpretability, and can handle large-scale datasets. Methods such as PCA, t-SNE, or auto encoders are commonly used for extensive learning. Clustering is a method for unsupervised learning that groups data instances into similar clusters based on their intrinsic similarities. It enables exploratory analysis and identification of underlying patterns in extensive datasets. Clustering methods, such as k-means, hierarchical clustering, or DENCLUE, are useful for extensive learning to gain insights into the data structure.

Graph-based learning represents data as a graph, where nodes represent instances and edges capture relationships or connections. By exploiting the graph structure, models can learn from the relationships between data points, uncovering hidden patterns or communities within the dataset. Graph-based learning methods, such as graph neural networks (GNNs) or random walk algorithms, are suitable for extensive learning in network or social network analysis. Reinforcement learning is a method that focuses on learning through interactions with an environment to maximize rewards. It is well suited for extensive learning in scenarios where actions have long-term consequences and sequential decision-making is required. Reinforcement learning algorithms, such as Q-learning or policy gradient methods, learn optimal strategies through trial-and-error interactions, making them applicable to various complex tasks.

Semi-structured data mining deals with data that contain both structured and unstructured components, such as text, XML, or JSON data. Techniques such as natural language processing, text mining, or information extraction are employed to extract knowledge from semi-structured data. These methods enable extensive learning from unstructured or loosely structured data sources. Deep reinforcement learning combines deep learning with reinforcement learning to address complex and high-dimensional problems. It leverages deep neural networks to learn representations and policies, enabling models to make decisions in high-dimensional state spaces. Deep reinforcement learning methods, such as deep Q-networks or deep policy gradients, have achieved significant success in extensive learning tasks, including game playing, robotics, and autonomous systems. Evolutionary algorithms mimic the process of natural evolution to search for optimal solutions in complex spaces. They are particularly useful for extensive learning when dealing with high-dimensional parameter optimization or combinatorial problems. Evolutionary algorithms, such as genetic algorithms or particle swarm optimization, can explore large solution spaces, find near-optimal solutions, and handle noisy or non-convex objective functions. Neural architecture search (NAS) aims to automate the process of designing and optimizing neural network architectures. NAS techniques explore a search space of potential architectures and use methods such as reinforcement learning or evolutionary algorithms to discover architectures that perform well on specific tasks. NAS enables extensive learning by automating the process of model design, allowing for the exploration of complex architectures in large-scale datasets.

Anomaly detection focuses on identifying rare or abnormal instances in a dataset. It is a critical method for extensive learning, especially in domains where detecting anomalies is of utmost importance, such as fraud detection or cybersecurity. Anomaly detection algorithms, such as isolation forests, support vector machines, or autoencoders, can learn normal patterns and identify deviations from them. Gaussian processes are probabilistic models that provide a flexible framework for modeling complex data relationships. They can capture nonlinear and nonparametric patterns, making them suitable for extensive learning tasks with uncertain or noisy data. Gaussian processes enable Bayesian learning and handle uncertainty well, allowing for robust predictions and efficient data analysis. Meta-learning focuses on learning to learn, where models aim to acquire knowledge or strategies to improve the learning process itself. Meta-learning algorithms explore multiple tasks or datasets and learn transferable knowledge that can be applied to new tasks. This method enhances extensive learning by enabling models to adapt quickly to new domains or datasets, reducing the need for extensive training. Active feature acquisition involves selecting or acquiring the most informative or relevant features for a learning task. It addresses the challenge of high-dimensional data by actively choosing the features that contribute the most to the learning process. Active feature acquisition methods, such as information gain, mutual information, or sequential feature selection, can reduce dimensionality, improve model performance, and enhance interpretability.

Data augmentation is a technique that generates additional training samples by applying transformations or perturbations to the existing data. It helps overcome the limitations of limited labeled data and enhances the generalization capabilities of the model. Data augmentation methods, such as rotation, scaling, or noise injection, create diverse training samples that improve model robustness and performance in extensive learning tasks. Time series analysis focuses on extracting patterns and trends from data collected over time. It is applicable in extensive learning scenarios where data are recorded sequentially, such as financial data, sensor data, or stock market data. Time series analysis methods, including autoregressive integrated moving average (ARIMA), RNNs, or hidden Markov models, capture temporal dependencies and enable forecasting or anomaly detection. Annotated data generation involves generating synthetic or artificial data with known labels or annotations. It helps overcome the challenges of limited labeled data by artificially expanding the labeled dataset. Generative models, such as generative adversarial networks (GANs) or variational autoencoders (VAEs), can be used to generate realistic and diverse synthetic data, allowing for extensive learning with a more extensive and diverse training set.

## 10.3.12 Large-scale datasets and advanced machine learning

Large-scale datasets pose unique challenges and opportunities for advanced machine learning techniques. It explores the intersection of large-scale datasets and advanced machine learning and discusses various methods and approaches to tackle the complexities of analyzing and deriving insights from such data [9].

Large-scale datasets, often referred to as Big Data, are characterized by their volume, velocity, and variety. Advanced machine learning techniques are essential to handle the vast amount of data, extract meaningful patterns, and gain actionable insights. Traditional machine learning algorithms may struggle to scale to large datasets due to memory and processing constraints. Advanced machine learning methods, such as distributed computing frameworks (e.g., Apache Spark) and parallel processing, allow for efficient processing and analysis of large-scale data. Large datasets often come with high dimensionality, which can lead to the curse of dimensionality and impact the performance of machine learning models. Advanced techniques like PCA or t-SNE help reduce the dimensionality while preserving essential information.

Deep learning, with its ability to learn complex patterns and hierarchical representations, excels in large-scale data analysis. Deep neural networks, such as CNNs and RNNs, have achieved remarkable success in various domains, including computer vision, natural language processing, and speech recognition. Transfer learning allows models to leverage knowledge learned from one domain and apply it to another, even when the datasets are different. This approach reduces the need for extensive labeled data in the target domain and speeds up the learning process. Ensemble learning combines multiple individual models to create a more accurate and robust prediction model. Techniques like random forests, gradient boosting, or stacking enable models to benefit from diverse perspectives and handle the complexities of large-scale datasets. Large-scale datasets often include streaming data, where data arrive continuously and in real time. Advanced machine learning methods for streaming data, such as online learning and incremental algorithms, allow for real-time analysis and decision-making.

Incremental learning techniques enable models to update and adapt as new data arrive, without retraining the entire model. These methods are valuable for large-scale datasets that evolve over time, as they efficiently incorporate new information without requiring a complete reanalysis. Unsupervised learning algorithms, such as clustering or anomaly detection, are valuable for large-scale datasets where labeled data may be scarce or expensive to obtain. These methods allow for the exploration and identification of patterns, structures, and outliers in the data. Semi-supervised learning utilizes a combination of labeled and unlabeled data for training. With large-scale datasets, there is often a vast amount of unlabeled data available. Semi-supervised learning methods leverage this unlabeled data to improve model performance and generalize better to unseen instances. Active learning is a method where the model interacts with a human annotator or expert to selectively acquire labels for the most informative or uncertain instances. This approach helps reduce the labeling effort required for large-scale datasets by focusing on the most critical instances. Parallel processing frameworks, such as MapReduce or Apache Hadoop, enable distributed computing across clusters of machines. These frameworks partition the data and distribute the computation, allowing for efficient analysis of large-scale datasets. Sampling techniques, such as random sampling or stratified sampling, can be used to obtain representative subsets of the large-scale data for model training and evaluation. These subsets reduce the computational requirements while preserving the statistical properties of the data. Advanced data preprocessing techniques, such as data cleaning, normalization, or feature engineering, are crucial for large-scale datasets. These preprocessing steps ensure data quality, reduce noise, and enhance the learning process.

Graph-based learning: Graph-based learning methods are particularly suitable for large-scale datasets with complex relationships. GNNs and graph clustering algorithms can capture dependencies and patterns within the data, enabling more accurate predictions and insights. Active feature selection techniques help identify the most relevant features from a large feature space. By focusing on the most informative features, model training and inference become more efficient and interpretable. Distributed representation learning techniques, such as word embeddings or node embeddings, enable the creation of compact and meaningful representations for large-scale data. These representations capture the semantic and structural information, facilitating subsequent analysis and learning tasks. Online anomaly detection methods monitor streaming data in real time to identify deviations from expected patterns. These methods are vital for large-scale datasets where the early detection of anomalies can have significant implications for security, fraud detection, or system monitoring. Large-scale deep learning models can be trained efficiently using distributed deep learning frameworks like TensorFlow or PyTorch. These frameworks leverage distributed computing resources, such as GPU clusters or distributed parameter servers, to train deep neural networks on massive datasets.

Large-scale machine learning models often require optimization over vast parameter spaces. Distributed optimization algorithms, such as stochastic gradient descent with parallel computing or parameter server architectures, enable efficient and scalable training of models on distributed systems. Approximate computing techniques trade off precision for computational efficiency, enabling faster processing and analysis of large-scale datasets. These techniques can be applied to certain machine learning algorithms, such as clustering or dimensionality reduction, where approximations do not significantly impact the final results.

Data compression methods, such as lossless or lossy compression algorithms, help reduce the storage requirements and computational costs associated with large-scale datasets. Compressed data can be efficiently stored, transmitted, and analyzed, enabling faster processing and minimizing resource usage. Automated machine learning (AutoML) frameworks automate the process of model selection, hyperparameter tuning, and feature engineering. These frameworks assist in handling large-scale datasets by streamlining the model development pipeline and reducing the manual effort required for experimentation and optimization. Reinforcement learning methods tackle large-scale environments, such as game simulations or robotic control, by using value-based or policy-based algorithms. These algorithms learn optimal strategies by interacting with the environment and are scalable to handle complex state and action spaces.

Large-scale datasets often require extensive hyperparameter tuning to optimize model performance. Parallel hyperparameter tuning techniques, such as grid search or Bayesian optimization, leverage distributed computing resources to speed up the process and efficiently explore the hyperparameter space. Federated learning enables model training on decentralized data sources, such as devices or edge nodes, without the need for data centralization. This approach is valuable for large-scale datasets distributed across multiple locations, as it preserves data privacy and reduces data transfer overheads. Once models are trained, distributing model serving across multiple nodes or edge devices enhances the scalability and real-time inference capabilities. Distributed model serving frameworks, such as TensorFlow Serving or Kubernetes, facilitate efficient model deployment and inference on large-scale data.

Probabilistic graphical models, such as Bayesian networks or Markov random fields, provide a framework to model and reason about uncertainty in large-scale datasets. These models capture probabilistic dependencies and allow for probabilistic inference, enabling robust decision-making and uncertainty quantification. Online learning techniques adapt to evolving data streams and concept drift in real time. These methods continuously update the model based on incoming data, making them suitable for large-scale datasets with shifting data distributions and changing patterns.

Large-scale datasets often contain sensitive or personally identifiable information. Advanced techniques for data anonymization, such as differential privacy or secure multiparty computation, protect privacy while enabling data analysis and machine learning on sensitive data. Deep reinforcement learning combines deep learning and reinforcement learning to handle large-scale sequential decision-making problems. It has shown success in domains such as robotics, autonomous vehicles, and game playing, where decision-making requires processing vast amounts of data over time. Active data cleaning methods automate the process of identifying and correcting errors or inconsistencies in large-scale datasets. These methods prioritize data cleaning efforts based on the impact of errors on subsequent analysis, reducing the manual effort required for data quality assurance. Time series analysis techniques capture temporal dependencies and patterns in large-scale time-stamped datasets. Methods such as autoregressive integrated moving average (ARIMA), RNNs, or long short-term memory (LSTM) networks are widely used to model and forecast time series data. Multimodal learning deals with large-scale datasets that include multiple modalities, such as images, text, and audio. Advanced machine learning methods, including multimodal fusion techniques and deep multi-modal architectures, enable the integration and analysis of information from diverse data sources. Active labeling methods aim to reduce the labeling effort required for large-scale datasets by selectively acquiring labels for the most informative or challenging instances. By focusing on critical instances, models can achieve high accuracy with a smaller labeled dataset. GNNs are designed to handle large-scale data with graph structures, such as social networks, citation networks, or knowledge graphs. GNNs capture graph relationships and enable node or graph-level predictions, facilitating tasks like node classification, link prediction, or graph generation.

Deep generative models, such as VAEs or GANs, generate new data samples that resemble the characteristics of the original large-scale datasets. These models provide powerful tools for data augmentation, data synthesis, and exploration of the underlying data distribution. Domain adaptation techniques help address the challenges of deploying machine learning models trained on one domain to another domain. With large-scale datasets, domain adaptation is crucial to ensure model generalization across different datasets or environments. Advanced techniques for hyperparameter optimization, such as Bayesian optimization or evolutionary algorithms, efficiently explore the hyperparameter space of machine learning models. These methods help identify optimal hyperparameters for large-scale datasets and improve model performance. Self-supervised learning is an approach where models learn to predict or reconstruct missing or masked parts of the data without relying on external labels. This technique is particularly valuable for large-scale datasets where obtaining labeled data are challenging or expensive.

Deep metric learning methods learn embeddings or distance metrics that capture semantic similarities between data instances. These techniques are well suited for large-scale datasets, enabling efficient retrieval, clustering, or classification based on similarity metrics. Time-to-event analysis, also known as survival analysis, focuses on modeling and predicting time until an event occurs. Advanced machine learning techniques, such as Cox proportional hazards models or deep learning-based survival models, are applied to large-scale datasets in domains like healthcare, finance, or customer churn prediction.

Uncertainty quantification methods estimate and quantify the uncertainty associated with machine learning models' predictions. With large-scale datasets, these techniques provide valuable insights into the reliability and confidence of model outputs. Causal inference methods aim to identify causal relationships from observational data. They are used to uncover cause-effect relationships and make informed decisions based on large-scale datasets, where controlled experiments may be impractical or unethical. Robust learning techniques aim to enhance model performance and resilience to adversarial attacks or outliers in large-scale datasets. Robust learning methods, such as adversarial training or outlier detection, ensure models are more reliable and less susceptible to perturbations. Compressed sensing techniques leverage the sparsity or low-dimensional structure of large-scale datasets to accurately recover the original signals from compressed or sampled measurements. These methods allow for efficient acquisition, storage, and processing of large-scale data. Analyzing the time complexity of machine learning algorithms is crucial when dealing with large-scale datasets. Advanced methods for time complexity analysis help estimate the computational requirements and scalability of algorithms to ensure efficient processing.

Automated feature engineering techniques automate the process of generating relevant features from large-scale datasets. These methods use domain knowledge or heuristics to derive informative features automatically, reducing the manual effort and expertise required for feature engineering. Interpreting large-scale machine learning models is challenging due to their complexity and size. Distributed model interpretability techniques, such as feature importance analysis or rule extraction, help understand and interpret models' predictions across distributed systems or massive datasets. Visualization plays a crucial role in understanding and exploring large-scale datasets. Advanced visualization techniques, such as interactive visualizations, dimensionality reduction plots, or network visualizations, aid in identifying patterns, outliers, and insights from the complex data structures.

### 10.3.13    Scale-up models

Scale-up models refer to the process of increasing the capacity and capabilities of a machine learning model to handle larger and more complex datasets. When the size of the data exceeds the processing capabilities of the existing model, scale-up models offer a solution by expanding the model's capacity without sacrificing performance. This involves optimizing the computational resources, memory, and algorithms used by the model to accommodate the increased data volume.

One common approach in scale-up models is to leverage parallel processing techniques. By distributing the computational workload across multiple machines or processing units, parallel processing enables the model to process and analyze larger datasets more efficiently. This can be achieved through frameworks like Apache Spark or by implementing distributed computing architectures. Additionally, scale-up models often involve optimizing the model's algorithms and data structures to handle the increased data size and complexity. This may include using more efficient data representations, implementing data compression techniques, or employing algorithms specifically designed for large-scale data processing. By scaling up models, organizations can unlock the potential of their data and extract valuable insights from vast and complex datasets [10].

### 10.3.14    Different approaches to fog analytics

Fog analytics refers to the analysis and processing of data at the edge of the network in a fog-computing environment. It enables real-time data analysis and decision-making close to the data source, reducing latency and network bandwidth requirements. There are several different approaches to fog analytics that can be employed based on the specific requirements and constraints of the application.

One approach is to use edge analytics, where data are processed and analyzed directly on the edge devices or gateway devices within the fog network. This approach enables immediate insights and decision-making at the edge, eliminating the need to send all data to a centralized cloud for analysis. Edge analytics is particularly useful in applications that require real-time responses, low latency, or data privacy and security. It can help filter and prioritize data, extract relevant features, and make localized decisions, reducing the amount of data that need to be transmitted and processed in the cloud.

Another approach is to leverage distributed analytics in the fog network. In this approach, the analytics tasks are distributed across multiple fog nodes or devices within the network. Each node processes a subset of the data and collaboratively analyzes the results. Distributed analytics allows for parallel processing and scalability, as the workload can be distributed across multiple devices. This approach is beneficial when dealing with large-scale datasets or computationally intensive analytics tasks. It can improve processing efficiency, reduce network congestion, and provide fault tolerance in case of node failures.

Overall, the different approaches to fog analytics offer flexibility in analyzing data at the edge of the network. By bringing analytics closer to the data source, fog computing enables real-time insights, reduced latency, and improved scalability for applications that rely on data analysis and decision-making at the edge. The choice of approach depends on factors such as the application requirements, the size and complexity of the data, and the available resources within the fog network.

### 10.3.15    Other goods and services

In addition to physical goods, the market also encompasses a wide range of other goods and services that contribute to various aspects of our lives. These include intangible products, digital services, and experiential offerings that cater to diverse needs and preferences.

One category of other goods and services includes digital products such as software applications, e-books, music, and video streaming services. These offerings provide convenience and accessibility, allowing users to access and enjoy content across various devices. Digital services have transformed industries like entertainment, education, and communication, enabling seamless access to information and entertainment from anywhere at any time.

Furthermore, experiential goods and services have gained prominence in recent years. This category includes activities such as travel, dining experiences, event tickets, and wellness services. Experiential offerings focus on creating memorable and enjoyable experiences for consumers, often targeting specific interests and lifestyles. These experiences contribute to personal growth, social interactions, and leisure activities, providing individuals with opportunities for relaxation, exploration, and enrichment.

The market for other goods and services continues to evolve, driven by technological advancements, changing consumer preferences, and the desire for unique experiences. It offers a diverse array of options beyond physical products, catering to the intangible, digital, and experiential aspects of our lives.

## 10.3.16    ParStream

ParStream is a real-time analytics platform designed for processing and analyzing large-scale streaming data. It is built to handle high-velocity, high-volume data streams, enabling organizations to extract valuable insights and make informed decisions in real time. ParStream utilizes a combination of compression, indexing, and distributed computing techniques to achieve fast query response times and efficient data storage.

The platform employs a columnar database structure that optimizes data storage and retrieval. It compresses the data to reduce storage requirements while maintaining query performance. ParStream's indexing capabilities allow for quick data retrieval by leveraging indexes based on the values within columns. This enables fast filtering and aggregation of data, making it ideal for applications that require real-time analytics, such as IoT sensor data analysis, cybersecurity monitoring, or financial market analysis.

Moreover, ParStream's distributed computing architecture enables scalable and parallel processing of data streams. It can distribute data and queries across multiple nodes to handle the high data volumes and provide fault tolerance. This scalability ensures that ParStream can accommodate growing data streams and maintain performance as the system expands.

## 10.3.17    Cloud-based analytics in the periphery

Cloud-based analytics in the periphery refers to the utilization of cloud computing resources and analytics capabilities at the edge of the network, closer to the data sources. This approach leverages the benefits of cloud computing, such as scalability, storage capacity, and computational power, while enabling real-time analytics and decision-making at the edge.

By deploying cloud-based analytics in the periphery, organizations can reduce latency and bandwidth requirements by processing and analyzing data locally. This is particularly advantageous in scenarios where real-time insights and immediate actions are crucial, such as in industrial IoT applications or autonomous systems. With cloud-based analytics in the periphery, data can be processed at the edge devices or gateways, allowing for faster response times, enhanced data privacy, and reduced reliance on cloud connectivity.

Furthermore, cloud-based analytics in the periphery enables efficient data filtering and aggregation. By performing initial data processing and analysis at the edge, organizations can reduce the amount of data that need to be transmitted and stored in the cloud. This helps minimize network congestion, optimize bandwidth usage, and reduce costs associated with data transfer and storage in the cloud. Additionally, local analytics at the periphery can enable real-time anomaly detection, predictive maintenance, or personalized experiences, providing immediate insights and actions based on the analyzed data.

## 10.4  Cloud Security Ontology

Cloud Security Ontology (CSO) is a comprehensive framework that provides a structured representation of cloud security concepts, relationships, and properties. It serves as a knowledge model for understanding and addressing security concerns in cloud computing environments.

CSO establishes a clear understanding of cloud security concepts by defining and organizing them in a structured manner. It provides a common language and taxonomy for discussing and analyzing cloud security issues. CSO covers a wide range of cloud security domains, including data security, network security, identity and access management (IAM), compliance, incident response, and more. It ensures that all critical aspects of cloud security are considered and addressed. CSO captures the relationships and dependencies between different security concepts. It helps identify the interdependencies among security controls, vulnerabilities, threats, and countermeasures, enabling a holistic view of the security landscape. CSO takes into account the contextual factors of cloud environments, such as multi-tenancy, virtualization, elasticity, and shared responsibility models. It ensures that security considerations align with the unique characteristics and challenges of cloud computing.

CSO is designed to accommodate the evolving nature of cloud security. It can be extended and updated to incorporate emerging security technologies, standards, and best practices, ensuring its relevance and applicability over time. CSO provides a framework for assessing and managing risks in cloud environments. It helps identify potential threats, vulnerabilities, and their associated impacts, facilitating the implementation of effective risk mitigation strategies.

CSO includes provisions for compliance and governance in cloud computing. It aligns security controls and practices with relevant regulatory frameworks, industry standards, and organizational policies, ensuring adherence to legal and operational requirements. CSO assists in decision-making by providing a structured representation of cloud security concepts and their relationships. It supports the evaluation of different security options, the selection of appropriate controls, and the identification of gaps or areas requiring improvement. CSO fosters knowledge sharing and collaboration among stakeholders involved in cloud security. It provides a common framework for communication, facilitates information exchange, and enables better coordination between different teams and organizations. CSO can be integrated with security tools and platforms to enhance automation and streamline security management processes. It enables the mapping of security controls to specific cloud services, facilitates security monitoring and incident response, and supports the automation of security-related tasks.

Table 10.1 presents the CSO, which serves as a foundational framework for understanding and addressing various aspects of cloud security. The first aspect,

*Table 10.1 Cloud Security Ontology (CSO)*

| Aspect | Description |
| --- | --- |
| Conceptual clarity | Provides a clear understanding of cloud security concepts |
| Comprehensive coverage | Covers a wide range of cloud security domains |
| Interconnections | Captures relationships and dependencies between security concepts |
| Contextual relevance | Considers the unique characteristics and challenges of cloud computing |
| Scalability and adaptability | Can be extended and updated to incorporate emerging security technologies |
| Risk assessment and mitigation | Provides a framework for assessing and managing risks in cloud environments |
| Compliance and governance | Aligns security controls with regulatory frameworks and organizational policies |
| Decision support | Assists in decision-making for selecting security controls and evaluating options |
| Knowledge sharing and collaboration | Facilitates communication and collaboration among stakeholders involved in cloud security |
| Tool integration and automation | Enables integration with security tools and platforms for automation and streamlined security management |

"Conceptual Clarity," highlights the CSO's ability to provide a clear and unambiguous understanding of cloud security concepts. This ensures that all stakeholders, from security professionals to business leaders, can effectively communicate and align their efforts to secure cloud-based systems. By establishing a common language and conceptual framework, the CSO enhances collaboration and decision-making in the context of cloud security. The CSO's "Comprehensive Coverage" is another crucial aspect, as it encompasses a wide range of cloud security domains. Cloud computing introduces unique security challenges due to its distributed nature and reliance on shared resources. The CSO addresses these challenges by capturing the diverse aspects of cloud security, including data protection, network security, IAM, and more. This comprehensive coverage allows organizations to adopt a holistic approach to securing their cloud environments, leaving no critical aspect unaddressed. Furthermore, the "Interconnections" aspect of the CSO is vital for understanding the relationships and dependencies between different security concepts. Cloud security is not isolated but interconnected, where actions in one area can affect others. The CSO's interconnections enable a deeper understanding of these relationships, guiding security practitioners to make informed decisions and implement robust security measures. By recognizing the complex interplay of security elements, organizations can better design, deploy, and manage secure cloud infrastructures. The "contextual relevance" attribute emphasizes that the CSO considers the unique characteristics and challenges of cloud computing. Cloud environments differ significantly from traditional on-premises setups, with varying deployment models (public, private, and hybrid), elasticity, and service models (IaaS, PaaS, and SaaS). The CSO takes these contextual factors into account, ensuring that security measures are tailored to fit the specific requirements of cloud-based deployments. This adaptability is essential in safeguarding data, applications, and services in the dynamic and evolving cloud landscape. The "scalability and adaptability" aspect ensures that the CSO can be extended and updated to incorporate emerging security technologies and best practices. Cloud security is an ever-evolving field, and new threats and technologies continuously emerge. The CSO's ability to scale and adapt allows it to remain relevant and effective over time, accommodating changes in the cloud ecosystem and enabling organizations to stay ahead of emerging threats. The "risk assessment and mitigation" attribute is particularly valuable in cloud security, where risk management is critical due to the shared nature of cloud resources and potential exposure to external threats. The CSO's framework for assessing and managing risks provides organizations with a structured approach to identify vulnerabilities and implement appropriate mitigation strategies, enhancing the overall security posture of their cloud deployments. Moreover, the "compliance and governance" aspect aligns cloud security controls with regulatory frameworks and organizational policies. Compliance is a key concern in cloud computing, where data privacy and protection regulations often apply. The CSO aids in meeting these compliance requirements by providing guidance on implementing security measures that adhere to relevant regulations and organizational governance principles. The "decision support" attribute of the CSO is invaluable for organizations facing choices in selecting security controls and evaluating different security options. With a wealth of cloud security measures available, decision-making can become overwhelming. The CSO streamlines this process by offering a structured and well-defined set of security options, making it easier for organizations to identify the most suitable solutions for their specific cloud security needs.

In Table 10.1, ontologies play a vital role in knowledge management, information retrieval, and data integration, as they provide a structured representation that facilitates efficient searching, organization, and discovery of relevant information. With the growing complexity of domains and the increasing volume of data, ontologies have become essential tools for knowledge representation and management, contributing to improved efficiency, accuracy, and collaboration across various fields of study and industries.

## 10.4.1   Create an ontology for safer cloud computing

Creating an ontology for safer cloud computing is a crucial step toward enhancing the security and trustworthiness of cloud-based systems. An ontology provides a structured representation of security concepts, relationships, and properties specific to the cloud computing domain. By developing an ontology for safer cloud computing, organizations can establish a common understanding and standardized framework for addressing security concerns.

The ontology should encompass various dimensions of cloud security, including data protection, access control, threat detection, incident response, and compliance. It should capture the interconnections and dependencies between these security aspects, enabling a holistic view of the security landscape. Additionally, the ontology should consider the unique characteristics of cloud computing, such as multi-tenancy, virtualization, and shared responsibility models, to ensure contextual relevance and alignment with industry best practices.

With a well-defined ontology, organizations can benefit in several ways. First, it provides a common language and taxonomy for communication and collaboration among stakeholders, including cloud service providers, customers, auditors, and regulators. This facilitates knowledge sharing, promotes consistent security practices, and enables effective coordination in addressing security challenges. Second, the ontology serves as a foundation for risk assessment, enabling organizations to identify and mitigate potential threats and vulnerabilities specific to cloud environments. It aids in the selection and implementation of appropriate security controls, ensuring robust protection of sensitive data and systems. Ultimately, a comprehensive and well-constructed ontology for safer cloud computing contributes to building trust, improving security posture, and fostering a safer cloud ecosystem.

## 10.4.2 Ontology: what it is and why it matters

An ontology is a structured representation of knowledge that captures concepts, entities, relationships, and properties within a specific domain. It serves as a common vocabulary and a shared understanding of the domain, enabling effective communication, knowledge sharing, and reasoning. Ontologies provide a formal and organized framework for representing knowledge, making it easier to capture, manage, and utilize information in a systematic manner.

The significance of ontologies lies in their ability to bring clarity and coherence to complex domains. By defining concepts and their relationships, ontologies facilitate knowledge integration, enable interoperability between different systems, and support reasoning and inference. They help overcome language barriers and promote a shared understanding of domain-specific concepts, allowing stakeholders to communicate more effectively and make informed decisions. In Table 10.2, ontologies play a vital role in knowledge management, information retrieval, and data

*Table 10.2  A simple ontology structure*

| Class | Subclass | Property | Description |
|---|---|---|---|
| **Person** | Employee | Name | Represents an individual |
| | | Age | Represents the age of the person |
| | | Position | Represents the job position of the employee |
| | Customer | Name | Represents a customer |
| | | Address | Represents the address of the customer |
| **Product** | Electronics | Brand | Represents the brand of an electronic product |
| | | Price | Represents the price of the electronic product |
| | Clothing | Brand | Represents the brand of a clothing product |
| | | Size | Represents the size of the clothing product |

integration, as they provide a structured representation that facilitates efficient searching, organization, and discovery of relevant information. With the growing complexity of domains and the increasing volume of data, ontologies have become essential tools for knowledge representation and management, contributing to improved efficiency, accuracy, and collaboration across various fields of study and industries.

### 10.4.3    CSO architecture as it is defined and operationalized

The CSO architecture defines the structure and components of the ontology and how it is operationalized within a cloud computing environment. It encompasses both the conceptual design and the technical implementation of the ontology. The architecture ensures that the CSO is effectively utilized to enhance cloud security.

At a conceptual level, the CSO architecture outlines the core elements of the ontology, such as classes, subclasses, properties, and relationships, which capture the security concepts relevant to cloud computing. It defines the hierarchy and organization of these elements, enabling a comprehensive representation of the security domain. Additionally, the architecture specifies the mappings and alignments of the CSO with existing security standards, frameworks, and regulatory requirements, ensuring its compatibility and interoperability within the broader security landscape.

From a technical perspective, the CSO architecture details the operationalization of the ontology within cloud computing environments. This includes considerations for data storage, querying, and reasoning mechanisms that support the efficient utilization of the CSO. It outlines the integration of the CSO with security management systems, tools, and platforms, enabling seamless incorporation of the ontology into existing security frameworks. Moreover, the architecture addresses scalability, extensibility, and versioning aspects of the CSO to accommodate evolving security requirements and advancements in cloud computing technologies.

The CSO architecture provides a road map for designing, implementing, and utilizing the ontology effectively. It ensures that the CSO is not only well-defined and aligned with security standards but also operationalized in a manner that maximizes its benefits in enhancing cloud security. By following the CSO architecture, organizations can effectively leverage the ontology to address security challenges, improve risk management, and foster a more secure cloud computing environment. Figure 10.1 in the CSO represents a visual depiction of the ontology structure and its key components. This figure provides an overview of the classes, subclasses, and relationships that constitute the CSO, offering a concise and organized representation of the cloud security concepts captured within the ontology. The visual depiction aids in understanding the hierarchical structure of the ontology, facilitating communication and comprehension of the security domain in a more intuitive and accessible manner. It serves as a valuable reference point for stakeholders involved in cloud security, enabling them to navigate and explore the CSO effectively.

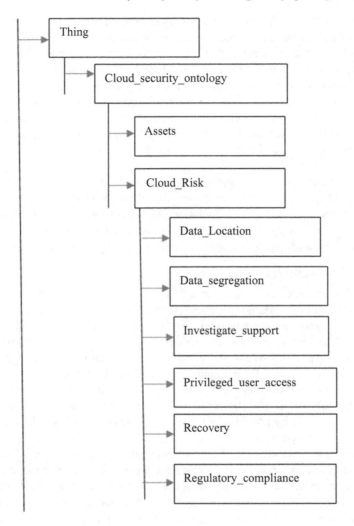

*Figure 10.1   CSO ontology*

## 10.4.4   Cloud computing security requirements

Cloud computing security requirements encompass a set of essential considerations that organizations must address to ensure the secure deployment and operation of their cloud based systems. These requirements are critical for safeguarding sensitive data, maintaining privacy, and mitigating potential risks in the cloud computing environment.

First, data protection is a fundamental security requirement. Organizations need to ensure that appropriate measures are in place to protect data confidentiality, integrity, and availability throughout its life cycle. This includes implementing robust encryption mechanisms, secure data storage, and access controls to prevent unauthorized access, disclosure, or modification of data.

Second, IAM is crucial in cloud computing environments. Organizations should establish strong authentication and authorization mechanisms to verify the identity of users and control their access to cloud resources. This includes employing multifactor authentication, role-based access control, and strong password policies to minimize the risk of unauthorized access.

Third, network security is vital to protect the communication channels and data transmission within the cloud environment. Secure network configurations, such as firewalls, intrusion detection and prevention systems, and virtual private networks, are necessary to safeguard against unauthorized network access, data interception, and malicious activities.

Lastly, compliance and regulatory requirements must be addressed in cloud computing. Organizations need to ensure that their cloud deployments adhere to relevant industry standards, legal regulations, and data protection laws. This includes complying with data residency and sovereignty requirements, conducting regular audits, and maintaining proper documentation of security controls and procedures.

### 10.4.5   Non-repudiation

Non-repudiation (NR) is a vital security concept that ensures the integrity and accountability of digital transactions and communications. It is the ability to provide evidence that a specific action or transaction took place and that the parties involved cannot deny their involvement or the authenticity of the exchanged information.

One key aspect of NR is the establishment of strong digital signatures or cryptographic techniques. Digital signatures provide a means to verify the integrity and origin of a digital message or document, making it impossible for the sender to deny their involvement. The use of public-key infrastructure and digital certificates further enhances NR by providing a trusted mechanism to validate the identities of the communicating parties.

Another important element of NR is the logging and preservation of transaction records and digital evidence. A comprehensive audit trail is maintained to track and document all relevant actions, communications, and transactions, including timestamps and associated metadata. This ensures that a reliable record of events is available to establish the sequence of activities and verify the authenticity of the transactions.

Furthermore, legal frameworks and regulations that recognize the validity and enforceability of digital signatures and the associated evidence often support NR. These regulations establish the legal basis for holding parties accountable for their actions and enable dispute resolution in case of repudiation.

NR is a critical security requirement in various domains, including e-commerce, financial transactions, legal agreements, and sensitive communications. It provides assurance and trust in the digital realm, protecting against fraudulent activities, disputes, and repudiation of actions. By ensuring NR, organizations and individuals can confidently engage in digital transactions and communications, knowing that the integrity and authenticity of their interactions are preserved and legally enforceable if necessary.

### 10.4.6   Conceptual software architecture

Conceptual software architecture (CSO) refers to the high-level design and structure of a software system, focusing on the conceptual components and their interactions.

It provides a blueprint for the software system's organization, functionality, and behavior, laying the foundation for the development and implementation phases.

The CSO defines the key conceptual elements of the software system, such as modules, components, layers, and interfaces, along with their responsibilities and relationships. It captures the overall structure and organization of the system, enabling developers to understand the system's architecture without delving into implementation details. The CSO serves as a communication tool between stakeholders, allowing them to discuss and align on the system's structure, functionality, and nonfunctional requirements.

The CSO also aids in system analysis and decision-making by providing an abstract representation of the software system. It allows for the identification of major system components, their interactions, and the flow of data or control within the system. This abstraction helps in identifying potential bottlenecks, architectural flaws, or areas for improvement before the actual development phase begins.

### 10.4.7  Domain and scope determination for CSO

Domain and scope determination for CSO involves identifying the specific domain of the software system and defining the boundaries and extent of the architecture's coverage. It is a crucial step in the development process as it sets the context and focus for designing the CSO.

Domain determination entails understanding the problem space in which the software system operates. It involves analyzing the requirements, stakeholders, and the business or technical domain in which the system will be used. This process helps identify the specific challenges, constraints, and goals that the CSO should address. By gaining a deep understanding of the domain, developers can design an architecture that aligns with the unique characteristics and requirements of the system.

Scope determination involves defining the boundaries and limits of the CSO. It outlines the functional and nonfunctional aspects of the system that the architecture will cover. This includes identifying the major components, modules, or subsystems that need to be included in the CSO, as well as determining the relationships and interactions between them. The scope also helps establish what is out of scope, setting boundaries for what the CSO does not need to address.

### 10.4.8  Identify the ontology's imperative keywords

Identifying the imperative keywords in an ontology is crucial for understanding the essential concepts and relationships within the domain. These keywords serve as building blocks for constructing the ontology and capturing the key elements that define the domain's structure and semantics.

The first step in identifying imperative keywords is to thoroughly analyze the domain and its associated literature, standards, and existing ontologies. This involves conducting domain research, consulting subject matter experts, and studying relevant documentation. By doing so, one can identify the important terms, concepts, and relationships that are frequently used and play a central role in the domain.

Once the domain analysis is complete, imperative keywords can be identified based on their significance in representing the core concepts and relationships of the ontology. These keywords typically include nouns that represent entities or classes, verbs that represent relationships or actions, and adjectives or adverbs that

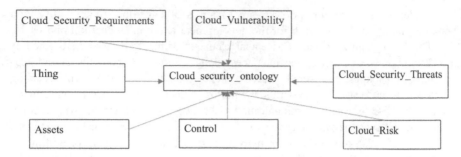

*Figure 10.2    Visualization (OntoGraf) of CSO*

describe properties or attributes. The imperative keywords should capture the essential components of the domain and be representative of the key concepts that need to be modeled within the ontology.

Figure 10.2, the visualization of CSO using OntoGraf, offers a graphical representation of the ontology's structure, concepts, and relationships. This visualization provides a visual overview of the CSO, facilitating a better understanding of its components and their interconnections. It presents a clear and intuitive depiction of the ontology, making it easier for stakeholders to grasp the complexity of the cloud security domain.

The visualization in Figure 10.2 showcases the classes, subclasses, and relationships within the CSO, highlighting the hierarchical organization and the connections between different concepts. Through visual cues such as nodes, edges, and labels, OntoGraf presents the ontology in a visually appealing and informative manner. This visualization enables stakeholders to navigate the CSO, explore its components, and comprehend the relationships between different security concepts.

By utilizing OntoGraf for visualizing CSO, stakeholders can gain valuable insights into the ontology's structure and semantics. They can visually explore the CSO, identify key classes, understand the inheritance hierarchy, and analyze the relationships between different concepts. This visualization aids in knowledge dissemination, promotes collaboration, and facilitates effective communication among stakeholders involved in cloud security discussions and decision-making processes.

## 10.5    Fog security and privacy

Building the CSO with OWL (Web Ontology Language) is a comprehensive process that involves carefully defining classes, properties, relationships, and rules to capture the essential elements of cloud security. Constructing the CSO using OWL enables a standardized and formal representation of cloud security concepts, allowing for effective knowledge representation, reasoning, and interoperability. The following paragraphs outline the key steps and considerations involved in building the CSO with OWL.

Clarify the specific domain and goals of the CSO, identifying the security concepts, standards, and best practices that need to be represented within the ontology. Conduct an in-depth analysis of relevant literature, security frameworks, and existing ontologies in the field of cloud security. This analysis helps identify established concepts, relationships, and terminology that can be leveraged in building the CSO. Identify the core classes that represent key cloud security concepts, such as "CloudProvider," "DataProtection," "AccessControl," and "ThreatDetection." Establish the hierarchical relationships between these classes by defining superclasses and subclasses, capturing specialization and generalization relationships. Determine the properties or attributes associated with each class. For example, the "CloudProvider" class may have properties such as "hasVendor," "hasServiceLevelAgreement," and "hasSecurityCertification." Define the relationships between classes using object properties. These properties represent how different classes are connected. For instance, an object property "hasDataProtection" can link the "CloudProvider" class with the "DataProtection" class.

Specify restrictions and cardinality constraints on properties to impose specific conditions or limitations. This ensures that relationships between classes adhere to desired rules and constraints. Define the domain and range of properties to restrict the types of classes that can be associated with them. This ensures the appropriate usage of properties within the CSO. Include axioms and rules within the CSO to enforce logical constraints, inferential rules, and consistency checks. These axioms and rules help maintain the integrity and coherence of the ontology. Incorporate metadata and annotations to provide additional information about classes, properties, and relationships. This includes adding labels, descriptions, and references to external resources.

Identify relevant external ontologies that can be integrated into the CSO to enhance interoperability and reusability. Align the CSO with established standards and ontologies in the field of cloud security. Perform iterative testing and validation of the CSO to ensure its accuracy, completeness, and adherence to domain requirements. Collaborate with domain experts to review and refine the ontology based on their expertise and feedback. Design the CSO to be scalable and extensible to accommodate future enhancements, evolving security requirements, and emerging technologies in cloud computing. If the CSO is intended for international use, consider providing multilingual support by incorporating language annotations and translations for labels and descriptions. Utilize the reasoning capabilities of OWL to infer implicit knowledge, identify inconsistencies, and perform automated checks on the CSO. Create comprehensive documentation that describes the purpose, structure, and usage guidelines of the CSO. This documentation serves as a reference for users, facilitating their understanding and utilization of the ontology.

Engage with the broader community of cloud security practitioners, researchers, and ontology experts to gather feedback, foster collaboration, and encourage the adoption of the CSO. Perform usability testing to evaluate the usability and effectiveness of the CSO. Incorporate user feedback and make iterative improvements to enhance the CSO's usability and user experience. Establish versioning and maintenance protocols to manage updates, revisions, and improvements to the CSO over time. Maintain a clear record of changes and ensure backward compatibility with previous versions. Develop visualization tools or use existing ones to generate graphical representations of the CSO, aiding in its understanding and interpretation by stakeholders.

Promote adoption and dissemination: Actively promote the adoption and dissemination of the CSO through publications, presentations, workshops, and collaborations. Encourage its integration into cloud security frameworks and standards. Establish governance mechanisms for the CSO to ensure its ongoing management, maintenance, and evolution. Encourage community participation in the development and evolution of the CSO through open contribution and collaboration. Test the interoperability of the CSO with other relevant ontologies, standards, and systems in the cloud security domain. Ensure seamless integration and interoperability with existing tools and platforms. Explore opportunities to integrate the CSO with established cloud security frameworks, such as ISO 27001, NIST Cybersecurity Framework, or CSA Security Guidance, to enhance compatibility and alignment. Optimize the performance of the CSO by considering efficient storage, retrieval, and querying techniques. Employ appropriate indexing and caching mechanisms for faster access to ontology data.

Ensure that the CSO appropriately addresses privacy concerns and handles sensitive information in compliance with relevant regulations and data protection standards.

Conduct comprehensive testing: Test the CSO extensively using a variety of scenarios, datasets, and use cases. Validate its effectiveness, accuracy, and performance under different conditions. Collaborate with domain experts and stakeholders in the field of cloud security to ensure that the CSO accurately represents the concepts and relationships specific to the domain. Seek peer review and expert feedback on the CSO to ensure its quality, accuracy, and adherence to ontology engineering principles. If the CSO is intended for global usage, ensure that it can be easily adapted and localized to different languages, regions, and cultural contexts. Foster a community of practice around the CSO, bringing together practitioners, researchers, and users to share experiences, best practices, and insights related to the CSO and cloud security. Keep up-to-date with emerging technologies, trends, and advancements in cloud security. Continuously assess and refine the CSO to align with evolving security requirements. Apply the CSO to real-world use cases and evaluate its effectiveness, applicability, and impact in solving cloud security challenges.

Ensure compliance with semantic web standards, such as RDF, RDFS, and OWL, to ensure interoperability and compatibility with other semantic web technologies and applications.

Address uncertainty and vagueness: Account for uncertainty and vagueness that may exist in cloud security concepts by incorporating fuzzy logic or probability-based approaches within the CSO. Consider cultural and legal differences when defining classes, properties, and relationships within the CSO. Ensure that the ontology remains inclusive and adaptable to diverse contexts. Engage with ontology communities, research groups, and organizations that focus on cloud security and ontological engineering. Collaborate and share knowledge to enhance the development and adoption of the CSO. Establish mechanisms to gather feedback from users and stakeholders of the CSO. Regularly assess the ontology's effectiveness and make iterative improvements based on user input and evolving requirements. Assess the performance and scalability of the CSO as the volume and complexity of cloud security knowledge grow. Optimize the ontology structure and reasoning mechanisms to ensure efficient and scalable operations.

Compare the CSO with other existing cloud security ontologies and frameworks to benchmark its effectiveness, coverage, and usability. Use the insights gained to further refine and enhance the CSO. Utilize ontology engineering tools, such as Protégé, to facilitate the development, management, and visualization of the CSO. These tools provide a range of functionalities to streamline ontology construction. Take into account domain-specific challenges, such as multi-tenancy, elasticity, and virtualization, when designing the CSO. Ensure that the ontology adequately represents the unique characteristics of cloud computing.

Promote semantic interoperability: Design the CSO to promote semantic interoperability by adhering to established standards and best practices in ontology engineering. Facilitate seamless integration and exchange of information with other systems and ontologies.

Continuously update and expand the CSO to address emerging security threats and vulnerabilities in cloud computing. Ensure that the ontology remains relevant and adaptable to changing security landscapes. Encourage collaboration and knowledge exchange between academia and industry in the development and utilization of the CSO. Bridge the gap between theoretical research and practical applications in cloud security. Design the CSO to be accessible and usable for a wide range of users, including security professionals, developers, auditors, and policymakers. Provide clear documentation and intuitive interfaces to enhance user experience. Incorporate semantic search and discovery capabilities within the CSO to enable efficient retrieval and discovery of cloud security knowledge. Facilitate the identification of relevant concepts, relationships, and best practices.

Ensure alignment with cloud computing standards: Align the CSO with established cloud computing standards, such as ISO 27017 (cloud security controls) or CSA's Cloud Control Matrix, to enhance its compatibility and compliance with industry best practices.

Establish processes and mechanisms for the continuous evolution and maintenance of the CSO. Incorporate feedback, adapt to evolving requirements, and ensure the long-term sustainability of the ontology. Actively engage with a community of CSO users to foster collaboration, gather insights, and facilitate knowledge sharing. Encourage users to contribute to the development, refinement, and extension of the CSO. Embrace a mindset of continuous improvement for the CSO. Regularly evaluate its effectiveness, collect feedback, and identify areas for enhancement. Strive for ongoing refinement and evolution to keep the CSO up-to-date with the evolving landscape of cloud security.

## 10.6　Conclusion

In conclusion, fog computing, coupled with deep learning capabilities, offers significant potential to improve Big Data analytics. The convergence of these technologies addresses the challenges of processing, analyzing, and deriving insights from massive volumes of data in a timely and efficient manner. Fog computing brings computing resources closer to the edge, enabling data processing and analytics to be performed at or near the source of data generation. This proximity reduces latency, bandwidth requirements, and dependency on cloud infrastructure, making it ideal for real-time and time-sensitive applications. Additionally, fog computing leverages distributed computing architectures, allowing for scalability, fault tolerance, and enhanced data privacy. The integration of deep learning capabilities within fog computing further enhances Big Data analytics. Deep learning algorithms, such as neural networks, excel in extracting complex patterns, relationships, and insights from large-scale datasets. By deploying deep learning models within the fog layer, real-time data analysis and decision-making can be performed directly at the edge, reducing the need for data transmission to a centralized cloud infrastructure. This approach enables faster and more efficient processing, especially in scenarios where low-latency response times are crucial.

The combination of fog computing and deep learning has the potential to revolutionize various industries and applications. From real-time monitoring and analysis of IoT devices to intelligent video surveillance, predictive maintenance, and personalized healthcare, the integration of fog computing and deep learning empowers organizations to harness the full potential of Big Data.

# References

[1] A. Vishwanath, R. Peruri, and J. Selena He, Security in Fog Computing through Encryption, *International Journal of Information Technology and Computer Science (IJITCS)*, 8, 28, 2016.

[2] C. Li, Z. Qin, E. Novak, and Q. Li, Securing SDN Infrastructure of IoTFog Networks from MitM Attacks, *IEEE Internet of Things Journal*, 4, 1156–1164, 2017.

[3] M. Tighe, G. Keller, M. Bauer, and H. Lutfiyya, DCSim: A Data Centre Simulation Tool for Evaluating Dynamic Virtualized Resource Management, in *8th International Conference on Network and Service Management (CNSM)*, 2012, pp. 385–392.

[4] Y. Jararweh, M. Jarrah, M. Kharbutli, Z. Alshara, M. N. Alsaleh, and M. Al-Ayyoub, CloudExp: A Comprehensive Cloud Computing Experimental Framework, *Simulation Modelling Practice and Theory*, 49, 180–192, 2014.

[5] H. Han, B. Sheng, C. C. Tan, Q. Li, and S. Lu, A Measurement Based Rogue AP Detection Scheme, in *IEEE INFOCOM*, 2009, pp. 1593–1601.

[6] H. Han, B. Sheng, C. C. Tan, Q. Li, and S. Lu, A Timing-Based Scheme for Rogue AP Detection, *IEEE Transactions on Parallel and Distributed Systems*, 22, 1912–1925, 2011.

[7] G. W. Kibirige and C. Sanga, A Survey on Detection of Sinkhole Attack in Wireless Sensor Network, *International Journal of Computer Science & Information Security*, 13, 48–52, 2015.

[8] S. Jain and A. Kajal, Effective Analysis of Risks and Vulnerabilities in Internet of Things, *International Journal of Computing and Corporate Research*, 5(2), 2015.

[9] A. TaheriMonfared and M. G. Jaatun, Handling Compromised Components in an IaaS Cloud Installation, *Journal of Cloud Computing*, 1, 1–21, 2012.

[10] C. Karlof and D. Wagner, Secure Routing in Wireless Sensor Networks: Attacks and Countermeasures, *Ad Hoc Networks*, 1, 293–315, 2003.

# Chapter 11

# Fog robotics

## Abstract

With the swift progress of robotics and the proliferation of edge computing technologies, fog computing has emerged as a promising paradigm to enable efficient data processing and decision-making capabilities for robotic systems in edge environments. This chapter provides a comprehensive overview of the background, scope, problem definition, aim, and analysis of fog computing in the realm of robotics.

**Background:** Fog computing leverages edge devices and cloud resources to enable real-time data processing and low-latency communication in close proximity to robotic systems. Robotics applications often require computational resources, large datasets, and real-time responsiveness, which can be challenging to achieve using centralized cloud-based architectures. Fog computing bridges the gap between cloud and edge computing by distributing data processing tasks, analytics, and decision-making closer to the robotic devices, resulting in enhanced performance and reduced network latency.

**Scope:** This chapter focuses on the utilization of fog-computing techniques in robotics applications, highlighting its potential in various domains such as industrial automation, smart cities, healthcare, and autonomous vehicles. The scope encompasses the integration of fog computing with robotic systems, including hardware platforms, software frameworks, communication protocols, and data management techniques. The analysis also covers the challenges, opportunities, and future directions in leveraging fog computing for robotics, including security concerns, resource allocation, scalability, and interoperability.

**Problem definition:** The increasing complexity and data-intensive nature of robotics applications pose challenges for traditional cloud-based architectures in terms of latency, bandwidth, and privacy. Robotic systems require real-time decision-making capabilities, which can be hindered by reliance on remote cloud servers. Fog computing addresses these issues by providing local processing and storage capabilities, enabling robotics to operate autonomously and efficiently in edge environments.

**Aim:** The aim of this chapter is to provide an in-depth understanding of fog computing and its application in robotics, emphasizing the benefits it offers in terms of low-latency data processing, real-time decision-making, and improved system performance. By exploring the potential use cases and challenges associated with fog computing in robotics, this study aims to assist researchers, practitioners, and policymakers in making informed decisions regarding the adoption and implementation of this paradigm. Additionally, this chapter aims to shed light on the integration of fog computing with robotic systems, highlighting the architectural considerations, communication protocols, and data management strategies required to achieve optimal performance and reliability.

**Analysis/observation on fog-computing robotics:** Fog computing enables robots to access real-time data processing capabilities at the network edge, reducing the reliance on centralized cloud infrastructures and improving overall system responsiveness. By leveraging fog computing, robotics applications can benefit from reduced latency, enhanced privacy, improved reliability, and efficient resource utilization. The integration of fog computing with robotics also opens up possibilities for collaborative decision-making, distributed sensing, and cooperative control, enabling advanced applications such as swarm robotics, multi-robot systems, and human–robot interaction in edge environments.

## 11.1   Introduction

Robotic systems have experienced significant advancements in recent years, enabling them to perform complex tasks and interact with the physical world more effectively. However, these advancements have also introduced new challenges, particularly in terms of real-time data processing, low-latency communication, and autonomous decision-making. In response to these challenges, fog computing has emerged as a powerful paradigm to address the limitations of centralized cloud architectures in the context of robotics. Fog computing extends the capabilities of edge computing by bringing computation, storage, and networking resources closer to the robotic devices. By leveraging a distributed computing infrastructure, fog computing enables robotics applications to overcome the limitations of cloud-centric architectures, such as network latency, bandwidth constraints, and reliance on remote servers. Fog computing provides a flexible and scalable framework for data processing and decision-making, empowering robots to operate autonomously and efficiently in edge environments [1].

The primary goal of this chapter is to explore the intersection of fog computing and robotics, investigating how fog computing can enhance the capabilities and performance of robotic systems. We will delve into the architectural considerations, communication protocols, data management techniques, and integration challenges that arise when combining fog computing with robotics applications. First, it provides an overview of fog computing, explaining its fundamental concepts, principles, and characteristics. We will explore its key components, including edge devices, fog nodes, and cloud resources, and discuss the role of fog computing in enabling efficient data processing and decision-making in robotics. Next, examine the specific challenges faced by robotics applications and the reasons why fog computing is particularly well suited to address these challenges. We will discuss the limitations of traditional cloud-based architectures in terms of latency, bandwidth, privacy, and real-time responsiveness and demonstrate how fog computing can mitigate these issues by leveraging local processing and storage capabilities [2].

This includes discussing the hardware platforms and software frameworks that support fog computing in robotics, as well as the communication protocols and data management strategies employed to ensure seamless connectivity, efficient resource utilization, and secure data exchange between robots and fog nodes. In addition to the technical aspects, we will explore the various application domains where fog-computing robotics can have a transformative impact. We will examine case studies and real-world examples of fog computing-enabled robotics applications in industrial automation, smart cities, healthcare, autonomous vehicles, and other relevant domains. The chapter will also address the challenges and open research areas in fog-computing robotics. We will discuss security concerns, including data privacy, integrity, and authentication, as well as the allocation of computational resources in a dynamic fog environment. We will explore scalability issues, interoperability challenges, and the need for standardized frameworks and protocols to facilitate the widespread adoption of fog-computing robotics. Furthermore, we will analyze the benefits and observations derived from the integration of fog computing and robotics. We will highlight the improved system performance, reduced latency, enhanced privacy, and energy efficiency that fog computing brings to robotic applications. We will also explore the possibilities for collaborative decision-making, distributed sensing, and cooperative control enabled by fog-computing robotics [3].

Figure 11.1 depicts the structure of deep learning robots, highlighting the intricate and interconnected components that enable these robots to learn and perform complex tasks. At a high level, the structure consists of three main components: perception, cognition, and action. This diagram provides a visual representation of how these components work together to create an intelligent and adaptable robotic system. The perception component, shown in the lower part of the figure, encompasses the sensory inputs and processing mechanisms that enable the robot to perceive and understand its environment. This includes sensors such as cameras, microphones, and tactile sensors, as well as algorithms for computer

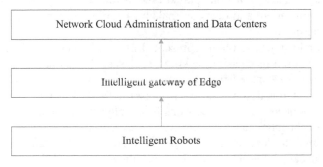

*Figure 11.1   Structure of deep learning robots*

vision, speech recognition, and sensor fusion. These perception capabilities allow the robot to gather relevant data about its surroundings and interpret it for further processing.

Moving to the middle part of the figure, we encounter the cognition component of deep learning robots. This component is responsible for higher-level processing, decision-making, and learning. It consists of various modules, such as artificial neural networks, deep learning algorithms, and reinforcement learning (RL) frameworks. These modules enable the robot to analyze the perceived data, extract meaningful patterns, make intelligent decisions, and learn from experiences. The cognition component is closely connected to the perception component, as it relies on the processed sensory information to generate knowledge and make informed decisions. The feedback loop between perception and cognition enables the robot to continually update its understanding of the environment and refine its decision-making capabilities. Lastly, the action component, depicted in the upper part of the figure, represents the physical manifestation of the robot's intelligent behavior. This component includes the actuators and mechanisms that enable the robot to interact with its environment, such as motors, grippers, and locomotion systems. The actions performed by the robot are based on the decisions made by the cognition component, allowing the robot to execute tasks, manipulate objects, and navigate its surroundings [4].

Overall, Figure 11.1 provides a comprehensive overview of the structure of deep learning robots, illustrating the integration of perception, cognition, and action components. This visual representation highlights the intricate interplay between these components, highlighting how deep learning algorithms and neural networks enable robots to perceive, reason, and act in their environment. Understanding the structure of deep learning robots is essential for developing and deploying intelligent robotic systems capable of learning and adapting to various tasks and scenarios.

## 11.2   Fog robotics

Fog robotics (FR) is an emerging field that combines the power of fog computing with robotics to enable intelligent and efficient operation of robots in edge environments. Mathematical functions play a crucial role in FR by providing tools for modeling, optimization, and decision-making. It explores some key mathematical functions used in FR.

The sigmoid function, often represented as $\sigma(x)$, is commonly used in FR to model the activation or decision-making processes. The sigmoid function maps a real-valued input to a value between 0 and 1, representing the level of activation or probability. This function is particularly useful for tasks such as thresholding, where the robot needs to make decisions based on certain conditions or activation levels. The exponential function, denoted as $\exp(x)$, plays a vital role in FR for modeling growth or decay over time. It is frequently used to represent data accumulation or decay in fog nodes. By utilizing the exponential function, robots can estimate the rate of data growth or decay and make informed decisions regarding offloading data to the cloud or performing local processing. Linear functions, represented as $f(x) = ax + b$, are extensively used in FR for various purposes. They are employed to model relationships among different parameters, such as energy consumption and distance traveled by a robot, or processing time and the number of robots allocated to a task. Linear functions are particularly useful for optimizing resource allocation, energy efficiency, and task assignment in fog-based robotic systems. Probabilistic functions, such as the Gaussian distribution, are essential in FR for handling uncertainties and modeling sensor noise. The Gaussian distribution, denoted as $N(\mu, \sigma^2)$, is a bell-shaped curve that describes the probability distribution of a continuous random variable. By incorporating probabilistic functions, robots can effectively model uncertainties in perception, localization, and decision-making tasks, improving robustness and reliability in uncertain and dynamic environments. Activation functions, such as the rectified linear unit (ReLU) or softmax, are employed in deep learning algorithms used in FR. These functions introduce nonlinearity into neural networks, enabling the models to learn complex patterns and make accurate predictions. Activation functions are crucial for tasks such as object recognition, speech processing, and natural language understanding. Optimization functions, such as gradient descent or evolutionary algorithms, are utilized in FR to optimize parameters and decision variables. These functions aim to find the optimal solution by iteratively adjusting the parameters based on a defined objective or cost function. Optimization functions are valuable for tasks like path planning, task scheduling, and resource allocation in fog-based robotic systems.

Figure 11.2 illustrates the architecture of FR, providing a visual representation of the key components and their interconnections. This architecture serves as a blueprint for designing and implementing intelligent robotic systems that leverage fog-computing capabilities in edge environments. The architecture of FR consists of three main layers: perception, fog, and cloud. These layers work together to enable efficient data processing, decision-making, and resource allocation. The perception layer represents the sensors and actuators that allow the robot to perceive and interact with its environment, including cameras, microphones, and various sensors for capturing data. Moving to the fog layer, we encounter the core

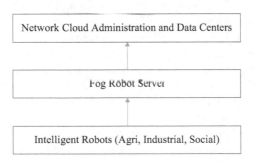

*Figure 11.2   Architecture of fog robotics*

of the FR architecture. This layer includes fog nodes, which are distributed computing devices located closer to the robotic systems. Fog nodes provide computational resources, storage capabilities, and networking capabilities for local data processing, decision-making, and communication. They play a crucial role in reducing latency, enhancing real-time responsiveness, and enabling efficient utilization of resources. Within the fog layer, there are also fog agents, which act as intermediaries between the perception layer and the cloud layer. Fog agents facilitate the communication and data exchange between robots and the cloud, ensuring seamless connectivity and coordination. They can perform data filtering, preprocessing, and analytics tasks to reduce the amount of data transmitted to the cloud and enable local decision-making. The cloud layer represents the centralized cloud infrastructure that provides additional computational power, storage, and advanced analytics capabilities. Cloud resources support tasks such as long-term data storage, complex data analytics, and training of deep learning models. The cloud layer plays a significant role in handling resource-intensive tasks and providing global insights to enhance the decision-making capabilities of the robotic systems. Arrows in the architecture represent the interconnections between the layers. These arrows depict the flow of data, commands, and feedback among the different layers. For instance, sensor data collected by the perception layer are processed and analyzed in the fog layer, where local decisions can be made based on real-time conditions. Results and selected data can then be transmitted to the cloud layer for further analysis, long-term storage, or model training.

## 11.2.1    Facilitating distributed and shared learning

Facilitating distributed and shared learning is a crucial aspect of collaborative and scalable learning in FR. This approach allows multiple robotic systems to learn from distributed data sources, share their knowledge, and collectively improve their performance. Essential principles and advantages of collaborative and distributed learning in the context of FR.

Distributed learning in FR involves training models using data that are distributed across multiple robotic systems or fog nodes. Instead of centralizing all the data in a single location, distributed learning leverages the computational power and local data availability of each system. By distributing the learning process, this approach enables efficient utilization of resources and mitigates privacy concerns associated with sharing sensitive data [5].

Shared learning refers to the collaboration between multiple robotic systems to collectively improve their learning outcomes. In shared learning, robots exchange information, model parameters, and experiences to enhance their individual learning processes. By sharing knowledge, the robots can collectively benefit from diverse perspectives and experiences, leading to improved generalization, faster convergence, and enhanced performance.

Facilitating distributed and shared learning in FR requires the development of suitable algorithms and protocols. For distributed learning, techniques like federated learning and collaborative learning can be employed to train models on local data while preserving data privacy. These approaches allow models to be trained collectively without requiring the raw data to leave the fog nodes or robotic systems.

Shared learning in FR can be facilitated through techniques such as transfer learning, model aggregation, and knowledge distillation. Transfer learning enables robots to leverage pretrained models or knowledge from other robots to accelerate their learning process. Model aggregation involves combining individual models or parameters from multiple robots to create a shared model with improved performance. Knowledge distillation allows a knowledgeable robot to transfer its acquired knowledge to less experienced robots, enabling them to learn more efficiently.

One of the key benefits of distributed and shared learning in FR is scalability. By distributing the learning process across multiple robotic systems, the computational burden can be divided, allowing for efficient utilization of resources and enabling learning in large-scale deployments. Additionally, shared learning leverages collective intelligence, enabling robots to learn from diverse data sources and experiences, leading to improved performance and adaptability.

Moreover, distributed and shared learning in FR promotes privacy and data security. Instead of sharing sensitive raw data, only model updates or aggregated information is exchanged between robots. This approach helps protect the privacy of individual data sources while still benefiting from collaborative learning. By preserving data privacy, FR can address concerns regarding data ownership, confidentiality, and compliance with privacy regulations [6].

## 11.2.2   Data security, confidentiality, and ownership

Data security, confidentiality, and ownership are critical considerations in FR, where sensitive data are processed and shared across distributed systems. Ensuring the protection of data and maintaining its integrity are vital for maintaining user trust and compliance with privacy regulations. In this comprehensive explanation, we will explore these concepts in detail. Data security refers to the measures and practices implemented to protect data from unauthorized access, modification, or disclosure. In the context of FR, data security involves safeguarding the data collected by robotic systems, ensuring that it remains confidential and is not vulnerable to cyber threats. Confidentiality relates to the protection of sensitive or private information from unauthorized access or disclosure. In FR, ensuring data confidentiality is crucial to protect user privacy, trade secrets, and proprietary information. Data ownership refers to the legal rights and control over the data collected or generated by a robotic system. Understanding data ownership is essential in FR, as it determines who has the authority to access, use, and make decisions based on the data.

To ensure data security, FR systems employ a range of techniques such as encryption, authentication, and access control mechanisms. Encryption techniques, such as symmetric and asymmetric cryptography, can be used to encrypt data in transit or at rest, preventing unauthorized access or eavesdropping. Authentication mechanisms, such as username-password combinations, biometrics, or digital certificates, help verify the identity of users or devices interacting with the FR system.

Strong authentication ensures that only authorized entities can access the data and system functionalities. Access control mechanisms play a crucial role in determining who can access and manipulate data within the FR system. Role-based access control (RBAC), access control lists (ACLs), or attribute-based access control (ABAC) can be implemented to restrict data access based on user roles, privileges, or specific attributes.

Data confidentiality in FR can be enhanced through techniques such as data anonymization, data minimization, and differential privacy. Data anonymization involves removing or obfuscating personally identifiable information (PII) from the dataset, ensuring that individuals cannot be directly identified. Data minimization focuses on collecting and retaining only the necessary data, reducing the risk of exposing sensitive information. By limiting data collection to what is essential for the robotic system's operation, the potential impact of a data breach or unauthorized access is reduced. Differential privacy is a concept that aims to protect individual privacy while allowing aggregate data analysis. It involves injecting random noise or perturbation into the data to prevent reidentification of individuals, thereby protecting their privacy. Regarding data ownership, it is crucial to establish clear policies and agreements to define the rights and responsibilities of data ownership within the FR ecosystem. Contracts or licenses can be utilized to clarify the ownership of data, specifying the scope of data usage and the rights of the data owners. In FR, data ownership may be shared among multiple entities, such as robot manufacturers, data providers, or end-users. This shared ownership requires transparent agreements and protocols to ensure that data are used ethically, respecting the rights and privacy of all stakeholders involved.

One approach to address data ownership concerns is through data governance frameworks. These frameworks define rules, processes, and responsibilities for managing and protecting data throughout its lifecycle, including its collection, storage, processing, and sharing. In the FR context, data governance frameworks can help establish data ownership rights, access controls, data retention policies, and procedures for data handling and disposal. In addition to technical measures and governance frameworks, legal and regulatory frameworks play a significant role in ensuring data security, confidentiality, and ownership in FR. Compliance with applicable privacy regulations, such as the General Data Protection Regulation (GDPR), ensures that data handling practices align with legal requirements and protects user privacy. Data security audits and assessments can be conducted to evaluate the effectiveness of security measures, identify vulnerabilities, and ensure compliance with data protection standards. Regular audits help maintain data security, identify potential risks, and address any issues promptly. Transparency and accountability are essential principles in maintaining data security, confidentiality, and ownership. FR systems should provide clear and transparent information to users about data collection practices, usage, and sharing, allowing them to make informed decisions and maintain control over their data [7].

Robust data backup and disaster recovery strategies are crucial in FR to mitigate the risks of data loss, corruption, or unauthorized access. Regular backups and redundant storage systems ensure data availability and quick recovery in the case of failures or security incidents. Ongoing monitoring and threat detection mechanisms are vital to identify and respond to potential security breaches or unauthorized access attempts promptly. Intrusion detection systems, log analysis, and anomaly detection techniques can be employed to detect and mitigate security threats in real-time. Education and awareness play a significant role in promoting data security, confidentiality, and ownership in the FR domain. Training users, developers, and system administrators on best practices, security protocols, and privacy-aware behaviors can significantly enhance the overall security posture. By adopting comprehensive data security, confidentiality, and ownership measures in FR, stakeholders can ensure the protection of sensitive data, maintain user trust, comply with privacy regulations, and foster a secure and ethical environment for data processing and sharing.

## 11.2.3 *Adaptability in resource allocation and placement*

Adaptability in resource allocation and placement is a crucial aspect of FR, enabling robotic systems to dynamically allocate resources and determine optimal locations for processing tasks based on changing conditions and requirements. This adaptability enhances efficiency, responsiveness, and scalability in fog-based environments. Here, we will explore the concepts and benefits of adaptability in resource allocation and placement in FR. Resource allocation in FR involves distributing computational, storage, and communication resources among robotic systems and fog nodes to fulfill their processing requirements. Adaptability in resource allocation enables dynamic adjustment of resource assignments based on factors such as workload, network conditions, energy constraints, and user demands. Dynamic resource allocation can be achieved through techniques like load balancing and resource provisioning. Load balancing aims to evenly distribute tasks or processing loads across available resources, ensuring efficient resource utilization and preventing bottlenecks. Resource provisioning involves dynamically allocating resources based on real-time demand, scaling up or down as needed.

Adaptability in resource allocation allows robotic systems to optimize resource utilization, improve system performance, and enhance responsiveness. By intelligently allocating resources, robots can avoid resource contention, reduce latency, and ensure that tasks are executed in a timely manner, leading to improved overall system efficiency. The placement of tasks or processing modules is another aspect of adaptability in FR. Task placement involves determining the optimal fog nodes or edge devices to execute specific tasks based on factors like proximity to data sources, network conditions, resource availability, and latency requirements. Dynamic task placement can be achieved through techniques like task offloading, where certain processing tasks are delegated to fog nodes or cloud resources to alleviate the computational burden on the robotic systems. Task placement decisions can be made in real-time based on the current system state and performance metrics, ensuring efficient and timely execution of tasks [8].

Adaptive resource allocation and placement algorithms in FR often employ machine learning and optimization techniques. Machine learning models can learn from past experiences, system behavior, and user preferences to predict resource requirements and make informed allocation decisions. Optimization algorithms, such as genetic algorithms or RL, can be utilized to find optimal resource allocation and placement strategies based on defined objectives and constraints. One of the key benefits of adaptability in resource allocation and placement is increased scalability. As the number of robotic systems and fog nodes grows, adaptability enables the system to dynamically scale resources, distribute workloads, and accommodate changing demands, ensuring efficient utilization of available resources. Adaptability also enhances system resilience and fault tolerance. By dynamically reallocating resources, the system can respond to failures, changes in network conditions, or resources unavailability, ensuring uninterrupted operation and maintaining desired levels of performance.

Furthermore, adaptability in resource allocation and placement allows for energy efficiency. By intelligently distributing tasks and processing loads, robots can optimize energy consumption and extend battery life, leading to increased operational time and reduced energy costs. Adaptability in resource allocation and placement is particularly beneficial in dynamic environments, where conditions and requirements may change rapidly. FR systems operating in domains such as autonomous vehicles, disaster response, or industrial automation can benefit from the ability to adaptively allocate resources and adjust task placement based on real-time conditions and user needs. However, there are challenges associated with adaptability in resource allocation and placement, including overhead in decision-making, resource monitoring, and system coordination. Efficient algorithms and protocols need to be developed to minimize computational complexity and ensure timely decision-making while considering system constraints and objectives. Additionally, privacy and security considerations should be taken into account when dynamically allocating resources and sharing data. Sensitive or confidential data should be protected during resource allocation and placement processes, ensuring compliance with privacy regulations and maintaining data confidentiality [9].

## 11.3    Comparison of fog and cloud robotics

Robotics in the fog and the cloud represent two distinct paradigms for deploying and operating robotic systems. While both approaches offer unique advantages, they differ significantly in terms of architecture, processing capabilities, latency, and resource allocation. Let's explore the contrasts between robotics in the fog and the cloud.

In FR, the architecture is decentralized and distributed. Computational resources and data processing capabilities are located closer to the robotic systems, typically in fog nodes or edge devices. This proximity enables low-latency communication, real-time decision-making, and local data processing. On the other hand, cloud robotics follows a centralized architecture, where computational resources and data processing occur in remote cloud servers. Cloud robotics relies on cloud connectivity for data exchange, analysis, and decision-making. FR offers significantly lower latency compared to cloud robotics. With fog computing, the proximity of fog nodes to robotic systems enables real-time data processing and faster response times. This low-latency communication is critical for time-sensitive applications such as autonomous vehicles, where rapid decision-making is necessary. In contrast, cloud robotics introduces higher latency due to the inherent delay in transmitting data to and from remote cloud servers. FR emphasizes local processing and edge computing capabilities. Fog nodes are equipped with computational resources that can handle real-time data processing, analytics, and decision-making closer to the robotic systems. This local processing enables faster response times, reduced dependence on cloud connectivity, and enhanced autonomy. Cloud robotics, on the other hand, leverages the vast computational power and storage capacity of cloud servers. Complex data analysis, machine learning, and resource-intensive tasks can be offloaded to the cloud for processing.

Resource allocation in FR focuses on distributed and localized resource utilization. Fog nodes and edge devices share computational resources and collaborate to optimize task execution and system performance. This approach reduces network congestion, enables efficient resource utilization, and enhances scalability. In cloud robotics, resource allocation is centralized and managed by the cloud infrastructure. Cloud servers allocate resources based on demand and availability, enabling elastic scaling but introducing potential bottlenecks in the network. FR places emphasis on local connectivity and the ability to operate in disconnected or intermittent network environments. Fog nodes can function autonomously even when the cloud connection is unavailable. This capability is valuable in scenarios where robots operate in remote or dynamic environments with limited or unreliable network connectivity. In contrast, cloud robotics relies heavily on constant and reliable network connectivity to access cloud resources and perform centralized data processing and analysis. Both fog and cloud robotics offer scalability, but they differ in their approaches. FR achieves scalability by distributing computational resources and processing capabilities closer to the robotic systems. This distributed architecture allows for flexible scaling based on the number of fog nodes and edge devices. Cloud robotics achieves scalability by leveraging the virtually unlimited computational power and storage capacity of the cloud infrastructure. Cloud servers can handle large-scale deployments and resource-demanding tasks efficiently.

Figure 11.3 depicts the structure of a fog robot, showcasing the various components that contribute to its operation in a fog-based environment. The diagram

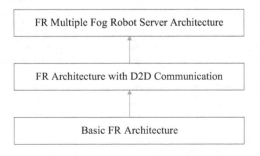

*Figure 11.3   Structure of fog robot*

provides a visual representation of the key elements that enable the fog robot to perform tasks efficiently and autonomously. The structure of a fog robot consists of three main components: perception, cognition, and action. The perception component includes sensors and actuators that enable the robot to perceive and interact with its surroundings. These sensors can include cameras, LIDAR, proximity sensors, and other environmental sensors. The data collected from these sensors are crucial for the robot to understand and navigate its environment effectively. The cognition component encompasses the intelligence and decision-making capabilities of the fog robot. This component includes algorithms for data processing, computer vision, machine learning, and navigation. It enables the robot to analyze the sensor data, make informed decisions, and adapt to changing circumstances. The cognition component is responsible for tasks such as object recognition, path planning, and task allocation. Finally, the action component represents the physical execution of tasks by the fog robot. It includes the robot's actuators, such as motors, grippers, or robotic arms, which enable it to manipulate objects, move within its environment, and perform specific actions. The action component is controlled by the decisions made by the cognition component, allowing the robot to autonomously carry out tasks and interact with its surroundings.

In Table 11.1, the action component represents the physical execution of tasks by the fog robot. It includes the robot's actuators, such as motors, grippers, or robotic arms, which enable it to manipulate objects, move within its environment, and perform specific actions. The action component is controlled by the decisions made by the cognition component, allowing the robot to autonomously carry out tasks and interact with its surroundings.

## 11.3.1 The fundamentals of FR design

Designing an FR system involves incorporating mathematical functions to enhance its efficiency, adaptability, and performance. Mathematical functions play a crucial role in various aspects of FR design, from data processing and decision-making to resource optimization and system performance.

*Table 11.1 Summarizing the contrasts between robotics in the fog and the cloud*

| Aspect | Robotics in the fog | Robotics in the cloud |
|---|---|---|
| Architecture | Decentralized and distributed | Centralized |
| Latency | Low-latency communication | Higher latency |
| Processing capabilities | Local processing and edge computing | Centralized processing in cloud servers |
| Resource allocation | Distributed and localized resource utilization | Centralized resource allocation in the cloud |
| Connectivity | Emphasizes local connectivity | Relies on constant and reliable network connectivity |
| Scalability | Distributed scaling with fog nodes and edge devices | Centralized scaling with cloud resources |

Mathematical functions, such as statistical functions and signal processing algorithms, are fundamental in FR for data processing and analysis. Functions like mean, median, standard deviation, and Fourier transforms enable robust data processing, noise reduction, feature extraction, and pattern recognition. These functions provide the foundation for analyzing sensor data and extracting meaningful information for decision-making. Mathematical functions are at the core of machine learning and artificial intelligence algorithms used in FR. Functions like activation functions (e.g., sigmoid and ReLU), loss functions (e.g., mean squared error and cross-entropy), and optimization functions (e.g., gradient descent) are employed in training neural networks and learning models. These functions enable learning, decision-making, and adaptive behavior of FR systems based on data inputs and training objectives. Mathematical optimization functions, such as linear programming, convex optimization, or genetic algorithms, are essential for resource allocation and optimization in FR design. These functions enable the system to find optimal solutions for task assignment, load balancing, energy management, and resource allocation. By formulating the resource allocation problem as an optimization function, the system can dynamically allocate resources based on objectives, constraints, and real-time conditions.

Sensor fusion and localization: Mathematical functions play a crucial role in sensor fusion and localization tasks in FR. Functions like Kalman filters, particle filters, or Bayesian estimation methods are employed to fuse data from multiple sensors and estimate the robot's position, orientation, or map of the environment. These functions integrate sensor measurements, probabilistic models, and motion dynamics to provide accurate and reliable estimates of the robot's state. Mathematical functions, such as queuing theory and network optimization algorithms, are essential in designing efficient communication and networking protocols for FR systems. These functions enable the analysis and optimization of data transmission rates, routing strategies, resource allocation, and congestion control in fog-based communication networks. By employing mathematical functions, FR systems can optimize communication efficiency, reduce latency, and improve overall network performance. Mathematical functions are used to evaluate and analyze the performance of FR systems. Functions like performance metrics (e.g., accuracy, precision, and recall) and simulation models (e.g., queuing models and Markov models) enable the assessment of system performance, scalability, and reliability. By utilizing these functions, FR designers can quantitatively measure the system's performance, identify bottlenecks, and optimize system parameters [10].

## 11.3.2 D2D communication in the FR architecture

Device-to-device (D2D) communication plays a significant role in FR architecture, enabling direct communication between robotic systems and edge devices without relying solely on cloud connectivity. D2D communication in FR offers several advantages, including reduced latency, improved reliability, enhanced privacy, and efficient resource utilization. It delves into how D2D communication fits into the FR architecture and its benefits.

In FR, D2D communication allows robotic systems to directly exchange data, commands, and information with nearby edge devices or other robotic systems. By eliminating the need to route data through distant cloud servers, D2D communication significantly reduces latency. This low-latency communication is crucial for time-critical tasks that require real-time responsiveness, such as autonomous navigation, collaborative operations, or immediate sensor data analysis. D2D communication enhances reliability in FR architecture by enabling direct communication between nearby devices, even in scenarios with intermittent or limited network connectivity. In environments with weak or unstable network coverage, D2D communication allows robotic systems to establish direct connections, ensuring continuous communication and reducing reliance on a centralized cloud infrastructure. This improves the overall reliability and robustness of the FR system. D2D communication in FR can enhance privacy and data security. By enabling local communication, sensitive data can be transmitted directly between devices without being exposed to the cloud or external networks. This minimizes the risk of unauthorized access or interception during data transmission. D2D communication can employ encryption, authentication, and access control mechanisms to ensure data privacy and maintain the confidentiality of sensitive information.

D2D communication optimizes resource utilization in FR architecture. Instead of constantly relying on cloud connectivity, nearby devices can collaborate and offload computation and data exchange tasks through direct communication. This distributed approach allows for local processing, reduces the amount of data transmitted over the network, and minimizes the load on cloud resources. It enables efficient resource allocation, reduces network congestion, and enhances overall system performance. D2D communication enables proximity-based collaboration among robotic systems in FR. Nearby devices can share information, exchange data, and coordinate their activities in a decentralized manner. This collaboration can facilitate cooperative tasks, such as collaborative mapping, swarm robotics, or coordinated decision-making. By leveraging D2D communication, FR systems can harness the collective intelligence and capabilities of nearby devices, leading to improved performance and adaptability. D2D communication adds flexibility and adaptability to the FR architecture. As the network topology changes, devices can establish new connections and adapt to the dynamic environment. This dynamic nature of D2D communication enables FR systems to reconfigure their communication links, adapt to failures, and ensure continuous operation. It also enables the deployment of ad hoc networks and facilitates communication in scenarios where infrastructure-based networks may be limited or unavailable.

## 11.3.3   In an FR architecture with many fog robot servers

In an FR architecture with multiple fog robot servers, the system benefits from increased scalability, distributed processing capabilities, and improved fault tolerance. It will explore the advantages and considerations of such an architecture.

Scalability: Having multiple fog robot servers allows for horizontal scalability, meaning that the system can handle a larger number of robotic systems and accommodate growing computational demands. As the number of robots and tasks increases, additional fog robot servers can be added to the architecture, distributing the workload and ensuring efficient resource utilization. This scalability enables the FR system to scale with the requirements of diverse applications and handle larger deployments. Distributed processing: Multiple fog robot servers provide distributed processing capabilities, allowing for parallel execution of tasks and faster data processing. Each fog robot server can handle a subset of the workload, enabling concurrent data analysis, decision-making, and resource allocation. This distributed processing approach reduces latency and improves overall system performance by leveraging the computational power of multiple servers. Fault tolerance: In a multi-fog robot server architecture, fault tolerance is enhanced as the system can withstand failures or disruptions. If one fog robot server encounters an issue or goes offline, the remaining servers can continue to operate, ensuring uninterrupted service. Additionally, data and tasks can be replicated across multiple servers, reducing the risk of data loss and enabling redundancy. This fault-tolerant design enhances the reliability and robustness of the FR system. Load balancing and resource allocation: Multiple fog robot servers enable load balancing and efficient resource allocation. Load-balancing algorithms can distribute tasks and workloads across the servers, ensuring that computational resources are utilized optimally. This dynamic resource allocation considers factors such as server capabilities, network conditions, and task requirements to achieve balanced and efficient processing. Load-balancing and resource allocation mechanisms ensure that no single server is overloaded, preventing performance bottlenecks and optimizing the overall system performance.

### 11.3.4 Delivery of social robots in this scenario

The delivery of social robots in an FR scenario introduces new opportunities for human–robot interaction and enhanced social interactions. Social robots, designed to engage with humans in social contexts, can leverage the benefits of the FR architecture to improve their capabilities and provide more personalized and adaptive interactions. It will explore the implications and advantages of delivering social robots within an FR framework.

In FR, social robots can benefit from the proximity and low-latency communication offered by fog nodes and edge devices. By leveraging D2D communication and local processing capabilities, social robots can engage in real-time interactions with humans. This proximity-based communication allows for faster response times, immediate feedback, and more natural conversational interactions. The reduced latency enhances the sense of presence and responsiveness, leading to more engaging and immersive social experiences. FR architecture enables social robots to access and process personalized data about individuals while respecting privacy regulations. By leveraging local data processing and edge analytics, social robots can adapt their behaviors, responses, and recommendations based on individual preferences, past interactions, and contextual information. This personalization enhances the quality of social interactions, making the robot more empathetic, relatable, and responsive to human needs.

Social robots within an FR framework can collaborate with other robotic systems, fog nodes, or edge devices to enhance their social capabilities. Collaborative algorithms and distributed intelligence mechanisms enable social robots to share knowledge, learn from each other, and collectively improve their social interaction skills. This collaboration fosters a rich and diverse social ecosystem, where robots can support each other and collectively provide a more comprehensive range of social services and experiences. FR architecture facilitates context awareness for social robots, enabling them to perceive and respond to the surrounding environment and human interactions. By integrating sensor data, environmental cues, and contextual information from fog nodes, social robots can adapt their behaviors, gestures, and speech patterns to better suit the current situation. This adaptability enhances the robot's social skills, allowing it to exhibit appropriate social etiquette, empathetic responses, and appropriate emotional expressions. FR architecture can contribute to ensuring safety and privacy in the delivery of social robots. By enabling local processing and decentralized data storage, sensitive personal information can be securely handled without the need for constant transmission to a central cloud server. Additionally, fog nodes can provide localized security measures, such as authentication and access control, to protect user privacy and prevent unauthorized access to personal data.

## 11.4    Deep learning-based robotics

Deep learning has revolutionized the field of robotics, empowering robots with the ability to learn and adapt to complex tasks and environments. Deep learning-based robotics combines the power of deep neural networks with robotic systems to enable autonomous perception, decision-making, and control. It will explore the key aspects and benefits of deep learning in robotics.

Deep learning algorithms have significantly advanced the perception capabilities of robots. Convolutional neural networks (CNNs) are widely used for tasks such as object recognition, image classification, and semantic segmentation. These networks allow robots to perceive and understand their environment by analyzing sensor data from cameras or depth sensors. Deep learning-based perception enables robots to recognize objects, interpret scenes, and extract meaningful information from sensor inputs. Deep learning facilitates learning and adaptation in robotic systems. RL algorithms, such as deep Q-networks (DQNs) and policy gradients, enable robots to learn optimal actions through trial and error. By interacting with the environment, robots can learn complex behaviors, adapt to dynamic conditions, and improve their performance over time. Deep learning-based adaptation enables robots to handle variations, uncertainties, and changes in the environment without the need for explicit programming. Deep learning techniques are also applied to motion planning and control in robotics. Recurrent neural networks (RNNs) and long short-term memory (LSTM) networks can model temporal dependencies and enable robots to learn sequential decision-making tasks. Deep learning-based control enables robots to perform tasks such as grasping objects, navigating in complex environments, or manipulating objects with dexterity. These networks learn complex motion patterns and generate control signals to execute precise and robust movements.

Deep learning enhances human–robot interaction by enabling robots to understand and respond to human gestures, speech, and emotions. Natural language processing (NLP) techniques combined with deep learning models enable robots to understand and generate humanlike speech. Deep learning-based sentiment analysis can enable robots to recognize and respond to human emotions, enhancing their ability to engage in meaningful social interactions. Deep learning enables transfer learning and generalization in robotics. Pretrained deep neural networks can be used as a starting point for new tasks or domains, allowing robots to leverage knowledge acquired from previous learning experiences. This transfer learning capability accelerates the learning process and improves performance in new scenarios with limited data. Deep learning-based generalization enables robots to apply learned knowledge to similar tasks, environments, or objects, saving time and resources in training. Deep learning plays a significant role in simulating and modeling robotic systems. Generative models, such as generative adversarial networks (GANs), can create realistic synthetic data for training robots in simulated environments. Deep learning-based simulations enable robots to learn and train in virtual environments, reducing the reliance on physical systems and facilitating safe and cost-effective experimentation.

## 11.4.1   Transferring simulation learning to the real world

Transferring simulation learning to the real world is a challenging but crucial aspect of robotics. While simulations provide a safe and cost-effective environment for training and testing robotic systems, the learned policies and behaviors may not directly translate to the real-world setting due to discrepancies between simulation and reality. It will explore the key considerations and techniques for effectively transferring simulation learning to the real world.

One approach to transferring simulation learning to the real world is domain adaptation. This involves minimizing the gap between the simulation and real-world domains by aligning their distributions. Techniques such as adversarial domain adaptation or discrepancy-based methods aim to learn a mapping from the simulation to the real-world domain, enabling the learned policies to generalize better in the target environment. Domain adaptation helps overcome the differences in visual appearance, dynamics, and sensory input between simulation and reality.

Transfer learning is another strategy for transferring simulation learning to the real world. Instead of directly applying the learned policies, transfer learning leverages knowledge acquired in the simulation to facilitate learning in the real world. Pretrained models or policies from the simulation can be fine-tuned or used as a starting point for training in the real world. Transfer learning allows robots to leverage prior knowledge while adapting and refining their behaviors in the target environment, reducing the required training time and improving performance.

Data augmentation techniques can bridge the gap between simulation and real-world data by introducing synthetic variations into the training process. Augmentation methods such as domain randomization or parameter perturbation introduce diversity and increase the robustness of learned policies. Hybrid approaches combine real-world data with simulated data during training, gradually transitioning from simulation to reality. By gradually introducing real-world experiences, the learned policies can adapt and generalize better in the real world.

Iterative refinement and real-world feedback: Iterative refinement is essential in the transfer of simulation learning to the real world. The initial policies learned in simulation can be refined through incremental training and fine-tuning in the real world. Collecting real-world data and incorporating it into the training process allow the system to learn from the specific characteristics and dynamics of the real-world environment. Additionally, gathering real-world feedback and using it to update the learned policies helps address the reality gap and improve performance. When transferring simulation learning to the real world, it is crucial to ensure safe and gradual deployment. Starting with simpler or lower-risk tasks in the real world allows the system to adapt and refine its behaviors while minimizing potential risks. Progressive deployment helps identify and address discrepancies or limitations between simulation and reality, enabling the system to gradually handle more complex tasks as it gains experience and robustness. Even after successful transfer, continuous learning and adaptation in the real world are essential. The real-world environment is dynamic and unpredictable, requiring the system to continually update and refine its policies. Techniques such as online learning, RL with model-based updates, or active learning can facilitate continuous adaptation and improvement in the real world.

### 11.4.2   Execution environment on a networked system

An execution environment on a networked system refers to the specific configuration and setup in which software applications or services are executed and run within a networked infrastructure. It encompasses the hardware, software, and network resources necessary to support the execution of applications and ensure their proper functioning. It will explore the key considerations and components of an execution environment on a networked system.

The hardware infrastructure forms the foundation of the execution environment. It includes servers, workstations, storage devices, and networking equipment that make up the networked system. The hardware components should be robust, scalable, and capable of meeting the computational and storage requirements of the applications or services running on the network.

The operating system (OS) and software stack provide the necessary runtime environment for applications to execute on the networked system. The OS manages the hardware resources and provides services such as process management, memory management, and device drivers. The software stack typically includes libraries, frameworks, and middleware that enable application development, networking, and data management. The network infrastructure plays a vital role in the execution environment as it facilitates communication and data exchange among different components and nodes within the networked system. It includes routers, switches, firewalls, and network cables that enable connectivity and data transfer. A reliable and high-performance network infrastructure is essential for ensuring efficient execution and seamless interaction between distributed applications.

Virtualization and containerization technologies provide flexibility and resource optimization in the execution environment. Virtualization allows for the creation of virtual machines (VMs) that encapsulate complete software environments, including the OS, applications, and dependencies. Containers, on the other hand, provide lightweight and isolated execution environments, enabling the deployment of applications with their dependencies in a more efficient and portable manner. Effective resource management and allocation are crucial for optimizing the execution environment. This involves monitoring and controlling the utilization of computational resources such as CPU, memory, and storage, ensuring fair distribution among applications or services. Resource allocation strategies, such as load balancing, dynamic scaling, and priority-based scheduling, help optimize performance, avoid bottlenecks, and ensure efficient utilization of available resources.

Security measures should be implemented to protect the execution environment from unauthorized access, data breaches, and malicious attacks. This includes implementing firewalls, encryption protocols, intrusion detection systems, and access control mechanisms to safeguard the networked system and the applications running within it. Regular security updates and patches should be applied to mitigate potential vulnerabilities. Monitoring and logging mechanisms are essential for tracking the performance and health of the execution environment. Monitoring tools collect and analyze metrics related to resource utilization, network traffic, and application performance. Log files record important events, errors, and activities, providing a valuable source of information for troubleshooting, performance optimization, and system auditing.

## 11.5 Fog robot architecture

The architecture of a fog robot refers to the overall design and structure of a robotic system that operates within a fog-computing environment. A fog robot architecture combines the capabilities of robotic systems with the computational power and data processing capabilities of fog-computing nodes or edge devices. It will explore the key components and characteristics of a fog robot architecture.

The fog robot architecture includes sensors and perception modules that enable the robot to perceive and interact with its environment. These sensors can include cameras, LIDAR, proximity sensors, IMU (inertial measurement unit), and other environmental sensors. The perception module processes the sensor data to extract relevant information about the surroundings, such as object detection, mapping, or localization. One of the central aspects of the fog robot architecture is the integration of edge processing and analytics capabilities. Fog nodes or edge devices located in close proximity to the robot provide computational resources for real-time data processing and analytics. The edge processing modules handle tasks such as sensor data fusion, feature extraction, object recognition, and decision-making. These modules leverage the computational power of fog nodes to enable local processing and reduce latency.

The fog robot architecture relies on communication and networking infrastructure to enable data exchange and coordination. D2D communication allows robots to directly communicate with nearby edge devices or other robotic systems without relying solely on cloud connectivity. This proximity-based communication reduces latency and improves real-time interactions. Communication protocols, networking technologies, and middleware facilitate seamless communication between the robot, fog nodes, and other components of the fog-computing environment.

The cognition and control components in the fog robot architecture encompass the intelligence and decision-making capabilities of the robot. This includes algorithms for data processing, computer vision, machine learning, and navigation. The cognition module analyzes the processed sensor data, interprets the environment, and makes informed decisions. The control module translates these decisions into actions, enabling the robot to move, manipulate objects, and interact with the surroundings. Resource optimization is a crucial aspect of the fog robot architecture. The architecture involves optimizing resource allocation and management across multiple fog nodes and edge devices. Load balancing algorithms, task offloading mechanisms, and resource provisioning techniques ensure efficient utilization of computational resources. These optimization strategies distribute the workload, minimize network congestion, and enhance overall system performance and scalability. The fog robot architecture integrates safety and security mechanisms to protect the robot and the overall system. Safety measures include collision avoidance, obstacle detection, and emergency stop mechanisms to ensure the physical well-being of the robot and its surroundings. Security measures include authentication, encryption, and access control to safeguard data privacy, prevent unauthorized access, and protect against cyber threats.

Figure 11.4 illustrates the architecture of FR, providing a visual representation of the key components and their interactions within the system. The diagram highlights the integration of robotic systems with fog-computing nodes and edge devices, highlighting the decentralized processing, real-time data analytics, and efficient resource allocation. The architecture emphasizes the perception, cognition, and action components of the fog robot, along with the communication and coordination among the fog nodes and the robot. The figure demonstrates how the fog-computing infrastructure enhances the capabilities of the robot by enabling local data processing, low-latency communication, and distributed intelligence. Overall, Figure 11.4 portrays the holistic design of FR, showcasing the seamless integration of robotic systems and fog-computing technologies to enable efficient and adaptive robotic operations in fog-based environments.

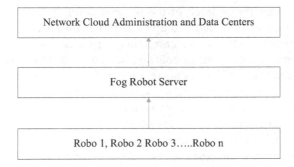

*Figure 11.4    Architecture of fog robotics*

## 11.6    Implementation of fog robotics

In the realm of cutting-edge technology, the implementation of FR stands as an avant-garde breakthrough that amalgamates the power of fog computing and robotics. This innovative fusion brings forth a new paradigm in the realm of automation and artificial intelligence. FR embodies the deployment of robotic systems augmented by fog nodes, which act as decentralized computing and processing units. The strategic positioning of these fog nodes in close proximity to robotic entities enables real-time data analysis, decision-making, and execution of tasks with unparalleled efficiency and responsiveness. The implementation of FR not only revolutionizes traditional robotics but also overcomes several limitations associated with centralized cloud-based architectures. By distributing computing resources closer to the robotic devices, latency is significantly reduced, allowing for swift and seamless data exchange. Furthermore, the extensive computational capabilities of fog nodes empower robots with enhanced cognitive abilities, enabling them to handle complex tasks autonomously and adapt to dynamic environments with utmost precision. In practical terms, the implementation of FR finds profound applications across diverse domains, such as industrial automation, smart cities, healthcare, and logistics. In manufacturing plants, fog-enabled robots collaborate harmoniously to optimize production processes, thereby enhancing productivity and cost-effectiveness. In smart cities, these robotic entities efficiently manage traffic control, waste management, and public safety, fostering a sustainable and secure urban environment. The seamless integration of fog computing and robotics paves the way for a future in which intelligent robotic systems efficiently coexist and coevolve with human society, revolutionizing industries and enriching lives in unparalleled ways.

## 11.7    Networking system with execution environment

This section in the context of fog computing delves into the sophisticated architecture that intertwines networking paradigms with dynamic execution environments. This amalgamation forms the bedrock of the fog-computing infrastructure, enabling seamless communication and computation in distributed and resource-constrained environments. At its core, this networking system establishes a highly interconnected network of fog nodes, equipped with diverse execution environments that foster efficient data processing and real-time decision-making. In this intricate ecosystem, fog nodes serve as pivotal intermediaries, orchestrating data flow, and resource management between edge devices and the cloud. The distributed nature of these nodes optimizes network performance, diminishing latency and bandwidth constraints. Each fog node boasts a versatile execution environment, encompassing a range of computational resources and virtualization techniques. This adaptability allows the networking system to dynamically allocate resources, ensuring optimal execution of diverse applications and services based on their specific requirements.

Furthermore, the integration of networking and execution environments fosters a robust ecosystem for the deployment of Internet of Things (IoT) devices. These interconnected devices leverage the fog-computing infrastructure to efficiently share data and collaborate on complex tasks, further enhancing the overall system's responsiveness and scalability. Additionally, this networking system with execution environment supports secure communication and data privacy, employing advanced encryption and authentication mechanisms to safeguard sensitive information as it traverses the network.

## 11.8    Advanced robotics using fog computing

This section delves into the cutting-edge convergence of two groundbreaking technologies: fog computing and robotics. This fusion marks a remarkable stride in the realm of automation and artificial intelligence, revolutionizing the capabilities of robotic systems in the modern era. By leveraging the power of fog computing, advanced robotics transcends traditional boundaries, unlocking a new realm of possibilities for intelligent machines. In this groundbreaking paradigm, fog computing acts as a transformative enabler for advanced robotics. By decentralizing computation and processing capabilities to fog nodes distributed closer to the robotic entities, real-time data analysis and decision-making become possible. This reduces latency and enhances the responsiveness of robotic systems, allowing them to handle complex tasks with unprecedented efficiency. The synergy between advanced robotics and fog computing facilitates seamless communication and coordination among robots, enabling them to collaborate and optimize their performance, even in resource-constrained environments. Moreover, the application of fog computing in advanced robotics revolutionizes the concept of autonomy. With access to vast computational resources, robots acquire sophisticated cognitive abilities, paving the way for adaptive learning and contextual understanding of their surroundings. This enhanced intelligence empowers robots to navigate dynamically changing environments, make autonomous decisions, and interact with humans and other robotic entities with a heightened level of precision and safety.

## 11.9 Applications of fog robotics

FR has a wide range of applications across various industries and domains. Some notable applications of FR:

(i) Industrial automation: FR finds significant application in industrial automation, where robots work alongside humans in manufacturing, assembly, and logistics processes. FR enables robots to perceive their environment, make real-time decisions, and collaborate with humans in a safe and efficient manner. These applications improve productivity, quality, and safety in industrial settings.

(ii) Smart agriculture: In the field of agriculture, FR plays a crucial role in automating tasks such as planting, harvesting, and monitoring crops. Robots equipped with sensors and vision systems can navigate fields, collect data on plant health, and perform targeted interventions such as pesticide application or irrigation. FR enables real-time data analysis, precise actions, and optimized resource allocation in agricultural operations.

(iii) Healthcare and assistive robotics: FR has applications in healthcare and assistive robotics, where robots can assist with patient care, rehabilitation, and support for the elderly or disabled. Robots equipped with sensors and AI algorithms can monitor vital signs, provide medication reminders, or assist with mobility. The fog-computing infrastructure enables real-time data analysis, secure communication, and personalized care in healthcare settings.

(iv) Smart cities and infrastructure: FR contributes to the development of smart cities by enabling intelligent infrastructure management. Robots equipped with sensors and actuators can monitor and maintain urban infrastructure, such as bridges, roads, and buildings. They can detect anomalies, perform inspections, and carry out maintenance tasks, improving the efficiency and longevity of critical infrastructure.

(v) Disaster response and search-and-rescue: FR has applications in disaster response scenarios, where robots can assist in search-and-rescue operations. Robots equipped with sensors and vision systems can navigate hazardous environments, detect survivors, and relay critical information in real time to emergency responders. FR enables efficient coordination, situational awareness, and timely response in high-risk situations.

(vi) Environmental monitoring and conservation: Robots integrated with fog-computing capabilities play a role in environmental monitoring and conservation efforts. They can collect data on air quality, water quality, and wildlife populations in remote or challenging environments. The fog-computing infrastructure enables real-time data analysis, remote monitoring, and decision-making to support conservation efforts and environmental management.

(vii) Personal robotics and entertainment: FR also finds application in personal robotics and entertainment, where robots provide companionship, entertainment, and assistance in homes or leisure settings. Robots equipped with

NLP, computer vision, and emotion recognition capabilities can interact with humans, entertain, and assist with daily tasks. FR enables personalized interactions, adaptive behaviors, and seamless integration with smart home devices.

## 11.10    Conclusion

Fog-computing robotics represents a transformative approach that combines the power of robotics and fog computing to enable efficient, adaptable, and intelligent robotic systems. By leveraging the computational resources and data processing capabilities of edge devices and fog nodes, fog-computing robotics overcomes the limitations of centralized cloud computing and empowers robots to perform complex tasks in real time, even in resource-constrained environments. The integration of fog computing into robotics brings several benefits. It enables low-latency communication, allowing robots to interact with their surroundings in real time and make rapid decisions based on local data processing. Fog-computing robotics also enhances scalability and fault tolerance by distributing computational tasks across multiple fog nodes and edge devices, enabling collaborative and resilient operation. With fog-computing robotics, robots can perform perception, decision-making, and control tasks more efficiently and autonomously. The integration of deep learning algorithms allows robots to learn from data, adapt to changing environments, and improve their performance over time. The proximity-based collaboration between robots and fog nodes facilitates knowledge sharing and collective intelligence, enabling robots to leverage the expertise of nearby devices for enhanced capabilities. Fog-computing robotics finds application in various domains, including industrial automation, healthcare, agriculture, smart cities, and disaster response. It brings automation, efficiency, and intelligence to these domains, enabling robots to perform complex tasks, enhance productivity, and improve safety.

## References

[1]  M. A. Hamid, M. O. Rashid, and C. S. Hong, Routing Security in Sensor Network: Hello Flood Attack and Defense, in *IEEE ICNEWS*, 2006, pp. 2–4.

[2]  O. Onolaja, R. Bahsoon, and G. Theodoropoulos, Conceptual Framework for Dynamic Trust Monitoring and Prediction, *Procedia Computer Science*, 1, 1241–1250, 2010.

[3]  T. Blasing, L. Batyuk, A. Schmidt, S. A. Camtepe, and S. Albayrak, An Android Application Sandbox System for Suspicious Software Detection, in *5th International Conference on Malicious and Unwanted Software*, 2010, pp. 55–62.

[4]  T. Abou-Assaleh, N. Cercone, V. Keselj, and R. Sweidan, N-Gram-Based Detection of New Malicious Code, in *Proceedings of the 28th Annual International Computer Software and Applications Conference*, 2, 41–42, 2004.

[5]  L. Martignoni, R. Paleari, and D. Bruschi, A Framework for Behavior-Based Malware Analysis in the Cloud, in *Information Systems Security*, 2009, pp. 178–192.

[6]  I. Burguera, U. Zurutuza, and S. Nadjm-Tehrani, Crowdroid: Behavior-Based Malware Detection System for Android, in *Proceedings of the 1st ACM Workshop on Security and Privacy in Smartphones and Mobile Devices*, 2011, pp. 15–26.

[7]  X. Wang, Y. Yang, Y. Zeng, C. Tang, J. Shi, and K. Xu, A Novel Hybrid Mobile Malware Detection System Integrating Anomaly Detection with Misuse Detection, in *Proceedings of the 6th International Workshop on Mobile Cloud Computing and Services*, 2015, pp. 15–22.

[8]  P. Ratha, D. Swain, B. Paikaray, and S. Sahoo, An Optimized Encryption Technique using an Arbitrary Matrix with Probabilistic Encryption, *Procedia Computer Science*, 57, 1235–1241, 2015.

[9]  N. Sathishkumar and K. Rajakumar, A Study on Vehicle to Vehicle Collision Prevention Using Fog, Cloud, Big Data and Elliptic Curve Security Based on Threshold Energy Efficient Protocol, in *Wireless Sensor Network in Second International Conference on Recent Trends and Challenges in Computational Models (ICRTCCM)*, 2017, pp. 275–280.

[10]  K. Ruan, J. Carthy, T. Kechadi, and M. Crosbie, Cloud Forensics, in *Advances in Digital Forensics VII*, 2011, pp. 35–46.

*Chapter 12*

# Cybernetic intelligence in fog computing

## Abstract

This chapter explores the concept of fog computing as an intelligent data-intensive environment for cyber intelligence. Fog computing leverages edge devices and infrastructure to enable real-time processing, analysis, and decision-making, bringing computation closer to the data source. This abstract provides a brief overview of the background, scope, problem definition, aim, and analysis related to the application of intelligent data intensive-based fog environment for cyber intelligence.

**Background:** Fog computing extends cloud computing by pushing processing capabilities to the edge of the network, reducing latency and improving response times. The exponential growth of data generated by Internet of Things (IoT) devices demands advanced computing paradigms to handle real-time data processing and analysis. Cyber intelligence requires timely and accurate insights to identify and mitigate potential threats, making fog computing an ideal platform to support such requirements.

**Scope:** This chapter focuses on the utilization of intelligent data intensive-based fog environment for cyber intelligence applications. The scope includes the integration of artificial intelligence and machine learning techniques to enable real-time analytics and decision-making at the network edge. Various data-intensive scenarios, such as network traffic analysis, anomaly detection, and threat identification, are considered within the context of fog computing for cyber intelligence.

**Problem definition:** Traditional centralized cloud architectures face challenges in handling the massive volume of data generated by IoT devices, leading to latency issues and potential privacy concerns. Timely processing and analysis of data are crucial for effective cyber intelligence, requiring a decentralized approach that brings computation closer to the data source. The integration of intelligent data-intensive techniques within fog-computing environments aims to address these challenges, enabling efficient cyber intelligence operations.

**Aim:** The primary aim of this chapter is to investigate and propose an intelligent data intensive-based fog environment for cyber intelligence to enhance real-time analysis and decision-making capabilities. By leveraging machine learning algorithms, artificial intelligence techniques, and distributed computing, the proposed approach aims to improve the efficiency and accuracy of cyber intelligence operations. The aim is to develop a scalable and robust framework that can handle large-scale data streams, ensure privacy and security, and provide actionable insights for effective cyber-threat detection and response.

**Analysis/observation:** The integration of intelligent data-intensive techniques within fog-computing environments enables real-time analysis and decision-making at the network edge, reducing latency and enhancing cyber intelligence capabilities. The use of machine learning algorithms and artificial intelligence techniques can assist in identifying patterns, anomalies, and potential threats in massive volumes of data generated by IoT devices. The proposed approach has the potential to improve the overall effectiveness of cyber intelligence operations, enabling faster response times, proactive threat mitigation, and improved situational awareness in dynamic and distributed environments.

## 12.1   Introduction

In recent years, the rapid proliferation of Internet of Things (IoT) devices has generated an unprecedented amount of data, posing significant challenges for traditional cloud-based architectures in terms of latency, scalability, and privacy concerns. To address these challenges, fog computing has emerged as a promising paradigm that brings computation, storage, and intelligence closer to the network edge. This chapter focuses on the application of an intelligent data intensive-based fog environment for cyber intelligence, leveraging the capabilities of fog computing to enhance real-time analysis and decision-making in the realm of cybersecurity.

This section provides an overview of the key concepts and motivations driving the need for an intelligent data-intensive fog environment for cyber intelligence. It highlights the shortcomings of centralized cloud architectures in handling the vast amount of data generated by IoT devices, which often leads to increased latency and privacy concerns. Additionally, it emphasizes the need for timely processing and analysis of data to detect and respond to cyber threats effectively.

Fog computing extends cloud computing by distributing computing resources to the edge of the network, leveraging edge devices, fog nodes, and local edge servers. By bringing computation closer to the data source, fog computing addresses the limitations associated with relying solely on centralized cloud infrastructure. This decentralized approach enables real-time data processing, analysis, and decision-making, reducing latency and bandwidth requirements.

Intelligent data-intensive techniques play a crucial role in the context of cyber intelligence. By integrating machine learning algorithms and artificial intelligence techniques into the fog environment, actionable insights can be extracted from the massive volumes of data generated by IoT devices. These techniques enable proactive threat detection, anomaly identification, and timely response, enhancing the overall efficiency, scalability, and accuracy of cyber intelligence operations [1].

The chapter aims to explore the technical aspects, implementation strategies, and evaluation of the intelligent data intensive-based fog environment for cyber intelligence. By leveraging the capabilities of fog computing and intelligent data-intensive techniques, the proposed environment has the potential to revolutionize cyber intelligence. Real-time analysis, faster response times, and improved situational awareness can be achieved in distributed and dynamic environments.

## 12.2 A model of cybernetic intelligence in fog environment

A model of cybernetic intelligence in fog environment unveils an innovative framework that embodies the seamless convergence of cybernetics and intelligent systems. This model represents a paradigm shift in the domain of fog computing, elevating the capabilities of interconnected devices and services to new heights. At its core, this model seeks to achieve a harmonious blend of human-like cognitive abilities and distributed computing, empowering fog computing with cybernetic intelligence.

Cybernetics is a multidisciplinary field that explores the mechanisms of control and communication in both living organisms and artificial systems. By integrating cybernetic principles into fog computing, this model aims to create adaptive, self-regulating systems capable of continuous learning and improvement. The cybernetic intelligence in fog computing hinges on the ability to process vast amounts of data efficiently. Fog nodes act as intelligent agents, employing machine learning algorithms to analyze data at the edge, facilitating real-time decision-making and reducing the burden on centralized cloud infrastructure. Cybernetic intelligence enables the model to dynamically allocate computing resources across the fog nodes based on the changing demands of connected devices and applications. This optimizes resource utilization, enhances responsiveness, and ensures smooth operation even in resource-constrained environments. Inspired by biological feedback loops, the model incorporates cognitive feedback mechanisms, enabling fog-computing systems to learn from experiences, adapt to new information, and continuously refine their decision-making processes. A vital aspect of this model is its emphasis on human–robot interaction. The cybernetic intelligence enables robots to understand human intentions, interpret natural language, and respond intelligently, fostering a more intuitive and efficient collaboration between humans and machines. Cybernetic intelligence in fog computing grants devices the ability to perceive their surroundings contextually. Fog nodes gather contextual data from various sensors and sources, enabling devices to adapt to dynamic environments with a heightened level of understanding.

By distributing control mechanisms across fog nodes, the model promotes fault tolerance and resilience. Even in scenarios where individual nodes fail, the system as a whole continues to function, mitigating risks and enhancing overall reliability. The model prioritizes security and privacy by employing cybernetic principles to monitor and regulate data flow, detect anomalies, and identify potential security threats. Fog computing entities become self-aware, actively safeguarding sensitive information within the network. Through the integration of cybernetic intelligence, fog computing devices gain autonomous decision-making capabilities. Robots can autonomously execute tasks, optimizing their actions based on real-time data and previously learned patterns. Inspired by the collective behavior of biological swarms, the model encourages swarm intelligence among robotic entities. This enables collaborative problem-solving, efficient task allocation, and adaptive behavior, particularly in large-scale applications. While embracing the principles of fog computing, the model emphasizes the symbiotic relationship between the edge and the cloud. Cybernetic intelligence ensures seamless integration and efficient data sharing between fog nodes and centralized cloud services. The cybernetic intelligence model promotes continual learning and adaptation. Fog-computing systems can evolve over time, learning from user interactions, environmental changes, and new data, resulting in ever-improving performance.

This model finds extensive application across numerous domains, including smart cities, autonomous vehicles, healthcare, and industrial automation. The amalgamation of cybernetic intelligence and fog computing redefines the possibilities of intelligent systems in real-world scenarios. With increased autonomy and decision-making capabilities, the model raises ethical concerns. As such, this book explores the responsible use of cybernetic intelligence in fog computing and addresses the implications for society. As the model of cybernetic intelligence in fog computing continues to evolve, it holds the promise of transforming industries and revolutionizing the way humans interact with technology. This book delves into the future prospects, potential challenges, and exciting opportunities that lie ahead in this captivating realm of cybernetic intelligence in the fog environment.

## 12.3   Data utility in cyborg

Data utility in the context of cyborgs refers to the relevance, value, and usefulness of data that is collected, processed, and utilized to enhance the functioning and capabilities of cyborg entities. Cyborgs, which are a combination of biological and artificial components, require a constant flow of data to facilitate seamless integration and interaction between the human and machine elements. The concept of data utility plays a crucial role in optimizing the performance and effectiveness of cyborgs in various aspects of their existence.

Cyborgs heavily rely on data gathered from biometric sensors to monitor and analyze the physiological state of the human components. This data includes vital signs, neural activity, and other biological indicators, which help regulate and adapt the artificial components for optimal performance and safety. Data utility ensures that the collected biometric information is accurately interpreted and utilized to maintain the cyborg's homeostasis and well-being. To enable cyborgs to interact seamlessly with their environment, data utility involves gathering information about the surrounding context. Sensors provide data about the external environment, including temperature, humidity, location, and object recognition. This contextual awareness is essential for cyborgs to respond appropriately and make intelligent decisions in real-time situations. Data utility plays a pivotal role in enhancing the cognitive capabilities of cyborgs. By constantly feeding relevant data to the artificial components, cyborgs can leverage machine learning algorithms to process and analyze information, learn from experiences, and improve decision-making abilities over time. The utility of data here lies in its ability to enable continuous learning and adaptation for the cyborg's cognitive functions.

For a cyborg to function harmoniously with its human counterpart, data utility ensures smooth user interaction and an enhanced user experience. Understanding and interpreting human gestures, speech, and emotions through data analysis fosters more intuitive communication and efficient collaboration between the human and machine components. Data utility in cyborgs must also address security and privacy concerns. Ensuring the confidentiality, integrity, and availability of sensitive data is crucial to protect the cyborg from potential threats, unauthorized access, and data breaches. Utilizing data encryption, access controls, and secure communication protocols are essential components of data utility in cyborgs. Data utility aids in optimizing resource allocation within cyborgs. Efficient use of computational resources, power management, and task prioritization based on data analysis contribute to increased energy efficiency, extending the operational life span of the cyborg. As cyborgs interact with the broader society, data utility must adhere to ethical and legal regulations concerning data collection, storage, and usage. This involves obtaining informed consent from users, ensuring data anonymization when necessary, and being transparent about the data processing practices.

### 12.3.1   Intelligent distributed computer network

An intelligent distributed computer network refers to a network infrastructure that leverages intelligent techniques and distributed computing to enhance performance, scalability, and efficiency. This explores the concept of intelligent distributed computer networks and their significance in various domains.

An intelligent distributed computer network utilizes advanced algorithms, machine learning, and artificial intelligence techniques to optimize resource allocation, improve decision-making, and enhance overall system performance. Distributed computing allows the network to distribute computational tasks across multiple nodes or devices, enabling parallel processing and faster execution of complex tasks. Intelligent distributed computer networks play a crucial role in large-scale data processing and analysis. By distributing data-intensive tasks across multiple nodes, the network can handle big datasets more efficiently, reducing processing time and enabling real-time analytics. In the context of cloud computing, intelligent distributed computer networks enable dynamic resource allocation and load balancing, ensuring optimal resource utilization and minimizing latency.

Intelligent distributed computer networks are particularly relevant in edge computing environments. By bringing computation closer to the network edge, these networks enable real-time data processing, reduce latency, and support applications that require low latency, such as IoT and real-time analytics. Security is a critical aspect of intelligent distributed computer networks. By leveraging intelligent techniques, such as anomaly detection and behavior analysis, these networks can enhance threat detection and response, ensuring the security of data and systems.

Intelligent distributed computer networks facilitate fault tolerance and reliability. By distributing tasks and data across multiple nodes, these networks can continue functioning even if individual nodes or components fail. Intelligent distributed computer networks enable collaborative computing, allowing multiple devices or entities to share resources, exchange information, and work together to solve complex problems. These networks are highly scalable, as new nodes can be easily added to the network to accommodate increased computational requirements or data volume.

Intelligent distributed computer networks are essential for real-time decision-making in time-sensitive applications, such as financial trading, autonomous vehicles, and industrial control systems. The use of intelligent techniques, such as machine learning and data mining, enables these networks to learn from past experiences and improve their performance over time. Intelligent distributed computer networks are relevant in the field of bioinformatics and genomics, where large-scale data analysis is crucial for understanding complex biological systems and accelerating scientific discoveries. These networks are instrumental in the field of distributed artificial intelligence, where multiple intelligent agents collaborate and communicate to solve complex problems and make collective decisions. Intelligent distributed computer networks support collaborative applications and platforms, enabling seamless collaboration among individuals or teams working on shared projects or documents.

In the field of robotics and autonomous systems, intelligent distributed computer networks enable distributed control and coordination, allowing multiple robots or devices to work together efficiently. Intelligent distributed computer networks are crucial for real-time monitoring and control systems, such as smart grids and environmental monitoring networks, ensuring efficient management of resources and timely response to events. These networks are essential for virtualization and cloud-based services, where distributed computing resources can be provisioned and managed dynamically to meet varying demands. Intelligent distributed computer networks facilitate data sharing and collaboration in distributed environments, enabling organizations and individuals to access and exchange data securely and efficiently. In the realm of scientific simulations and modeling, intelligent distributed computer networks enable the parallel execution of computationally intensive simulations, accelerating scientific discoveries and improving accuracy. Intelligent distributed computer networks are at the forefront of research and development, driving innovation in areas such as IoT, artificial intelligence, cybersecurity, and smart cities, by providing scalable and efficient computing infrastructures to support these technologies.

## 12.3.2    A model for data-intensive applications in fog environment

In the era of Big Data, data-intensive applications require efficient and scalable computing infrastructures. The fog-computing paradigm has emerged as a promising solution, enabling real-time processing and analysis at the network edge.

This section presents a model for data-intensive applications in a fog environment. The proposed model leverages the capabilities of fog computing to handle large volumes of data generated by IoT devices, reducing latency and enhancing overall system performance.

The model encompasses the entire data life cycle, including data acquisition, processing, storage, analysis, and decision-making. It takes into account the unique characteristics of fog computing, such as distributed computing, edge intelligence, and proximity to data sources. Data acquisition in the model involves collecting data from various IoT devices, sensors, and other sources at the network edge. The data is then processed and aggregated locally before being transmitted to the cloud or central data center. In the processing stage, the model employs edge computing techniques to perform real-time data filtering, transformation, and preprocessing, reducing the amount of data sent to the cloud and conserving network bandwidth.

The model emphasizes the importance of intelligent data analysis techniques, such as machine learning and artificial intelligence, to extract actionable insights from the data. These techniques enable real-time analytics, anomaly detection, predictive modeling, and other data-intensive tasks at the edge of the network. The model incorporates efficient data storage mechanisms in the fog environment. It employs a combination of local storage on edge devices, edge servers, and cloud storage to manage and store data based on its criticality, access requirements, and compliance regulations. Security and privacy are integral components of the proposed model. It includes mechanisms for data encryption, access control, and secure communication to ensure the confidentiality and integrity of data in transit and at rest. The model emphasizes the dynamic allocation of computational resources in the fog environment. It leverages resource management techniques to allocate computing resources based on data processing demands, network conditions, and energy constraints.

The model includes mechanisms for data synchronization and coordination between edge devices, fog nodes, and the cloud. It ensures consistency and coherence across distributed data sources and enables seamless collaboration among various components in the fog environment. Scalability is a key consideration in the model. It takes into account the ability to scale the infrastructure, computing resources, and data processing capabilities to handle the growing volume and velocity of data generated by IoT devices. The model incorporates fault tolerance and resilience mechanisms to handle failures and disruptions in the fog environment. It includes redundancy, replication, and failover strategies to ensure continuous availability and reliability of data-intensive applications. The model addresses the challenge of interoperability and integration in the fog environment. It provides standardized interfaces, protocols, and Application Program Interface (APIs) to facilitate seamless integration of different devices, platforms, and applications.

Energy efficiency is a critical aspect of the proposed model. It includes energy-aware algorithms and optimization techniques to minimize energy consumption in the fog environment, extending the battery life of edge devices and reducing operational costs. The model emphasizes the importance of real-time decision-making in data-intensive applications. It enables rapid response and actions based on real-time insights generated at the network edge, reducing latency and enabling time-critical applications. The model takes into account the heterogeneity of edge devices, fog nodes, and cloud infrastructure. It provides mechanisms for adaptive computing, dynamic configuration, and resource orchestration to accommodate diverse hardware and software capabilities.

The model promotes a collaborative approach between edge devices, fog nodes, and the cloud. It enables distributed computation, data sharing, and workload offloading to optimize overall system performance and resource utilization. The model incorporates analytics-driven feedback loops to continuously improve data-intensive applications in the fog environment. It leverages data analytics to monitor application performance, optimize resource allocation, and refine data processing strategies. The model considers the trade-off between data locality and data movement in the fog environment. It aims to minimize data movement and transmission to reduce latency, bandwidth consumption, and operational costs. Overall, the proposed model provides a comprehensive framework for developing and deploying data-intensive applications in a fog environment. By leveraging the unique characteristics of fog computing, the model enables efficient data processing, real-time analytics, and intelligent decision-making at the network edge, paving the way for scalable and responsive data-intensive applications.

### 12.3.3    Resources

Resources in a fog environment refer to the computational, storage, and networking capabilities that enable the execution of applications and services at the network edge. These resources are distributed across edge devices, fog nodes, and cloud infrastructure to support various functionalities and meet the requirements of fog computing. Edge devices: Edge devices, such as IoT devices, sensors, smartphones, and gateways, are the primary resources in a fog environment. They generate data, perform local computations, and act as data sources. These devices often have limited computational power, storage capacity, and energy resources. Fog nodes: Fog nodes are intermediate computing nodes that sit between edge devices and the cloud. They provide additional processing and storage capabilities, enabling edge devices to offload computational tasks and share resources. Fog nodes can be deployed in proximity to edge devices, such as in access points, routers, or local servers. Cloud infrastructure: Cloud infrastructure, including data centers and servers, complements the fog environment by providing additional computational and storage resources. Cloud resources are typically located remotely and accessed through the network. The cloud is responsible for handling heavy computations, large-scale data storage, and centralized management.

Edge servers: Edge servers are powerful computing nodes located at the network edge, closer to edge devices. They offer higher computational capabilities and storage capacity than edge devices, enabling more resource-intensive tasks to be processed locally. Edge servers can run specialized software, middleware, and applications. Network infrastructure: The network infrastructure plays a vital role in a fog environment, connecting edge devices, fog nodes, edge servers, and cloud infrastructure. It provides the necessary bandwidth, low latency, and reliable connectivity for data transmission, resource sharing, and communication. Storage resources: Storage resources in a fog environment include local storage on edge devices, storage on fog nodes, and cloud-based storage. These resources are used to store data generated by edge devices, intermediate results of computations, and applications' data. Computational resources: Computational resources in a fog environment refer to the processing capabilities of edge devices, fog nodes, edge servers, and cloud infrastructure. These resources enable the execution of computational tasks, data analytics, machine learning algorithms, and other resource-intensive operations. Memory resources: Memory resources, including RAM and cache, are critical for storing data and temporary results during computations. Edge devices, fog nodes, and edge servers require sufficient memory capacity to support efficient data processing and analysis.

Power and energy resources: Power and energy resources are essential considerations in a fog environment, especially for resource-constrained edge devices. Energy-efficient designs, power management techniques, and energy harvesting technologies are employed to optimize energy consumption and extend battery life. Security resources: Security resources in a fog environment encompass mechanisms, protocols, and technologies to ensure data confidentiality, integrity, and availability. These resources include encryption algorithms, authentication mechanisms, access control policies, and intrusion detection systems. Monitoring and management resources: Monitoring and management resources are utilized to monitor the health, performance, and availability of edge devices, fog nodes, and edge servers. These resources enable remote management, monitoring of resource utilization, and troubleshooting in the fog environment. Virtualization resources: Virtualization technologies are employed to create virtual instances of resources, such as virtual machines or containers, in the fog environment. Virtualization allows for efficient resource allocation, isolation, and scalability, enabling multiple applications to run simultaneously on shared resources.

Orchestration resources: Orchestration resources facilitate the coordination and management of distributed resources in a fog environment. Orchestration platforms automate resource provisioning, workload distribution, and task scheduling to optimize resource utilization and meet application requirements. Communication resources: Communication resources include wired and wireless network infrastructure, protocols, and technologies. These resources enable seamless data transmission, interconnectivity between edge devices and fog nodes, and communication with the cloud. Sensor resources: Sensor resources refer to the various sensors embedded in edge devices, capable of collecting data such as temperature, humidity, motion, or environmental parameters. Sensors are integral to data acquisition and enable real-time monitoring and contextual awareness in the fog environment. Software resources: Software resources encompass operating systems, middleware, application frameworks, and development tools used in the fog environment. These resources enable the development, deployment, and execution of applications, services, and algorithms.

Analytics and machine learning resources: Analytics and machine learning resources include algorithms, libraries, and tools for data analysis, machine learning, and predictive modeling. These resources enable real-time analytics, anomaly detection, pattern recognition, and decision-making in the fog environment. Service discovery and composition resources: Service discovery and composition resources enable the identification, discovery, and composition of services and resources in the fog environment. These resources facilitate service discovery protocols, APIs, and platforms to enable seamless integration and interaction between services. Quality of service (QoS) resources: QoS resources encompass mechanisms and policies to ensure the desired QoS for applications and services in the fog environment. These resources include latency guarantees, throughput optimization, reliability assurances, and prioritization mechanisms.

Resource management and orchestration platforms: Resource management and orchestration platforms provide centralized or distributed management capabilities for the allocation, monitoring, and optimization of resources in the fog environment. These platforms ensure efficient resource utilization, load balancing, and scalability.

## 12.3.4 Data source

A data source refers to the origin or location from which data is collected or generated. It can be any system, device, sensor, application, or entity that produces or provides data for storage, processing, analysis, and utilization. Data sources play a critical role in various domains and industries, as they provide the raw material for deriving insights, making informed decisions, and driving innovation. This section explores different types of data sources.

IoT devices, such as sensors, actuators, wearables, and smart devices, are a significant source of data. These devices collect and transmit data about physical and environmental conditions, machine statuses, user behaviors, and other relevant information. Sensors are specialized devices that measure and detect physical, chemical, or biological parameters. They can include temperature sensors, pressure sensors, humidity sensors, motion sensors, GPS sensors, and many others. Sensors are commonly used in various applications, such as environmental monitoring, industrial automation, and healthcare. Social media platforms, such as Facebook, Twitter, Instagram, and LinkedIn, are rich sources of user-generated data. They provide insights into user demographics, preferences, behaviors, opinions, and social interactions. This data is valuable for market research, customer analytics, sentiment analysis, and personalized advertising.

The World Wide Web and the Internet as a whole are vast sources of data. Websites, blogs, forums, online news portals, and other online platforms generate substantial amounts of structured and unstructured data. Web scraping and crawling techniques are often used to extract data from web pages and analyze it for various purposes. Enterprise systems, such as customer relationship management systems, enterprise resource planning systems, and supply chain management systems, generate data related to business processes, transactions, sales, inventory, and customer interactions. This data provides insights into operational efficiency, customer behavior, and overall business performance. Various organizations, research institutions, and government agencies provide publicly available datasets for research, analysis, and innovation. Examples include data repositories like Kaggle, US government data portals, and scientific research databases. These datasets cover diverse domains, such as healthcare, climate, transportation, and finance.

Machine-generated data refers to data produced by automated systems, machinery, or devices. This data can include logs, system metrics, error reports, performance indicators, and machine-generated events. Machine-generated data is commonly used in system monitoring, diagnostics, and predictive maintenance. Mobile devices, such as smartphones and tablets, are a significant source of data. They generate data through applications, GPS, call records, text messages, multimedia content, and device sensors. Mobile data provides insights into user behavior, location-based services, and personalized recommendations. Biological and genetic data sources include DNA sequencing data, gene expression data, protein interaction data, and medical records. These sources are crucial in bioinformatics, genomics, and medical research, helping to understand diseases, discover new treatments, and advance personalized medicine.

Open government data: Governments around the world are increasingly making datasets available to the public. Open government data includes information on demographics, public services, transportation, environment, health, crime, and more. It enables transparency, innovation, and the development of data-driven public policies.

Geospatial data sources provide information about geographic locations, land features, maps, and satellite imagery. This data is used in fields such as urban planning, logistics, navigation systems, and environmental monitoring. Financial institutions generate vast amounts of financial data, including transaction records, stock market data, credit card transactions, and banking records. This data is utilized for fraud detection, risk analysis, investment strategies, and financial forecasting. Healthcare data encompasses electronic health records, medical imaging data, patient vitals, clinical trials' data, and genetic information. It plays a crucial role in medical research, patient care, disease management, and public health initiatives. Environmental data sources provide information about weather conditions, air quality, water quality, biodiversity, and ecological systems. This data is essential for climate research, environmental monitoring, natural resource management, and disaster response. Wearable devices, such as fitness trackers, smartwatches, and health monitoring devices, collect data related to physical activities, biometrics, sleep patterns, and personal health. This data is used for personal wellness, healthcare monitoring, and behavior analysis.

Audio and video data sources include recorded media, surveillance footage, video streams, and voice recordings. This data is analyzed for speech recognition, video analytics, sentiment analysis, and content recommendation. Satellite imagery and remote sensing data provide detailed information about Earth's surface, climate patterns, vegetation, and natural resources. This data is utilized in fields like agriculture, urban planning, disaster management, and environmental monitoring.

Historical data sources include archived records, historical documents, and historical datasets. This data provides insights into past trends, patterns, and events, enabling historical analysis, trend forecasting, and predictive modeling. Government records, such as census data, tax records, property records, and public documents, are valuable sources of demographic, economic, and legal information. Government records contribute to research, public policy, and demographic analysis. Personal data refers to data collected from individuals, including their demographics, preferences, behaviors, and online activities. Personal data is utilized for personalization, targeted advertising, recommendation systems, and user profiling.

### 12.3.5   Tasks

Tasks in a data-intensive environment refer to the activities and operations performed to process, analyze, manipulate, and utilize data. These tasks are aimed at extracting valuable insights, making informed decisions, and achieving specific goals. In the context of data-intensive applications, tasks can range from simple data processing operations to complex analytics and machine learning algorithms. This explores different types of tasks commonly performed in a data-intensive environment [2].

Data collection tasks involve gathering data from various sources, such as sensors, databases, APIs, and external datasets. This task includes acquiring, aggregating, and preprocessing data to make it ready for further analysis and processing. Data cleaning and preprocessing tasks involve removing inconsistencies, errors, and missing values from the collected data. This task includes data deduplication, data validation, handling outliers, and normalizing data formats. Data integration tasks involve combining data from multiple sources or datasets to create a unified view. This task includes mapping and transforming data from different schemas, resolving semantic conflicts, and ensuring data consistency and coherence.

Data transformation and enrichment: Data transformation and enrichment tasks involve converting raw data into a more usable and meaningful format. This task includes feature engineering, data normalization, data aggregation, and deriving new variables or attributes from existing data.

Data analysis and exploration tasks involve examining data to discover patterns, trends, correlations, and insights. This task includes descriptive statistics, data visualization, exploratory data analysis, and hypothesis testing to gain a deeper understanding of the data. Statistical analysis tasks involve applying statistical techniques to data to infer relationships, estimate parameters, and test hypotheses. This task includes tasks such as regression analysis, hypothesis testing, clustering, and time-series analysis. Machine learning tasks involve training models and algorithms on data to make predictions, classifications, or uncover patterns. This task includes supervised learning, unsupervised learning, reinforcement learning, and deep learning. Predictive analytics tasks involve using historical data and statistical modeling techniques to make predictions about future events or outcomes. This task includes forecasting, demand prediction, risk assessment, and recommendation systems.

Anomaly detection: Anomaly detection tasks involve identifying rare or abnormal patterns in data that deviate from the expected behavior. This task includes tasks such as outlier detection, fraud detection, intrusion detection, and anomaly scoring.

Data visualization tasks involve creating visual representations of data to communicate information and insights effectively. This task includes tasks such as charts, graphs, dashboards, and interactive visualizations to present data in a visually appealing and intuitive manner. Data mining tasks involve discovering patterns, relationships, and hidden insights in large datasets. This task includes association rule mining, cluster analysis, text mining, and pattern recognition. Natural language processing (NLP) tasks involve processing and understanding human language data, including text and speech. This task includes tasks such as sentiment analysis, text classification, named entity recognition, and machine translation. Real-time processing tasks involve analyzing and processing data in real time or near real time to enable immediate actions or responses. This task includes streaming data analysis, event processing, and real-time decision-making. Data compression and storage tasks involve reducing the size of data and optimizing its storage to minimize storage costs and improve efficiency. This task includes data compression algorithms, file formats, and data archiving strategies. Data privacy and security tasks involve ensuring the confidentiality, integrity, and availability of data. This task includes data encryption, access control, data anonymization, and vulnerability assessment. Data governance and management tasks involve establishing policies, procedures, and frameworks for data quality, data governance, and data life cycle management. This task includes data cataloging, data lineage, data stewardship, and data governance frameworks.

Data querying and retrieval tasks involve extracting specific information or subsets of data from large datasets. This task includes tasks such as SQL queries, data indexing, and search algorithms to efficiently retrieve relevant data. Model training and evaluation tasks involve training machine learning models on labeled data, tuning model parameters, and assessing model performance. This task includes cross-validation, model evaluation metrics, and hyperparameter optimization. Deployment and integration tasks involve integrating data-intensive applications and models into existing systems, platforms, or workflows. This task includes deploying models in production, creating APIs, and integrating with other software systems. Monitoring and maintenance tasks involve continuously monitoring the performance, health, and quality of data-intensive systems and applications. This task includes performance monitoring, error handling, system upgrades, and data quality checks.

## 12.3.6 Use of data in cloud computing

The use of data in cloud computing has revolutionized the way organizations store, process, and utilize their data. Cloud computing provides a scalable and flexible infrastructure that enables efficient data management and analysis. In this paradigm, organizations can leverage the vast storage capacity and computing resources of cloud service providers to handle large volumes of data. Data can be securely stored in the cloud, eliminating the need for on-premises infrastructure and reducing operational costs. With cloud-based data processing and analytics tools, organizations can perform complex data analysis, generate insights, and make data-driven decisions in real time. The use of data in cloud computing also enables collaboration and data sharing among teams and organizations, facilitating innovation and improving productivity.

Additionally, cloud computing offers advanced data processing capabilities, such as distributed computing and parallel processing, that allow organizations to process massive datasets quickly and efficiently. This empowers organizations to unlock the value hidden in their data by extracting actionable insights, detecting patterns, and making accurate predictions. The cloud also provides scalable data storage solutions, enabling organizations to store and access their data on demand without concerns about storage capacity limitations. Cloud-based data solutions also offer high availability and reliability, ensuring that data is accessible at all times and protected from data loss. Overall, the use of data in cloud computing provides organizations with the agility, scalability, and analytical power needed to leverage their data assets effectively and drive innovation.

## 12.3.7   Situational aspects

Situational aspects refer to the contextual factors and conditions that influence a particular situation or scenario. These aspects provide the backdrop for understanding and analyzing the circumstances, dynamics, and constraints within which a situation unfolds.

Environmental factors, such as weather conditions, geographical location, and physical surroundings, can significantly influence a situation. For example, extreme weather conditions may affect transportation, outdoor activities, and disaster response. Economic factors, including market conditions, resource availability, and financial constraints, play a crucial role in shaping a situation. Economic factors impact business operations, investment decisions, and socio-economic outcomes. Social factors encompass cultural norms, societal values, and social structures that influence human behavior and interactions. Social factors can shape social relationships, power dynamics, and community responses in a given situation. Technological factors refer to the advancements, capabilities, and limitations of technology in a specific situation. Technological factors can enable or hinder certain actions, affect communication, and drive innovation.

Legal and regulatory factors encompass laws, regulations, and policies that govern a situation. Compliance with legal requirements and adherence to regulations are crucial in areas such as business operations, healthcare, and data privacy. Political factors relate to the influence of political systems, governance structures, and political dynamics on a situation. Political factors can shape decision-making processes, policy implementation, and power struggles. Organizational factors pertain to the internal dynamics, structures, and processes within an organization that impact a situation. These factors include organizational culture, leadership styles, and resource allocation. Demographic factors, such as age, gender, ethnicity, and population characteristics, can significantly influence a situation. Demographic factors can affect market segmentation, social dynamics, and public policy. Psychological factors encompass individual and collective psychological states, attitudes, and behaviors that impact a situation. Psychological factors influence decision-making, motivation, and interpersonal dynamics. Time constraints refer to the limitations and pressures imposed by time in a situation. Time constraints can influence decision-making, project management, and resource allocation. The urgency and priority of a situation dictate the immediate attention and action it requires. Urgent and high-priority situations may demand rapid response, resource mobilization, and decision-making. Complexity refers to the intricacy and inter-dependencies of elements in a situation. Complex situations may involve multiple variables, stakeholders, and decision factors that require careful analysis and problem-solving. Uncertainty refers to the lack of predictability or clarity about future events or outcomes in a situation. Uncertainty can affect decision-making, risk assessment, and planning. Stakeholder dynamics encompass the relationships, interests, and influence of different individuals or groups involved in a situation. Understanding stakeholder dynamics is crucial for effective communication, collaboration, and conflict resolution.

Power imbalances occur when certain individuals or groups have more influence, control, or resources than others do in a situation. Power imbalances can affect decision-making, negotiations, and social dynamics. Resource constraints refer to limitations in terms of financial, human, or material resources in a situation. Resource constraints can affect project implementation, service delivery, and innovation. Communication channels determine how information flows within a situation. The choice of communication channels can impact the effectiveness of information sharing, collaboration, and decision-making. Ethical considerations relate to moral principles and values that guide behavior and decision-making in a situation. Ethical considerations are particularly relevant in fields such as healthcare, research, and governance. Trust and credibility: Trust and credibility play a vital role in interpersonal and institutional relationships within a situation. Establishing trust and credibility is crucial for effective collaboration, cooperation, and conflict resolution. Cultural sensitivity involves understanding and respecting diverse cultural perspectives, values, and practices within a situation. Cultural sensitivity is essential for effective communication, teamwork, and inclusivity. Geographic constraints refer to limitations imposed by physical location, terrain, or geographic features in a situation. Geographic constraints can impact transportation, logistics, and resource accessibility.

Health and well-being factors encompass physical and mental health considerations within a situation. Health and well-being factors influence productivity, decision-making, and overall quality of life. Education and knowledge levels of individuals involved in a situation can affect understanding, communication, and problem-solving capabilities. Access to education and knowledge resources is vital for informed decision-making and innovation. Cultural norms and traditions shape behavior, interactions, and expectations within a situation. Understanding and respecting cultural norms are essential for effective communication and collaboration. Collaboration and cooperation among individuals or groups can facilitate problem-solving, innovation, and shared decision-making in a situation.

Conflict and competition can arise in situations where there are divergent interests, goals, or perspectives. Managing conflict and competition requires effective communication, negotiation, and conflict resolution skills. Infrastructure availability refers to the presence or absence of physical, technological, or social infrastructure in a situation. Adequate infrastructure is crucial for transportation, communication, and service delivery. Geopolitical considerations relate to the impact of geopolitical factors, such as international relations, conflicts, and alliances, on a situation. Geopolitical considerations can affect decision-making, trade, and resource allocation. Media coverage and public perception can shape the narrative and public response to a situation. Media and public perception influence public opinion, reputation management, and crisis communication. Data accessibility refers to the availability and ease of access to relevant data in a situation. Data accessibility is essential for evidence-based decision-making, research, and analysis. Scalability refers to the ability of a system, process, or solution to handle increasing demands, workload, or complexity in a situation. Scalability is crucial for accommodating growth, changing circumstances, and resource requirements.

Regulatory compliance involves adhering to legal and industry-specific regulations, standards, and guidelines in a situation. Regulatory compliance ensures ethical practices, data security, and risk management. Cultural diversity refers to the presence of individuals with diverse cultural backgrounds, perspectives, and experiences within a situation. Cultural diversity enhances creativity, innovation, and problem-solving capabilities.

Access to information: Access to information is the availability and ability to obtain relevant and accurate information within a situation. Access to information is crucial for informed decision-making, research, and analysis. Emotional intelligence refers to the ability to recognize, understand, and manage emotions in oneself and others. Emotional intelligence influences interpersonal dynamics, leadership effectiveness, and conflict resolution.

Disaster preparedness: Disaster preparedness involves planning, infrastructure, and procedures in place to mitigate risks and respond to emergencies in a situation. Disaster preparedness is crucial for public safety, resilience, and recovery. Cross-cultural communication involves effective communication across different cultural contexts and languages. Cross-cultural communication skills are essential for global collaborations, diversity management, and international relations. Gender dynamics refer to the social, cultural, and power relations between genders within a situation. Understanding and addressing gender dynamics are crucial for equality, inclusivity, and empowerment. Customer preferences and behavior impact market demand, product development, and marketing strategies in a situation. Understanding customer preferences and behavior enables effective customer engagement and satisfaction.

Technological readiness: Technological readiness refers to the preparedness and ability to adopt and utilize technology within a situation. Technological readiness influences digital transformation, innovation, and competitiveness. Intellectual property rights involve legal protections for intellectual creations, inventions, and innovations. Respect for intellectual property rights fosters innovation, creativity, and fair competition. Workforce skills and expertise influence the capabilities, productivity, and innovation potential within a situation. Developing and utilizing the skills and expertise of the workforce enhances performance and competitiveness.

Public opinion and sentiment reflect the collective attitudes, beliefs, and sentiments of the general public within a situation. Public opinion and sentiment shape public policy, reputation management, and decision-making. Accessibility and inclusivity refer to the availability and equal participation of individuals with diverse abilities and backgrounds in a situation. Accessibility and inclusivity promote equality, social justice, and human rights. Data privacy and security considerations involve protecting personal and sensitive information from unauthorized access or misuse. Ensuring data privacy and security builds trust, compliance, and reputation. The promotion of innovation and creativity within a situation encourages novel ideas, problem-solving, and continuous improvement. Creating an environment that fosters innovation and creativity drives progress and competitiveness. Economic development considerations focus on strategies and actions that foster economic growth, job creation, and prosperity within a situation. Economic development enhances living standards, infrastructure, and opportunities. Emergency response capabilities involve the capacity to respond promptly and effectively to emergencies or crises within a situation. Strong emergency response capabilities save lives, minimize damages, and facilitate recovery.

Collaborating with stakeholders, including government agencies, communities, NGOs, and businesses, fosters collective problem-solving, shared decision-making, and holistic approaches within a situation. Continuity planning involves preparing for and managing potential disruptions or contingencies within a situation. Continuity planning ensures the resilience, stability, and uninterrupted operation of critical processes.

## 12.3.8 Data utility

Data utility refers to the value or usefulness derived from data. It represents the extent to which data can meet the needs, goals, and requirements of individuals, organizations, or systems. Data utility is essential for making informed decisions, driving innovation, and achieving desired outcomes. Here are ten paragraphs highlighting different aspects of data utility:

Data utility plays a critical role in decision-making processes. By providing relevant and reliable information, data enables individuals and organizations to make well-informed decisions based on evidence and insights derived from data analysis. Data utility lies in the ability to extract meaningful insights and conduct valuable analysis from data. Through data analysis techniques such as data mining, statistical modeling, and machine learning, data can reveal patterns, trends, and correlations, allowing for informed decision-making and strategic planning. Data utility supports problem-solving by providing the necessary information and context to identify issues, understand root causes, and develop effective solutions. Analyzing data can reveal patterns and anomalies that help identify problems and guide problem-solving efforts. Data utility is vital for monitoring and evaluating performance. By collecting and analyzing relevant data, individuals and organizations can assess their progress, identify areas of improvement, and make data-driven adjustments to enhance performance.

Data utility allows organizations to gain a deeper understanding of their customers. By analyzing customer data, organizations can identify preferences, behavior patterns, and trends, enabling targeted marketing strategies, personalized experiences, and improved customer satisfaction. Data utility fuels innovation and product development. By leveraging data, organizations can identify emerging trends, market gaps, and customer needs, allowing for the creation of new products, services, and business models. Data utility supports risk management by providing insights into potential risks and threats. Through data analysis, organizations can identify and assess risks, make risk-informed decisions, and implement mitigation strategies.

Data utility enables efficient resource allocation and optimization. By analyzing data on resource usage, organizations can identify areas of waste, inefficiency, and bottlenecks, allowing for improved resource allocation and cost savings. Data utility facilitates forecasting and predictive analytics. By analyzing historical data, organizations can develop models and algorithms to predict future trends, anticipate market changes, and make proactive decisions.

Data utility is crucial for continuous improvement efforts. By collecting and analyzing data on performance, processes, and customer feedback, organizations can identify areas for improvement, implement changes, and monitor the impact of those changes over time.

## 12.3.9    Data life cycle

The data life cycle in a fog environment refers to the stages that data go through from its creation or acquisition to its eventual disposal or archiving. The fog environment, which combines edge devices, fog nodes, and cloud infrastructure, introduces unique considerations and challenges to the data life cycle. The stages of the data life cycle in a fog environment are as follows:

The data life cycle begins with data generation, where data is created or collected by edge devices, sensors, or other data sources in the fog environment. This can include sensor readings, user interactions, or machine-generated data. The distributed nature of the fog environment means that data is generated at the edge, closer to the source, enabling real-time and context-aware data collection. Once data is generated, it needs to be ingested into the fog infrastructure for further processing and analysis. Data ingestion involves transferring the data from edge devices to fog nodes or cloud infrastructure for storage and subsequent processing. In a fog environment, data ingestion needs to consider the limitations of edge devices, such as limited bandwidth and intermittent connectivity, and ensure efficient and reliable transfer of data. After data ingestion, the next stage is data processing and analysis. Fog nodes and cloud infrastructure leverage computational resources to perform various operations, including data filtering, aggregation, transformation, and analytics. Data processing and analysis in the fog environment aim to extract meaningful insights, detect patterns, and make real-time decisions based on the processed data. Data storage is a critical stage in the data life cycle, where processed data is persistently stored for future retrieval and analysis. In a fog environment, data storage can be distributed across edge devices, fog nodes, and cloud infrastructure. It requires considering factors such as data replication, data placement strategies, and data consistency to ensure efficient and reliable storage.

Data transmission and communication play a crucial role in the data life cycle within a fog environment. This stage involves the transfer of data between edge devices, fog nodes, and cloud infrastructure. It requires reliable and low-latency communication protocols to enable efficient data sharing, synchronization, and collaboration among the various components of the fog environment. Data privacy and security are paramount considerations throughout the data life cycle in a fog environment. Data need to be protected from unauthorized access, tampering, or disclosure. Encryption, access control mechanisms, authentication protocols, and secure data transmission are essential to ensure the privacy and security of data in transit and at rest. Data analytics and decision-making stages involve leveraging processed data to extract insights, perform advanced analytics, and make informed decisions. Fog nodes and cloud infrastructure enable data-intensive operations, including machine learning algorithms, predictive modeling, and real-time analytics, to support intelligent decision-making at the edge. Data visualization and presentation are important stages in the data life cycle to convey insights and findings to stakeholders. Visual representations such as charts, graphs, and dashboards help to communicate complex information in a clear and intuitive manner. In a fog environment, data visualization can be performed at the edge or centralized in the cloud, depending on the specific requirements and constraints.

Data archiving and retention involve storing data for long-term preservation, compliance, or historical analysis. In a fog environment, archiving strategies need to consider the life span of the data, storage capacity, and retrieval requirements. Archiving can be performed in the cloud or distributed across fog nodes and edge devices based on factors such as data size, access frequency, and compliance regulations. The final stage of the data life cycle is data disposal, which involves securely and permanently removing data that are no longer needed or have reached the end of its life cycle. Data disposal practices need to comply with relevant data privacy regulations and ensure that data is properly erased to prevent unauthorized access or data leakage.

### 12.3.10   Using the data utility model

Using the data utility model provides a systematic approach to maximizing the value and usefulness of data in various domains and contexts.

The data utility model guides decision-making by ensuring that data is relevant, accurate, and timely. Decision-makers can use the model to assess the utility of different datasets and prioritize data sources that provide the most value for informed decision-making. The data utility model enables the assessment of data quality to ensure that data meets the required standards for accuracy, completeness, and consistency. By evaluating data quality dimensions, such as reliability, validity, and timeliness, organizations can make informed decisions based on high-quality data. The data utility model facilitates data integration by considering the compatibility, consistency, and relevance of data from different sources. By integrating data effectively, organizations can derive valuable insights from a holistic view of the data landscape. Implementing the data utility model helps organizations establish robust data governance practices. This includes defining data ownership, ensuring data privacy and security, and establishing data management policies and procedures to enhance the overall utility of data.

The data utility model promotes collaboration among stakeholders by facilitating data sharing and cooperation. It establishes mechanisms for sharing data assets, knowledge, and insights across teams, departments, or organizations, maximizing the utility of data through collective efforts. Using the data utility model, organizations can focus on data visualization techniques that effectively convey insights and enhance understanding. Visualizing data in a meaningful and intuitive manner enhances its utility, enabling stakeholders to grasp complex information quickly. The data utility model guides the selection and application of appropriate data analysis techniques based on the specific objectives and requirements of the situation. Whether it's descriptive statistics, predictive modeling, or machine learning algorithms, the model ensures that the chosen techniques maximize the utility of data. By leveraging the data utility model, organizations can drive innovation through data-driven initiatives. The model helps identify areas where data can be utilized creatively to discover new opportunities, optimize processes, or develop novel solutions. Targeted marketing: The data utility model supports targeted marketing efforts by enabling organizations to analyze customer data and identify relevant segments for personalized marketing campaigns. This maximizes the utility of data in driving customer engagement and conversions. Using the data utility model, organizations can allocate resources effectively by considering the utility of data sources and analysis efforts. This ensures that resources are optimally invested in areas where data provides the greatest value and impact.

The data utility model facilitates continuous improvement efforts by establishing a feedback loop to monitor data utility and drive ongoing enhancements. Regular assessment of data sources, analytics techniques, and decision outcomes helps organizations improve their data-driven processes over time. The data utility model assists in risk management by providing insights into potential risks and facilitating informed decision-making. By analyzing data and evaluating risk indicators, organizations can proactively identify and mitigate risks. Organizations can enhance the customer experience by utilizing the data utility model to gain insights into customer behavior, preferences, and pain points. This allows for tailored products, services, and interactions that maximize customer satisfaction. The data utility model contributes to operational efficiency by analyzing data to identify inefficiencies, bottlenecks, and areas for improvement. This enables organizations to optimize processes, streamline operations, and enhance productivity. Using the data utility model, organizations can leverage predictive analytics to forecast trends, anticipate customer behavior, and make proactive decisions. Predictive analytics maximizes the utility of data by providing insights into future outcomes. The data utility model helps organizations explore opportunities for data monetization. By identifying valuable data assets, organizations can create new revenue streams through data products, data-as-a-service offerings, or partnerships. The data utility model ensures regulatory compliance by considering legal and ethical obligations related to data usage. It helps organizations align data practices with privacy regulations, data protection laws, and industry standards. The data utility model enables resource optimization by evaluating the costs and benefits associated with data acquisition, storage, processing, and analysis. It guides organizations in efficiently allocating resources to maximize the utility of data. The data utility model supports real-time decision-making by leveraging data streams and real-time analytics. Organizations can use this model to prioritize relevant data sources and implement real-time data processing capabilities for timely decision-making.

Using the data utility model, organizations can assess the performance and impact of their data-driven initiatives. By tracking key performance indicators, organizations can measure the utility of data in achieving desired outcomes. The data utility model incorporates ethical considerations and privacy protections in data utilization. It ensures that data usage aligns with ethical principles, respects individual privacy rights, and maintains data confidentiality. The data utility model accommodates scalability requirements by considering the scalability of data sources, storage, and processing capabilities. It helps organizations plan for future growth and scalability to maintain data utility as the volume and complexity of data increase. The data utility model establishes feedback loops to continuously assess and improve data utility. By collecting feedback from stakeholders, users, and decision-makers, organizations can refine their data practices and enhance data utility over time. The data utility model facilitates the development of data collaboration frameworks that promote sharing, reuse, and interoperability of data assets. This enhances data utility by enabling collaboration among diverse stakeholders.

The data utility model guides organizations in effectively disseminating data and insights to stakeholders. By considering the needs and preferences of different user groups, organizations can deliver data in formats that maximize its utility and accessibility. Using the data utility model, organizations can implement data validation and verification processes to ensure the accuracy and reliability of data. This enhances the utility of data by minimizing errors and inconsistencies. The data utility model helps organizations define data-driven performance metrics that align with their strategic objectives. By establishing relevant metrics, organizations can measure the utility of data in achieving desired outcomes. The data utility model promotes collaboration with data providers, such as third-party vendors, partners, or open data initiatives. Organizations can establish partnerships to access high-quality data sources that enhance the overall utility of data. The data utility model emphasizes the importance of data accessibility to maximize its utility. Organizations can adopt data accessibility measures, such as data catalogs, data APIs, and user-friendly interfaces, to enable easy data discovery and retrieval. Using the data utility model, organizations can manage the life span of data assets effectively. This includes defining data retention periods, archival processes, and disposal strategies to ensure data utility while adhering to legal and compliance requirements. The data utility model promotes a culture of data-driven innovation within organizations. By embedding data utilization practices and fostering a mindset that values data-driven decision-making, organizations can maximize the utility of data for innovation and growth. The data utility model encourages organizations to explore opportunities for transforming data into valuable products or services. By analyzing data assets and market demands, organizations can create data products that provide utility and value to customers. The data utility model emphasizes the importance of context in data utilization. Organizations can consider the specific context, such as industry trends, customer demographics, or environmental factors, to tailor data utilization approaches for maximum utility.

The data utility model supports the adoption of data-driven collaboration platforms that facilitate data sharing, collaboration, and knowledge exchange. These platforms enhance data utility by enabling seamless collaboration among stakeholders. The data utility model underscores the importance of data training and literacy within organizations. By promoting data literacy, organizations can enhance the utility of data by empowering individuals to effectively work with and interpret data. The data utility model encourages organizations to adopt data-centric performance management practices. By incorporating data-driven metrics into performance evaluations, organizations can assess the utility of data in driving individual and organizational performance. Using the data utility model, organizations can extract valuable customer insights from data. By analyzing customer, behavior, preferences, and feedback, organizations can enhance customer understanding and tailor products and services to maximize customer utility. The data utility model promotes agile data management practices that enable organizations to quickly adapt and respond to changing data needs. Agile methodologies enhance data utility by facilitating iterative data processing, analysis, and decision-making.

The data utility model guides organizations in preserving and archiving data assets for long-term utility. Organizations can establish data preservation strategies to retain valuable historical data that can be utilized for future analysis and insights. The data utility model aids organizations in optimizing supply chain operations by leveraging data. By analyzing supply chain data, organizations can identify inefficiencies, optimize logistics, and enhance overall supply chain utility. The data utility model enables personalization and customization of products, services, and experiences. By leveraging customer data, organizations can tailor offerings to individual preferences, maximizing customer utility and satisfaction. The data utility model promotes the establishment of data-driven collaboration networks that connect organizations, academia, and research institutions. These networks facilitate knowledge sharing, data exchange, and collaborative projects to maximize data utility. The data utility model emphasizes user-centric data design principles. Organizations can consider user needs, preferences, and workflows to design data structures, interfaces, and visualizations that enhance the utility and usability of data. Using the data utility model, organizations can optimize processes and workflows based on data insights. By analyzing process data, organizations can identify bottlenecks, streamline operations, and enhance overall process utility.

The data utility model encourages organizations to leverage data for social impact initiatives. By analyzing social data, organizations can identify areas of need, design interventions, and measure the impact of social programs to maximize societal utility. The data utility model supports the integration of sustainability considerations into decision-making processes. By analyzing environmental data and impact assessments, organizations can develop data-driven sustainability strategies that maximize utility and minimize environmental footprint. The data utility model aids organizations in leveraging data for knowledge management initiatives. By capturing, organizing, and analyzing data, organizations can extract knowledge, best practices, and lessons learned to enhance decision-making and innovation. The data utility model assists organizations in monitoring and ensuring compliance with regulations and industry standards. By analyzing data and implementing compliance monitoring mechanisms, organizations can maximize the utility of data while meeting legal and ethical obligations. Using the data utility model, organizations can optimize talent management practices. By analyzing employee data, organizations can identify talent gaps, optimize workforce allocation, and implement data-driven strategies to enhance talent utility and engagement. The data utility model helps organizations enhance stakeholder engagement and satisfaction. By analyzing stakeholder data, organizations can tailor communications, products, and services to maximize utility and meet the diverse needs of stakeholders.

## 12.4   Content-aware intelligent systems fog computing in cybernetics intelligence

Cybernetic threat intelligence (CTI) refers to the process of collecting, analyzing, and sharing information about cyber threats and adversaries to enable proactive threat detection, prevention, and response. CTI combines elements of cybersecurity, intelligence analysis, and data analytics to provide actionable intelligence to organizations and security teams [3].

In today's interconnected digital landscape, organizations face a constant barrage of cyber threats. CTI plays a critical role in enhancing cybersecurity defenses by providing organizations with timely and relevant information about potential threats and vulnerabilities. CTI gathers information from various sources, including open-source intelligence (OSINT), dark web monitoring, threat intelligence feeds, security vendor reports, incident data, and collaboration with other organizations and government agencies. This broad range of sources helps provide a comprehensive picture of the threat landscape. CTI involves the collection and processing of vast amounts of data related to potential threats. This includes indicators of compromise (IoCs), malware samples, vulnerability data, hacker forums, social media platforms, and other sources. The data is then analyzed to identify patterns, trends, and emerging threats.

CTI analysts perform in-depth analysis of collected data to identify the motivations, tactics, techniques, and procedures of threat actors. This analysis helps organizations understand the nature and severity of potential threats and enables them to develop effective countermeasures. CTI encourages the sharing of threat intelligence among organizations, industry groups, and government agencies. Collaborative sharing allows for the rapid dissemination of threat information, enabling collective defense against cyber threats. CTI focuses on identifying IoCs, which are artifacts or evidence that indicate the presence of a threat. These may include IP addresses, domain names, file hashes, and patterns of behavior associated with malicious activities. By detecting and sharing IoCs, organizations can proactively defend against threats. CTI supports proactive threat hunting, where analysts actively search for potential threats within an organization's networks and systems. Through advanced analytics and continuous monitoring, threat hunters identify anomalies and IoCs that may indicate a breach or ongoing attack.

CTI plays a crucial role in incident response by providing real-time intelligence and actionable insights to incident response teams. This enables faster and more effective incident containment, mitigation, and recovery. Organizations often leverage specialized cyber-threat intelligence platforms to automate data collection, analysis, and dissemination of threat intelligence. These platforms enhance the efficiency and effectiveness of CTI operations by aggregating and correlating data from multiple sources. CTI feeds provide real-time or near real-time updates on the latest threats, vulnerabilities, and malicious activities. These feeds, offered by commercial providers or open-source initiatives, help organizations stay ahead of emerging threats and bolster their defensive capabilities. CTI focuses on identifying and profiling different threat actors, such as individual hackers, organized cybercriminal groups, state-sponsored entities, and hacktivist collectives. Understanding the motives, capabilities, and tactics of these threat actors helps organizations better defend against targeted attacks. CTI attempts to attribute cyber threats to specific threat actors or groups. While attribution can be challenging, it provides valuable insights into the motivations, intent, and potential future activities of threat actors, allowing organizations to better prepare and respond. CTI includes the analysis of malware samples to understand their functionality, behavior, and potential impact. Malware analysis helps identify IoCs, detect new attack vectors, and develop effective mitigation strategies. CTI supports vulnerability management efforts by providing intelligence on newly discovered vulnerabilities, exploits, and patch updates. This information helps organizations prioritize and remediate vulnerabilities before threat actors exploit them. CTI enables organizations to conduct comprehensive risk assessments by incorporating threat intelligence into their risk management processes. This ensures that security investments and measures align with the most relevant and imminent threats.

CTI helps establish early warning systems by continuously monitoring the threat landscape and providing timely alerts on emerging threats, vulnerabilities, or attack campaigns. Early warnings enable organizations to take proactive measures to prevent or mitigate potential attacks. CTI enhances the capabilities of security operations centers by providing them with actionable intelligence for detecting and responding to threats. This helps SOC teams prioritize incidents, allocate resources efficiently, and respond effectively to cyber threats. CTI supports threat-modeling exercises, where organizations simulate potential attack scenarios to identify vulnerabilities and devise appropriate defenses. By integrating threat intelligence, organizations can ensure that threat-modeling exercises reflect real-world threats. CTI enables organizations to adopt proactive defense strategies by leveraging threat intelligence to anticipate and prevent attacks. This includes implementing threat hunting, threat intelligence-driven patch management, and proactive vulnerability scanning. CTI emphasizes continuous monitoring of networks, systems, and data to detect and respond to threats in real time. This proactive approach allows organizations to identify potential threats before they cause significant damage.

## 12.4.1 Social media analytics

Social media analytics, also known as SOCMINT (social media intelligence), refers to the process of collecting, analyzing, and extracting valuable insights from social media data. It involves using specialized tools and techniques to monitor, track, and analyze social media platforms to gain insights into public sentiment, trends, customer behavior, and brand reputation [4]. Here are ten paragraphs providing an overview of SOCMINT:

With the proliferation of social media platforms, SOCMINT has become crucial for organizations to understand customer preferences, market trends, and public sentiment. It helps businesses make data-driven decisions, enhance marketing strategies, manage brand reputation, and improve customer engagement. SOCMINT involves the collection of data from various social media platforms such as Facebook, Twitter, Instagram, LinkedIn, YouTube, and more. Data collection methods include web scraping, API integration, and social media monitoring tools that capture public posts, comments, likes, shares, and other user-generated content. SOCMINT employs text and sentiment analysis techniques to extract meaningful insights from social media data. NLP algorithms are used to analyze text, detect sentiment, and identify keywords, topics, and trends. This analysis helps organizations understand public opinion, customer sentiment, and emerging issues.

SOCMINT enables organizations to monitor and manage their brand reputation on social media. By tracking mentions, reviews, and comments related to their brand, organizations can address customer concerns, respond to feedback, and take proactive measures to protect their brand image. SOCMINT provides valuable customer insights by analyzing social media conversations, posts, and profiles. It helps organizations understand customer preferences, behavior, and sentiment, allowing for personalized marketing campaigns, targeted messaging, and improved customer experiences. SOCMINT helps identify influencers and opinion leaders within specific industries or target audiences. By analyzing social media data, organizations can identify individuals or accounts with significant followers, engagement, and impact. Collaborating with influencers can enhance brand visibility and reach. SOCMINT plays a crucial role in crisis management by monitoring social media for mentions of potential crises, identifying emerging issues, and tracking public sentiment during a crisis. Organizations can use this real-time information to develop timely responses, mitigate reputational damage, and manage crises effectively. SOCMINT enables organizations to conduct competitive analysis by monitoring and analyzing social media activities of competitors. This helps organizations gain insights into their competitors' strategies, customer interactions, and market positioning, allowing for informed decision-making and strategic planning.

SOCMINT helps organizations identify and analyze social media trends. By monitoring popular hashtags, viral content, and user conversations, organizations can stay informed about emerging topics, industry trends, and consumer preferences. This information can drive innovation, product development, and marketing campaigns. SOCMINT includes social listening, which involves monitoring social media conversations and public sentiment around specific keywords, brands, or topics. By listening to customer feedback and identifying patterns in social media conversations, organizations can gain insights to improve products, services, and customer satisfaction. SOCMINT enables organizations to assess the effectiveness of their social media advertising campaigns. By analyzing engagement metrics, sentiment, and customer responses, organizations can evaluate the impact of their ads, optimize targeting strategies, and measure return on investment (ROI). SOCMINT helps in detecting potential crises by monitoring social media for early warning signs. By analyzing spikes in negative sentiment, customer complaints, or mentions of critical issues, organizations can take preventive measures and proactively address potential crises. SOCMINT allows organizations to analyze social media data based on geolocation and demographic factors. This helps in understanding regional preferences, cultural differences, and target audience segmentation, enabling personalized marketing strategies. SOCMINT provides insights into the performance and impact of social media campaigns. By analyzing engagement metrics, sentiment analysis, and conversion rates, organizations can evaluate the success of their campaigns, identify areas for improvement, and refine their social media strategies.

SOCMINT plays a significant role in influencer marketing. By analyzing the reach, engagement, and sentiment associated with influencers, organizations can identify the right influencers for collaboration, measure the effectiveness of influencer campaigns, and track their impact on brand awareness and customer engagement. SOCMINT serves as a valuable tool for market research. By monitoring social media conversations, organizations can gain insights into customer preferences, opinions, and emerging market trends. This information helps in identifying market gaps, refining product offerings, and developing effective marketing strategies. SOCMINT enables organizations to provide timely customer service and support by monitoring social media platforms for customer inquiries, complaints, or feedback. By promptly responding to customer concerns, organizations can enhance customer satisfaction, build brand loyalty, and improve overall customer experience. SOCMINT helps organizations manage relationships with influencers by monitoring their activities, measuring their impact, and assessing their alignment with brand values. This facilitates effective influencer engagement, collaboration, and long-term partnerships. SOCMINT supports organizations in simulating social media crisis scenarios. By analyzing past crises and their social media impact, organizations can develop crisis response strategies, train their teams, and enhance preparedness to effectively manage future crises. SOCMINT assists organizations in monitoring social media for compliance with industry regulations, advertising standards, and legal requirements. By identifying non-compliant or risky content, organizations can mitigate legal and reputational risks.

## 12.4.2 Technical intelligence

Technical intelligence (TECHINT) is a discipline that focuses on the collection, analysis, and interpretation of technical information related to military capabilities, weapons systems, infrastructure, and emerging technologies [5]. It involves the examination of scientific, engineering, and technical data to gain insights into adversaries' capabilities, vulnerabilities, and potential threats. Here are five paragraphs providing an overview of TECHINT:

TECHINT involves the collection and analysis of technical information from various sources such as satellite imagery, intercepted communications, technical specifications, patents, scientific publications, and field reports. This information is meticulously analyzed to extract valuable insights related to adversaries' military capabilities, weapon systems, infrastructure, and technological advancements. TECHINT focuses on the analysis of weapons and systems employed by adversaries. It examines the design, performance, operational characteristics, and vulnerabilities of military hardware and equipment. By understanding the technical aspects of these systems, TECHINT provides critical information for threat assessments, defense planning, and countermeasures development. TECHINT plays a crucial role in assessing emerging technologies that have potential military applications. It involves monitoring scientific research, industry developments, and technological trends to identify advancements that could impact national security. By analyzing these emerging technologies, TECHINT helps anticipate future threats, evaluate countermeasures, and guide research and development efforts. TECHINT encompasses the analysis of infrastructure, including transportation networks, communication systems, power grids, and industrial facilities. By examining technical details and vulnerabilities in these critical infrastructures, TECHINT provides insights into potential targets, potential points of failure, and opportunities for disruption or exploitation. TECHINT provides valuable support to counterintelligence efforts by identifying and countering adversary technical collection activities. It helps detect and assess hostile intelligence operations aimed at acquiring technical information or compromising sensitive technologies. TECHINT supports counterintelligence measures to protect classified information, intellectual property, and defense capabilities.

## 12.4.3 Measurement and signature intelligence

Measurement and signature intelligence (MASINT) is a discipline within the field of intelligence that involves the collection, analysis, and interpretation of distinctive physical characteristics, signals, and emissions from various sources. It focuses on detecting and identifying unique signatures or patterns that provide valuable insights into the capabilities, intentions, and activities of adversaries.

MASINT relies on advanced sensor technologies to collect and analyze data from a wide range of sources, including radar, sonar, electro-optical systems, nuclear detectors, seismic sensors, and chemical and biological sensors. These sensors capture distinctive signatures such as electromagnetic emissions, acoustic signals, radiation levels, or other physical characteristics that can be exploited for intelligence purposes. MASINT emphasizes the analysis of signatures and patterns to extract meaningful intelligence. Analysts examine the unique characteristics of signatures, such as their frequency, amplitude, modulation, spatial distribution, or temporal behavior, to identify and correlate specific activities, targets, or phenomena of interest. This analysis helps in understanding adversary capabilities, weapons systems, movements, and potential threats. MASINT goes beyond traditional intelligence sources by leveraging unconventional sources of information. It includes sources such as spectrometry data, radio frequency emissions, seismic activity, chemical traces, and even subtle variations in environmental factors. By monitoring and analyzing these unconventional sources, MASINT provides insights that are not readily available through other intelligence disciplines.

MASINT complements other intelligence disciplines by providing unique insights and filling gaps in understanding. It integrates with disciplines such as imagery intelligence (IMINT), signals intelligence (SIGINT), and human intelligence (HUMINT) to create a comprehensive intelligence picture. By combining multiple sources of intelligence, analysts can enhance their understanding of the operational environment and adversary activities. MASINT relies on advanced analytics techniques and technology to process and analyze large volumes of complex data. Machine learning, pattern recognition, data fusion, and data mining are employed to identify and extract relevant signatures, correlate data from different sources, and uncover hidden patterns or anomalies. This enables analysts to derive actionable intelligence and support decision-making processes.

## 12.4.4   Human intelligence

HUMINT is a crucial discipline within the field of intelligence that focuses on collecting information through direct human interaction. HUMINT involves gathering intelligence from human sources, such as informants, agents, or individuals with access to valuable information.

HUMINT relies on recruiting and cultivating human sources who have access to specific knowledge or information of interest. These sources can be recruited from various backgrounds, including government agencies, military personnel, diplomatic circles, academic institutions, or local communities. HUMINT operators establish relationships with these sources to gather intelligence, validate information, and obtain insights into adversaries' intentions, plans, and activities. HUMINT operators possess strong interpersonal skills to establish rapport, build trust, and elicit information from human sources. They employ various techniques such as active listening, effective questioning, and empathy to gain cooperation and valuable intelligence. The ability to navigate cultural differences, language barriers, and complex social dynamics is critical for successful HUMINT operations.

HUMINT often involves covert operations where intelligence operatives work undercover or clandestinely to collect sensitive information. These operations require careful planning, risk assessment, and adherence to legal and ethical guidelines. Covert HUMINT operations aim to gather intelligence in high-risk or denied areas where other intelligence collection methods may be limited.

HUMINT operators conduct debriefings with human sources to extract relevant information and insights. Debriefings involve structured interviews, documentation, and analysis of collected information. HUMINT operators handle sources with utmost care, ensuring source protection, confidentiality, and ethical treatment. Building a secure and trusting relationship with sources is crucial for ongoing cooperation and the acquisition of accurate intelligence. HUMINT provides unique and firsthand information that complements other intelligence disciplines. HUMINT reports and insights contribute to the overall intelligence picture, providing valuable context, human perspectives, and understanding of the intentions, capabilities, and vulnerabilities of adversaries. HUMINT intelligence is analyzed and, correlated with other sources, integrated into comprehensive intelligence assessments, allowing decision-makers to formulate informed strategies and policies.

## 12.4.5 Finding humming in the dark

Finding humming in the dark is a metaphorical expression that emphasizes the pursuit of positivity, hope, and light even in challenging or difficult circumstances. It suggests the importance of seeking and embracing moments of joy, beauty, and inspiration amidst darkness or adversity.

Finding humming in the dark encourages individuals to cultivate resilience and inner strength during challenging times. It acknowledges that darkness and difficulties are inevitable aspects of life, but within those moments, there is an opportunity to discover resilience and tap into our inner resources. By embracing resilience, we can find the strength to overcome obstacles and keep moving forward. Finding humming in the dark invites us to appreciate and cherish the small joys and positive moments that may be present even in difficult times. It reminds us to pay attention to the simple pleasures that can bring light to our lives, such as the laughter of loved ones, a beautiful sunset, or a heartfelt conversation. These moments of joy can provide solace, inspiration, and a reminder of the beauty that still exists amidst darkness. Finding humming in the dark suggests that challenging circumstances can be transformative opportunities for personal growth and self-discovery. In moments of darkness, we can develop resilience, empathy, compassion, and a deeper understanding of ourselves and others. By embracing the lessons and growth that come from difficult experiences, we can find a sense of purpose and meaning even in the darkest times. Finding humming in the dark encourages the practice of gratitude as a way to shift our focus from negativity to positivity. It invites us to intentionally seek out and appreciate the blessings, kindness, and beauty that surround us, no matter how small or seemingly insignificant. Cultivating gratitude allows us to reframe our perspective and find moments of joy and appreciation, even in challenging circumstances. Finding humming in the dark emphasizes the importance of nurturing hope, even in the face of adversity. It acknowledges that hope can be a guiding light that helps us navigate through difficult times and inspires us to keep moving forward. By nurturing hope, we maintain a positive outlook, cultivate resilience, and find the strength to persevere, even when the path ahead seems uncertain or obscured.

## 12.5    Using fog/edge computing for context-aware intelligence

Fog/edge computing refers to the paradigm of bringing computational capabilities closer to the data source, enabling real-time processing, analysis, and decision-making at the edge of the network. When applied to context-aware intelligence, fog/edge computing offers several advantages in terms of speed, efficiency, and responsiveness. The benefits and applications of using fog/edge computing for context-aware intelligence are as follows:

Fog/edge computing enables real-time data processing and analysis at the edge devices or local fog nodes. This capability is crucial for context-aware intelligence, as it allows for immediate extraction of insights from sensor data, video feeds, or other contextual information. By processing data closer to the source, organizations can achieve low latency and make timely decisions based on the most up-to-date information. Context-aware intelligence often involves processing large volumes of data, such as sensor data from IoT devices or video streams. By utilizing fog/edge computing, data can be processed and filtered locally, reducing the need to transmit all the raw data to a central server or cloud. This approach minimizes network traffic and bandwidth consumption, optimizing resource utilization and reducing communication costs. Fog/edge computing enhances security and privacy in context-aware intelligence applications. By processing sensitive data locally at the edge, organizations can reduce the risk of data breaches or unauthorized access during data transmission. Additionally, sensitive information can be anonymized or encrypted locally, providing an extra layer of privacy protection before data is sent to the cloud or a centralized server.

Fog/edge computing enables the integration of context-aware intelligence directly into edge devices or fog nodes. This localization of intelligence allows for real-time analysis of contextual information, such as location, environmental conditions, or user behavior. By leveraging this contextual data, organizations can derive more accurate and actionable insights, leading to personalized services, optimized resource allocation, and improved user experiences. Fog/edge computing provides the ability to operate in disconnected or low-connectivity environments, ensuring the availability of context-aware intelligence even when network connectivity is limited or intermittent. By processing and storing relevant data locally, edge devices can continue to provide intelligence and make informed decisions even during network outages or in remote areas. This offline availability enhances system resilience and supports critical applications in various domains, such as healthcare, transportation, or industrial settings.

## 12.6    Types of cybernetics intelligence

Cybernetic intelligence encompasses various types, each representing a distinct aspect of the integration of cybernetics principles with intelligent systems. These types of cybernetic intelligence form the foundation for building adaptive, self-regulating systems that can continuously learn and improve. Here are some key types of cybernetic intelligence:

Feedback control intelligence: Feedback control is a fundamental concept in cybernetics. This type of cybernetic intelligence involves continuous monitoring and analysis of system outputs and using the feedback to adjust system behaviors or parameters in real time. This ensures that the system remains stable and achieves desired performance goals despite external disturbances or changes in the environment.

Adaptive intelligence: Adaptive intelligence in cybernetics refers to the ability of a system to learn and modify its behaviors or strategies based on experiences. These systems can adjust their internal models or decision-making processes to improve their performance or cope with changing circumstances, leading to increased efficiency and responsiveness.

Cognitive intelligence: Cognitive intelligence in cybernetics focuses on the emulation of human-like cognitive processes, such as perception, learning, reasoning, and decision-making. By incorporating cognitive abilities into intelligent systems, cybernetic intelligence enables them to understand complex patterns, adapt to new information, and make informed choices based on a combination of data and internal knowledge.

Swarm intelligence: Inspired by the collective behavior of biological swarms, swarm intelligence in cybernetics involves the coordination and cooperation of a large number of simple agents to achieve complex tasks collectively. These systems leverage local interactions and feedback loops to self-organize and adapt to changing conditions, enabling robust and scalable problem-solving capabilities.

Autonomous intelligence: Autonomous intelligence is a key feature of cybernetic systems that enables them to operate independently and make decisions without direct human intervention. By integrating feedback mechanisms and adaptive learning, autonomous cybernetic intelligence empowers systems to navigate dynamic environments, carry out tasks, and interact with the world autonomously.

Social intelligence: Social intelligence in cybernetics focuses on understanding and modeling social interactions between intelligent systems or between humans and machines. These systems can analyze social cues, interpret emotions, and adapt their behaviors to foster more natural and effective communication and collaboration.

Resilient intelligence: Resilient intelligence in cybernetics refers to the ability of systems to withstand disruptions, adapt to unexpected changes, and recover from failures or damages. By employing feedback loops and redundancy mechanisms, these systems can maintain essential functionalities and recover quickly from adverse events.

Contextual intelligence: Contextual intelligence involves the capability of cybernetic systems to perceive and interpret information within the context of their environment. This type of intelligence allows the system to understand the significance of data and adapt its responses based on the current context, enhancing its effectiveness and relevance in different situations.

Emotional intelligence: Emulating emotional intelligence in cybernetic systems enables them to recognize and respond to human emotions, making interactions more empathetic and human-centric. This type of intelligence can be vital in applications involving human–robot interaction, healthcare, and assistive technologies.

Predictive intelligence: Predictive intelligence involves the use of historical data and patterns to anticipate future events or trends. By leveraging predictive models and machine learning algorithms, cybernetic systems can proactively adjust their behaviors or provide useful insights to assist decision-making processes.

## 12.7  Conclusion

The available data sources continue to increase in recent years. Many aspects of our lives may now be captured as digital data thanks to advancements in technology and software. Data-intensive technology can examine this information to help with decision-making, innovation, and process optimization. For software development, it is not always helpful to have access to several data sources. It may be difficult for them to locate the appropriate resources that will allow them to realize their goals. In this chapter, we introduce the notion of data utility, which may evaluate the value of a data source in light of its application. Data source and application deployments are contextualized by the current state of the system and the requirements of the developers. Our method is geared for data-heavy apps that function in a fog setting. The flexibility of computing and storage resources is taken into account while building a data utility, since it may be necessary to move jobs and data sources between cloud or edge resources in such a scenario. The offered addition presently supports the data utility–driven selection of data sources at the task level. Considerations like task interdependencies and deployment constraints raise problems regarding how a program's total value may be assessed. The relevance of fog-computing technology and its wide-ranging applications to cybernetic intelligence were the main topics of this chapter. Fog networks connect edge networks and cloud topologies, opening up a new field of study rich with potential research directions even as this chapter's overall goal is to make sense of data in any fog setting. The newly proposed fog networks may allow for intelligent connections to be made among objects, people, processes, data, and other elements in hierarchical IoT networks. The fog concepts and their execution improved the latency, bandwidth, reliability, security, and overall performance of the Internet of edge network for cybernetic intelligence. Since effective threat intelligence management is an ongoing process, researchers have been looking at the most secure and trustworthy methods for firms to share and discuss cyber-threat intelligence

(CTI). Cybernetic CTI systems and the development of cybernetic CTI frameworks have, however, been severely lacking. OSINT, SOCMINT, HUMINT, and TECHINT are just some of the CTI mechanisms and methods currently in use, all of which collect intelligence from data stored in the cloud, fog, or edge networks and report on specific threat actors. If these reports and information on threat actors are not shared with other public and commercial groups, more supply chains might be at risk. There are a large and varied number of dangers, and their numbers are continually growing. As time goes on, it becomes harder to identify malicious activity because bad actors use a wider range of strategies, tools, and infrastructure. The ever-evolving nature of the technology, strategies, and platforms used by threat actors necessitates a reevaluation of the defensive measures taken by authorities, governments, companies, and all other stakeholders in the digital market.

# References

[1]  Y. Wang, T. Uehara, and R. Sasaki, Fog Computing: Issues and Challenges in Security and Forensics, in *IEEE 39th Annual Computer Software and Applications Conference*, 3, 53–59, 2015.

[2]  S. Basudan, X. Lin, and K. Sankaranarayanan, A Privacy-Preserving Vehicular Crowdsensing-Based Road Surface Condition Monitoring System Using Fog Computing, *IEEE Internet of Things Journal*, 4, 772–782, 2017.

[3]  Q. Yaseen, Y. Jararweh, M. Al-Ayyoub, and M. AlDwairi, Collusion Attacks in Internet of Things: Detection and Mitigation using a Fog based Model, in *IEEE Sensors Applications Symposium (SAS)*, 2017, pp. 1–5.

[4]  S. A. Soleymani, A. H. Abdullah, M. Zareei, *et al.*, A Secure Trust Model Based on Fuzzy Logic in Vehicular Ad Hoc Networks with Fog Computing, *IEEE Access*, 5, 15619–15629, 2017.

[5]  S. Yu, C. Wang, K. Ren, and W. Lou, Achieving Secure, Scalable, and Fine-Grained Data Access Control in Cloud Computing, in *Proceedings IEEE INFOCOM*, 2010, pp. 1–9.

*Chapter 13*

# Further application of fog computing

## Abstract

As the digital landscape evolves, the demand for real-time, data-intensive applications has surged, necessitating the exploration of novel paradigms such as fog computing. This chapter presents an in-depth analysis of fog computing, focusing on its background, scope, problem definition, aim, and applications.

**Background:** The exponential growth of connected devices and the Internet of Things (IoT) has led to an unprecedented surge in data generation at the network edge. Fog computing, an extension of cloud computing, aims to overcome the limitations of centralized cloud architectures by distributing computation, storage, and networking resources closer to the data source. By leveraging the capabilities of fog computing, edge devices can process and analyze data in real time, reducing latency, improving scalability, and enhancing overall system performance.

**Scope:** This study explores the key components and architectural principles of fog computing, including fog nodes, fog infrastructure, and fog-based services. This chapter investigates the challenges associated with fog computing, such as resource constraints, security and privacy concerns, and network heterogeneity. The analysis encompasses various applications of fog computing, including smart cities, healthcare, industrial automation, and autonomous vehicles, highlighting its transformative potential.

**Problem definition:** The centralized nature of cloud computing introduces latency, which hampers the real-time processing requirements of time-sensitive applications. Resource-constrained edge devices struggle to handle the computational demands of data-intensive tasks, leading to performance degradation. Its concerns arise when sensitive data are transmitted and stored in remote cloud servers, necessitating a more localized and distributed approach.

**Aim:** The aim of this chapter is to provide a comprehensive understanding of fog computing and its potential to revolutionize edge intelligence for next-generation applications. By addressing the challenges and limitations of fog computing, this study aims to identify potential solutions and future research directions. Ultimately, this research aims to inspire the development and adoption of fog-computing techniques, empowering edge devices to process and analyze data efficiently, securely, and in real time.

**Analysis/observations on application of fog computing:** Fog computing enables real-time analytics and decision-making for smart city infrastructure, optimizing resource allocation, traffic management, and enhancing citizen services. In healthcare, fog computing facilitates real-time monitoring, analysis, and diagnosis, improving patient care, remote consultations, and emergency response systems. The application of fog computing in industrial automation enhances productivity, predictive maintenance, and quality control, enabling agile and efficient manufacturing processes.

## 13.1　Introduction

In the era of digital transformation, the proliferation of connected devices and the Internet of Things (IoT) has generated an unprecedented amount of data at the network edge. This data explosion poses challenges in terms of processing, analyzing, and deriving actionable insights in real time. To address these challenges, fog computing has emerged as a promising paradigm that extends cloud-computing capabilities to the network edge. Fog computing, also known as edge computing, aims to distribute computational resources, storage, and networking closer to the data source, reducing latency and enhancing overall system performance. By bringing computing resources closer to the edge devices, fog computing enables real-time data processing, analytics, and decision-making, opening up a wide range of innovative applications. None of the prominent applications of fog computing lies in the realm of smart cities. With the rapid urbanization and the growing need for efficient resource management, fog computing can play a pivotal role in optimizing various aspects of smart city infrastructure. For instance, fog computing can enable real-time traffic management systems, leveraging data from sensors and cameras deployed on roads, intersections, and public transportation to alleviate congestion and enhance commuter experience.

In addition to traffic management, fog computing in smart cities can facilitate energy management, enabling intelligent monitoring and control of energy distribution systems. By integrating real-time data from smart meters, buildings, and renewable energy sources, fog computing can help optimize energy usage, reduce wastage, and improve the overall sustainability of cities. Another application domain where fog computing has significant implications is healthcare. Fog computing can enable real-time monitoring of patients, allowing health-care professionals to remotely access and analyze vital signs, ensuring timely intervention, and reducing the need for hospital visits. Furthermore, fog computing can enhance the efficiency of health-care systems by facilitating telemedicine and remote consultations, especially in rural and underserved areas. Fog computing can also revolutionize industrial automation by enabling edge intelligence. In manufacturing environments, fog computing can empower real-time data analytics and predictive maintenance, facilitating proactive equipment monitoring, minimizing downtime, and optimizing production processes. Additionally, fog computing can enhance quality control by analyzing sensor data in real time, ensuring product consistency and reducing defects. Autonomous vehicles represent another domain where fog computing can make a significant impact. By leveraging fog-computing capabilities, autonomous vehicles can augment their onboard processing power with the ability to offload complex computations to nearby fog nodes. This distributed computing approach reduces latency, enables faster decision-making, and enhances the overall safety and reliability of autonomous systems.

The retail industry is yet another domain that can benefit from fog computing. With the rise of e-commerce and the demand for personalized shopping experiences, fog computing can support real-time inventory management and personalized recommendations. By analyzing customer preferences, purchase history, and contextual data, fog computing can enable retailers to offer tailored promotions, optimize stock levels, and provide a seamless shopping experience across online and offline channels. Fog computing also holds great potential in the field of agriculture, often referred to as smart farming or precision agriculture. By deploying sensors and IoT devices in the field, fog computing can enable real-time monitoring of soil conditions, weather patterns, and crop health. The collected data can be analyzed locally to provide farmers with valuable insights, such as optimal irrigation schedules, pest detection, and crop yield predictions, facilitating efficient resource allocation and maximizing agricultural productivity. The deployment of fog computing in the energy sector can revolutionize power grid management and enhance the integration of renewable energy sources. By leveraging real-time data from smart grids, weather sensors, and energy consumption patterns, fog computing can enable dynamic load balancing, predictive maintenance of power infrastructure, and efficient utilization of renewable energy resources, ultimately leading to a more sustainable and resilient energy ecosystem.

Fog computing also finds applications in the realm of public safety and emergency response. By deploying fog nodes in critical infrastructure and disaster-prone areas, real-time data from sensors, surveillance cameras, and social media feeds can be processed locally to enable early detection of emergencies, efficient resource allocation, and timely response. This can significantly enhance the effectiveness of emergency services and improve public safety. In the financial sector, fog computing can enable secure and real-time transaction processing. By deploying fog nodes in financial institutions and retail outlets, real-time fraud detection and prevention can be performed at the edge, reducing the need to transmit sensitive data to centralized servers. This approach enhances security, minimizes response time, and ensures uninterrupted financial services even in the event of network disruptions. Fog computing can also transform the field of augmented reality (AR) and virtual reality (VR). By leveraging fog-computing resources, AR/VR applications can offload computationally intensive tasks such as rendering and scene analysis, resulting in improved user experience, reduced latency, and greater immersion. This opens up new possibilities for applications such as interactive training, remote collaboration, and immersive gaming. The entertainment industry can also benefit from fog computing in various ways. Fog computing can enable real-time content delivery and streaming, reducing latency and ensuring smooth playback of high-quality media. Additionally, fog computing can support personalized content recommendations, analyzing user preferences, viewing habits, and contextual data to deliver tailored content and enhance user engagement.

Fog computing can play a crucial role in the advancement of smart grid technologies. By deploying fog nodes in power distribution networks, real-time monitoring and control of grid assets can be performed locally, enabling efficient fault detection, load balancing, and power quality management. Moreover, fog computing can facilitate peer-to-peer energy trading among prosumers, optimizing energy distribution and fostering a decentralized energy ecosystem. The transportation sector can benefit from fog computing by enabling real-time vehicle monitoring and fleet management. By integrating data from sensors, global positioning system (GPS) devices, and traffic monitoring systems, fog computing can optimize route planning, fuel efficiency, and maintenance schedules. Furthermore, fog computing can enhance transportation safety by analyzing real-time data to detect and mitigate potential hazards. Fog computing can also have a significant impact on the field of environmental monitoring and conservation. By deploying fog nodes in remote areas, natural reserves, and ecosystems, real-time data from environmental sensors can be processed locally, facilitating early detection of environmental changes, endangered species monitoring, and adaptive conservation strategies. Fog computing can enhance the effectiveness of supply chain management by enabling real-time tracking and monitoring of goods. By integrating data from radio frequency identification (RFID) tags, GPS devices, and warehouse sensors, fog computing can provide supply chain stakeholders with accurate and up-to-date information on inventory levels, shipment status, and delivery routes, improving logistics efficiency and reducing costs.

In the field of public transportation, fog computing can optimize transit systems, enabling real-time passenger information, efficient route planning, and intelligent scheduling. By integrating data from vehicles, ticketing systems, and passenger feedback, fog computing can enhance the overall quality of public transportation services, resulting in improved user satisfaction and increased ridership. Finally, fog computing can facilitate personalized and context-aware marketing and advertising. By analyzing user profiles, location data, and behavior patterns, fog computing can deliver targeted advertisements and promotional offers in real time, enhancing the relevance and effectiveness of marketing campaigns [1].

## 13.2   Geospatial technology with fog computing and IoT in agriculture

Precision agriculture, enabled by the IoT, has emerged as a game-changer in the agricultural industry. By harnessing the power of IoT devices and sensors, precision agriculture aims to optimize crop production, increase yield, and minimize resource wastage. IoT applications in precision agriculture encompass a wide range of capabilities, including real-time monitoring, data analytics, and automated decision-making.

One key IoT application in precision agriculture is the deployment of sensor networks to monitor various environmental factors. These sensors can collect data on soil moisture levels, temperature, humidity, and nutrient content. The collected data are then transmitted to a central hub or cloud-based platform for analysis. By continuously monitoring these environmental parameters, farmers can make data-driven decisions regarding irrigation schedules, fertilization practices, and crop health management. This proactive approach ensures that resources are allocated efficiently, reducing water consumption, minimizing chemical usage, and optimizing crop growth conditions.

Furthermore, IoT applications in precision agriculture also involve the use of aerial drones equipped with sensors and cameras. These drones can capture high-resolution images and collect data on crop health, vegetation indices, and pest infestations. By analyzing the captured data, farmers can identify areas of the field that require attention, such as disease outbreaks or nutrient deficiencies. With this information, targeted interventions can be implemented, such as applying pesticides or adjusting nutrient levels, leading to improved crop health and yield. Additionally, drones can also be used to monitor large fields quickly and efficiently, enabling farmers to cover vast areas and identify issues that may not be visible from the ground. Overall, IoT applications in precision agriculture empower farmers with actionable insights, allowing them to optimize their farming practices and achieve sustainable, efficient, and profitable outcomes.

## 13.2.1 *System to monitor irrigation*

Implementing a system to monitor irrigation is crucial in optimizing water usage, improving crop yield, and conserving resources. Such a system can leverage IoT technologies to provide real-time monitoring and control, ensuring that crops receive the appropriate amount of water at the right time.

A typical system to monitor irrigation incorporates soil moisture sensors placed strategically throughout the field. These sensors continuously measure the moisture content of the soil at different depths. The sensor data are then transmitted wirelessly to a central control unit or cloud-based platform. By analyzing the soil moisture data, farmers can determine when and how much water should be applied to the crops. This information enables precise irrigation scheduling and prevents over- or under-irrigation, which can lead to water wastage or crop stress. Additionally, the system can send alerts or notifications to farmers when the soil moisture levels deviate from the desired range, allowing for immediate corrective actions to be taken.

In addition to soil moisture sensors, a comprehensive irrigation monitoring system may also include weather sensors and evapotranspiration (ET) calculations. Weather sensors measure environmental factors such as temperature, humidity, wind speed, and solar radiation. Combined with ET calculations, which estimate the amount of water lost through evaporation and transpiration, these sensors provide valuable insights into the water requirements of the crops. By integrating weather data with soil moisture readings, the irrigation system can dynamically adjust irrigation schedules and volume based on current weather conditions. This adaptive approach ensures that irrigation is aligned with the specific needs of the crops and minimizes water wastage during periods of rain or high humidity.

Overall, a system to monitor irrigation utilizing IoT technologies empowers farmers to make informed decisions, optimize water usage, and enhance agricultural productivity.

### 13.2.2    Treatment for insect and disease problems

Addressing insect and disease problems is essential for maintaining healthy and productive crops. Effective treatment strategies can help minimize yield losses and ensure the overall well-being of agricultural plants. Various approaches, including both chemical and biological methods, are employed to combat insect pests and diseases.

Chemical treatment is a common method used to control pests and diseases in agriculture. Insecticides and fungicides are applied to crops to target specific pests or pathogens. These chemical treatments can help suppress insect populations and inhibit the growth of harmful fungi, preventing the spread of diseases. However, it is important to use these chemicals judiciously, following proper guidelines and regulations, to minimize environmental impact and potential risks to human health. Integrated pest management (IPM) practices, which involve the strategic use of chemicals along with other control methods such as cultural practices and biological control, are often adopted to ensure sustainable pest and disease management.

Biological control is an alternative approach that utilizes natural enemies to combat insect pests and diseases. Beneficial organisms such as predators, parasitoids, and pathogens are introduced into the ecosystem to regulate pest populations. For instance, predatory insects like ladybugs or lacewings feed on harmful pests, while parasitoids lay eggs inside pest insects, eventually killing them. Additionally, certain bacteria or fungi can be employed as biological control agents, infecting and eliminating specific pathogens. Biological control methods offer a more environmentally friendly and sustainable solution, reducing the reliance on chemical treatments and preserving natural ecosystem balances. However, successful implementation of biological control often requires careful consideration of factors such as target species, release timing, and compatibility with existing pest management strategies.

### 13.2.3    Controlled fertilizer usage

Controlled fertilizer usage is a critical aspect of modern agricultural practices aimed at optimizing nutrient application, minimizing environmental impact, and ensuring efficient plant growth. By implementing strategies to precisely regulate the amount, timing, and placement of fertilizers, farmers can achieve higher crop yields while reducing nutrient runoff and soil degradation.

One approach to controlled fertilizer usage is the adoption of precision agriculture techniques. This involves utilizing technologies such as GPS, remote sensing, and soil mapping to gather data on soil fertility and crop nutrient requirements. With this information, farmers can create site-specific fertilizer management plans tailored to the needs of individual field areas. By applying fertilizers only where and when they are needed, excess nutrient application is minimized, reducing the risk of nutrient leaching into water bodies and contributing to harmful algal blooms. Precision agriculture also enables the use of variable-rate application systems, where fertilizers are distributed at different rates across the field based on variations in soil conditions. This precise and targeted approach ensures that crops receive the right amount of nutrients, promoting optimal growth while reducing fertilizer waste.

Another strategy for controlled fertilizer usage is the adoption of nutrient management practices such as split applications and slow-release fertilizers. Split applications involve dividing the total fertilizer dose into multiple smaller doses applied at different growth stages of the crop. This approach ensures that nutrients are provided to the plants in a timely manner, matching their specific requirements during different growth phases. By avoiding excessive nutrient loading at any given time, split applications help minimize nutrient losses through leaching or volatilization. Similarly, slow-release fertilizers are designed to release nutrients gradually over an extended period, aligning with the nutrient uptake patterns of the plants. This controlled release mechanism reduces nutrient runoff and enhances nutrient use efficiency, resulting in improved plant growth and reduced environmental impact [2].

### 13.2.4 Monitoring of greenhouse gases

Monitoring greenhouse gases is a crucial component of understanding and addressing climate change. Greenhouse gases, such as carbon dioxide ($CO_2$), methane ($CH_4$), and nitrous oxide ($N_2O$), trap heat in the atmosphere, contributing to the greenhouse effect and global warming. Monitoring these gases helps assess their sources, levels, and trends, providing valuable insights into the effectiveness of emission reduction efforts and informing climate policy decisions.

One common method for monitoring greenhouse gases is through the use of atmospheric monitoring stations. These stations are strategically located across the globe and equipped with sophisticated instruments that measure the concentration of greenhouse gases in the atmosphere. The collected data are transmitted to central databases, where it is analyzed and used to calculate emission estimates. These monitoring stations play a crucial role in capturing global and regional variations in greenhouse gas levels, as well as detecting sources and sinks of these gases. Additionally, satellite-based remote sensing techniques are also employed to monitor greenhouse gas concentrations from space, providing a broader coverage and a comprehensive understanding of global atmospheric dynamics.

Furthermore, monitoring greenhouse gases extends beyond atmospheric measurements to include other sectors such as energy production, transportation, and agriculture. Emission monitoring systems are implemented to measure and track the release of greenhouse gases from industrial facilities, power plants, vehicles, and agricultural operations. These systems utilize a combination of on-site measurements, data logging, and real-time monitoring to quantify and report emissions accurately. By continuously monitoring emissions from various sources, policymakers and organizations can identify high-emitting sectors, assess the effectiveness of emission reduction strategies, and develop targeted mitigation plans to curb greenhouse gas emissions.

## 13.2.5    Cattle tracking and monitoring

Cattle tracking and monitoring systems play a crucial role in modern livestock management, providing valuable insights into the health, location, and behavior of individual animals. These systems utilize various technologies, including RFID, GPS, and sensor-based monitoring, to track and monitor cattle in real time.

RFID-based tracking systems involve the placement of RFID tags on cattle, which can be read using RFID readers. These tags contain unique identification numbers that allow farmers and ranchers to keep detailed records of each animal's movements, health history, and breeding information. By scanning the RFID tags, farmers can quickly and accurately identify individual animals, monitor their movement within the herd, and track their location within the grazing area or barn. This data is invaluable for optimizing herd management, ensuring proper feeding and healthcare, and improving overall productivity.

GPS technology is also utilized in cattle tracking systems to monitor the location and movement of animals over large grazing areas. GPS-enabled collars or ear tags are attached to cattle, enabling real-time tracking of their positions. This allows farmers to monitor grazing patterns, prevent straying or theft, and manage rotational grazing systems effectively. Additionally, GPS tracking can aid in locating cattle during round-ups or in emergency situations, such as natural disasters or disease outbreaks. By leveraging GPS technology, farmers can enhance operational efficiency, reduce the risk of livestock losses, and ensure the safety and welfare of their cattle.

In conjunction with tracking technologies, sensor-based monitoring systems are utilized to gather data on the health and well-being of cattle. These systems may include sensors for measuring parameters such as body temperature, heart rate, rumination activity, and feeding behavior. The collected data can be analyzed to detect early signs of illness, monitor reproductive cycles, and ensure optimal feeding practices. By continuously monitoring the health and behavior of cattle, farmers can promptly identify and address health issues, prevent disease spread, and implement appropriate management strategies for individual animals or the entire herd.

## 13.2.6    Assert the need of tracking and farming systems monitoring

The need for tracking and monitoring systems in farming is paramount in modern agriculture. These systems provide critical information and data that enable farmers to make informed decisions, optimize resource allocation, and enhance overall farm management.

Tracking systems, such as GPS-enabled technologies and RFID tagging, allow farmers to monitor the movement and location of livestock or farm machinery. This enables better management of grazing areas, prevents theft, and ensures the safety and well-being of animals. By accurately tracking the movement of livestock or machinery, farmers can also optimize logistical operations, such as planning efficient routes for machinery or identifying areas where animals have not grazed adequately. These results in improved productivity, reduced labor costs, and enhanced farm operations.

Monitoring systems provide real-time data on various aspects of farming operations, including environmental conditions, crop health, and livestock behavior. Sensor-based monitoring systems can measure parameters such as soil moisture, temperature, humidity, and pest presence. By monitoring these variables, farmers can make data-driven decisions regarding irrigation schedules, pest control measures, and crop management practices. Additionally, monitoring systems can track livestock health, feed consumption, and reproductive cycles. This allows farmers to detect early signs of illness, optimize feeding programs, and implement timely breeding strategies. Overall, tracking and monitoring systems empower farmers with actionable insights, enabling them to improve efficiency, reduce costs, and maximize agricultural productivity.

### 13.2.7    *Agriculture and information and communications technologies*

Information and communications technologies (ICT) have revolutionized the agriculture industry, transforming the way farmers and stakeholders manage and optimize agricultural practices. The integration of ICT in agriculture has brought forth numerous benefits, including improved efficiency, enhanced decision-making, and increased productivity.

ICT enables farmers to access real-time information on weather conditions, market prices, and best agricultural practices. Weather forecasting applications and sensors provide accurate and timely weather data, enabling farmers to make informed decisions regarding irrigation, fertilization, and pest management. Market information systems, accessible through mobile applications or online platforms, provide farmers with up-to-date pricing and market trends, enabling them to make informed decisions about crop selection, harvesting timing, and sales strategies. Furthermore, ICT tools facilitate knowledge sharing and capacity-building among farmers by providing access to agricultural databases, online forums, and training resources. This exchange of information empowers farmers with the latest techniques, innovations, and best practices, ultimately improving their farming methods and overall productivity.

ICT also plays a crucial role in supply chain management, connecting farmers with buyers, processors, and consumers. Electronic systems for tracking and traceability ensure transparency and accountability throughout the supply chain, promoting food safety and quality assurance. Moreover, ICT tools enable efficient logistics and transportation planning, optimizing routes and reducing post-harvest losses. By streamlining the supply chain and reducing information asymmetry, ICT contributes to fairer pricing, increased market access, and improved profitability for farmers.

### 13.2.8    *IoT's functions*

The IoT encompasses a wide range of functions that contribute to its transformative impact across various industries. Two key functions of IoT are data collection and automation.

Data collection: IoT devices are equipped with sensors that collect and transmit data from the physical world. These sensors can measure various parameters such as temperature, humidity, pressure, motion, and more. The data collected by IoT devices provide valuable insights into the environment, processes, and behaviors of objects or systems. For example, in agriculture, soil moisture sensors can collect data on soil moisture levels, enabling farmers to optimize irrigation practices. In healthcare, wearable devices can monitor vital signs and collect patient health data, facilitating remote patient monitoring and personalized healthcare. The data collected by IoT devices are often transmitted to cloud-based platforms for storage, analysis, and further processing, enabling businesses and organizations to make data-driven decisions and gain actionable insights.

Automation: IoT enables automation by connecting devices and systems, allowing them to communicate and interact with each other. Through the use of sensors, actuators, and connectivity, IoT devices can collect data, analyze it, and trigger actions or responses based on predefined rules or algorithms. For instance, in smart homes, IoT devices such as thermostats, lighting systems, and security cameras can be interconnected to automate temperature control, lighting adjustments, and security monitoring based on occupancy or time of day. In industrial settings, IoT enables predictive maintenance by monitoring equipment conditions in real time, detecting anomalies, and automatically triggering maintenance actions to prevent breakdowns. Automation through IoT not only improves efficiency and productivity but also enhances safety and convenience in various domains, enabling smarter and more autonomous systems.

## 13.2.9  Big data's place in the Internet of Things

Big Data plays a significant role in the IoT ecosystem, enabling the extraction of valuable insights from the massive amounts of data generated by IoT devices. With the proliferation of IoT devices and sensors, there is an exponential increase in data volume, velocity, and variety. Big Data technologies provide the infrastructure and tools to handle and process this vast amount of data, unlocking its potential for meaningful analysis and decision-making.

One key aspect of Big Data in IoT is the storage and management of large-scale datasets. Traditional data storage and processing methods may not be sufficient to handle the sheer volume and variety of IoT data. Big Data technologies, such as distributed file systems and NoSQL databases, provide scalable and flexible solutions for storing and managing massive amounts of data generated by IoT devices. These technologies allow for data ingestion, real-time processing, and long-term storage, ensuring that the data generated by IoT devices are effectively captured, stored, and made accessible for analysis.

Moreover, Big Data analytics techniques are applied to IoT data to uncover patterns, trends, and correlations that provide valuable insights. With advanced analytics algorithms, such as machine learning and data mining, Big Data can be leveraged to derive actionable insights and make data-driven decisions. For example, in smart cities, Big Data analytics can analyze data from various IoT sources, such as sensors and social media, to optimize traffic flow, improve energy efficiency, and enhance public safety. In industrial settings, predictive analytics using Big Data can enable predictive maintenance of machinery by analyzing sensor data, minimizing downtime, and optimizing maintenance schedules. Big Data's ability to process and analyze large volumes of IoT data empowers organizations to make informed decisions, optimize operations, and unlock new opportunities for innovation and efficiency.

## 13.2.10    The Internet of Things and cloud and fog computing

The IoT relies heavily on cloud and fog computing to enable its full potential. Cloud computing serves as a central hub for storing, processing, and analyzing the vast amount of data generated by IoT devices. By leveraging the scalability and computing power of cloud infrastructure, IoT systems can offload data storage and computational tasks, allowing for efficient data management and analysis. Cloud computing also provides a platform for deploying IoT applications and services, enabling remote access, monitoring, and control of connected devices. With cloud-based IoT solutions, organizations can leverage the benefits of centralized data storage, real-time analytics, and seamless scalability to enhance their IoT deployments.

Fog computing, on the other hand, complements cloud computing in the IoT ecosystem by bringing computation and storage closer to the network edge. Fog computing enables data processing and analytics to be performed at or near the edge devices themselves, reducing latency and improving real-time decision-making capabilities. This is particularly crucial in scenarios where low latency and high responsiveness are essential, such as in autonomous vehicles, industrial automation, or health-care applications. By distributing computational resources and data storage closer to the IoT devices, fog computing enables faster data processing, reduced bandwidth requirements, and enhanced privacy and security. Fog computing also enables edge intelligence, where edge devices can perform data preprocessing and analysis, sending only relevant information to the cloud, thereby optimizing network traffic and reducing the burden on cloud infrastructure. The combination of cloud and fog computing in the IoT ecosystem creates a powerful architecture that enables efficient data processing, real-time insights, and seamless connectivity across a wide range of IoT applications and use cases.

## 13.2.11    Sensors associated with plants

Sensors associated with plants play a crucial role in monitoring and understanding the growth, health, and environmental conditions of plants. These sensors provide valuable data that help farmers, researchers, and gardeners make informed decisions about plant care, optimize resource allocation, and enhance overall plant productivity.

One commonly used sensor associated with plants is a soil moisture sensor. These sensors measure the moisture content in the soil, providing information about the water availability to plants. By monitoring soil moisture levels, farmers and gardeners can optimize irrigation practices, ensuring that plants receive adequate water without overwatering. This helps conserve water resources, prevent waterlogging, and promote healthy root development.

Another important sensor associated with plants is a light sensor or a photo-synthetically active radiation (PAR) sensor. These sensors measure the intensity of light available for photosynthesis, providing insights into the light conditions experienced by plants. Light sensors are particularly crucial in indoor or controlled environment settings, where artificial lighting is used to support plant growth. By monitoring light levels, growers can optimize the duration and intensity of artificial lighting to promote optimal photosynthesis and growth. Additionally, light sensors are also used in shade systems and crop canopies to assess light penetration and adjust shading accordingly to prevent light stress or optimize light exposure for different plant species [3].

## 13.2.12    The GPS's function

The GPS plays a fundamental role in providing precise location and navigation information worldwide. GPS uses a constellation of satellites in orbit around the Earth to accurately determine the position, velocity, and time synchronization of receivers on the ground. The primary function of GPS is to provide real-time and continuous positioning information to users across various sectors.

One of the key functions of GPS is navigation. GPS receivers receive signals from multiple satellites and use the time it takes for the signals to reach the receiver to calculate the distance to each satellite. By triangulating the distances from multiple satellites, the GPS receiver can determine its precise position on the Earth's surface. This allows individuals and organizations to navigate and plan routes efficiently, whether it's for land, air, or maritime transportation. GPS navigation systems have become ubiquitous in vehicles, smartphones, and handheld devices, providing turn-by-turn directions, real-time traffic updates, and precise positioning information to users.

Another important function of GPS is timing and synchronization. GPS satellites carry highly accurate atomic clocks, and their signals are used as a reference for timekeeping. GPS receivers can synchronize their internal clocks with the precise time signal from GPS satellites. This synchronization is crucial for various applications that require precise timing, such as telecommunications, financial transactions, power grid synchronization, and scientific research. By utilizing GPS timing, organizations can ensure coordinated operations, accurate data logging, and synchronization of distributed systems.

## 13.3    Big Data-based intelligent fog computing

The field of IoT presents various research challenges and issues that researchers and industry professionals are actively addressing. These challenges arise from the complex nature of IoT systems and the vast amount of data generated by interconnected devices. Two key research challenges in IoT are security and privacy concerns and the scalability and interoperability of IoT systems.

Security and privacy are major concerns in IoT due to the interconnected nature of devices and the sensitive data they generate. IoT devices are vulnerable to security threats such as unauthorized access, data breaches, and device tampering. Ensuring the confidentiality, integrity, and availability of data across the IoT ecosystem is crucial. Researchers are exploring encryption techniques, authentication mechanisms, and secure communication protocols to address these challenges. Additionally, privacy concerns arise due to the extensive data collection and potential for personal information exposure in IoT systems. Developing privacy-preserving methods and robust data anonymization techniques are important research areas to protect user privacy while still enabling the benefits of IoT.

Scalability and interoperability are significant challenges in IoT systems as they involve the integration of diverse devices, protocols, and platforms. IoT networks consist of a wide range of devices with varying capabilities, communication protocols, and data formats. Ensuring seamless interoperability and data exchange between different IoT devices and systems is critical for creating cohesive IoT ecosystems. Researchers are focusing on developing standardized protocols, middleware, and data models to facilitate device compatibility, data integration, and interoperability. Additionally, scaling IoT systems to accommodate the massive influx of data and the growing number of connected devices is a research challenge. Finding efficient ways to handle and process Big Data generated by IoT devices while maintaining system performance and reliability is an ongoing area of investigation.

## 13.3.1 Computerized information management

Computerized information management refers to the process of collecting, organizing, storing, and retrieving data using computer systems and software applications. It involves the use of digital tools and technologies to efficiently manage and utilize information resources within organizations. Two key aspects of computerized information management are data organization and accessibility.

Data organization is essential for effective information management. Computerized systems enable the categorization, indexing, and structuring of data, making it easier to locate and retrieve information when needed. With the use of databases and data management systems, organizations can store and organize large volumes of data in a structured and systematic manner. This allows for efficient data retrieval, reducing the time and effort required to access specific information. Additionally, computerized information management systems often incorporate advanced search and filtering capabilities, enabling users to quickly find relevant data based on specific criteria, such as keywords, dates, or categories. By organizing data in a computerized manner, organizations can optimize information management processes, streamline workflows, and enhance overall productivity.

Accessibility of information is another crucial aspect of computerized information management. Computer systems enable the sharing and dissemination of information across various platforms and networks. With centralized data repositories and networked systems, authorized users can access information from different locations and devices, facilitating collaborative work and decision-making. Computerized information management systems also provide security and access controls, ensuring that sensitive or confidential data are accessible only to authorized individuals. Furthermore, computerized information management facilitates real-time updates and version control, allowing multiple users to work on the same document or database simultaneously. This enhances information accessibility and promotes efficient collaboration within organizations, ultimately leading to improved communication, knowledge sharing, and decision-making processes.

### 13.3.2    *Big Data analysis and processing*

Big Data analysis and processing refers to the techniques and technologies used to extract meaningful insights from large and complex datasets. As the volume, velocity, and variety of data continue to grow exponentially, traditional data processing methods become insufficient for handling and extracting value from these massive datasets. Big Data analysis and processing techniques offer solutions to overcome the challenges associated with large-scale data.

One key aspect of Big Data analysis is the use of advanced analytics techniques such as machine learning, data mining, and predictive modeling. These techniques enable the identification of patterns, trends, and correlations within the data that may not be readily apparent. By applying these analytics methods to Big Data, organizations can gain valuable insights and make data-driven decisions. For example, in healthcare, Big Data analysis can be used to identify disease patterns, predict patient outcomes, and optimize treatment strategies. In marketing, Big Data analysis can uncover consumer preferences and behaviors, enabling targeted marketing campaigns and personalized customer experiences.

The processing of Big Data often requires distributed computing and parallel processing techniques to handle the enormous volume and complexity of the data. Distributed storage systems, such as Hadoop and Apache Spark, enable the storage and processing of data across multiple machines or nodes. These systems divide the data into smaller chunks, distribute them across the cluster, and process them in parallel. This parallel processing approach allows for faster and more efficient analysis of Big Data. Additionally, technologies such as in-memory computing and stream processing enable real-time analysis of Big Data, providing instant insights and allowing organizations to respond to events and trends as they occur.

### 13.3.3    *The role of the cloud in Big Data*

The cloud plays a pivotal role in the realm of Big Data by providing the necessary infrastructure and resources to store, process, and analyze large volumes of data. With the exponential growth of data, traditional on-premises solutions often struggle to handle the scale and complexity of Big Data. Cloud computing offers scalable and flexible solutions that can seamlessly accommodate the demands of Big Data workloads.

One of the primary roles of the cloud in Big Data is data storage. Cloud storage services, such as Amazon S3, Google Cloud Storage, or Microsoft Azure Blob

Storage, provide virtually unlimited storage capacity for businesses to store their Big Data sets. This eliminates the need for organizations to invest in expensive on-premises storage infrastructure and allows them to scale their storage resources as needed. Additionally, cloud storage offers durability, data redundancy, and accessibility from anywhere, enabling efficient and reliable data management for Big Data projects.

Moreover, the cloud provides a powerful computing environment for Big Data processing and analytics. Cloud-based platforms, such as Amazon Web Services (AWS) Elastic MapReduce (EMR) or Google Cloud Dataproc, offer distributed computing capabilities that can handle the computational demands of Big Data workloads. These platforms allow organizations to provision and configure clusters of virtual machines (VMs) to process data in parallel, significantly reducing processing time. Furthermore, cloud-based analytics services, such as AWS Athena or Google BigQuery, provide scalable and on-demand query capabilities for analyzing Big Data without the need for upfront infrastructure investment. The cloud's ability to provide scalable computing resources and on-demand analytics tools empowers organizations to process and analyze Big Data efficiently, extract valuable insights, and derive actionable intelligence from their datasets.

## 13.3.4   Cloud computing and geospatial data

Cloud computing and geospatial data are a perfect match, offering numerous benefits for managing and analyzing spatially referenced information. Geospatial data, which includes geographic coordinates and associated attributes, is increasingly being generated by various sources such as satellite imagery, GPS sensors, and location-based services (LBS). Cloud computing provides an ideal platform for storing, processing, and analyzing this vast amount of geospatial data.

One significant advantage of cloud computing in relation to geospatial data is its scalability and storage capacity. Cloud storage services allow organizations to store and manage massive amounts of geospatial data without the need for extensive on-premises infrastructure. Cloud storage systems provide virtually unlimited storage space, ensuring that geospatial datasets can be readily accessed and efficiently managed. This scalability is particularly valuable in the context of geospatial data, which often involves large file sizes and complex datasets. Cloud-based storage also facilitates easy data sharing and collaboration, enabling geospatial professionals, researchers, and decision-makers to access and work with the same datasets in a collaborative environment.

Furthermore, cloud computing offers powerful computational capabilities that are essential for processing and analyzing geospatial data. With cloud-based processing, organizations can leverage high-performance computing resources to perform complex spatial analysis, image processing, and geospatial modeling. Cloud platforms provide the computational power needed to handle geospatial tasks that require significant processing capabilities, such as spatial data mining, machine learning algorithms, or large-scale geoprocessing workflows. Additionally, cloud-based geospatial tools and services, such as cloud-based geographic information

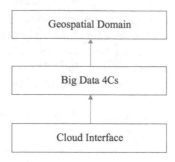

*Figure 13.1   Geospatial domain-based cloud structure*

system (GIS) platforms, provide intuitive interfaces and ready-to-use algorithms for geospatial analysis, making it more accessible for users without extensive technical expertise. Overall, cloud computing empowers organizations to unlock the full potential of geospatial data, enabling advanced spatial analysis, informed decision-making, and innovative applications across various domains, including urban planning, agriculture, environmental monitoring, and disaster management.

In Figure 13.1, a geospatial domain-based cloud structure, the focus is on leveraging cloud computing technologies and infrastructure to support geospatial data management, processing, and analysis. The structure involves the integration of geospatial technologies, such as GISs, with cloud computing resources to meet the specific requirements of geospatial applications and workflows.

The structure typically includes components such as geospatial data storage, geospatial processing services, and geospatial analytics capabilities. Geospatial data storage involves cloud-based repositories that provide scalable and accessible storage for geospatial datasets, which may include satellite imagery, topographic data, geospatial databases, and other spatial data sources. Geospatial processing services encompass cloud-based platforms or tools that enable geospatial analysis, geoprocessing, and spatial modeling tasks. These services can support operations such as spatial queries, spatial indexing, overlay analysis, and proximity analysis. Geospatial analytics capabilities leverage cloud-based computing power and algorithms to perform advanced analytics on geospatial data, enabling tasks like spatial pattern recognition, predictive modeling, and geospatial data mining.

## 13.3.5   Big geographical data

Big Geographical Data refers to large-scale and complex datasets that contain geographic or spatial information. It encompasses massive volumes of data generated from various sources such as satellite imagery, remote sensing, GPS, social media, sensor networks, and geospatial databases. These datasets consist of spatially referenced information, including geographic coordinates, boundaries, topographic features, and attributes related to location.

The unique characteristic of Big Geographical Data lies in its size, variety, and velocity. These datasets often contain terabytes or even petabytes of information, requiring specialized storage, processing, and analysis techniques. Additionally, Big Geographical Data encompasses diverse data types, including satellite imagery, geospatial databases, point cloud data, 3D models, and real-time sensor data. Managing and integrating these different data sources pose significant challenges. Moreover, the velocity of data generation is another crucial aspect. With the advent of remote sensing technologies and LBS, large volumes of geospatial data are generated at a rapid pace, requiring efficient processing and analysis methods to derive meaningful insights.

The analysis and utilization of Big Geographical Data offer immense opportunities across various domains. It enables advanced spatial analysis, such as spatial pattern recognition, hotspot identification, and predictive modeling, which have applications in fields such as urban planning, environmental monitoring, transportation, and emergency response. Big Geographical Data also contributes to the development of smart cities, precision agriculture, climate modeling, and disaster management. The insights derived from these datasets help organizations and policymakers make informed decisions, optimize resource allocation, and improve operational efficiency. However, effectively harnessing the potential of Big Geographical Data requires scalable infrastructure, sophisticated data management techniques, powerful computing capabilities, and advanced analytics methods tailored to handle the unique characteristics of these large and complex geospatial datasets [3].

### 13.3.6    Technical measures for thermostatic regulation

Technical measures for thermostatic regulation involve the use of various technologies and techniques to control and maintain desired temperature levels in heating, ventilation, and air conditioning (HVAC) systems. These measures aim to improve energy efficiency, occupant comfort, and overall system performance.

One common technical measure for thermostatic regulation is the use of programmable or smart thermostats. These thermostats allow users to set specific temperature schedules based on their preferences and occupancy patterns. Programmable thermostats enable pre-programming temperature settings for different times of the day, allowing for energy-saving setbacks during periods when spaces are unoccupied or when lower temperatures are acceptable. Smart thermostats take this a step further by utilizing advanced sensors, occupancy detection, and learning algorithms to adapt temperature settings automatically based on occupants' behavior and environmental conditions. These thermostats can also be controlled remotely through mobile applications, enabling users to adjust settings even when they are not physically present. By providing precise and flexible temperature control, programmable and smart thermostats help optimize energy consumption and provide personalized comfort.

Another technical measure is the use of zoning systems in HVAC setups. Zoning systems divide a building into different zones or areas, each with its own independent temperature control. This allows for customized temperature regulation in different parts of the building based on individual needs and usage patterns.

Zoning systems utilize dampers or valves in ductwork to control airflow and direct conditioned air to specific zones. Each zone is equipped with its own thermostat, allowing occupants to set desired temperature levels independently. Zoning systems help eliminate energy waste by avoiding over-conditioning of unoccupied areas or spaces with varying thermal requirements. By providing localized temperature control, zoning systems enhance occupant comfort and reduce energy consumption by directing conditioned air only where it is needed.

### 13.3.7    Efficient and eco-friendly structures are called "green buildings"

Efficient and eco-friendly structures are commonly referred to as "green buildings." Green buildings are designed and constructed with a focus on minimizing environmental impact, conserving resources, and promoting sustainability. These buildings employ various strategies and technologies to enhance energy efficiency, reduce water consumption, improve indoor air quality, and utilize renewable materials.

One key aspect of green buildings is energy efficiency. They incorporate energy-efficient systems and features such as insulation, high-performance windows, efficient HVAC systems, and LED lighting. By reducing energy consumption for heating, cooling, and lighting, green buildings help lower greenhouse gas emissions and decrease reliance on fossil fuels. Additionally, green buildings often integrate renewable energy technologies such as solar panels or wind turbines to generate on-site renewable energy, further reducing their environmental footprint.

Water conservation is another critical component of green buildings. They incorporate water-efficient fixtures, such as low-flow toilets, faucets, and showerheads, as well as rainwater harvesting systems for non-potable water uses. These measures help minimize water consumption, alleviate strain on water resources, and reduce the energy required for water treatment and distribution.

Furthermore, green buildings prioritize indoor environmental quality by using low-emission materials, proper ventilation systems, and abundant natural light to create a healthy and comfortable indoor environment. By reducing indoor air pollutants and providing ample daylight, green buildings promote occupant well-being and productivity.

### 13.3.8    Geospatial data influences thermal comfort in buildings

Geospatial data play a significant role in influencing thermal comfort in buildings by providing insights into the external environmental factors that affect indoor temperature conditions. Geospatial data include information such as solar radiation, outdoor air temperature, wind patterns, and shading analysis, which are crucial for understanding and managing thermal comfort within buildings.

Solar radiation data allow building designers and occupants to assess the amount of solar heat gain that a building is likely to experience. By analyzing geospatial data on solar radiation, it becomes possible to optimize building orientation, window placement, and shading devices to control the amount of direct sunlight entering the building. This helps prevent overheating in warm climates while maximizing solar gains during colder periods, contributing to better thermal comfort and reduced energy consumption for heating and cooling.

Outdoor air temperature data obtained through geospatial sources enable building designers to determine the appropriate sizing and capacity of HVAC systems for maintaining comfortable indoor temperatures. By analyzing historical temperature patterns and climate data, designers can accurately predict the thermal load requirements and design HVAC systems that efficiently regulate indoor temperature. Geospatial data also allow for the identification of outdoor temperature variations across different regions, which can influence building design and thermal comfort strategies specific to the location [4].

### 13.3.9 Thermostatic consistency of building equipment

Thermostatic consistency refers to the ability of building equipment, particularly HVAC systems, to maintain consistent and stable indoor temperatures within a desired range. Achieving thermostatic consistency is crucial for providing optimal comfort conditions for occupants and maximizing energy efficiency.

Building equipment, such as air conditioning units and heating systems, are equipped with thermostats that control the operation of these systems based on temperature settings. Thermostatic consistency ensures that the equipment responds accurately and consistently to changes in temperature, minimizing temperature fluctuations and providing a stable indoor climate.

To achieve thermostatic consistency, building equipment must be properly calibrated and maintained. Regular calibration of thermostats helps ensure their accuracy in sensing and controlling temperature. Additionally, routine maintenance of HVAC systems, including cleaning filters, checking refrigerant levels, and inspecting ductwork, is essential for optimal performance and temperature control.

Another aspect of thermostatic consistency is the integration of building automation systems and advanced controls. These systems use sensors and actuators to monitor and regulate indoor temperature conditions. By utilizing advanced control algorithms and feedback mechanisms, building automation systems can continuously adjust HVAC settings to maintain consistent temperatures throughout different zones or areas of a building.

### 13.3.10 Building materials made locally

Using locally sourced building materials refers to the practice of utilizing construction materials that are obtained from nearby sources, reducing the environmental impact associated with transportation and supporting local economies. There are several benefits to using locally sourced building materials in construction projects.

First, using locally sourced materials reduces the carbon footprint associated with transportation. By sourcing materials from nearby locations, the distance traveled to transport the materials to the construction site is minimized. This results in lower energy consumption and greenhouse gas emissions compared to materials sourced from distant locations. Additionally, the use of local materials reduces the need for long-distance transportation infrastructure, such as highways or shipping routes, which further contributes to environmental sustainability.

Second, utilizing locally sourced building materials supports local economies and communities. When materials are procured from local suppliers, it stimulates the local economy by generating employment opportunities and supporting local businesses. This, in turn, fosters economic growth and strengthens community resilience. Moreover, using locally sourced materials can promote cultural preservation and reflect regional identity by incorporating materials that are characteristic of the local area, such as indigenous stone, timber, or clay. This adds a unique and authentic touch to the built environment while celebrating local heritage and craftsmanship.

### 13.3.11　Technologies and protocols for the Internet of Things overview

Technologies and protocols for the IoT play a crucial role in enabling the seamless connectivity, communication, and interoperability of IoT devices and systems. Several key technologies and protocols form the foundation of IoT deployments.

One important technology is wireless communication protocols, which facilitate the exchange of data between IoT devices and networks. Some commonly used wireless protocols for IoT include Wi-Fi, Bluetooth, Zigbee, Z-Wave, and LoRaWAN. These protocols provide various advantages such as high data transfer rates, low power consumption, long-range connectivity, and support for different use cases and device types. The selection of a wireless protocol depends on factors such as the range of communication, power requirements, data transfer speed, and the specific IoT application.

Another crucial technology for the IoT is cloud computing. Cloud platforms offer scalable computing resources and storage capabilities that can accommodate the massive amounts of data generated by IoT devices. Cloud computing provides a centralized and scalable infrastructure for data storage, processing, and analysis. It allows IoT devices to offload computational tasks, store and access data remotely, and leverage advanced analytics tools and machine learning algorithms. Cloud computing also facilitates the integration of IoT devices with other systems and services, enabling seamless data sharing and interoperability.

Furthermore, IoT security protocols and technologies are essential for ensuring the privacy, integrity, and authentication of data exchanged between IoT devices and networks. These security measures include authentication and access control mechanisms, encryption techniques, secure communication protocols, and device management frameworks. Robust security protocols are critical to protect sensitive data, prevent unauthorized access, and mitigate potential security threats in IoT deployments.

### 13.3.12　Technologies of information and communication and of physical location

The technologies of information and communication, combined with physical location technologies, are instrumental in enabling the seamless integration of data and spatial context. These technologies play a vital role in various applications and industries, including navigation, transportation, logistics, asset tracking, and LBS.

Information and communication technologies encompass a wide range of tools and systems, including wireless communication protocols, Internet connectivity, data storage and processing, and software applications. These technologies facilitate the exchange, storage, and analysis of vast amounts of data, enabling real-time communication and decision-making. They provide the backbone for collecting, transmitting, and managing information, allowing organizations to leverage data-driven insights for improved operations and service delivery.

Physical location technologies, on the other hand, focus on capturing and utilizing spatial information. These technologies include global navigation satellite systems (GNSS), such as GPS, Galileo, and GLONASS, which provide accurate positioning and navigation capabilities. Additionally, technologies like GISs, remote sensing, and spatial databases enable the collection, integration, and analysis of geospatial data. These tools allow organizations to understand the spatial relationships and characteristics of objects, events, and phenomena, enhancing their ability to make informed decisions and optimize resource allocation based on location-based insights.

When these technologies are combined, they enable the integration of information and spatial context, creating a powerful synergy. For example, LBS utilizes information and communication technologies to deliver location-specific information and services to users. These services rely on physical location technologies to accurately determine the user's position and provide relevant and personalized information based on their location. This integration enables a wide range of applications, from navigation and mapping services to targeted advertising, smart city management, and real-time asset tracking [5].

## 13.3.13 Detection and monitoring techniques

Detection and monitoring techniques refer to the methods and technologies used to identify, track, and monitor specific objects, events, or conditions. These techniques are crucial in various fields, including surveillance, environmental monitoring, industrial processes, and healthcare. They enable real-time data collection, analysis, and decision-making, leading to improved safety, efficiency, and quality in diverse applications.

One commonly used technique is sensor-based detection and monitoring. Sensors are devices that can measure and detect physical or environmental parameters such as temperature, pressure, humidity, motion, or chemical composition. They convert these measurements into electrical signals that can be analyzed and interpreted. Sensors can be deployed in various forms, including wireless sensors, IoT devices, and embedded sensors in equipment or structures. They provide continuous or periodic data acquisition, allowing for real-time monitoring and detection of changes or anomalies. Sensor-based techniques find applications in areas such as environmental monitoring for air quality, structural health monitoring for buildings and infrastructure, and condition monitoring in industrial processes.

Another technique is image and video-based detection and monitoring. This technique involves the use of cameras and imaging systems to capture visual information and analyze it for specific patterns, objects, or events. Image processing algorithms and computer vision techniques are used to detect and track objects, recognize patterns, and extract relevant information from images or video streams. Image and video-based detection and monitoring have wide-ranging applications, including surveillance and security systems, traffic monitoring, object recognition in robotics, and medical imaging. These techniques enable automated analysis and interpretation of visual data, enabling timely response and decision-making based on real-time or recorded images.

### 13.3.14    The Internet of Things in the cloud

The integration of the IoT with cloud computing is a powerful combination that offers numerous benefits and opportunities. The IoT generates vast amounts of data from interconnected devices, while cloud computing provides scalable and flexible infrastructure to store, process, and analyze this data. By leveraging the cloud, the IoT becomes more efficient, secure, and capable of delivering advanced services and applications.

One key advantage of combining IoT with cloud computing is the ability to handle the massive scale of data generated by IoT devices. Cloud platforms provide the necessary storage capacity and computational resources to manage and process large volumes of IoT data. This eliminates the need for organizations to invest in on-premises infrastructure and enables them to scale their IoT deployments as needed. The cloud also allows for real-time data processing and analysis, enabling organizations to gain actionable insights from IoT data and make informed decisions promptly.

Another benefit is enhanced security and data privacy. The cloud offers robust security measures, including encryption, access controls, and data backups, which help protect IoT data from unauthorized access and ensure data integrity. Cloud-based security solutions can provide end-to-end encryption and secure communication channels between IoT devices and the cloud, mitigating the risk of data breaches. Additionally, cloud platforms enable organizations to implement centralized device management and security policies, simplifying the monitoring and control of IoT devices across a distributed network.

Moreover, the cloud provides a platform for deploying IoT applications and services. Cloud-based IoT platforms offer tools and frameworks for developing and managing IoT solutions, including device connectivity, data ingestion, analytics, and visualization. These platforms enable organizations to rapidly develop and deploy IoT applications without the need for extensive infrastructure setup, reducing time to market and overall costs. Furthermore, cloud-based analytics and machine learning capabilities allow for advanced data analysis, predictive modeling, and real-time decision-making, unlocking the full potential of IoT data.

### 13.3.15    IoT with the advent of Big Data and the cloud

The combination of the IoT with Big Data and the Cloud has revolutionized the way data are collected, processed, and analyzed, leading to unprecedented opportunities for insights and innovation. The IoT generates massive amounts of data from interconnected devices, while Big Data technologies enable the storage, management, and analysis of these large datasets. The cloud provides scalable infrastructure and computing resources to handle the volume and complexity of IoT-generated data, making it a perfect platform for managing and leveraging Big Data in the context of IoT.

With the advent of Big Data and the cloud, organizations can effectively capture, store, and process the vast amounts of data generated by IoT devices. The cloud provides the necessary scalability and flexibility to accommodate the ever-increasing data volume, variety, and velocity of the IoT. Big Data technologies, such as distributed storage systems and data processing frameworks like Apache Hadoop and Spark, enable efficient handling and analysis of IoT-generated data. This allows organizations to uncover valuable insights, identify patterns, trends, and correlations, and make data-driven decisions. The cloud also provides the ability to store and access historical IoT data, enabling retrospective analysis and long-term data retention for future analysis or compliance purposes.

Furthermore, the cloud's computational power and advanced analytics capabilities enable real-time and predictive analytics on IoT data. Organizations can leverage Big Data processing and machine learning algorithms in the cloud to gain real-time insights and make immediate decisions based on IoT-generated data. This empowers businesses to optimize operations, improve efficiency, and deliver personalized experiences. The cloud also facilitates the integration of diverse data sources, such as IoT data, social media data, and enterprise data, enabling cross-domain analysis and comprehensive insights. With the combination of IoT, Big Data, and the cloud, organizations can unlock the full potential of data-driven innovation, transforming industries and creating new business models, products, and services.

### 13.3.16 Computing on the cloud: from fog to cloud

Computing on the cloud encompasses a range of technologies and services that enable the storage, processing, and analysis of data in remote data centers. Over time, the computing landscape has evolved from a centralized cloud model to include distributed architectures like fog computing.

Fog computing is an extension of cloud computing that brings computation, storage, and networking capabilities closer to the edge of the network, closer to where data are generated and consumed. This enables faster data processing, reduced latency, and improved performance for applications that require real-time or near-real-time responses. Fog computing leverages edge devices, such as routers, switches, and gateways, to perform localized computation and data storage. It complements cloud computing by offloading some of the processing tasks from the centralized cloud to the edge, reducing the amount of data that need to be transferred to the cloud for processing. Fog computing is particularly useful in IoT applications, where there is a need for real-time analytics, low latency, and bandwidth efficiency.

While fog computing extends the capabilities of cloud computing to the edge, the centralized cloud still plays a critical role in the overall computing ecosystem. The cloud provides vast storage and computing resources, advanced analytics capabilities, and scalable infrastructure. It serves as the central hub for data aggregation, long-term storage, and resource-intensive processing tasks that may not be feasible at the edge. The cloud offers the flexibility to scale resources up or down based on demand, allowing organizations to adapt to changing computational needs. Moreover, the cloud enables seamless collaboration, data sharing, and integration across different devices and applications.

## 13.4    Fog computing in health-care systems

Conceptualizing a unified fog-computing security platform for the IoT cloud health-care system involves developing a comprehensive framework that addresses the unique security challenges and requirements of health-care environments where IoT devices and cloud computing technologies are interconnected. The goal is to ensure the confidentiality, integrity, and availability of sensitive health-care data, protect against potential cyber threats, and maintain the trust and privacy of patients' information.

The security platform should encompass multiple layers of security measures. At the network layer, robust authentication and access control mechanisms should be implemented to ensure that only authorized devices and users can access the health-care system. Encryption techniques and secure communication protocols should be employed to protect data in transit and prevent eavesdropping or tampering. Additionally, intrusion detection and prevention systems can be deployed to monitor network traffic and detect any suspicious activities or potential attacks.

At the fog-computing layer, security measures should focus on securing the edge devices and gateways that interact with the IoT devices. This includes implementing device-level authentication, firmware validation, and secure boot processes to ensure that only trusted devices can connect to the fog-computing infrastructure. Data encryption and integrity checks can be applied to protect data stored or processed at the edge. Moreover, the fog-computing layer can incorporate anomaly detection algorithms and machine learning techniques to identify unusual behavior and potential security breaches.

At the cloud layer, the security platform should include measures such as strong access controls, data encryption, and regular vulnerability assessments and patch management to safeguard the cloud infrastructure. Privacy-preserving techniques, like differential privacy, can be employed to protect sensitive patient data during data analytics and processing. Additionally, compliance with industry regulations and standards, such as the Health Insurance Portability and Accountability Act (HIPAA), should be ensured to maintain regulatory compliance and patient trust.

By conceptualizing a unified fog-computing security platform, health-care organizations can address the unique security challenges posed by IoT devices and cloud computing in health-care environments. This platform should provide end-to-end security, from the IoT devices at the edge to the cloud infrastructure, ensuring the protection of sensitive health-care data and the uninterrupted delivery of critical health-care services.

### 13.4.1 The proposed system's core functionality discerning the equipment

The proposed system's core functionality revolves around discerning the equipment in a given environment. This entails utilizing various technologies and techniques to accurately identify and classify the different types of equipment present. The system aims to provide real-time insights and information about the equipment, enabling better asset management, maintenance planning, and operational efficiency.

To achieve this, the system may utilize machine learning algorithms and computer vision techniques. By training the system with a large dataset of equipment images, it can learn to recognize specific equipment types based on visual features and patterns. Computer vision algorithms can then be applied to analyze live video feeds or images captured in the environment to identify and classify the equipment present. This allows for automatic detection and categorization of equipment, eliminating the need for manual inspection and reducing human effort.

Additionally, the proposed system may integrate with sensor-based technologies. By deploying sensors on the equipment or in the surrounding environment, the system can capture relevant data such as vibration, temperature, or power consumption. These sensor readings can be analyzed and correlated with the identified equipment to provide insights into equipment health, performance, and usage patterns. This enables proactive maintenance planning, timely fault detection, and optimization of equipment utilization.

### 13.4.2 Disposables identification, location, and tracking

Disposables identification, location, and tracking involve the use of technology to accurately identify, track, and monitor disposable items within a given environment. Disposables refer to items that are designed for single-use or limited use, such as medical supplies, consumables, or other disposable assets. The goal of identification, location, and tracking systems is to enhance inventory management, improve workflow efficiency, and ensure the availability of essential disposable items when needed.

One approach to disposables identification and tracking is through the use of RFID technology. RFID tags can be attached to disposable items, allowing for their unique identification and tracking throughout their lifecycle. RFID readers placed strategically in the environment can detect and record the presence and movement of tagged disposables in real time. This enables accurate inventory management, automates restocking processes, and helps prevent stockouts or excess inventory. RFID-based tracking systems also provide visibility into usage patterns, helping organizations optimize disposables utilization and reduce costs.

Another technology that can be utilized for disposables identification and tracking is barcode scanning. Disposable items can be labeled with unique barcodes that can be easily scanned using barcode readers or mobile devices. The scanned barcode data can then be linked to a centralized system, allowing for accurate tracking of disposables' location and usage. Barcode scanning provides a cost-effective and efficient method for identifying and tracking disposable items, particularly in health-care settings where disposable medical supplies are critical for patient care.

### 13.4.3   Functionality and design of the proposed system

The proposed system aims to provide an innovative solution that offers advanced functionality and a well-designed user experience. The system's functionality revolves around efficient data collection, processing, and analysis, along with seamless integration and user-friendly interfaces.

At its core, the system facilitates data collection through various sensors, devices, or data sources relevant to the application domain. This may include IoT devices, wearable sensors, environmental sensors, or other data-capturing mechanisms. The system ensures reliable data capture, data validation, and data storage, ensuring the availability of accurate and high-quality data for further processing.

The proposed system also focuses on efficient data processing and analysis. It leverages advanced algorithms, machine learning techniques, and statistical models to extract valuable insights and actionable information from the collected data. This enables real-time or near-real-time analytics, anomaly detection, predictive modeling, or other relevant data processing tasks specific to the application domain. The system's architecture is designed to handle large volumes of data, ensuring scalability, speed, and accuracy in data processing.

In terms of design, the proposed system emphasizes a user-centric approach. The user interfaces are designed to be intuitive, visually appealing, and easy to navigate. The system provides interactive visualizations, dashboards, and reports to present the analyzed data in a meaningful way. This allows users to gain insights at a glance, make informed decisions, and interact with the system in a seamless manner. Additionally, the system's design ensures compatibility and integration with existing technologies or software systems, promoting interoperability and ease of deployment.

### 13.4.4   The future of networking devices

The future of networking devices is poised for significant advancements as technologies continue to evolve and reshape the way we connect and communicate. Several trends and innovations are expected to shape the future of networking devices.

First, the emergence of 5G networks will revolutionize networking devices by providing faster speeds, lower latency, and increased capacity. 5G technology will enable a seamless and robust connectivity experience, supporting a wide range of devices and applications. Networking devices will leverage 5G capabilities to enable real-time data transfer, enhance IoT connectivity, and power emerging technologies like autonomous vehicles, smart cities, and AR.

Another key trend is the proliferation of edge computing. Edge devices, located closer to the data source or user, will play a crucial role in processing and analyzing data in real time, reducing latency, and enhancing the overall network performance. Networking devices will increasingly integrate edge computing capabilities to offload processing tasks, enable faster response times, and support applications that require real-time decision-making.

Furthermore, the future of networking devices will see the rise of software-defined networking (SDN) and network virtualization. SDN enables centralized network management and control, allowing for greater flexibility, scalability, and efficiency in network operations. Networking devices will leverage SDN principles to enable dynamic network configurations, efficient resource allocation, and improved network security.

In terms of device design, networking devices will become more compact, energy-efficient, and highly adaptable. Miniaturization of networking components will lead to smaller, more portable devices that can be seamlessly integrated into various environments. Energy efficiency will be a key consideration, enabling networking devices to operate with reduced power consumption and contribute to sustainable practices.

Additionally, networking devices will embrace advanced security features to address the growing cybersecurity challenges. Robust encryption, authentication mechanisms, and intrusion detection systems will be embedded in networking devices to safeguard data and protect against emerging threats.

## 13.4.5   The field of network analysis

The field of network analysis encompasses the study and evaluation of complex networks, including social networks, computer networks, biological networks, and more. It involves analyzing the structural properties, interactions, and dynamics of networks to gain insights into their behavior, performance, and functionality. Network analysis provides a powerful framework for understanding the intricate relationships and patterns within networks and enables the identification of key nodes, communities, and influential factors.

One key aspect of network analysis is the study of network topology, which examines the structure and connectivity of nodes and edges in a network. This involves analyzing measures such as degree centrality, betweenness centrality, and clustering coefficient to understand the importance and influence of individual nodes and groups of nodes. Network analysis also encompasses the study of network dynamics, exploring how information, influence, or disease spread within a network over time. It employs techniques such as diffusion models, epidemic modeling, and cascading processes to simulate and understand the behavior and dynamics of complex networks.

Furthermore, network analysis provides insights into network resilience and robustness. By identifying critical nodes and analyzing the connectivity patterns, researchers can understand the vulnerabilities and potential failure points in a network. This knowledge can then be utilized to design more robust and resilient networks that can withstand failures, disruptions, or attacks. Network analysis also aids in optimizing network performance and efficiency by identifying bottlenecks, optimizing routing algorithms, and improving resource allocation.

### 13.4.6    Implied hardware

Implied hardware refers to the concept of virtual or abstracted hardware components that are not physically present but are inferred or simulated by software or virtualization technologies. It allows software applications to interact with virtual hardware components that mimic the behavior and functionality of real hardware, providing a flexible and scalable computing environment.

One example of implied hardware is VMs or virtualized environments. Virtualization technology enables the creation of multiple virtual instances of hardware, including processors, memory, storage, and network interfaces. These virtual instances can run on a single physical server, allowing for the consolidation of resources and the efficient utilization of hardware. Each VM behaves like an independent computer system, running its own operating system and applications, while sharing the underlying physical resources. This enables organizations to optimize hardware utilization, reduce costs, and increase scalability and flexibility in deploying and managing software applications.

Another example of implied hardware is SDN. SDN decouples the control plane from the underlying network infrastructure, allowing network administrators to control and manage network behavior through software-based controllers. The network functions that were traditionally implemented in hardware devices, such as routers and switches, are now abstracted and realized through SDN components. This abstraction allows for greater flexibility and programmability in managing network resources, routing protocols, and traffic flows. With SDN, network administrators can dynamically configure and manage the network infrastructure, optimizing performance, and responding to changing business needs without the need for physical hardware reconfiguration.

## 13.5    Protecting individuality within the paradigm of a recommender system

This section explains the notion of privacy, a reference model for cloud-based recommendation services, and the security and privacy problems. We will talk about the threat model we used in this study in the last part. The concept of privacy is difficult to grasp conceptually. Legislation, use restrictions, and societal conventions all have a role in this issue, so it's not just a technological one. Privacy is a concept that might change based on the user's perspective. Two prevalent incentives for consumers to share their personal information include tailored content and discount vouchers. The term "private" typically refers to information that the end-user feels the need to keep secret for fear of being subjected to prejudice, humiliation, or damage to their professional or personal reputations. External parties' perceptions of private information might change over time and in different settings, which impacts the degree to which it is made available to others. In this study, there are a variety of opinions that encompass the notion of privacy. This part, on the other hand, will touch on the most essential ideas that are required to go on with this project. "The right to be left alone" was defined by Warren and Brandeis as privacy. According to Westin, in the era of information and communication technology, privacy may be split into two categories: informational privacy and geographical privacy. A user's ability to manage how, when, and to what degree personal information about him or her is disclosed is referred to as "informational privacy." Personal data like a person's name, age, phone number, or email address are often connected with this.

Another facet of privacy in the physical world is the user's ability to choose which sensory inputs are prioritized. Privacy, according to the authors of this research, is neither rule-based nor fixed. Contrary to this belief, "a fine-grained coordination between activity and revelation of that action happens, and depends on the social context, goal, and the fine-grained coordination of action and disclosure." Privacy was described as the ability of services to get lawful knowledge without knowing who the underlying users were. The results of this investigation were noteworthy. It's safe to conclude that the term "privacy" today has many meanings, depending on the context. The most critical concern for privacy-enhancing methods is the investigation of their potential drawbacks. As a result, our idea of privacy is quite close to the original definition, as it also takes into account the desire for privacy and the possibility of valid results.

### 13.5.1 The cloud-based recommendation service reference model

The cloud-based recommendation service reference model outlines a framework for designing and implementing recommendation systems that leverage cloud computing capabilities. This model provides a structured approach to building recommendation systems that can handle large-scale data processing, real-time recommendations, and personalized user experiences.

At the core of the reference model is the cloud infrastructure, which provides the necessary scalability, storage, and computational resources to handle the vast amounts of data required for recommendation systems. The cloud allows for elastic scaling, enabling recommendation engines to process and analyze massive datasets efficiently. It also facilitates data storage and retrieval, ensuring that historical user data and item information can be accessed and utilized in real time.

The model incorporates data processing and analytics components that leverage cloud-based Big Data technologies. These components enable the extraction of insights from user behavior data, item metadata, and contextual information to generate accurate and relevant recommendations. Advanced analytics techniques, such as collaborative filtering, content-based filtering, and machine learning algorithms, are employed to analyze the data and generate personalized recommendations for users.

Additionally, the model includes components for real-time recommendation generation and delivery. This involves leveraging cloud-based streaming and event processing capabilities to capture and process user interactions in real time. By continuously analyzing user actions, the recommendation system can adapt and provide up-to-date recommendations that align with users' preferences and current context.

Moreover, the reference model emphasizes the importance of user interfaces and application programming interfaces (APIs) to enable seamless integration and interaction with the recommendation system. User interfaces can be web-based or mobile-based, providing intuitive interfaces for users to view and interact with recommendations. APIs enable integration with other applications or services, allowing recommendations to be incorporated into various platforms and user experiences.

## 13.5.2    Definition of risk

Risk can be defined as the potential for harm, loss, or undesirable outcomes resulting from uncertainties and hazards. It represents the possibility of an event or situation occurring that may have negative consequences for individuals, organizations, or systems. Risk is inherent in various aspects of life and spans across different domains, including finance, health, environment, and technology.

In a general sense, risk involves the interaction between potential threats or hazards and vulnerabilities. Threats are external factors or events that have the potential to cause harm or negative outcomes. Vulnerabilities, on the other hand, refer to weaknesses or shortcomings that increase the likelihood of experiencing adverse consequences. The assessment and management of risk often involve identifying and analyzing potential threats, assessing vulnerabilities, and implementing strategies to mitigate or reduce the impact of risks.

Risk can be quantified and evaluated using various methodologies and frameworks. This includes risk assessment, which involves the systematic identification and analysis of potential risks, their likelihood of occurrence, and their potential impacts. Risk management is the process of identifying, assessing, and prioritizing risks and implementing measures to reduce, transfer, or accept those risks. It aims to strike a balance between risk reduction and the cost or effort associated with risk mitigation.

## 13.5.3    Formulation of the issue

The formulation of an issue involves defining and structuring the problem in a clear and concise manner. It entails identifying the key components, variables, and relationships associated with the issue at hand. The formulation serves as the foundation for problem-solving, analysis, and decision-making processes.

To effectively formulate an issue, it is essential to identify and articulate the problem statement. This involves clearly stating the problem or challenge that needs to be addressed, including its scope, context, and desired outcomes. The problem statement should be specific, measurable, attainable, relevant, and time-bound (SMART), providing a clear focus for problem-solving efforts.

Next, the formulation of the issue requires identifying the relevant variables and parameters involved. These variables represent the factors that influence or contribute to the issue. They can be qualitative or quantitative, and their relationships and dependencies should be explicitly defined. This step often involves conducting a thorough analysis of the issue, gathering relevant data and information, and considering various perspectives and stakeholders.

Once the variables are identified, they can be represented using mathematical equations, models, or frameworks. This enables a quantitative and structured approach to analyzing and addressing the issue. Mathematical formulations allow for the application of analytical techniques, simulations, or optimization methods to gain insights, make predictions, or identify solutions.

### 13.5.4    Modifications of the FMCP protocols

Modifications of the FMCP (Fuzzy Multi-Criteria Programming) protocols involve making adjustments or enhancements to the existing protocols to improve their effectiveness, efficiency, or applicability in solving multi-criteria decision-making problems. These modifications can be made based on specific requirements, domain expertise, or advancements in the field of decision analysis. The aim is to refine the FMCP protocols to better handle complex decision scenarios and provide more accurate and robust results.

One common modification is the incorporation of additional decision criteria or factors into the FMCP protocols. The original FMCP protocols may consider a limited set of criteria, but in practice, decision-making problems often involve multiple dimensions and diverse factors. By expanding the criteria set, the modified FMCP protocols can capture a broader range of decision aspects, allowing decision-makers to evaluate options based on a more comprehensive set of attributes. This modification enhances the decision analysis process and provides a more holistic view of the problem.

Another modification is the integration of advanced computational techniques or algorithms into the FMCP protocols. This includes incorporating optimization algorithms, machine learning approaches, or metaheuristic methods to enhance the efficiency and accuracy of the decision-making process. These computational techniques can help automate complex calculations, optimize the trade-offs between criteria, or handle larger decision spaces more effectively. By leveraging advanced computational techniques, the modified FMCP protocols can provide more robust and efficient solutions, enabling decision-makers to make informed and optimal choices.

### 13.5.5    PRR protocol for private relevancy scoring

The PRR (private relevancy scoring) protocol is a mechanism designed to calculate relevancy scores while preserving privacy and data confidentiality. In traditional relevancy scoring systems, the calculation of scores often requires access to sensitive user data or information, raising privacy concerns. The PRR protocol addresses these concerns by providing a privacy-preserving solution for calculating relevancy scores without compromising the privacy of user data.

The PRR protocol employs techniques such as secure multiparty computation or homomorphic encryption to enable the calculation of relevancy scores while keeping the underlying data encrypted. This ensures that no party involved in the computation, including the service provider or third parties, can access or decipher the actual data. Instead, they can perform computations on encrypted data and obtain the relevancy scores without exposing any sensitive information.

The PRR protocol guarantees privacy by design, as it ensures that the relevancy scores are calculated in a privacy-preserving manner, even when the data are distributed across multiple parties. This allows for collaborative filtering, personalized recommendations, or other relevancy-based systems to be implemented while protecting the privacy and confidentiality of user data. By utilizing the PRR protocol, organizations can address privacy concerns, build trust with users, and comply with privacy regulations while still delivering accurate and personalized relevancy scores.

### 13.5.6 *PGD protocol for private group discovery (private group discovery protocol)*

The PGD (private group discovery) protocol is a privacy-enhancing mechanism designed to facilitate the discovery of groups or communities while preserving the privacy of individual participants. Traditional group discovery methods often require participants to disclose sensitive information or reveal personal attributes, raising privacy concerns. The PGD protocol addresses these concerns by providing a privacy-preserving solution that allows individuals to discover and join relevant groups without compromising their privacy.

The PGD protocol utilizes cryptographic techniques such as secure multiparty computation or differential privacy to enable group discovery while keeping individual information private. These techniques ensure that the group discovery process is conducted in a privacy-preserving manner, where no party involved can learn specific details about individual participants or their attributes. Instead, the protocol allows participants to share limited information or aggregate statistics that contribute to the group discovery process without disclosing sensitive details.

By leveraging the PGD protocol, individuals can discover relevant groups, communities, or social networks while maintaining their privacy. The protocol ensures that participants can join groups based on common interests, shared characteristics, or other criteria without revealing personal information that could be used to identify them. This privacy-preserving approach fosters trust among participants, encourages participation, and addresses privacy concerns in group discovery scenarios.

## 13.6    Conclusion

Patients' information may be exchanged with care facilities and patient-side fog-based middleware (FMCP) that allows users to communicate with support groups without disclosing their choices to third parties. The recommended procedures were given a quick rundown. The recommended techniques were tested on a real dataset to see how well they performed. The experimental and analytical findings suggest that the proposed technique may achieve better degrees of privacy in recommending support groups without sacrificing accuracy. The cloud-based recommendation service has several difficulties that need to be addressed. Support-group suggestions should also take into account reputation management approaches. Precision agriculture relies on the IoT to improve agricultural output, keep tabs on environmental factors, and gauge the quality of water and soil. Agriculture operations, such as watering plants, maintaining greenhouses, and inspecting for pests, can all be carried out remotely thanks to the IoT technology. These components and technologies, as well as their strengths, problems, and concerns, all come to light here in the chapter on the IoT. Geospatial data are considered in relation to IoT. Climate change, pollution, global warming, and blights are just some of the environmental issues that need to be addressed in this chapter. It also gives an understanding of the numerous technologies involved in precision agriculture. As a result of this idea, more people will be aware of precision farming and the abundance of available control software toolkits. As a consequence, farmers may check in with the zone management office, have their crop data updated automatically, and have access to data that give them more agency, such as how much water to use or what nutrients to provide. If the proposed framework is developed as a model and used in practice, it will lead to a revolution in agriculture.

# References

[1]   M. Tebaa and S. E. Hajji, Secure Cloud Computing through Homomorphic Encryption, *International Journal of Advancements in Computing Technology (IJACT)*, 5, 29–38, 2014.

[2]   S. Sharma, J. Powers, and K. Chen, Privacy Preserving Spectral Analysis of Large Graphs in Public Clouds, in *Proceedings of the 11th ACM on Asia Conference on Computer and Communications Security*, 2016, pp. 71–82.

[3]   S. Narayan, M. Gagne, and R. Safavi-Naini, Privacy Preserving EHR System Using Attribute-based Infrastructure, in *Proceedings of the 2010 ACM Workshop on Cloud Computing Security Workshop*, 2010, pp. 47–52.

[4]   R. Lu, X. Liang, X. Li, X. Lin, and X. Shen, EPPA: An Efficient and Privacy-Preserving Aggregation Scheme for Secure Smart Grid Communications, *IEEE Transactions on Parallel and Distributed Systems*, 23, 1621–1631, 2012.

[5]   X. Liu, R. H. Deng, Y. Yang, H. N. Tran, and S. Zhong, Hybrid Privacy-Preserving Clinical Decision Support System in Fog-Cloud Computing, *Future Generation Computer Systems*, 78, 825–837, 2017.

# Chapter 14
# Future research directions

## Abstract

This chapter presents an overview of fog computing, a paradigm that extends cloud computing capabilities to the edge of the network. It explores the background, scope, problem definition, aim, and potential future research directions in the field of fog computing.

**Background:** The rapid growth of Internet of Things (IoT) devices and the demand for real-time data processing have led to the emergence of fog computing. Fog computing enables the decentralization of computation and storage resources, bringing computing closer to the edge of the network, thereby reducing latency and bandwidth requirements. It leverages the collaborative processing capabilities of edge devices, fog nodes, and cloud resources to provide efficient and low-latency data processing solutions.

**Scope:** This chapter focuses on the key components and architecture of fog computing, including edge devices, fog nodes, and cloud infrastructure. It discusses the challenges and opportunities in deploying fog computing in various application domains such as smart cities, industrial automation, healthcare, and transportation. It explores the integration of fog computing with other emerging technologies like machine learning, artificial intelligence (AI), and blockchain to enhance its capabilities.

**Problem definition:** The increasing volume and velocity of data generated by IoT devices pose significant challenges for traditional cloud computing architectures in terms of latency, bandwidth, and scalability. The centralized nature of cloud computing results in higher response times and network congestion, which can limit the effectiveness of real-time applications. Efficiently distributing computation and storage resources across the network while ensuring data security, privacy, and reliability is a complex problem in fog computing.

**Aim:** The aim of this chapter is to provide a comprehensive understanding of the fog-computing paradigm, its benefits, and its potential applications. It aims to highlight the research challenges and opportunities in the field of fog computing, including resource management, security, privacy, and energy efficiency. This chapter also aims to inspire future research efforts in developing innovative algorithms, protocols, and architectures to address the emerging requirements of fog computing.

**Analysis/observation on future research directions:** Future research should focus on developing intelligent resource management algorithms for efficient load balancing, task scheduling, and data placement in fog-computing environments. Security and privacy remain critical concerns in fog computing. Future research should explore novel techniques for secure data transmission, access control, and privacy preservation. The integration of fog computing with emerging technologies like machine learning, AI, and blockchain opens up exciting avenues for future research, including context-aware decision-making, data analytics at the edge, and decentralized trust mechanisms.

## 14.1   Introduction

Fog computing has gained significant attention in recent years as a promising paradigm that extends the capabilities of cloud computing to the edge of the network. With the proliferation of Internet of Things (IoT) devices and the need for real-time data processing, fog computing has emerged as a powerful solution to address the challenges of latency, bandwidth, and scalability. While significant progress has been made in this field, there are several exciting research directions that hold great potential for further advancements and improvements in fog computing.

Intelligent resource management: One important area of future research lies in developing intelligent resource management techniques for efficient load balancing, task scheduling, and data placement in fog-computing environments. These algorithms should dynamically allocate resources based on real-time demands and optimize the utilization of computing and storage resources across the network.

Security and privacy: Security and privacy are critical concerns in fog computing. Future research should focus on developing robust security mechanisms, including secure data transmission, access control, and privacy preservation techniques. Encryption, authentication, and intrusion detection systems tailored for the fog-computing environment need to be explored further.

Edge analytics and machine learning: The integration of fog computing with machine learning and analytics presents exciting opportunities for future research. Developing edge analytics techniques that enable real-time data analysis and decision-making at the edge of the network can enhance the efficiency and effectiveness of fog-computing applications. Furthermore, exploring the use of machine learning algorithms for intelligent data processing and predictive analytics in fog-computing environments holds great promise.

Energy efficiency: Fog computing involves a distributed architecture with numerous edge devices and fog nodes. Therefore, energy efficiency is a crucial aspect that requires further investigation. Future research should focus on designing energy-aware algorithms and protocols to optimize resource usage, minimize power consumption, and prolong the battery life of edge devices.

Edge-to-cloud collaboration: Fog computing and cloud computing are complementary paradigms. Research efforts should be directed toward establishing effective collaboration and resource orchestration mechanisms between the fog layer and the cloud layer. This collaboration should ensure seamless data transfer, efficient task offloading, and resource sharing between the fog and the cloud, considering factors like latency, cost, and network conditions.

Quality of service (QoS): Ensuring QoS in fog-computing environments is a challenging task. Future research should explore QoS-aware resource management techniques, including dynamic service provisioning, traffic prioritization, and fault tolerance mechanisms. These techniques should guarantee reliable and timely delivery of services and data in diverse application domains.

Heterogeneity and interoperability: Fog computing encompasses a diverse range of edge devices, fog nodes, and cloud resources. Ensuring interoperability and seamless integration among these heterogeneous components is a crucial research direction. Developing standardized protocols, data formats, and middleware frameworks can facilitate interoperability and enable efficient communication and collaboration in fog-computing ecosystems.

Fog computing for smart cities: Smart cities are one of the most promising application domains for fog computing. Future research should explore the potential of fog computing in enhancing the efficiency of smart city services, such as traffic management, energy optimization, and public safety. Novel approaches leveraging edge intelligence, data analytics, and IoT integration can revolutionize the way smart cities operate.

Fog computing for Industry 4.0: Fog computing has the potential to transform industrial automation and manufacturing processes. Future research should focus on developing fog-computing solutions tailored for Industry 4.0, including real-time monitoring, predictive maintenance, and decentralized control systems. Integration with technologies like robotics, augmented reality, and digital twin can further enhance the capabilities of fog computing in industrial settings.

Scalability and resilience: As fog-computing networks grow larger and more complex, ensuring scalability and resilience becomes critical. Future research should explore scalable architectures, fault tolerance mechanisms, and self-healing algorithms to handle the increasing scale, dynamicity, and heterogeneity of fog-computing deployments. Additionally, investigating the impact of failures, network disruptions, and cyberattacks on fog-computing systems and developing resilient solutions is of paramount importance.

## 14.2   Cloud of things: cloud–IoT integration

The cloud of things (CoT) refers to the integration of cloud computing and the IoT technologies, enabling devices to connect, communicate, and share data with cloud-based platforms. CoT provides a scalable and flexible infrastructure for IoT devices, allowing them to leverage the computing power and storage capabilities of the cloud. By integrating IoT devices with the cloud, CoT enables real-time data processing, analysis, and storage, facilitating efficient decision-making and actionable insights. Cloud–IoT integration allows for seamless connectivity and interoperability among various IoT devices, sensors, and applications, enhancing their overall functionality.

With CoT, IoT devices can offload resource-intensive tasks to the cloud, reducing the processing burden on the devices and extending their battery life. Cloud-based analytics and machine learning algorithms can be applied to the vast amounts of data generated by IoT devices, enabling predictive and prescriptive analytics for improved decision-making. CoT enables centralized management and control of IoT devices, making it easier to monitor and maintain a large-scale IoT deployment. The cloud provides a secure environment for storing and accessing IoT data, offering robust authentication, encryption, and access control mechanisms. By leveraging the cloud's elasticity, CoT enables IoT deployments to scale up or down dynamically based on demand, ensuring optimal resource allocation.

CoT enhances data collaboration and sharing among IoT devices, enabling them to work together to accomplish complex tasks or solve problems collectively. With cloud–IoT integration, businesses can gain valuable insights into customer behavior, preferences, and usage patterns, leading to improved product development and personalized experiences. CoT enables remote monitoring and control of IoT devices, allowing users to access and manage their devices from anywhere at any time. By leveraging cloud-based machine learning capabilities, CoT can enable IoT devices to learn from data patterns, optimize performance, and adapt to changing environments. Cloud-based storage and backup services ensure the resilience and reliability of IoT data, minimizing the risk of data loss or device failures.

CoT enables real-time data streaming from IoT devices to cloud platforms, facilitating rapid response and proactive decision-making. The cloud provides a cost-effective solution for IoT deployments, as it eliminates the need for extensive on-premises infrastructure and allows for pay-as-you-go pricing models. CoT opens up opportunities for cross-industry collaborations and innovations, as IoT devices from different domains can be integrated and leveraged together in the cloud. Cloud-based platforms offer a rich set of tools and services for data visualization, reporting, and analytics, enabling users to derive meaningful insights from IoT data. With CoT, IoT devices can benefit from cloud-based firmware updates and software patches, ensuring they are always up-to-date with the latest features and security enhancements. Cloud–IoT integration enables seamless integration with other emerging technologies such as artificial intelligence (AI), blockchain, and edge computing, unlocking new possibilities for IoT applications.

CoT enhances the scalability of IoT deployments, allowing organizations to expand their IoT infrastructure without significant upfront investments in hardware or infrastructure. Cloud-based machine learning models can be deployed to IoT devices through CoT, enabling them to perform advanced analytics and inference locally. CoT simplifies the development and deployment of IoT applications by providing ready-to-use cloud services, APIs, and development frameworks. Cloud-based data lakes and data warehouses can store and process massive volumes of IoT data, enabling long-term analysis and historical trend identification. With CoT, organizations can leverage cloud-based anomaly detection and predictive maintenance algorithms to proactively identify and address issues with IoT devices.

Cloud-based integration platforms provide connectors and adapters for seamless integration among IoT devices, cloud services, and enterprise systems.

CoT enables rapid prototyping and experimentation with IoT solutions, as cloud-based resources can be quickly provisioned and deprovisioned as needed. Cloud-based dashboards and control panels allow users to monitor and manage their IoT devices in real time, providing insights into device status, performance, and operational metrics. CoT facilitates data sharing and collaboration between multiple stakeholders, enabling ecosystem-wide insights and collaborative decision-making. Cloud-based simulations and digital twins can be used in CoT to model and simulate IoT deployments, allowing organizations to test and optimize their solutions before deployment. CoT enhances data privacy and security by providing centralized management of access control, encryption, and identity management for IoT devices and data. Cloud-based location services can be integrated with IoT devices through CoT, enabling location-based services and geospatial analytics.

CoT enables the integration of IoT devices with cloud-based voice assistants and natural language processing technologies, enabling voice control and interaction with IoT devices. Cloud-based data preprocessing and filtering can be performed in CoT, reducing the amount of data transmitted by IoT devices and optimizing bandwidth usage. CoT enables real-time monitoring and analysis of environmental data collected by IoT sensors, facilitating environmental sustainability initiatives and compliance reporting. Cloud-based data fusion and integration services can be leveraged in CoT to combine data from multiple IoT devices and sources, providing a holistic view of the system. CoT enhances the interoperability of IoT devices by providing standardized APIs, protocols, and data formats for seamless communication and data exchange. Cloud-based data marketplaces and exchanges can be built on top of CoT, enabling organizations to monetize their IoT data and collaborate with external partners.

CoT enables the integration of IoT devices with cloud-based business process automation platforms, streamlining and optimizing enterprise workflows. Cloud-based streaming analytics can be applied in CoT to detect and respond to critical events or anomalies in real time, enabling proactive decision-making. CoT facilitates the integration of edge computing capabilities with the cloud, enabling IoT devices to offload data processing to edge nodes and reduce latency. Cloud-based data governance frameworks and policies can be applied in CoT to ensure compliance with regulatory requirements and industry standards. CoT enables the creation of digital ecosystems where IoT devices, cloud services, and applications can seamlessly interact and interoperate. Cloud-based AI services can be leveraged in CoT to analyze and extract insights from unstructured data generated by IoT devices, such as images or text.

CoT provides a scalable and resilient infrastructure for disaster recovery and business continuity planning for IoT deployments. Cloud-based data analytics platforms can be integrated with CoT to perform real-time anomaly detection, fraud detection, or predictive maintenance for IoT systems.

CoT enables the integration of IoT devices with cloud-based asset management systems, providing organizations with real-time visibility into their assets and inventory. Cloud-based digital transformation platforms can be utilized in CoT to drive innovation and optimize business processes through IoT-driven insights. CoT facilitates the integration of IoT devices with cloud-based supply chain management systems, improving inventory management, logistics, and demand forecasting. Cloud-based data anonymization and de-identification techniques can be applied in CoT to protect the privacy of individuals and comply with data protection regulations. CoT enables the integration of IoT devices with cloud-based energy management systems, optimizing energy consumption and reducing carbon footprints. Cloud-based recommendation engines can be integrated with CoT to provide personalized recommendations based on the data collected from IoT devices. CoT facilitates the integration of IoT devices with cloud-based health-care platforms, enabling remote patient monitoring, telemedicine, and personalized health-care services.

Cloud-based data marketplaces can be utilized in CoT to enable the sharing and trading of IoT data between organizations, fostering data-driven collaborations. CoT enables the integration of IoT devices with cloud-based smart city platforms, facilitating urban planning, traffic management, and sustainability initiatives. Cloud-based sentiment analysis can be applied in CoT to analyze social media and customer feedback data collected from IoT devices, providing valuable insights for marketing and brand management. CoT facilitates the integration of IoT devices with cloud-based asset tracking and management systems, improving inventory visibility and reducing operational costs. Cloud-based data classification and tagging services can be leveraged in CoT to organize and categorize the vast amounts of IoT data generated by different devices. CoT enables the integration of IoT devices with cloud-based weather forecasting systems, improving weather prediction, and supporting decision-making in agriculture, transportation, and other sectors. Cloud-based data governance platforms can be integrated with CoT to manage data quality, metadata, and data lineage for IoT deployments.

CoT facilitates the integration of IoT devices with cloud-based smart home platforms, enabling automation, energy efficiency, and enhanced home security. Cloud-based data anonymization and pseudonymization techniques can be applied in CoT to protect the privacy of individuals while allowing data analysis and insights. CoT enables the integration of IoT devices with cloud-based predictive analytics platforms, supporting demand forecasting, predictive maintenance, and proactive decision-making. Cloud-based data visualization tools can be integrated with CoT to create interactive dashboards and reports, enabling stakeholders to gain insights from IoT data at a glance. CoT facilitates the integration of IoT devices with cloud-based inventory management systems, improving inventory accuracy, replenishment, and order fulfillment. Cloud-based social network analysis can be applied in CoT to analyze social interactions and relationships between IoT devices, uncovering hidden patterns and insights. CoT enables the integration of IoT devices with cloud-based industrial automation systems, optimizing manufacturing processes and improving productivity. Cloud-based data discovery and cataloging services can be utilized in CoT to enable efficient search and discovery of IoT data assets within an organization.

CoT facilitates the integration of IoT devices with cloud-based predictive maintenance platforms, reducing equipment downtime and improving asset reliability. Cloud-based data virtualization techniques can be leveraged in CoT to provide a unified view of IoT data from multiple sources, simplifying data integration and analysis. CoT facilitates the integration of IoT devices with cloud-based fleet management systems, optimizing route planning, fuel consumption, and vehicle maintenance, thereby enhancing overall operational efficiency and enabling real-time monitoring and decision-making for fleet managers. Cloud-based natural language processing can be applied in CoT to enable voice-controlled interactions with IoT devices and intelligent virtual assistants. CoT facilitates the integration of IoT devices with cloud-based customer relationship management systems, enabling personalized marketing campaigns and improved customer experiences. Cloud-based data replication and synchronization services can be utilized in CoT to ensure data consistency and availability across distributed IoT deployments. CoT enables the integration of IoT devices with cloud-based smart grid systems, optimizing energy distribution, load balancing, and renewable energy integration. Cloud-based data governance frameworks can be integrated with CoT to enforce data access controls, privacy policies, and data retention policies for IoT data.

CoT facilitates the integration of IoT devices with cloud-based building management systems, enabling energy-efficient buildings, and improving occupant comfort. Cloud-based time-series databases can be leveraged in CoT to store and query time-stamped IoT data, supporting real-time analytics and trend analysis. CoT enables the integration of IoT devices with cloud-based e-commerce platforms, enabling personalized recommendations, inventory management, and order fulfillment. Cloud-based data lineage and auditing services can be utilized in CoT to track and trace the origin and processing of IoT data, ensuring data integrity and compliance. CoT facilitates the integration of IoT devices with cloud-based predictive analytics platforms, enabling proactive maintenance, demand forecasting, and optimization. Cloud-based data synchronization services can be integrated with CoT to ensure consistency and availability of IoT data across multiple cloud and edge nodes. CoT enables the integration of IoT devices with cloud-based asset tracking systems, improving supply chain visibility, theft prevention, and inventory management. Cloud-based streaming data processing frameworks can be leveraged in CoT to analyze and transform real-time data from IoT devices, enabling rapid insights and decision-making.

CoT facilitates the integration of IoT devices with cloud-based risk management systems, enabling real-time monitoring, and mitigation of operational risks. Cloud-based data governance platforms can be integrated with CoT to enforce data privacy policies, consent management, and data sharing agreements for IoT data. CoT enables the integration of IoT devices with cloud-based video analytics platforms, supporting real-time video surveillance, object detection, and facial recognition. Cloud-based data archiving and retention services can be utilized in CoT to store and manage long-term historical data generated by IoT devices. CoT facilitates the integration of IoT devices with cloud-based agriculture management systems, optimizing irrigation, crop monitoring, and yield prediction. Cloud-based data transformation and enrichment services can be applied in CoT to cleanse, normalize, and enrich IoT data for further analysis and processing. CoT enables the integration of IoT devices with cloud-based smart transportation systems, optimizing traffic flow, public transit, and logistics operations. Cloud-based data governance frameworks can be integrated with CoT to ensure data quality, data lineage, and data ownership for IoT deployments.

CoT facilitates the integration of IoT devices with cloud-based health-care analytics platforms, enabling population health management, disease surveillance, and early intervention. Cloud-based data replication and backup services can be leveraged in CoT to ensure data durability and recoverability for IoT deployments. CoT enables the integration of IoT devices with cloud-based inventory optimization systems, improving stock availability, order fulfillment, and inventory turnover. Cloud-based stream processing frameworks can be utilized in CoT to perform real-time analysis and filtering of IoT data streams, enabling immediate actions and responses. CoT facilitates the integration of IoT devices with cloud-based asset performance management systems, enabling predictive maintenance and asset optimization. Cloud-based data governance platforms can be integrated with CoT to enforce data access controls, data masking, and data classification for IoT data. CoT enables the integration of IoT devices with cloud-based intelligent transportation systems, improving traffic management, road safety, and navigation. Cloud-based data anonymization techniques can be applied in CoT to protect sensitive information in IoT data while preserving its utility for analysis and insights.

## 14.3    Conclusion

Many additional wireless applications, such as those related to other areas seeing rapid growth, include VANETs, smart cities, health-care, cyber-physical systems, ITS, and the IoT. To keep up with the ever-increasing demands, wireless networks need to be expandable. Researchers are looking at IoT–cloud systems that work together to accomplish this goal. Cloud-based IoT applications may use the almost limitless resources of the cloud, while the cloud itself can broaden its service offering by integrating IoT nodes and apps. However, a basic cloud–IoT integration solution cannot meet the QoS requirements of various current and emerging wireless applications. It is possible to offload resource-constrained nodes by using fog as middleware to conduct time-sensitive operations locally. Fog architecture and its advantages and disadvantages are discussed in detail in this chapter. Performance assessment findings and analyses in this research raise the question of whether fog is appropriate for a given activity depending on its size and complexity. Finally, we identify and explore several fog research issues that must be solved in the future if fog is to become an attractive and practical option for new services with a wide range of needs.

# Index

access control lists (ACLs) 288

adaptive intelligence in cybernetics 337

adaptive XSS monitoring systems 151

advanced fog-computing architecture 49

  collaboration with cloud computing 50

  edge intelligence 50

  fog nodes 49

  hierarchy and scalability 49

  low latency and real-time processing 49–50

  reliability and resilience 50

  security and privacy 50

Advanced Packaging Tool (APT) protocol 106–8

  working of 109–10

advantages of fog computing 40–2

analytic and performance parameters for fog/edge nodes 68–9

anomaly detection 260

application management in fog-computing environments 248

  application performance 249–50

  approach distributed data flow 250–1

application of fog computing 27, 341

  Big Data-based intelligent fog computing 352–64

  geospatial technology with fog computing and IoT in agriculture 344–52

  health-care systems, fog computing in 364–8

  recommender system 368–72

application programs, management of 11

applications, fog-computing 87–90

architectonics 16

artificial intelligence (AI) 34, 97

attribute-based access control (ABAC) 288

augmented reality (AR) 88

automated machine learning (AutoML) frameworks 263

automobiles, network of 13

autonomous intelligence 337

behavior-based XSS monitoring systems 151

behavior of fog computing 66–8

Big Data 8, 23

Big Data base analysis 251

  associative mining in real time 257–8

  cloud-based analytics in the periphery 267–8

  DBSCAN 256

  decision trees with distributed nodes 255

  DENCLUE 256

  different approaches to fog analytics 265–6

extensive learning, methods for
258–61
goods and services 266–7
large-scale datasets and advanced
machine learning 261–5
learning under guidance 254–5
methods for clustering large data
255–6
mining association rules in large
datasets 257
ParStream 267
scale-up models 265
streaming data, processing of 252–3
tree-based incremental clustering
256–7
Big Data-based intelligent fog
computing 352
analysis and processing 354
building materials made locally
359–60
cloud computing and geospatial data
355–6
computerized information
management 353–4
computing on the cloud: from fog to
cloud 363–4
detection and monitoring techniques
361–2
efficient and eco-friendly structures
are called "green buildings" 358
geospatial data influences thermal
comfort in buildings 358–9
Internet of Things in the
cloud 362
IoT with the advent of Big Data and
the cloud 362–3
role of the cloud in Big Data 354–5
technical measures for thermostatic
regulation 357–8
technologies and protocols for IoT
360

technologies of information and
communication and of physical
location 360–1
thermostatic consistency of building
equipment 359
Big Geographical Data 356–7
blockchain technology 85–6
Border Gateway Protocol (BGP) 38–9

cache placement and management
127–8
cellular networks 64
cellular-V2X 134
centralized tree structure models 73
challenges of fog environments 77–81
characteristics of fog computing 76–7
CityPulse project, sensor data in
211–13
cloud-based recommendation service
reference model 369–70
cloud-based XSS monitoring systems
151
cloud computing 1, 14
fog computing versus 14
security requirements 273–4
use of data in 319–20
cloud data centers' learning mode
151–3
CloudFIT architecture stack 100–1
cloud infrastructure 314
cloud of things (CoT) 377–82
cloud radio access network (CRAN) 6
Cloud Security Ontology (CSO) 268
architecture 272–3
conceptual software architecture
274–5
create an ontology for safer cloud
computing 270–1
domain and scope determination for
275

identify the ontology's imperative keywords 275–6

non-repudiation (NR) 274

cloud technology 14

clustering techniques 99–100

CoAP (Constrained Application Protocol) 38–9

code embedded in JavaScript 157–8

cognitive intelligence in cybernetics 337

Comment Comparison Tool 161

communication between devices 16

computational skills 16

computation offloading 221–2

computations, management of 10–11

concept of fog computing 2–3

conditional logic with predicates 240–2

connected data processing, advantages of 98

connectivity technologies 63–6

containerization and virtualization technologies 97

content-aware intelligent systems fog computing in cybernetics intelligence 329

finding humming in the dark 335–6

human intelligence (HUMINT) 334–5

measurement and signature intelligence (MASINT) 333–4

social media analytics 331–3

technical intelligence (TECHINT) 333

content caching and delivery

performance evaluation and analysis 128

virtualization for 128

content caching in vehicular fog computing 127

content delivery in vehicular fog computing 128

content delivery networks (CDNs) 197

context-aware intelligence, using fog/edge computing for 336

context-aware services 123

context-aware work stealing scheme 229

Docker images, transfer of 232–3

Docker image transfer, performance of 231–2

extension for context-awareness 229–30

fog nodes, distribution of tasks to 233–4

responsibilities, distribution of 234–5

task management skills 230–1

Context Finder 162–3

contextual intelligence 338

convolutional neural networks (CNNs) 296

cost of fog computing 9

coworkers, networking with 227–9

cross-site scripting (XSS) attack 142–5, 158

cutting-edge computing technologies 97

cybernetic intelligence in fog computing 307

content-aware intelligent systems 329

finding humming in the dark 335–6

human intelligence (HUMINT) 334–5

measurement and signature intelligence (MASINT) 333–4

social media analytics 331–3

technical intelligence (TECHINT) 333

context-aware intelligence, using fog/edge computing for 336

cyborg, data utility in 310
  cloud computing, use of data in
    319–20
  data-intensive applications, model
    for 312–14
  data life cycle 324–5
  data source 316–18
  data utility 323–4
  data utility model, using 325–9
  intelligent distributed computer
    network 311–12
  resources 314–16
  situational aspects 320–3
  tasks 318–19
  model of cybernetic intelligence
    309–10
  types of 337–8
cybernetic threat intelligence (CTI)
  329–31
cyborg, data utility in 310, 323–4
  cloud computing, use of data in
    319–20
  data-intensive applications, model
    for 312–14
  data life cycle 324–5
  data source 316–18
  data utility model, using 325–9
  intelligent distributed computer
    network 311–12
  resources 314–16
  situational aspects 320–3
  tasks 318–19

data, management of 11–12
data access 101–2
Data as a Service (Daas) 89–90
data augmentation techniques 298
data collection module 154
data compression methods 263
data confidentiality in FR 288

data encryption 13
data-intensive applications, model for
  312–14
data life cycle 324–5
data lifecycle management 90
data loss (DL) 233
data ownership 287
data processing 16, 22–3
data retention and lifecycle
  management 90
data speed and delay, sensitivity to
  23–4
data utility 323–9
data velocity 23
DBSCAN (density-based spatial
  clustering of applications with
  noise) 256
decision trees with distributed nodes
  255
deep generative models 264
deep learning 252, 260
deep learning algorithms 250–1
deep learning-based robotics 296
  execution environment on a
    networked system 298–9
  transferring simulation learning to
    the real world 297–8
deep metric learning methods 264
deep reinforcement learning methods
  260
demerits of fog computing 26–7
DENCLUE (DENsity-based
  CLUstEring) 256
denial-of-service (DoS) attack 13
device-to-device (D2D)
  communication 293–4
Diffie–Hellman protocol 159
dimensionality reduction methods 256
disaster preparedness 322
distributed hash tables (DHTs) 101

distributed learning 286
distributed tree structure models 73
distributed with the fog 20–1
distributed XSS monitoring systems 151
Docker image transfer 232–3
  performance of 231–2
domain adaptation techniques 264

edge analytics 266
edge analytics and machine learning 376
edge and pervasive computing, developing a platform for 98–9
edge-based XSS monitoring systems 151
edge caching 70
edge-cloud collaboration 81
edge computing 1, 3, 97
edge computing, fog computing and 17
  fog computing and IoT app development in action 17
  healthcare sector 17
  in a nutshell 17–18
  video games, playing 17
edge device caching 83
edge devices 314
edge equipment 4
edge intelligence 70
  integration 52
  and machine learning 137
edge servers 314–15
edge-to-cloud collaboration 376–7
emotional intelligence 322
emulating emotional intelligence in cybernetic systems 338
encryption techniques 287
energy and environmental impact, consumption of 8–9

energy efficiency 313, 376
  and sustainability 137
energy resources, management of 12
environment model 47
  network layers 48–9
  tree-based computing paradigm 48
evolutionary algorithms 260
execution costs 8
Extensible Messaging and Presence Protocol (XMPP) 38–9

feature extraction module 154
features of fog computing 192–5
feedback control intelligence 337
Fisher's LDA (FLDA) 171
5G networks 81–3, 85, 366
FMCP (Fuzzy Multi-Criteria Programming) protocols 371
fog data analytics and use cases 86–7
fog deployment model 18–20
Fog-Infrastructure-as-a-Service (FogIaaS) 21
fog layer 35
fog networking 1
fog nodes 6, 34, 60–3
  distribution of tasks to 233–4
Fog Platform as a Service (FogPaaS) 21
fog radio access network (FRAN) 82
fog robotics (FR) 281, 284
  advanced robotics using 302
  applications of 303–4
  comparison wiith cloud robotics 290
  delivery of social robots in this scenario 295–6
  device-to-device (D2D) communication 293–4
  FR architecture with many fog robot servers 294–5

fundamentals of FR design 292–3
data security, confidentiality, and
    ownership 287–9
deep learning-based robotics 296
    execution environment on a
        networked system 298–9
    transferring simulation learning to
        the real world 297–8
    facilitating distributed and shared
        learning 286–7
    fog robot architecture 299–300
    implementation of 301
    networking system with execution
        environment 301–2
    resource allocation and placement,
        adaptability in 289–90
fog security and privacy 276–9
Fog-Software-as-a-Service (FogSaaS)
    21–2
Fog-to-Cloud (F2C) protocol 39
forecast 106
function-as-a-service 22
future research directions 375
    cloud of things (CoT) 377–82

Gaussian distribution 285
generic fog-computing architecture 39
    advantages 40–2
    basic rules of IoT with fog 42–4
    models of fog computing 44
        devices for creating a haze 46–7
        infrastructure design for general-
            ized fog computing 44–5
        Internet of Things sensors and
            actuators 45–6
        resources management 47
geopolitical considerations 322
geospatial data sources 317
geospatial technology with fog comput-
    ing and IoT in agriculture 344

agriculture and information and
    communications technologies
    349
asserting the need of tracking and
    farming systems monitoring
    348–9
Big Data's place in the Internet of
    Things 350–1
cattle tracking and monitoring 348
controlled fertilizer usage 346–7
GPS's function 352
greenhouse gases, monitoring of 347
Internet of Things and cloud and fog
    computing 351
IoT's functions 349–50
sensors associated with plants 351–2
system to monitor irrigation 345–6
treatment for insect and disease
    problems 346
GPS technology 348
graph-based learning methods 259, 262
ground zero, stations at 6

Hamming code 159–60
haze machines 46–7
healthcare sector 17
health-care systems, fog computing in
    364
    disposables identification, location,
        and tracking 365–6
    functionality and design of the
        proposed system 366
    implied hardware 368
    network analysis, field of 367–8
    networking devices, future of 366–7
    proposed system's core functionality
        discerning the equipment 365
heating, ventilation, and air condition-
    ing (HVAC) systems 357
heterogeneity and interoperability 377

history of fog computing 1–2
human intelligence (HUMINT) 334–5
hybrid cloud-fog architectures 86
hybrid XSS monitoring systems 151
hyperspectral feature partitioning
    179–83
hyperspectral images, supervised
    feature extraction in 174
  experimental evaluation 183
    description of datasets 183–5
    parameter measures modified
      MMC-based approach 186–7
    performance measures 185
  hyperspectral feature partitioning
    179–83
  maximum margin criterion (MMC)-
    based feature extraction method
    177–8
  modified Fisher's linear discriminant
    analysis (MFLDA)-based
    feature 175–6
  partitioned maximum margin
    criterion (PMMC) method 178–9
  prototype space feature extraction
    (PSFE) method 176–7
hyperspectral imaging and
    dimensionality reduction 173
  math functions 174
hyperspectral remote sensing (HSR)
    170–2

ICON 237
  design principles 239–40
  fog-computing system architecture
    for ICON-based smart house
    243–4
  implementation of 242–4
incremental learning techniques 262
Industrial Internet Consortium 40
Industrial Internet of Things
    (IIoT) 88, 96

Industry 4.0
  fog computing for 377
information and communications
    technologies (ICT) 349
information sharing 219
  computation offloading 221–2
  conditional logic with predicates
    240–2
  context-aware work stealing scheme
    229
    Docker images, transfer of 232–3
    Docker image transfer,
      performance of 231–2
    extension for context-awareness
      229–30
    fog nodes, distribution of tasks to
      233–4
    responsibilities, distribution of
      234–5
    task management skills 230–1
  ICON 237
    design principles 239–40
    fog-computing system architecture
      for ICON-based smart house
      243–4
    implementation of 242–4
  Internet of Things (IoT) -based smart
    home 235–6
  load balancing and efficient
    deployment 223–4
  mobility-aware edge computing
    224–5
  result routing 222–3
  smart home scenario 236–7
  system design 225
    coworkers, networking with 227–9
    potential employees, selection of
      226–7
infrared (IR) sensors 76
infrastructure design for generalized
    fog computing 44–5

input field, analyzer of 156–7
integrated pest management (IPM)
    practices 346
intelligent distributed computer
    network 311–12
intelligent resource management 376
intelligent vehicles 6
intelligent XSS monitoring systems,
    different types of 150–1
internet, devices for connecting to 6
internet-based platform for the
    distribution of content 13
Internet of Things (IoT) 12, 31
    -based smart home 235–6
    Big Data's place in 350–1
    in the cloud 362
    and cloud and fog computing 351
    cloud–IoT integration 377–82
    models of fog computing 33
        basic structure of fog computing
            34–5
        literature analysis with the help of
            scientific publications 36–8
    protocol of fog computing 38
        advanced fog-computing
            architecture 49–50
        fog-computing environment model
            47–9
        generic fog-computing
            architecture 39–47
        tree model 50–2
    protocols 134
    sensors and actuators 45–6
    technologies and protocols for 360
Internet of Things (IoT), fog
    computing and 15
    architectonics 16
    communication between devices 16
    computational skills 16
    continuous services 16

data processing 16
enhanced security 15–16
facilities 15
frequency performance of the
    network 16
low delay 16
maximum business flexibility 15
quantity of nodes 16
sustainable urban 15
user experience, enhanced 16
interoperability 45, 137

JavaScript
    analysis on 159
    comment comparison tool for 160–2

large-scale deep learning models 262
large-scale machine learning models
    262–3
latency control of fog computing 9
learning under guidance 254–5
LiDAR (Light Detection and Ranging)
    systems 76
Lightweight Machine-to-Machine
    (LWM2M) 39
linear discriminant analysis (LDA) 170
load balancing and efficient
    deployment 223–4
load balancing techniques 70
long short-term memory (LSTM)
    networks 296

machine-generated data 317
machine learning (ML) 34, 97, 137,
    150–1, 154, 253–4
magnetic sensors 76
management and orchestration
    (MANO) 71, 85
mapping 116–18
master–slave nodal cooperation 7

math functions 174

maximum margin criteria (MMC) 171, 177–8

measurement and signature intelligence (MASINT) 333–4

merits of fog computing 26

message-oriented middleware (MOM) 22

Message Queue Telemetry Transport (MQTT) 38–9

middlewares 22

mobile devices/mobile phones, access networks for 12

mobile edge computing (MEC) 81–2

mobility-aware edge computing 224–5

models of fog computing 33, 44
  devices for creating a haze 46–7
  infrastructure design for generalized fog computing 44–5
  Internet of Things sensors and actuators 45–6
  literature analysis with the help of scientific publications 36–8
  resources management 47
  structure of fog computing 34–5

modified Fisher's linear discriminant analysis (MFLDA) 175–6

multiple sources of information 24

natural language processing (NLP) techniques 297, 319

network, management of 10

network function virtualization (NFV) 10, 64, 70, 83–4, 128
  orchestration and management 129
  performance evaluation and analysis 129–30
  Software-Defined Networking (SDN) and: *see* Software-Defined Networking (SDN) and Network Function Virtualization (NFV) technology

vehicular fog computing, NFV infrastructure in 129

vehicular NFV use cases 129

Network Function Virtualization infrastructure (NFVI) 71

networking systems, usefulness of 12

network layers 48–9

network operating system, SDN controller and 131

network virtualization protocols 135

neural architecture search (NAS) 260

node level, collaboration at 6–7

node-to-node communication 5

non-repudiation (NR) 274

northbound interfaces and application ecosystem 132

online mode of virtualized network of fog computing 153–4

OntoGraf 276

ontology 271–2

OpenFlow protocol and southbound interfaces 132

OpenFog Consortium 2, 40

Open Fog Consortium Reference Architecture (OFCA) 38–9

operating expenses 9

operating system (OS) 298

orchestration resources 315

OSE (outlier, spike, and event) detection 105–6

paradigm of fog/edge computing 56–60

parallel hyperparameter tuning techniques 263

ParStream 267

partitioned maximum margin criterion (PMMC) method 178–9

passive optical network, power line communications via 12–13

pay-as-you-go (PaaS) model 4, 18

peer-to-peer (P2P) pervasive grid 6–7,
    93, 257
  Advanced Packaging Tool (APT)
    protocol 106–8
    working of 109–10
  context and scheduling 102–3
  coordination and clustering 99–101
  cryptographic protection 114–15
  data access 101–2
  data forwarding 111–12
  default mappers 110–11
  design principles 108–9
  edge and pervasive computing,
    developing a platform for 98–9
  failure detection and recovery
    112–13
  forecast 106
  incremental deployment 115–16
  input preprocessing 104–5
  mapping 116–18
  mapping distribution protocol
    113–14
  mapping information 111
  monitoring ozone events for UV
    alerts 103–4
  OSE (outlier, spike, and event)
    detection 105–6
  proximity services with edge
    computing and pervasive
    grids 97
    connected data processing,
      advantages of 98
    cutting-edge computing
      technologies 97
    ubiquitous networks 97
  routing policy 116–18
  time-series analysis 105
  traditional and pervasive
    environments 94
    background 96

  case study analysis 96
  Industrial Internet of Things (IIoT)
    fog computing 96
  pervasive environment 95–6
  routing scalability 96
  traditional fog-computing
    environment 94–5
  tunneling architecture 96
performance enhancement techniques
    69–74
performance parameters for fog/edge
    nodes 68–9
pervasive computing 1
PGD (private group discovery)
    protocol 372
photo-synthetically active radiation
    (PAR) sensor 352
potential employees, selection of
    226–7
power and energy resources 315
power line communications via passive
    optical network 12–13
precision agriculture 344
predictive intelligence 338
preprocessing module 154
principal component analysis (PCA)
    170
privacy, sensitivity to the importance
    of 24–5
probabilistic graphical models 263
process automation data 23
protocol generation 159–60
protocol of fog computing 38
  advanced fog-computing
    architecture 49
    collaboration with cloud
      computing 50
    edge intelligence 50
    fog nodes 49
    hierarchy and scalability 49

low latency and real-time processing 49–50
reliability and resilience 50
security and privacy 50
fog-computing environment model 47
network layers 48–9
tree-based computing paradigm 48
generic fog-computing architecture 39
advantages 40–2
basic rules of IoT with fog 42–4
models of fog computing 44–7
tree model 50
edge intelligence integration 52
fault tolerance and redundancy 51
hierarchical structure 50–1
intermediate fog nodes 51
leaf nodes 51
root node 51
scalability 51
task distribution 51
prototype space feature extraction (PSFE) method 176–7
proximity services with edge computing and pervasive grids 97
connected data processing, advantages of 98
cutting-edge computing technologies 97
ubiquitous networks 97
PRR (private relevancy scoring) protocol 371–2
public opinion and sentiment 323

quality of experience (QoE) 79
quality of service (QoS) 45, 135, 377
assurance 79
goals for 9
management 70

parameters 79–80
resources 316
and service provisioning 136
vehicular fog computing and 135
virtualization in fog computing and 135–6
queueing theory 166

radar sensors 76
Radio Access Network (RAN) 12
radio frequency identification (RFID) 19, 348, 365
real-time processing 123
real-time XSS monitoring systems 151
recurrent neural networks (RNNs) 296
reinforcement learning methods 259, 263
remote sensing imaging 171
hyperspectral 171–2
supervised features extraction 172
types of 171
resilient intelligence in cybernetics 337
resource optimization 300
resources management 47, 250
and optimization 136
response time 165
responsibilities, distribution of 234–5
result routing 222–3
risk, definition of 370
robotic systems: *see* fog robotics (FR)
role-based access control (RBAC) 288
round-trip times (RTTs) 197
routing policy 116–18
rule-based XSS monitoring systems 150

satellite connectivity 64
scalable architectures 377
security and privacy 376
security and privacy challenges in fog computing 247

application management in fog-
     computing environments
     248–51
Big Data base analysis 251–68
Cloud Security Ontology (CSO)
     268–76
fog security and privacy 276–9
sensor data 189
  in CityPulse project 211–13
  pre-cleaned datasets for exploration
       in Internet of Things, fog, and
       cloud 215–16
  in smart city 213–15
  in SmartME project 192
     ability and instruction 208–9
     adopted technology 204–5
     analysis sensor data formats in
          smart cities 210
     aspects of the natural setting 209–10
     cloud environment 199–200
     construction measurement of fog
          computing 205–6
     data availability, interoperability
          for 201–2
     enhanced heterogeneity 197–9
     enhanced level of service 195–6
     features of fog computing 192–5
     infrastructure, connectivity, and
          availability 209
     latency, reduction in 196
     location 210
     mobility, support for 196–7
     nature, protection for 200–1
     organization, aspects of 206–7
     privacy and security 209
     reduced complicacy and
          customizability 209
     sensor data 210–11
     supporting governance adopt new
          technology 202–4

     top-down administrative backing
          207–8
Service Level Objectives (SLOs) 5, 9
shared learning 286–7
short-range communication 134
sigmoid function 284
signature-based XSS monitoring
     systems 150
smart cities
  fog computing for 377
  sensor data in 213–15
smart home scenario 236–7
SmartME project, sensor data in 192
  ability and instruction 208–9
  adopted technology 204–5
  analysis sensor data formats in smart
       cities 210
  aspects of the natural
       setting 209–10
  cloud environment 199–200
  construction measurement of fog
       computing 205–6
  data availability, interoperability for
       201–2
  enhanced heterogeneity 197–9
  enhanced level of service 195–6
  features of fog computing 192–5
  infrastructure, connectivity, and
       availability 209
  latency, reduction in 196
  location 210
  mobility, support for 196–7
  nature, protection for 200–1
  organization, aspects of 206–7
  privacy and security 209
  reduced complicacy and
       customizability 209
  sensor data 210–11
  supporting governance adopt new
       technology 202–4

top-down administrative backing 207–8

smart XSS attack monitoring system 147
  extracted web page module 148–9

smart XSS attack surveillance system for fog computing 141
  cross-site scripting (XSS) attack 143–5
  key contribution XSS 145
    related work 146–7
  performance analysis 165–6

smart XSS monitoring system 155
  components of 163
    conceptualization 164
    development 164–5
    testing 165
  modes of 154
    code embedded in JavaScript 157–8
    Context Finder 162–3
    input field, analyzer of 156–7
    JavaScript, analysis on 159
    JavaScript, comment comparison tool for 160–2
    protocol generation 159–60

smart XSS surveillance system 149
  cloud data centers' learning mode 151–3
  intelligent XSS monitoring systems, different types of 150–1
  online mode of virtualized network of fog computing 153–4

social intelligence in cybernetics 337

social media analytics: *see* SOCMINT (social media intelligence)

SOCMINT (social media intelligence) 331–3

software-defined networking (SDN) 10, 64, 70, 83, 130, 367

network operating system, SDN controller and 131

northbound interfaces and application ecosystem 132

OpenFlow protocol and southbound interfaces 132

performance evaluation and analysis 132

vehicular fog computing, SDN use cases in 130–1

Software-Defined Networking (SDN) and Network Function Virtualization (NFV) technology 55, 83–6

advanced fog-computing applications 87–90

analytic and performance parameters for fog/edge nodes 68–9

challenges of fog environments 77–81

characteristics of fog computing 76–7

connectivity technologies 63
  cellular networks 64
  satellite connectivity 64
  software-defined networking (SDN) technology 64
  wired connectivity technologies 63–4
  wireless connectivity technologies 64

5G connecting technology and the fog architecture 81–3

fog computing use cases 74–6

fog data analytics and use cases 86–7

fog nodes 60–3

paradigm of fog/edge computing 56–60

performance enhancement techniques 69–74

structure and behavior of fog computing 66–8

standards organizations 40
Stream Data 254
Stream Data Analysis 253–4
streaming data, processing of 252–3
structure and behavior of fog
    computing 66–8
structure of fog computing 34–5
supervised feature extraction in
        hyperspectral images 174
    experimental evaluation 183
        description of datasets 183–5
        parameter measures modified
            MMC-based approach 186–7
        performance measures 185
    hyperspectral feature partitioning
        179–83
    maximum margin criterion (MMC)-
        based feature extraction method
        177–8
    modified Fisher's linear discriminant
        analysis (MFLDA)-based fea-
        ture 175–6
    partitioned maximum margin criter-
        ion (PMMC) method 178–9
    prototype space feature extraction
        (PSFE) method 176–7
supervised feature extraction methods
        170–1
    evaluation of 171
supervised learning: *see* learning under
        guidance
sustainability, energy efficiency and 137
swarm intelligence 337

task management skills 230–1
taxonomy of fog computing 5
    application programs, management
        of 11
    computations, management of 10–11
    controlling the costs 9

cost 8
data 7–8
data, management of 11–12
data encryption 13
denial-of-service (DoS) attack 13
energy and environmental impact,
        consumption of 8–9
energy resources, management of 12
fear for one's safety 13
future directions 14
goals for the quality of service 9
ground zero, stations at 6
intelligent vehicles 6
internet, devices for connecting to 6
internet-based platform for the
        distribution of content 13
internet of things 12
latency control 9
master–slave nodal cooperation 7
mobile devices/mobile phones,
        access networks for 12
network, management of 10
networking systems, usefulness of 12
network of automobiles 13
node level, collaboration at 6–7
power line communications via
        passive optical network 12–13
time 7
user authentication 13
technical intelligence (TECHINT) 333
technological readiness 322
Terminal Data (TD) system 74
throughput 165
time-series analysis 105
transfer speed (TS) 231–2
transfer time (TT) 231–2
tree-based computing paradigm 48
tree-based incremental clustering
        256–7

tree model, fog-computing 50
  edge intelligence integration 52
  fault tolerance and redundancy 51
  hierarchical structure 50–1
  intermediate fog nodes 51
  leaf nodes 51
  root node 51
  scalability 51
  task distribution 51
tree structure models 73

ultrasonic sensors 76
use cases, fog computing 74–6
user authentication 13
UV alerts, monitoring ozone events for
  103–4

vehicular and virtualization fog
  computing 123
  application of 134
    cellular-V2X 134
    Internet of Things (IoT) protocols
    134
    network virtualization protocols 135
    short-range communication 134
  applications and services 125–6
  communication infrastructure 125
  data processing and analytics 125
  fog nodes 125
  roadside infrastructure 125
  vehicular nodes 124–5
  virtualization in fog computing 123–4
  virtualization layer 125
vehicular fog computing (VFC) 10
  enhanced reliability and resilience
  133
  improved scalability and resource
  utilization 132–3
  low latency and real-time
  responsiveness 132

SDN use cases in 130–1
vehicular fog computing and
  virtualization 121
  cache placement and management
  127–8
  content caching and delivery
    performance evaluation and
    analysis 128
    virtualization for 128
  content caching in vehicular fog
  computing 127
  content delivery in vehicular fog
  computing 128
  network function virtualization
  (NFV) 128
    NFV infrastructure in vehicular
    fog computing 129
    orchestration and management 129
    performance evaluation and
    analysis 129–30
    vehicular NFV use cases 129
  quality of service (QoS) 135–6
  research vehicular and virtualization
  in fog computing 136
    edge intelligence and machine
    learning 137
    energy efficiency and
    sustainability 137
    quality of service (QoS) and
    service provisioning 136
    resource management and
    optimization 136
    security and privacy 136–7
    standardization and
    interoperability 137
    vehicular mobility modeling and
    analysis 137
  software-defined networking (SDN)
  130
    northbound interfaces and
    application ecosystem 132

OpenFlow protocol and
southbound interfaces 132
performance evaluation and
analysis 132
SDN controller and network
operating system 131
SDN use cases in vehicular fog
computing 130–1
vehicular mobility models 126
data analysis and evaluation 127
data collection and preprocessing 126
iterative refinement 127
model initialization 126
selection of mobility model 126
simulation execution 126–7
video games 17
virtualization in fog computing 123–4
efficient resource management 133
improved fault isolation and security
133

service agility and rapid deployment
133
*see also* vehicular fog computing and
virtualization
Virtualized Network Functions (VNFs)
71
virtual machines (VMs) 9, 123, 355
virtual network functions (VNFs) 128
virtual reality (VR) 88
vision-based sensors 76

wearable devices 317
wired connectivity technologies 63–4
wireless connectivity technologies 64
working of fog computing 4–5
workload, characteristics of 25–6

zoning systems 357–8

Printed in the USA
CPSIA information can be obtained
at www.ICGtesting.com
JSHW011506221024
72173JS00005B/1222